Jinnah, Pakistan and Islamic identity

'I hugely enjoyed the book … a welcome and much needed reassessment of Jinnah's reputation after decades of ill-informed propaganda and criticism.'

Andrew Roberts, author of *Eminent Churchillians*

'A courageous book, based on careful and original research. Professor Ahmed has rendered all persons of goodwill an extremely important service.'

Dr Julius Lipner, Director of the Dharam Hinduja Institute of Indic Research, University of Cambridge

'Every generation needs to reinterpret its great men of the past. Akbar Ahmed, by revealing Jinnah's human face alongside his heroic achievement, both makes this statesman accessible to the current age and renders his greatness even clearer than before.'

Professor Francis Robinson, University of London

'A *Mahabharata* … readable, human orientated, multi-dimensional. Unique. Superb.'
Professor Sharif al Mujahid, founder Director of Quaid-i-Azam Academy, Karachi

Four men shaped the end of British rule in India: Nehru, Gandhi, Mountbatten and Jinnah. We know a great deal about the first three, but Mohammed Ali Jinnah, the founder of Pakistan, has mostly either been ignored or in the case of Richard Attenborough's hugely successful film, *Gandhi*, portrayed as a cold megalomaniac, bent on the bloody partition of India.

Akbar Ahmed's major study tells a different story of heroism and tragedy and of backstage manoeuvring among the governing élite of the Raj, and argues for Jinnah's continuing relevance as contemporary Islam debates its future direction.

Akbar S. Ahmed is a Fellow of Selwyn College, Cambridge, and the author of many books, including *Discovering Islam* (1988), *Postmodernism and Islam* (1992), and *Living Islam* (1993). He is the executive producer of a feature film and a documentary on Jinnah.

Jinnah, Pakistan and Islamic Identity

The search for Saladin

Akbar S. Ahmed

Routledge
Taylor & Francis Group

LONDON AND NEW YORK

First published 1997
by Routledge
11 New Fetter Lane, London EC4P 4EE

Simultaneously published in the USA and Canada
by Routledge
29 West 35th Street, New York, NY 10001

Reprinted 2000, 2001, 2002, 2004

Routledge is an imprint of the Taylor & Francis Group

© 1997 Akbar S. Ahmed

Typeset in Palatino by Solidus (Bristol) Limited
Printed and bound in Great Britain by
TJ International Ltd, Padstow, Cornwall

British Library Cataloguing in Publication Data
A catalogue record for this book is available from the British Library

Library of Congress Cataloguing in Publication Data
Ahmed, Akbar S.
Jinnah, Pakistan and Islamic identity: the search for Saladin / Akbar S. Ahmed.
p.   cm.
Includes bibliographical references and index.
1. Jinnah, Mohammed Ali, 1876–1948.   2. India—Politics and
government—1919–1947.   3. Pakistan—History—1947–   4. Islam and
state—Pakistan.   5. Statesmen—Pakistan—Biography.   I. Title.
DS385.J5A69   1997
954.03′5′092—dc21   97-10613
                                                                            CIP

ISBN 0-415-14965-7 (hbk)
ISBN 0-415-14966-5 (pbk)

For Mina, Amineh and Arsallah
with love

Contents

Contents

Plates

Plates

Preface

In August 1947 I found myself on a slow train to Pakistan. My parents had decided to follow Mr Jinnah to the promised land of Pakistan, the land of the pure. Like millions of others they were following the call of the Quaid-i-Azam, as Jinnah was – and is – known by his admirers. To them, as an Englishman said, he was the King of England, the Prime Minister and the Archbishop of Canterbury rolled into one. For Muslims, he was like the Saladin of the age, the victor of Jerusalem, the defender of the oppressed.

Theirs was an act of blind faith. They were losing a home but found solace in the belief that they were gaining a country. They had no idea where they were going or what they would find at their journey's end. Many did not make it through the communal violence that waited for them in the plains of the Punjab. Our story here is tied to the bloody creation of Pakistan.

It was a sultry, oppressive summer and death was in the air. If my mother had not exercised what my father called a woman's intuition we might not have made it at all. She insisted we catch a later train. Later we heard that the passengers on the earlier train had all been killed by Sikhs somewhere in the Punjab. My family survived intact, although the journey was agonizingly slow. But almost two million people were not so lucky, for Muslims, Hindus and Sikhs were killing each other in shameless acts of savagery.

We were among some 15 million people who were transferring themselves from one part of the subcontinent to the other – Hindus and Sikhs to India, Muslims to Pakistan. Mountbatten and to an extent his friend Nehru, we believed, were responsible for much of the suffering. On our arrival in Karachi from Delhi we found there was as much adulation of Jinnah as there was hatred of the leaders we had left behind. Gandhi was seen as the evil genius, Nehru the scheming Brahmin and Mountbatten the wicked Englishman determined to ruin Pakistan. These images reflected those across the border, where Jinnah was the object of hatred for Indians. It was not an auspicious start to relations between India and Pakistan.

Jinnah, Mountbatten, Nehru, Gandhi – already my young life was in danger of being overwhelmed by these larger-than-life names. I put them in the back of my mind where they remained for most of my life. Now, with half a century gone, I felt I needed to return to that time. In doing so I found myself faced with questions of leadership, statehood, security and identity in the context of plural societies – issues that remain central to all of us as the new millennium approaches. Clearly Jinnah's story is of relevance to our lives today.

The story points to the links with the past and the attendant disruption and transformation. When Jinnah was leading the Pakistan movement in the 1940s I was a child. He was born in 1876 just two decades after the last Mughal emperor, Zafar Shah, sat on his throne in Delhi. One of Zafar's literary tutors was the poet Mirza Ghalib, who in turn acknowledged as his master the poet Mir Taqi Mir. Mir, who was alive when Ghalib was a young child, was born only a few years after the death of the last of the great Mughal emperors, Aurangzeb, in 1707. The span of time from Aurangzeb's death in 1707 to Jinnah's death in 1948 covers two centuries of disintegration and changing political fortunes for Muslims in South Asia (for a visual impression of this, see maps 1–4, 'The Shrinking World of the Muslims'). This uncertainty is reflected in the character of Muslims and the nature of their society today.

One of the objectives of this study is to add an anthropological dimension to the account of events – and of leaders – in the 1940s. Accordingly I have drawn partly on oral interviews with ordinary people who lived through the drama to discover what Pakistan and Jinnah meant to them and what they mean now, in terms also of culture, clothes, marriage, rituals and the everyday. Such evidence tends to be omitted from traditional political accounts.

I talked to many of the British involved in the events of 1947, including the daughters of Lord Mountbatten, the Countess Mountbatten and Lady Pamela Hicks, as well as Christopher Beaumont and Alan Campbell-Johnson. British historians and politicians like Tony Benn, Gordon Johnson, Alastair Lamb, Neville Maxwell, Andrew Roberts and Francis Robinson were also generous with their time. I am also grateful to the insights of those Pakistanis who knew or met Jinnah: G. M. Adamjee, the late Malik Ahsan, Yahya Bakhtiar, Wajid Shamsul Hasan, Shaukat Hyat, Shaista Ikramullah, Colonel S. G. Mahdi, Lady Viqarunissa Noon, S. S. Pirzada, Makhdoom Sajjad Hussain Qureshi, Zeenat Rashid, Hashim Raza, Sahibzada Yaqub, Ijlal Zaidi and Dr Z. H. Zaidi.

These Pakistanis are an important source of information about Mr Jinnah. Most of them are now about eighty years old; some died during the years I was working on the Jinnah project. Their impressions and perceptions of those times also help us to understand the impact of Jinnah on the Muslims. Their descriptions of him do not tally with the prevailing negative image of Jinnah. To those Pakistanis who knew him he is a towering, charismatic hero. He looked like the conqueror of Delhi, one of them remarked. He was like God, said another, aware of the sacrilegious nature of the comparison. Yet today Jinnah appears a remote, cold and inaccessible figure in books and films. Which is the correct image?

Other people keen to divest themselves of their memories included non-Pakistanis too. Their generosity was inspiring. For example, out of the blue I received a letter from Douglas Crook, who had been a young Royal Air Force officer at Karachi when Jinnah first landed there as Governor-General in 1947. He visited me in Cambridge and kindly gave me the unpublished photographs he had taken on that occasion with his small camera. Similarly, Yahya Bakhtiar let me have private photographs of Jinnah that he had taken during the 1940s.

I am grateful to the Pakistani historians, such as Professor Riaz Ahmad, Ayesha Jalal, Sharif al Mujahid, S. S. Pirzada and Dr Z. H. Zaidi for their support. I also benefited from the knowledge and insight of some outstanding Indian scholars. In particular, I should like to mention Professor Bhiku Parekh, H. M. Seervai, Professor A. M. Khusro, Dr Ashis Nandy, Rajmohan Gandhi and Anita Graham. I was saddened by the death of H. M. Seervai of Bombay in early 1996, since I had been looking forward to meeting him. His book (1990) was a landmark in the study of partition: he had overturned the traditional British and Indian way of looking at personalities and events connected with partition; Jinnah had emerged on top and Mountbatten was exposed.

It is assumed by Pakistanis that among Indians there is a negative perception of Jinnah which is monolithic. This is not correct: to many Indians, Jinnah is a great South Asian leader. Dr Krishna Gamre, one of the leaders of the Dalit movement in India, is one such person. To him Jinnah is a far greater hero in Indian history than Gandhi or Nehru. Indeed, he blames the latter for having created Pakistan through their intransigence and neglect of the genuine fears of the minorities and he has provided me with substantial material to support his view.

Some of the most personal revelations about Jinnah came from his only child Dina Wadia. I was fortunate in being able to meet her and talk to her over the years I was working on this project and learned much about Dina and her father that was previously unknown. Other biographers including Professor Stanley Wolpert and Ayesha Jalal had been unable to interview her.

This book is part of a bigger project on Jinnah which I began in 1993 and hoped to complete in 1997, the fiftieth year of Pakistan's birth. The project developed into a feature film called *Jinnah*, a television documentary and a graphic novel under the title *The Quaid: Jinnah and the Story of Pakistan* (published by Oxford University Press, Ahmed 1997b). This ambitious project on Jinnah became my full-time obsession; its scope, nature and global implications created periods of immense pressure for me. (The shooting of the film *Jinnah* in Pakistan from March to May, under almost impossible conditions, was fraught with tension (see 'Rebirth of a Nation' by Lucy Hodges in *The Times Higher Education Supplement*, 23 May 1997). It is a story worth telling in itself as much for a comment on the making of the film as on contemporary Pakistan. A TV documentary called *The Making of Jinnah* has already been made for release in 1997.)

The following people assisted and encouraged me in my work on Jinnah in different ways: Nighat and Mueen Afzal, Professor Khurshid Ahmad, Ilyas and Mohsin Akhtar, Muazzam Ali, Sardar Asseff Ahmed Ali, Sheikh Omar Ali, Muhammad Ashraf, Dr Nasim Ashraf, Tariq Azim, Sir Nicholas Barrington, Imtiaz Rafi Butt, Dr Lionel Carter, Amir and Almas Chinoy, Akram Choudhry, Jamil Dehlavi, Farrukh Dhondy, Prince Muhammad al Faisal al Saud of Saudi Arabia, Marina and Shaukat Fareed, Sharif Farooq, Sir Oliver Forster, Najma and Jamil Hamdani, Ejaz ul-Haq, Hussain and Hameed Haroon, Sadruddin Hashwani, Crown Prince Hassan of Jordan, Shagufta and Sayyed Azmat Hassan, Irshad Ahmed Haqqani, Iran Ispahani, Dr Shafqat Shah Jamote, General Jehangir Karamat, Shameem and Ash Karim, General Ali Quli Khan, Imran Khan, Mumtaz Khan, Nasreen and Asad Hayat Khan, Dr Julius Lipner, Dr Maleeha

Lodhi, Ruby Malik, Dr Ghazanfar Mehdi, Liaquat Merchant, Crown Prince Sidi Mohamed of Morocco, Hugh Purcell, Moeen Qureshi, Jamshed Rahim, Nadir Rahim, Lady and Sir Julian Ridsdale, Ameena Saiyid, Azra and Wasim Sajjad, Victoria Schofield, Farooq Shah, Mian Hussein Sharif, James Shera, Kamal Siddiqui, Dr André Singer and S. M. Zafar.

The support of the President of Pakistan, Sardar Farooq Khan Leghari, was exemplary. His confidence in my work never wavered and was a source of strength in the dark days. I wish to express warm gratitude to Selwyn College, Cambridge – and its Fellows – for the Fellowship awarded to me. A special word of thanks to my editors Mari Shullaw and Linden Stafford; together they improved the book and provided me with support and insight as it developed. My wife Zeenat as always stood by me, working round the clock. She was overheard telling her sister that she had the best possible of husbands until he became obsessed with Jinnah; my love and gratitude to her for having faith that I would return to normality. She is the real heroine of my film and book project on Jinnah.

Some of the material has appeared in my chapter 'Social Structure and Flows', in W. E. James and S. Roy (eds), *Foundations of Pakistan's Political Economy* (1992), in *Modern Asian Studies* (Cambridge), *History Today* (London), in *The World Today* (London) and *Ethnic and Racial Studies* (London); they are gratefully acknowledged.

In the cultural context of the subcontinent names of respected leaders are often preceded by titles. Thus Nehru is Pandit Jawaharlal Nehru; Gandhi is Mahatma Gandhi; Jinnah is Quaid-i-Azam Mohammed Ali Jinnah. It is considered rude to call them only by their last names. Without wishing to be provocative, however, I shall refer to them mainly by their surnames. No offence is intended. It is merely a question of logistics in a book that needs to save space. Thus Pandit Jawaharlal Nehru will be Nehru; Mahatma Mohandas Karamchand Gandhi will be Gandhi; and Quaid-i-Azam Mohammed Ali Jinnah will be Jinnah.

This book is dedicated to my granddaughter, Mina, and her parents, Amineh and Arsallah. Mina's life will take shape in the early years of the next century and will be exposed to the turbulence and cross-currents of cultures and civilizations clashing, colliding and synthesizing. Mina is a good example of the South Asian global diaspora, the pattern that is forming. Her father was born in Hoti Mardan, in North Pakistan, her mother in Jinnah's city, Karachi, on the coast of the Arabian Sea. Mina was born in Cambridge; her maternal grandmother was born in Saidu Sharif, Swat, in the northern hills of the subcontinent, her grandfather in Allahabad, deep in the Gangetic plain. Her own blood is a similar mixture: the blood of the holy Prophet of Islam, the blood of the Nawabs of Hoti, of the Wali of Swat, of her Pathan ancestry. With this book I give Mina all my love and blessings for her millennial journey.

Akbar S. Ahmed
Cambridge, 5 June 1997

Introduction: Seeking Saladin

The approaching millennium promises to accelerate the processes of globalization which are already irreversible and advancing dizzily before our eyes to envelop even the most remote people of the world in a suffocating embrace. Structures, values and ideas that we took for granted for most of this century are disintegrating. Global answers are required if we are to adjust to and understand one another.

A host of broad questions which have a universal echo will therefore be raised in this book. How can different world cultures learn to live with each other? How can local cultures retain their sense of identity and dignity in the face of the global onslaught of non-stop satellite television transmission, instant high-tech communications, and so on? How can the less privileged in society, including minorities, feel secure as the power of the state becomes increasingly intrusive? Can the modern state justify its legitimacy in the face of widespread accusations of violence and corruption? Will religion be a force for good or the cause of destruction? Will the new millennium bring unity, a better understanding or sharper conflict between different peoples?

For Muslims, a number of related questions also require answers. Who speaks for Islam? How do the negative media images of Islam affect Muslim leaders? What model of political leadership could best resolve the issue of Muslim identity while ensuring the safety of the citizens? Can a satisfactory balance be found between tradition and the modern world?

Muslim leaders and the quest for identity

As we near the end of the millennium we can identify several distinct Muslim responses to these questions (see Ahmed 1988, 1996a and 1996b). The Muslim leaders engaged in this exercise in the late twentieth century have comprised many different types. These include religious clerics, like Ayatollah Khomeini in Iran; dynastic kings, such as the rulers of Saudi Arabia or Kuwait; military dictators (of whom there are many in the Arab world); leaders of resistance movements (such as the Palestine Liberation Organization leader Yasser Arafat, or the Chechen resistance leader Dzhokhar Dudayev); and various revolutionary, charismatic and idiosyncratic figures. None of these types of leader has achieved a new or modern Muslim state without oppression, bloodshed or devastation suffered by the people and their country.

Those rulers who believe in a balance between tradition and modernity, between Islam and the West, have been strong in South Asia, and Jinnah was one of these. In the particular circumstances of the 1940s, he took a different path from the kinds of leaders I have listed above, and this book will explore how he set about his task.

The world media, especially in the West, know only three or four Muslim leaders – Arafat, Khomeini, Gaddafi and Saddam – whom they have made the most hated villains in contemporary global culture. This fuels the 'clash of civilizations' argument that Islam is intrinsically an enemy of the West (Ahmed 1992a, 1993a, 1993d, 1995a, 1996b; Fukuyama 1992; Huntington 1993; Mestrovic 1994); but it is both dangerous reductionism on the part of the West and cultural humiliation for Muslims (since these leaders are by no means universally accepted by Muslims themselves). Yet how many in the West know of other Muslim leaders like Jinnah? For Muslims today Jinnah's relevance is therefore great in providing not only a response to negative media images but an authentic model of leadership.

Late in the twentieth century the Muslim world faces a new crisis of leadership, but this time there is a far greater urgency, for several reasons. The world has shrunk; it is more intolerant; there is a growing feeling that civilizations are heading for a final showdown. This may sound apocalyptic but one has only to pick up the 'quality' newspapers published in Washington, London and Paris to sense the mood. Often the most pernicious ethnic, racial and religious prejudices are paraded as serious political commentary. We see this and we despair.

It is not an easy time to be a Muslim. To be Muslim and male in the 1990s in many parts of the world is to attract hostility. Even where Muslims live in large numbers it seems to make little difference. In Karachi it can mean being kidnapped or killed; but things are not much better across the border in India. Indeed, given the choice, the Muslim male may be marginally better off in Karachi: in Bombay during a communal riot the mob may force his trousers down to see if he is circumcised and then stab him.

One answer is to seek asylum, like the ruler of Afghanistan in the last century who, exasperated by his people, said he would rather be a grass-cutter in the British camp than a king in his own land. Today many members of the Muslim élite appear to be saying the same when they apply to settle in the USA or UK.

Muslims are responding individually to political crises. They belong either to a party with loyalties to a corrupt or despotic leader who is the source of their patronage, or to a sect which is increasingly introspective, or else to an inward-looking lineage or clan. These are not good signs. When they need to be united on a broader platform they fall into the black hole of parochial divisions.

But this is not how the rest of the world sees Muslims. Whatever their political, sectarian or ethnic affiliations, the world regards them as 'Muslim'. They were being hounded in Bosnia, Central Asia and India because they were identified as 'Muslim'. Even the most lukewarm, the most 'secular' Muslims have been condemned as 'Muslim fanatics' by critics and thus were being persecuted simply because of their genealogy. Yet they themselves are largely unaware of the nature of the hatred and how to formulate a meaningful response to it.

It is a monumental failure of imagination and organization. Muslims are failing to connect different points in the global political and cultural landscape. This failure is costing them the loss of land, power and dignity. They seem almost paralysed, vulnerable – people to be kicked and humiliated at will on the world stage.

Although Muslims have been branded as fanatics, terrorists and extremists, they have been, by and large, benevolent rulers when in power in the past. Philosophically, theologically and culturally they have protected minorities and provided justice. Muslims point out that had they been fanatics they would have annihilated the Christians in the Iberian peninsula and in the Balkans when they ruled there. In fact it was the Christians in Spain who wiped out the Muslims in Renaissance Europe; in the Balkans a similar attempt was made by non-Muslims in recent times. In the subcontinent, when the British ruled and numbers were counted for the census, it became clear the great majority of the population were Hindus. Had the Muslims been fanatical and determined to change the demographic balance they would have succeeded.

Muslims have been killed in vast numbers in the 1990s by non-Muslim armies and state paramilitary forces using high-tech weaponry. The numbers, although difficult to ascertain exactly, are appalling: over 50,000 each in Kashmir, in Chechniya and in Bosnia. Hundreds of thousands of Muslims have been displaced, bombed and uprooted in Palestine and Lebanon (and let us not forget the Christian Arabs). But some Muslims have themselves been equally harsh with other Muslims. In Algeria in the last few years another 50,000, perhaps more, have been killed; the dispossessed Kurds have been brutally persecuted by several Muslim countries; in Karachi, Muslims have killed and tortured each other in thousands. It is a bad time to look at Muslim civilizations; more critical thinking needs to be done by its writers, policy planners and leaders to prepare for the way ahead.

The search for Saladin

Muslim heroes in history are sometimes men of ideas like Al-Beruni (in the tenth–eleventh century) and Ibn Khaldun (fourteenth–fifteenth century) but are usually men of action like Tariq, who conquered Spain in the eighth century, or Babar, who established the Mughal dynasty in sixteenth-century India. The heroes who are immortalized are those who combine Muslim tradition and a dramatic victory at a time of general crisis, such as Saladin.

Saladin is the leader *par excellence*, as described in the preface to a popular book written by a Muslim author, *Hundred Great Muslims*: 'Saladin the Great (Sultan Salahuddin Ayyubi) ... was a symbol of Muslim unity and solidarity, piety and strength' (J. Ahmed 1977). Contemporary Muslims everywhere look for Saladin, whether in Britain (Werbner 1990: 55) or in India (Kakar 1995: 221) or in the Arab world (see the article by David Hirst in the *Guardian*, 'Divided Muslim peoples yearn for a new Saladin', 12 December 1992); even Saddam Hussein exploited this yearning by encouraging his press to project him as another Saladin during the Gulf War.

Introduction

Among Muslims, Saladin's name is synonymous with courage, compassion, integrity and respect for culture. My use of Saladin in the sociological imagination is not to be taken literally; it is a metaphor, a cultural construct, an ideal-type. In this manner an analogy can be made between Saladin and Jinnah.

Saladin and Jinnah are both known in history for their victory – Saladin recapturing Jerusalem, Jinnah winning Pakistan. Although they are an unlikely pair, none the less they have much in common. Both were outsiders in mainstream Muslim society. Saladin was not an Arab in a world dominated by the Arabs and their language; indeed, he was a Kurd, a tribal people with their own culture and language. Jinnah did not belong to the culture of the United Provinces (UP) and Punjab which dominated the Muslims of India. He was from the Sind, originally Gujarat, and was a member of one of the minor sects within Islam. He did not speak Urdu, the main language of North India; nor did he dress or behave like those who lived in the UP and the Punjab. Both Saladin and Jinnah took on the most renowned opponents of their age, almost mythical in stature. Saladin fought against Richard the Lionheart and Jinnah challenged Mountbatten, Gandhi and Nehru.

Saladin and Jinnah both tried to echo the ultimate leadership model for Muslims: that of the holy Prophet. Unlike Jesus Christ, who was crucified before his followers established the Christian religion and who never sought to gain material power on earth, the holy Prophet not only introduced a new religion and saw it spread throughout the land, but ended his days as the head of a new Islamic state. That, for every Muslim, would be the ideal: triumph and success here on earth; the balance between *din* (religion) and *dunya* (the world).

Jinnah may have preferred to speak English and worn Savile Row suits but for the Muslims he was none the less, in the popular imagination, a modern Saladin (Ahmed 1993a, 1994, 1996a, 1997a, 1997b). Dr Jaffar Qureshi, an Indian Muslim from Hyderabad, referred to Jinnah in this way. I was curious why he regarded Jinnah as a Saladin rather than as another Gandhi, another Mandela, or another de Gaulle. The answer was simple: Qureshi was looking at Jinnah from the point of view of a Muslim.

Discovering Jinnah and his Pakistan

To many Pakistanis in 1947, the founding of the state of Pakistan itself was a moment of attaining the impossible, a nation and a people dedicated to working for a higher and noble cause. Today Pakistan is a shrunken travesty of what its supporters demanded on the basis of population and history half a century ago. Both its provinces, Sind and the North-West Frontier Province, were created this century from districts and agencies carved out of larger provinces, Bombay and Punjab respectively. Its provinces were therefore made up of truncated parts of the older British provinces. The two full provinces Jinnah insisted on, Punjab and Bengal, were divided by the British in spite of his warnings; untold misery and communal violence followed. Even the chopped-up Pakistan Jinnah was offered has now been further mutilated: Bengal is no longer part of Pakistan and only bits of Kashmir belong in it.

But Pakistan meant more than just territory, more than a defined area with boundaries; Pakistan meant a culmination of a Muslim movement rooted in history, the quest for a mystical homeland, a Pakistan, a land of the pure. That is why the reality of the violence, corruption, nepotism, mismanagement and materialism of Pakistan in the 1990s is so painful. Mosques are not sacred, public places, private homes, nowhere is safe especially in its main city Karachi. If the creation itself is so poor, asked critics, how could the creator have had any merit?

In the 1990s Jinnah's name continues to evoke controversy across the world (in December 1996 he was attacked in special features by *Time* magazine, in an article by Carl Posey in the issue of 23 December, and in the *Khilafah*, the journal of the Hizb-ut-Tahrir in the UK). In Pakistan he remains the very symbol of the state, the father of the nation, the saviour of the Muslims, the man who created a homeland for them and led his community to it. In India he is also a symbol, but a symbol of the ultimate betrayal: the partition of Mother India.

In Britain too his image is contradictory for Muslims. For the Hizb-ut-Tahrir, the extremist Muslim organization, and Dr Kalim Siddiqui of the so-called Muslim Parliament, he is the epitome of a man who sold his soul to the West: the 'imperialist collaborator', he is billed on Hizb posters. They see his Anglicized appearance and condemn him (see *Khilafah*, December 1996). They fail to recognize the scale of his achievement or understand its cultural and religious context. But most Pakistanis in Britain respect Jinnah; many who seek a point of reference in an alien land perceive him as a man of extraordinary spiritual authority. In Manchester, Pakistani mullahs talk of him as a saint (see the work of the British anthropologist Pnina Werbner).

There are many people even in Pakistan who have little time for Jinnah. Corrupt democrats and military dictators because of his integrity, Marxists because they find him too religious, narrow-minded clerics who find him too broadminded and tolerant a Muslim, ignorant journalists and lazy scholars – all these find it easier either to ignore Jinnah or to create in their own minds a self-serving image.

The élite of Pakistan are happy to keep Jinnah in the official portraits and on banknotes but not heed his example. The autocratic rulers of Pakistan have been equally happy to pay him little more than lip-service – like Banquo's ghost at the banquet he is a potent reminder of their shortcomings. We need to ask the rulers of Pakistan some questions. Has there been a plan to marginalize him? Has there been a conspiracy to tarnish Jinnah's image? What is the record of Pakistan in promoting Jinnah's standing on the international stage?

I also wish to challenge many of the myths about the Pakistan movement: that Jinnah was unreasonable and robot-like, obsessed with Pakistan, that only Muslims supported him in the movement, that the entire Muslim body stood behind him like a monolith, that Gandhi was the apostle of non-violence, that Lord Mountbatten was fair and just in distributing the lands that would become India and Pakistan, that Lady Mountbatten's affair with Nehru was justifiably concealed and had little impact on the partition process. I also suggest that the Muslims of India in the 1940s regarded Jinnah as a heroic figure. In retrospect, however, it is difficult to imagine that he received adulation from the Muslim masses through the length and breadth of India, and that he had already begun to create an international pan-Islamic network.

Several anthropological questions are raised in the study of Jinnah. Why did Muslims respond positively to a man who did not dress and behave like them? Why did they see in him a saviour of their community when he was not even an orthodox Muslim? What sociological and historical factors explain their increasing reverence towards him today?

But is it really so simple? Do popular mythologies really approximate to reality? Some of the finest and most objective writing on Jinnah has come from India recently; many in Pakistan have serious reservations about him and wish to undermine him, his personality and his message. There are undercurrents in the analysis of Jinnah which are not at first visible. If Pakistan falls apart in the next few years, as many commentators appear to think, then Jinnah's role in history will be reduced to a footnote. For those who disagree, Jinnah's name in Bangladesh is a salutary example. Until 1971 the main buildings and roads of the towns and cities were named after Jinnah, but after 1971 his name disappeared from the map. This may perhaps be his fate in what is now Pakistan.

Alongside the many benighted contemporary Asian leaders, Jinnah seems surprisingly modern. All the major issues of our times – women's rights, human rights, minority rights, upholding the constitution and the rule of law – were espoused by him with passion. His financial and moral integrity was acknowledged even by his adversaries (nothing could buy him off, not even the offer of the job of first Prime Minister of India, made by both Mountbatten and Gandhi, if he gave up his idea of Pakistan).

Yet Jinnah's story is in danger of being forgotten; it has been buried under layers of propaganda, lies and plain ignorance. Jinnah is depicted as an 'enigma' by non-Pakistanis; even Pakistani writers, those who should know him, have failed to penetrate the seemingly impersonal exterior. This book will be an attempt to understand Jinnah.

Discussion

We can read this book on several levels. It is the biography of Jinnah; and it is a discussion of the state that he founded, Pakistan. It is also autobiography, in that it reflects my own citizenship and identity as a Pakistani. The search for identity is complicated by the pull between the forces of tradition and of modernity, a struggle expressed in heightened awareness of ethnicity and religion. But it is not a simple quest; neighbours too search for their own identity, in the process creating the suggestion of the clash of civilizations. The continuing search for identity, both mystical in its atavistic resonance and concrete in the urgent need to find security, forms a central theme of this discussion.

The book is about a subcontinent which in demographic, cultural, political and economic terms is one of the most important regions on earth; about one-quarter of humanity, over a billion people, live there. The Muslims of the subcontinent, over one-third of Islam's billion followers, have produced philosophers, poets and politicians, men of ideas and action. Together with the founding fathers of India – Gandhi, Nehru, Patel, Dr Ambedkar, Bose, and so on – they are chiselled on the Mount Rushmore of our subcontinental imagination.

But South Asia is in ethnic and religious turmoil. From Kabul to Kandy, from Karachi to Cox's Bazaar, issues of identity, ethnic and religious revivalism, nationhood and communal violence are still front-page news. Those who imagine the subcontinent to be a land of gentle mystics and spiritual eccentrics will be disturbed by the facts that I will present and the analysis that will follow. Many stereotypes will be challenged.

After the destruction of the mosque at Ayodhya in 1992 Hindu temples in the UK were damaged. Clearly the passions and conflicts of the subcontinent have involved its communities living in the UK, the USA and elsewhere. Their influence far exceeds their numbers. In the arts, in literature, in the cinema, in sport they have made an international mark. Indian restaurants and cinema are now part of British cultural life. In the 1990s there is a global dimension to the study of South Asia.

This book is thus about several civilizations living side by side, sometimes synthesizing, sometimes clashing. I shall examine these civilizations through the prism of one man's life: that of Jinnah. Thus our study becomes a complex examination of interpenetrating cultures and political systems. This is neither traditional biography nor traditional history; it is not a mechanistic recounting of dates and major events. I shall explain how the ongoing political and cultural confrontations in the subcontinent are rooted in history, how the endemic tension between India and Pakistan reflects the pattern of history that has formed. To study Jinnah is to open the wounds of history.

When a leader who commands respect in the Muslim community appears, and can focus on a cause, Muslims are capable of moving mountains. When there is no leadership or the leadership is corrupt, the reverse is true and Muslim society begins to disintegrate; cynicism and disillusionment prevail.

Muslim society, in responding to modernity, when confronted with two clear choices of leadership in the last century rejected both. The first was traditionalist, orthodox and exemplified by the *ulema*, the clerics and religious figures of Islam. The second type of leadership rejected Islam altogether either by adopting extreme forms of Sufistic or unorthodox behaviour or by mimicking other cultures like the British or the Hindu. There was a third way: a synthesis of several principles. While holding on to the main tenets of Islam it also interacted with other civilizations, particularly the West, then exemplified by the British. Jinnah may be considered a personification of the model of synthesis; but is it still valid? Does the fact that this is a weak model in the late twentieth century explain how both groups can so easily distort his message and significance and/ or then crudely appropriate him?

The structure of the book

In chapter 1, I will give a brief account of Jinnah's life. I shall also discuss the people who mattered to him; they will assist us in understanding his personal life which he guarded so carefully. Images of Jinnah in the literature and in the media will be examined with reference to the different perspectives, especially the British, Indian and Pakistani. Chapter 2 will outline the history of the subcontinent, focusing on the developments that made Jinnah's movement possible. I shall explain the clash between the British, Hindu and Muslim civilizations and ask: was there always a confrontation between Hindus and Muslims or were there areas of synthesis?

Chapters 3 and 4 will trace Jinnah's conversion from ambassador of Hindu–Muslim unity to Muslim champion. It was clearly not a case of the blinding light on the road to

Damascus but a slow, if inevitable, process. Several developments in the 1920s which explain Jinnah's conversion will be explored. At the same time the following questions will be borne in mind. How are we to penetrate the formal, enigmatic exterior that Jinnah deliberately cultivated most of his life? How can we understand a man who was so reticent, who did not leave any memoirs or a wealth of anecdotes? Can we find clues in his dress and in his speeches? Were Jinnah's ideas influenced by those of the poet-philosopher Allama Iqbal and what evidence do we possess?

In chapter 5, I shall discuss Mountbatten's role as the last Viceroy of India and the part he played in the creation of Pakistan in 1947. In so doing I shall ask why the British and Hindu leaders – Mountbatten, Nehru and Gandhi – saw Jinnah and the Muslims as an obstacle in their path. Lord and Lady Mountbatten's relationship with Nehru and its bearing on Jinnah will feature in chapter 6. Not only did both Mountbattens have a close friendship with Nehru but during the summer of 1947 a love affair developed between Nehru and Edwina Mountbatten. I shall explore the relationship's sociological implications in terms of race and culture, its political ramifications and its possible effect, direct or indirect, on decision-making in 1947. What was its impact on the future of India and Pakistan? Why did historians – South Asian and British – fail for almost half a century to comment on the liaison? If they knew what was going on, why is there no hint of it in their work? The chapter concludes with an account of the horrifying violence that broke out in the aftermath of partition.

Chapters 7 and 8 discuss the creation of Pakistan and its subsequent history, raising many questions. For example, how did Jinnah envisage an Islamic identity for the nation? Did he favour a secular or a fundamentalist state? Chapter 8 will examine Jinnah's relevance in modern-day Pakistan. It will also discuss India and the situation of the Muslims there. I shall ask why in India, where Jinnah is seen as a villain, any Muslim leader demanding rights is contemptuously called a 'second Jinnah'. Finally I investigate the link between Jinnah and Bangladesh, which was part of Pakistan until 1971, and the crisis of Muslim disunity in South Asia.

The epilogue will ask where South Asians are heading as the new millennium approaches. As I shall point out, at the end of the twentieth century there is an urgent need for dialogue, for reassessment, for greater harmony between India and Pakistan, between Hindu and Muslim. We must look to the future and try to overcome the prejudices of the past for the sake of the coming generations. We can achieve this, however, only if we are able to look at the past clearly and dispassionately, not using it for propaganda. Otherwise life in South Asia will turn to barbarism and savagery, negating the ideas of Jinnah, Nehru and Gandhi. We need to recognize the possibility that the states of the subcontinent could become locked in eternal confrontation, in a struggle that neither side could completely win: a pattern that has been all too painfully evident over the last half-century.

In conclusion I suggest steps to be taken to improve understanding and increase dialogue. The common ground needs to be strengthened. The differences must not be minimized but need to be understood. If the South Asian nations are to fulfil their economic and political destiny they must re-examine their origins and their founding fathers like Jinnah. On the threshold of the next millennium it is an appropriate time for stock-taking, for looking at the past and contemplating the coming years. It is in the spirit of reconciliation and dialogue that I write this book, secure in the knowledge that across the border, in India, there are others who share this spirit. A half-century is a good pretext for reassessment: 1997 is the fiftieth anniversary of Pakistan's birth. Fifty years on, India and Pakistan must now reach out to each other.

Methodology

Throughout this book I have attempted to simplify complex issues and paint with a broad brush in order to highlight what is of greatest relevance today. Diverse themes are raised – themes as varied as gender, sexual relationships, race, empire, Islam, secularism versus fundamentalism, the nature of nationhood, ethnic and religious identity, the problems of minorities and the overpowering influence of the media. These topical themes will be connected through my analysis and interpretation of Jinnah's life and related events. The focus will remain on Jinnah but I shall range widely, to place his life within a broader context than is usual in a traditional biography. Besides, I wish to explore old ground with new insight and new interpretations, including the perspectives generated by the notions of globalization and postmodernity (Ahmed 1992a, 1993d, 1996b; Ahmed and Donnan 1994; Ahmed and Shore 1995; Turner 1994).

This book is not conventional history or biography. We already have standard political, biographical and historical accounts; my study will use the methodology of cultural anthropology, semiotics and media studies. In keeping with anthropological methods I have asked ordinary people to give their comments on the extraordinary figures and events they witnessed. This has allowed a certain informal, folk perspective on history, while nevertheless including larger themes and climactic moments.

We shall examine the photographs taken at the time. They tell us a lot. We learn through body language and dress how people projected themselves and what they wished to say about themselves. We shall also examine how television and cinema have depicted the last days of the British Raj.

With so much propaganda against Islam in the world media and the incoherent responses from within Islam, it is more than ever imperative to explain the actual position, to go back to the sources. The source in this particular case leads us to a thorough account of Jinnah. We therefore need to remove the layers of demonology and hagiography that have been accumulated around him by critics and admirers respectively. It is not an easy task because it challenges many cherished ideas and long-held prejudices. Not only emotions but academic reputations are also affected. This makes it a difficult but even more urgent enterprise.

The standard literature on Jinnah is over a decade old (Jalal 1985; Talbot 1984; Wolpert 1984). Some of the information now available to us alters the image of Jinnah: for instance, until recently it was assumed – and it is still assumed in many quarters – that Jinnah was not really 'Islamic'; that he had no contact with his daughter Dina after she married against his wishes and that he had virtually no relationship with the Muslim community, interacting with people only in meetings and committee rooms, working with the skill of a lawyer on constitutional drafts. Allegations that Mountbatten was hostile to Jinnah and Pakistan and therefore out to damage both, once dismissed as a figment of the dark Pakistani imagination, have now been confirmed, thanks to the evidence provided by people like Christopher Beaumont (who was secretary to Sir Cyril

Radcliffe, the man responsible for dividing India in 1947).

    I am aware of the danger that some of my comments on Jinnah and the Pakistan movement will be misconstrued as an attempt at whitewash, as a reflexive defence by a Pakistani. I shall therefore support my case with extensive references from non-Muslim and non-Pakistani sources. There is literature around Jinnah which can be mined for the arguments that I will present. It is the arguments that will be new, not the facts and figures. I am reinterpreting history, not reinventing it.

Maps

The Shrinking World of the Muslims

Kabul ●
Ghazni ●
KASHMIR
Lahore ●
PUNJAB
● Panipat
RAJPUTANA
● Delhi
BALUCHISTAN
● Agra
AVADH
SIND
Ajmer ●
Benaras ●
BENGAL
Dhaka ●
MUGHAL EMPIRE
DECCAN
ARABIAN SEA
BAY OF BENGAL

☐ Muslim Empire/
area of influence

Map 1   The Mughal Empire, *c.* 1707, at the time of Aurangzeb's death

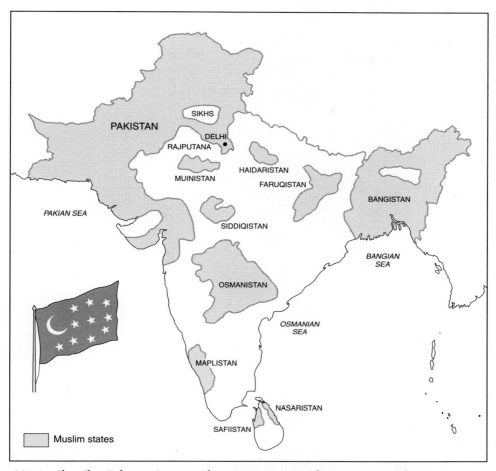

Map 2   Chaudhry Rahmat Ali's map: The Pak Commonwealth of Nations and their flag, *c*. 1940

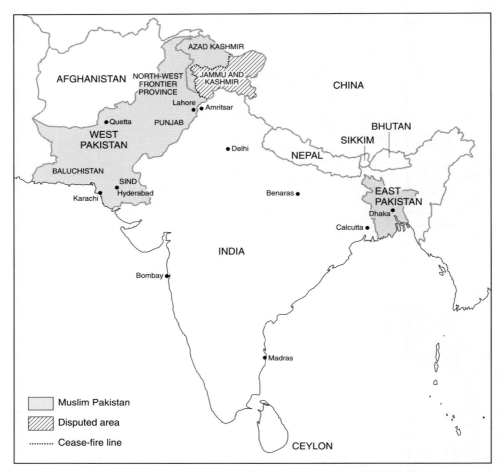

Map 3   Pakistan in 1947 (East and West including Azad Kashmir)

Map 4   Pakistan in 1997 (including Azad Kashmir)

Part I

Who's Afraid of
Mr Jinnah?

CHAPTER 1

Understanding Jinnah

God cannot alter the past, but historians can.

(Samuel Butler)

Islam gave the Muslims of India a sense of identity; dynasties like the Mughals gave them territory; poets like Allama Iqbal gave them a sense of destiny. Jinnah's towering stature derives from the fact that, by leading the Pakistan movement and creating the state of Pakistan, he gave them all three. For the Pakistanis he is simply the Quaid-i-Azam or the Great Leader. Whatever their political affiliation, they believe there is no one quite like him.

Jinnah: a life

Mohammed Ali Jinnah was born to an ordinary if comfortable household in Karachi, not far from where Islam first came to the Indian subcontinent in AD 711 in the person of the young Arab general Muhammad bin Qasim. However, Jinnah's date of birth – 25 December 1876 – and place of birth are presently under academic dispute.

Just before Jinnah's birth his father, Jinnahbhai Poonja, had moved from Gujarat to Karachi. Significantly, Jinnah's father was born in 1857 – at the end of one kind of Muslim history, with the failed uprisings in Delhi – and died in 1901 (F. Jinnah 1987: vii).

Jinnah's family traced its descent from Iran and reflected Shia, Sunni and Ismaili influences; some of the family names – Valji, Manbai and Nathoo – were even 'akin to Hindu names' (F. Jinnah 1987: 50). Such things mattered in a Muslim society conscious of underlining its non-Indian origins, a society where people gained status through family names such as Sayyed and Qureshi (suggesting Arab descent), Ispahani (Iran) and Durrani (Afghanistan). Another source has a different explanation of Jinnah's origins. Mr Jinnah, according to a Pakistani author, said that his male ancestor was a Rajput from Sahiwal in the Punjab who had married into the Ismaili Khojas and settled in Kathiawar (Beg 1986: 888). Although born into a Khoja (from *khwaja* or 'noble') family who were disciples of the Ismaili Aga Khan, Jinnah moved towards the Sunni sect early in life. There is evidence later, given by his relatives and associates in court, to establish that he was firmly a Sunni Muslim by the end of his life (Merchant 1990).

One of eight children, young Jinnah was educated in the Sind Madrasatul Islam and the Christian Missionary Society High School in Karachi. Shortly before he was sent to London in 1893 to join Graham's Shipping and Trading Company, which did business with Jinnah's father in Karachi, he was married to Emibai, a distant relative (F. Jinnah 1987: 61). It could be described as a traditional Asian marriage – the groom barely 16 years old and the bride a mere child. Emibai died shortly after Jinnah left for London; Jinnah barely knew her. But another death, that of his beloved mother, devastated him (ibid.).

Jinnah asserted his independence by making two important personal decisions. Within months of his arrival he left the business firm to join Lincoln's Inn and study law. In 1894 he changed his name by deed poll, dropping the 'bhai' from his surname. Not yet 20 years old, in 1896 he became the youngest Indian to pass. As a barrister, in his bearing, dress and delivery Jinnah cultivated a sense of theatre which would stand him in good stead in the future.

It has been said that Jinnah chose Lincoln's Inn because he saw the Prophet's name at the entrance. I went to Lincoln's Inn looking for the name on the gate, but there is no such gate nor any names. There is, however, a gigantic mural covering one entire wall in the main dining hall of Lincoln's Inn. Painted on it are some of the most influential lawgivers of history, like Moses and, indeed, the holy Prophet of Islam, who is shown in a green turban and green robes. A key at the bottom of the painting matches the names to the persons in the picture. Jinnah, I suspect, was not deliberately concealing the memory of his youth but recalling an association with the Inn of Court half a century after it had taken place. He had remembered there was a link, a genuine appreciation of Islam. Had those who have written about Jinnah's recollection bothered to visit Lincoln's Inn the mystery would have been solved. However, knowledge of the pictorial depiction of the holy Prophet would certainly spark protests; demands from the active British Muslim community for the removal of the painting would be heard in the UK.

In London Jinnah had discovered a passion for nationalist politics and had assisted Dadabhai Naoroji, the first Indian Member of Parliament. During the campaign he became acutely aware of racial prejudice, but he returned to India to practise law at the Bombay Bar in 1896 after a brief stopover in Karachi. He was then the only Muslim barrister in Bombay (see plate 1).

Jinnah was a typical Indian nationalist at the turn of the century, aiming to get rid of the British from the subcontinent as fast as possible. He adopted two strategies: one was to try to operate within the British system; the other was to work for a united front of Hindus, Muslims, Christians and Parsees against the British. He succeeded to an extent in both.

Jinnah's conduct reflected the prickly Indian expression of independence. On one occasion in Bombay, when Jinnah was arguing a case in court, the British presiding

4

Plate 1   Jinnah as a young barrister

judge interrupted him several times, exclaiming, 'Rubbish.' Jinnah responded: 'Your honour, nothing but rubbish has passed your mouth all morning.' Sir Charles Ollivant, judicial member of the Bombay provincial government, was so impressed by Jinnah that in 1901 he offered him permanent employment at 1,500 rupees a month. Jinnah declined, saying he would soon earn that amount in a day. Not too long afterwards he proved himself correct.

Stories like these added to Jinnah's reputation as an arrogant nationalist. His attitude towards the British may be explained culturally as well as temperamentally. He was not part of the cultural tradition of the United Provinces (UP) which had revolved around the imperial Mughal court based in Delhi and which smoothly transferred to the British after they moved up from Calcutta. Exaggerated courtesy, hyperbole, dissimulation, long and low bows, salaams that touched the forehead repeatedly – these marked the deference of courtiers to imperial authority. Even Sir Sayyed Ahmad Khan, one of the most illustrious champions of the Muslim renaissance in the late nineteenth century, came from a family that had served the Mughals, but had readily transferred his loyalties to the British.

Jinnah often antagonized his British superiors. Yet he was clever enough consciously to remain within the boundaries, pushing as far as he could but not allowing his opponents to penalize him on a point of law. In short he learned to use British law skilfully against the British.

At several points in his long career, Jinnah was threatened by the British with imprisonment on sedition charges for speaking in favour of Indian home rule or rights. He was frozen out by those British officials who wished their natives to be more deferential. For example, Lord Willingdon, Viceroy of India in 1931–6, did not take to him, and even the gruff but kindly Lord Wavell, Viceroy in 1943–7, was made to feel uncomfortable by Jinnah's clear-minded advocacy of the Muslims, even though he recognized the justice of Jinnah's arguments. The last Viceroy, however, Lord Mountbatten, could not cope with what he regarded as Jinnah's arrogance and haughtiness, preferring the natives to be more friendly and pliant.

Ambassador of Hindu–Muslim unity

On his return from England in 1896, Jinnah joined the Indian National Congress. In 1906 he attended the Calcutta session as secretary to Dadabhai Naoroji, who was now president of Congress. One of his patrons and supporters, G. K. Gokhale, a distinguished Brahmin, called him 'the best ambassador of Hindu–Muslim unity'. He was correct. When Bal Gangadhar Tilak, the Hindu nationalist, was being tried by the British on sedition charges in 1908 he asked Jinnah to represent him.

On 25 January 1910 Jinnah took his seat as the 'Muslim member from Bombay' on the sixty-man Legislative Council of India in Delhi. Any illusions the Viceroy, Lord Minto, may have harboured about the young Westernized lawyer as a potential ally were soon laid to rest. When Minto reprimanded Jinnah for using the words 'harsh and cruel' in describing the treatment of the Indians in South Africa, Jinnah replied: 'My Lord! I should feel much inclined to use much stronger language. But I am fully aware of the constitution of this Council, and I do not wish to trespass for one single moment. But I do say that the treatment meted out to Indians is the harshest and the feeling in this country is unanimous' (Wolpert 1984: 33).

Jinnah was an active and successful member of the (mainly Hindu) Indian Congress from the start and had resisted joining the Muslim League until 1913, seven years after its foundation. None the less, Jinnah stood up for Muslim rights. In 1913, for example, he piloted the Muslim Wakfs (Trust) Bill through the Viceroy's Legislative Council, and it won widespread praise. Muslims saw in him a heavyweight on their side. For his part, Jinnah thought the Muslim League was 'rapidly growing into a powerful factor for the birth of a United India' and maintained that the charge of 'separation' sometimes levelled at Muslims was extremely wide of the mark. On the death of his mentor, Gokhale, in 1915, Jinnah was struck with 'sorrow and grief' (Bolitho 1954: 62), and in May 1915 he proposed that a memorial to Gokhale be constructed. A few weeks later in a letter to *The Times of India* he argued that the Congress and League should meet to discuss the future of India, appealing to Muslim leaders to keep pace with their Hindu 'friends'.

Jinnah was elected president of the Lucknow Muslim League session in 1916 (from now he would be one of its main leaders, becoming president of the League itself from 1920 to 1930 and again from 1937 to 1947 until after the creation of Pakistan). Jinnah's political philosophy was revealed in the Lucknow conference in the same year when he helped bring the Congress and the League on to one platform to agree on a common scheme of reforms. Muslims were promised 30 per cent representation in provincial councils. A common front was constructed against British imperialism. The Lucknow Pact between the two parties resulted. Presiding over the extraordinary session, he described himself as 'a staunch Congressman' who had 'no love for sectarian cries' (Afzal 1966: 56–62).

This was the high point of his career as ambassador of the two communities and the closest the Congress and the Muslim League came. About this time, he fell in love with a Parsee girl, Rattanbai (Ruttie) Petit, known as 'the flower of Bombay'. Sir Dinshaw Petit, her father and a successful businessman, was furious, since Jinnah was not only of a different faith but more than twice her age, and he refused his consent to the marriage. As Ruttie was under-age, she and Jinnah waited until she was 18, in 1918, and then got married. Shortly before the ceremony Ruttie converted to Islam. In 1919 their daughter Dina was born.

By this time even the British recognized Jinnah's abilities. Edwin Montagu, the Secretary of State for India, wrote of him in 1917: 'Jinnah is a very clever man, and it is, of course, an outrage that such a man should have no chance of running the affairs of his own country' (Sayeed 1968: 86).

Jinnah cut a handsome figure at this time, as described in a standard biography by an American professor: 'Raven-haired with a moustache almost as full as Kitchener's and lean as a rapier, he sounded like Ronald Coleman, dressed like Anthony Eden, and was adored by most women at first sight, and admired or envied by most men' (Wolpert 1984: 40). A British general's wife met him at a viceregal dinner in Simla and wrote to her mother in England:

> After dinner, I had Mr. Jinnah to talk to. He is a great personality. He talks the most beautiful English. He models his manners and clothes on Du Maurier, the actor, and his English on Burke's speeches. He is a future Viceroy, if the present system of gradually Indianizing all the services continues. I have always wanted to meet him, and now I have had my wish. (Raza 1982: 34)

Mrs Sarojini Naidu, the nationalist poet, was infatuated: to her, Jinnah was the man of the future (see her 'Mohammad Ali Jinnah – ambassador of Hindu–Muslim unity', in J. Ahmed 1966). He symbolized everything attractive about modern India. Although her love remained unrequited she wrote him passionate poems; she also wrote about him in purple prose worthy of a Mills and Boon romance:

Tall and stately, but thin to the point of emaciation, languid and luxurious of habit, Mohammad Ali Jinnah's attenuated form is a deceptive sheath of a spirit of exceptional vitality and endurance. Somewhat formal and fastidious, and a little aloof and imperious of manner, the calm hauteur of his accustomed reserve but masks, for those who know him, a naïve and eager humanity, an intuition quick and tender as a woman's, a humour gay and winning as a child's. Pre-eminently rational and practical, discreet and dispassionate in his estimate and acceptance of life, the obvious sanity and serenity of his worldly wisdom effectually disguise a shy and splendid idealism which is of the very essence of the man. (Bolitho 1954: 21–2)

However, Gandhi's emergence in the 1920s – and the radically different style of politics he introduced which drew in the masses – marginalized Jinnah. The increasing emphasis on Hinduism and the concomitant growth in communal violence worried Jinnah. Throughout the decade he remained president of the Muslim League but the party was virtually non-existent. The Congress had little time for him now, and his unrelenting opposition to British imperialism did not win him favour with the authorities. As we shall see in later chapters, he was a hero in search of a cause.

In 1929, while Jinnah was vainly attempting to make sense of the uncertain political landscape, Ruttie died. Jinnah felt the loss grievously. He moved to London with his daughter Dina and his sister Fatima, and returned to his career as a successful lawyer. At this point, Jinnah's story appeared to have concluded as far as the Indian side was concerned.

Securing a financial base

Jinnah had successfully resolved the dilemma of all those who wished to challenge British colonialism. He had secured himself financially. Sir Sayyed Ahmad Khan had to compromise; Jinnah did not. This difference was made possible by developments in the early part of the century: Indians could now enter professions which gave them financial and social security irrespective of their political opinions. Earlier, Indians had been seen as either friendly or hostile natives. The former were encouraged, the latter were victimized, often losing their lands and official positions.

Jinnah's lifestyle resembled that of the upper-class English professional. Jinnah prided himself on his appearance. He was said never to wear the same silk tie twice and had about 200 hand-tailored suits in his wardrobe. His clothes made him one of the best-dressed men in the world, rivalled in India perhaps only by Motilal Nehru, the father of Jawaharlal. Jinnah's daughter called him a 'dandy', 'a very attractive man'. Expensive clothes, perhaps an essential accessory of a successful lawyer in British India, were Jinnah's main indulgence. In spite of his extravagant taste in dress Jinnah remained careful with money throughout his life (he rebuked his ADC for over-tipping the servants at the Governor's house in Lahore in 1947 – G. H. Khan 1993: 81). Dina recounts her father commenting on the two communities: 'If Muslims got ten rupees they would buy a pretty scarf and eat a biriani whereas Hindus would save the money.'

Understanding Jinnah

In the early 1930s Jinnah lived in a large house in Hampstead, London, had an English chauffeur who drove his Bentley and an English staff to serve him. There were two cooks, Indian and Irish, and Jinnah's favourite food was curry and rice, recalls Dina. He enjoyed playing billiards. Dina remembers her father taking her to the theatre, pantomimes and circuses.

In the last years of his life, as the Quaid-i-Azam, Jinnah increasingly adopted Muslim dress, rhetoric and thinking. Most significant from the Muslim point of view is the fact that the obvious affluence was self-created. Jinnah had not exploited peasants as the feudal lords had done, nor had he made money like corrupt politicians through underhand deals, nor had he been bribed by any government into selling his conscience. What he owned was made legally, out of his skills as a lawyer and a private investor. By the early 1930s he was reportedly earning 40,000 rupees a month at the Bar alone (Wolpert 1984: 138) – at that time an enormous income. Jinnah was considered, even by his opponents like Gandhi, one of the top lawyers of the subcontinent and therefore one of the most highly paid. He also had a sharp eye for a good investment, successfully dabbling in property. His houses were palatial: in Hampstead in London, on Malabar Hill in Bombay and at 10 Aurangzeb Road in New Delhi, a house designed by Edwin Lutyens. His wealth gave him an independence which in turn enabled him to speak his mind.

Paradoxically, Jinnah's behaviour reflected as much Anglo-Indian sociology as Islamic theology. His thriftiness to the point of being parsimonious, his punctuality, his integrity, his bluntness, his refusal to countenance *sifarish* (nepotism) were alien to South Asian society (see chapter 4). Yet these were the values he had absorbed in Britain. He later attempted to weld his understanding of Islam to them. His first two speeches in the Constituent Assembly of Pakistan in 1947 reflect some of the ideas of a Western liberal society and his attempts to find more than an echo of them in Islamic history from the time of the holy Prophet (see chapter 7). Jinnah was attempting a synthesis.

Creating a country

In the early 1930s several important visitors came to Jinnah's Hampstead home, requesting him to return to India to lead the Muslim League. Eventually he was persuaded and finally returned in 1935. With little time for preparation, he led the League into the 1937 elections. Its poor showing did not discourage him; instead, he threw himself into reorganizing it. The Muslim League session in 1937 in Lucknow was a turning point and generated wide enthusiasm (see chapter 3). A snowball effect became apparent. In 1939, now in his early sixties, Jinnah made his last will, appointing his sister Fatima, his political lieutenant Liaquat Ali Khan and his solicitor as joint executors and trustees of his estate. Although Fatima was the main beneficiary, he did not forget his daughter Dina and his other siblings. He also remembered his favourite educational institutions, especially Aligarh, which helped lay the foundations for Pakistan.

Jinnah's fine clothes and erect bearing helped to conceal the fact that he was in poor physical health. From 1938 onwards he was to be found complaining of 'the tremendous strain' on his 'nerves and physical endurance' (Jinnah's letter to Hassan Ispahani written on 12 April of that year in the *Ispahani Collection*). From then on he regularly fell ill, yet that was carefully hidden from the public. He remained unwell for much of the first half of 1945. Later in the year he admitted: 'The strain is so great that I can hardly bear it' (to Ispahani, 9 October 1945, *Ispahani Collection*). His doctors, Dr Jal Patel and Dr Dinshah Mehta, ordered him to take it easy, to rest, but the struggle for Pakistan had begun and Jinnah was running out of time.

Although by now called the Quaid-i-Azam, the Great Leader, Jinnah never courted titles. He had refused a knighthood and even a doctorate from his favourite university:

> In 1942, when the Muslim University, Aligarh, had wished to award him an honorary Degree of Doctor of Laws, he refused saying: 'I have lived as plain Mr. Jinnah and I hope to die as plain Mr. Jinnah. I am very much averse to any title or honours and I will be more happy if there was no prefix to my name.' (Zaidi 1993: volume I, part I, xlv)

Not all Muslims looked up to Jinnah. Many criticized him, some because they found him too Westernized, others because he was too straight and uncompromising. One young man, motivated by religious fervour and belonging to the Khaksars, a religious party, attempted to assassinate him on 26 July 1943. Armed with a knife he broke into Jinnah's home in Bombay and succeeded in wounding him before he was overpowered. Jinnah publicly appealed to his followers and friends to 'remain calm and cool' (Wolpert 1984: 225). The League declared 13 August a day of thanksgiving throughout India.

In 1940 Jinnah presided over the League meeting in which the Lahore Resolution was moved calling for a separate Muslim homeland. In 1945–6 the Muslim League triumphed in the general elections. The League was widely recognized as the third force in India along with the Congress and the British. Even Jinnah's opponents now acknowledged him: Gandhi addressed him as Quaid-i-Azam. The Muslim masses throughout India were now with him, seeing in him an Islamic champion.

By the time Mountbatten came to India as Viceroy in 1947 Jinnah was dying; he would be dead in 1948. Neither the British nor the Congress suspected the gravity of Jinnah's illness. Many years later Mountbatten confessed that had he known he would have delayed matters until Jinnah was dead; there would have been no Pakistan.

There were several dramatic twists and turns on the way to Pakistan, with Jinnah trying to negotiate the best possible terms to satisfy the high expectations and emotions of the Muslims. Pakistan was finally conceded in the summer of 1947, with Jinnah as its Governor-General. It was, in his words, 'moth-eaten' and 'truncated', but still the largest Muslim nation in the world. In Karachi, its capital, as Governor-General Jinnah delivered two seminal speeches to the Constituent Assembly on 11 and 14 August (see chapter 7). Suddenly, at the height of his popularity, Jinnah resigned the presidency of the League.

Despite his legendary reserve and the seriousness of his position, Jinnah retained his quiet sense of humour. As Governor-General, when he was almost worshipped in Pakistan, he was told that a certain young lady had said she was in love with his hands (Bolitho 1954: 213). Shortly afterwards, she was seated near him at a function, and Jinnah mischievously asked her not to keep looking at his hands. The lady was both thrilled and embarrassed at having amused the Quaid-i-Azam.

By now his health was seriously impaired. He was suffering from tuberculosis, and his heavy smoking – fifty cigarettes a day of his favourite brand, Craven A – and punishing work schedule had also taken their toll. Jinnah died on 11 September 1948 at the age of 71. The nation went into deep mourning (see plates 4 and 15). Quite spontaneously, hundreds of thousands of people joined the burial procession – a million people, it was estimated. They felt like orphans; their father had died. Dina, on her only visit to Pakistan, recalls 'the tremendous hysteria and grief'.

The grief was genuine. Those present at the burial itself or those who heard the news still look back on that occasion as a defining moment in their lives. They felt an indefinable sense of loss, as if the light had gone out of their lives. (As a typical example take the case of Sartaj Aziz, a distinguished Pakistani statesman. He remembers the impact that hearing of Jinnah's death had on him. He had fainting fits for three days. His mother said that he did not respond in the same manner to his own father's death.) A magnificent mausoleum in Karachi was built to honour Jinnah.

This, then, is the bare bones of Jinnah's life.

The role of Jinnah's family

The closest members of Jinnah's family were his sister Fatima, his wife Ruttie and their daughter, their only child, Dina. Ruttie and Dina are problematic for many Pakistanis, especially for sociological and cultural reasons. For the founder of the nation – the Islamic Republic of Pakistan – to have married a Parsee appears inexplicable to most Pakistanis. Jinnah's orthodox critics taunted him, composing verses about him marrying a *kafirah*, a female infidel (Khairi 1995: 468; see also G. H. Khan 1993: 77): 'He gave up Islam for the sake of a *Kafirah* / Is he the *Quaid-i-Azam* [great leader] or the *Kafir-i-Azam* [great *kafir*]?'

Dina is seen by many as the daughter who deserted her father by marrying a Christian. Because she did not go to live in Pakistan Dina is regarded as 'disloyal'. Pakistanis have blotted out Ruttie and Dina from their cultural and historical consciousness. Thus Professor Sharif al Mujahid, a conscientious and sympathetic biographer and former director of the Quaid-i-Azam Academy in Karachi, does not mention either woman in his 806-page volume (1981). Nor did the archives, pictorial exhibitions and official publications contain more than the odd picture of the two. Someone appears to have been busy eliminating their photographs.

It is almost taboo to discuss Jinnah's personal life in Pakistan; Ruttie and Dina, his beloved wife and daughter, have both been blacked out from history. None the less, it is through a study of his family that we see Jinnah the man and understand him more than at any other point in his life because that is when he exposes his inner feelings to us.

Fatima: sister of Jinnah

The relationship between Jinnah and his sister Fatima (see plate 2) is important in helping us to understand Jinnah, the Muslim movement leading to Pakistan and Pakistan history. Her name of course comes from that of the Prophet's daughter and symbolizes traditional Muslim family life. Born in 1893, Fatima was a constant source

Plate 2 Jinnah with his sister Fatima, on his right, and Dina, his daughter, on his left

of strength to her brother, and after his death she remained the symbol of a democratic Pakistan true to his spirit, a symbol of modern Muslim womanhood. Closest to Jinnah of his siblings in looks and spirit, Fatima is known as the Madr-e-Millat, Mother of the Nation, in Pakistan.

After their father's death in 1901, Jinnah became her guardian, first securing her education as a boarder at a convent when she was nine in 1902 and then enrolling her in a dental college in Calcutta in 1919. In 1923 he helped her set up a clinic in Bombay. All this was done in the face of opposition at home because Muslim society of the time discouraged Western education and Western professions for its women (F. Jinnah 1987: xvii). When Ruttie died, Fatima gave up her career as a dentist at the age of 36 and moved into Jinnah's house to run it and look after Dina; she then accompanied Jinnah on his voluntary exile in London. She accepted the role of her brother's confidante, friend, assistant and chief ally.

Fatima attended the League session in 1937 and all the annual sessions from 1940 onwards when she took on the role of organizing women in favour of the League. She was with her brother on his triumphant plane journey to Pakistan from Delhi and stepped out with him on the soil of the independent nation that he had created in August 1947.

In the last years she was anxious that Jinnah was burning himself out in the pursuit of Pakistan. When she expressed concern for his health he would reply that one man's health was insignificant when the very existence of a hundred million Muslims was threatened. 'Do you know how much is at stake?' he would ask her (F. Jinnah 1987: 2). She was the last person to see him on his deathbed.

Yahya Bakhtiar, a senator from Baluchistan who was sensitive to the issue of notions of women's honour in Baluch society, pointed out that in those days not even British male politicians encouraged their womenfolk to take a public role as Jinnah did. After Pakistan had been created he asked Fatima Jinnah to sit beside him on the stage at the Sibi Darbar, the grand annual gathering of Baluch and Pukhtun chiefs and leaders at Sibi. He was making a point: Muslim women must take their place in history. The Sibi Darbar broke all precedents.

Fatima's behaviour echoed that of her brother. Zeenat Rashid, daughter of Sir Abdullah Haroon, a leader of Sind who was one of Jinnah's followers, said that although the Jinnahs stayed in her family home in Karachi for weeks at a time there was never a hint of moral or financial impropriety. They would never accept presents; indeed no one would dare to give any. There was no lavish spending at government expense. On the contrary, the joke was that when Fatima Jinnah was in charge of the Governor-General's house after the creation of Pakistan the suppliers would be in dismay. 'She has ordered half a dozen bananas ... or half a dozen oranges because six people will have lunch,' they would moan. The ADCs would ring Zeenat Rashid and say they wished to come to her house for a good meal; they were hungry. Jinnah's broad Muslim platform was also echoed by his sister years after his death, as quoted by Liaquat Merchant: 'I said, "Miss Jinnah even you are born a Shia." To this she remarked, "I am not a Shia, I am not a Sunni, I am a Mussalman." She also added that the Prophet of Islam has given us Muslim Religion and not Sectarian Religion' (Merchant 1990: 165).

Later in life, retired and reclusive, she once again entered public life. In the mid-1960s, as a frail old woman she took on Field Marshal Ayub Khan, then at the height of his power, in an attempt to restore democracy. To challenge a military dictator is a commendable act of courage in Pakistan. She came very close to toppling him, in spite of the vote-rigging and corruption:

> A combined opposition party with Fatima Jinnah, sister of the Quaid-i-Azam (Founder of the Nation), Mohammed Ali Jinnah, as its candidate won a majority in three of the country's sixteen administrative divisions – Chittagong, Dacca, and Karachi. Despite a concerted political campaign on the part of the government, Fatima Jinnah received 36 percent of the national vote and 47 percent of the vote in East Pakistan. (Sisson and Rose 1990: 19)

Fatima was bitter about the way Pakistan had treated her and dishonoured the memory of her brother by the use of martial law, and by corruption and mismanagement. The strain of the campaign hastened her end and she died in 1967, just after the elections, at the age of 74. She is buried within the precincts of Jinnah's mausoleum in Karachi. Fatima Jinnah remains an unsung heroine of the Pakistan movement. A fierce nationalist, a determined woman of integrity and principle, she reflected the characteristics of her brother.

Who's Afraid of Mr Jinnah?

Ruttie: Jinnah's wife

Rattanbai Petit, Jinnah's wife, remains a mystery (see plate 3). Dina Wadia remembers her mother as 'warm, intelligent, wonderful. She was humorous and loved poetry and the arts.' She campaigned to abolish the brothels of Bombay and against cruelty to animals especially dogs. Since Jinnah said and wrote little about his personal life, we can only guess why he married her and how the relationship developed. But Ruttie hints at the human side of Jinnah – in love, vulnerable, unsure, in pain.

Although Ruttie had married Jinnah against her father's wishes, waiting until she was old enough to be married without his consent, he quite quickly forgave the couple afterwards (M. A. H. Dossa, 'Roots of the Quaid', *Dawn*, 25 December 1994; also confirmed by Dina). According to Dina, Lady Petit 'adored' Jinnah. Sir Dinshaw Petit had understandably been furious when his friend Jinnah proposed to his daughter. The Parsees were a wealthy and sophisticated Westernized community who dominated Bombay life (Luhrmann 1996), and Ruttie could have had the pick of the young men from her people. Ruttie converted to Islam before she married; eleven years later when she died she was buried according to Muslim ritual.

One well-known story illustrates the Jinnahs' attitude to officialdom. Lord Willingdon,

Plate 3 Photograph of Ruttie, wife of Jinnah

then the Governor of Bombay, and his wife invited the Jinnahs for a formal dinner. Lady Willingdon, eyeing Ruttie's fashionable new dress which showed more of her than the Governor's wife thought proper, asked the butler to bring a shawl for Mrs Jinnah as she was cold. Mr Jinnah, always quick to perceive an insult, immediately rose from his seat and said if Mrs Jinnah wished for a shawl she would ask for it herself. Offering his arm to Ruttie, he led her from the table and the Jinnahs made a magnificent exit, leaving an astounded party behind. In another story Ruttie heard the Viceroy recount his experiences on a recent visit to Europe. In Germany he had not been welcome because he was a foreigner. 'Then why are you here?' asked Ruttie sweetly.

The marriage was based on mutual affection but eventually disintegrated because of increasingly divergent interests and temperaments. To make matters worse Ruttie became ill. Jinnah was now caught between developments threatening his political life and the tragedy engulfing his personal life. On the one hand, he was increasingly struggling to find a place in a political firmament redefined by Gandhi's arrival; on the other hand, he was trying to devote himself to his ailing wife. As Ruttie's health deteriorated, her curiosity began to wander into books about seances and the afterlife. She was drifting into a mystical world of her own.

The Jinnahs had separated during the last few years but came together again when Jinnah learned of her illness. Even when ill she would tell their mutual friend Kanji to 'go and see Jinnah' (Beg 1986: 313). She would complain that 'now that I am not there to bother and tease him, he will be worse than ever' (ibid.). She went to Paris for treatment and Jinnah followed. He stayed with her in a nursing home for over a month and, as Ruttie told Kanji, he ate the same food as she did. During the separation she wrote to him: 'I have loved you, my darling, as it is given to few men to be loved. I only beseech you that the tragedy which commenced with love should also end with it. Darling, good night and good bye' (ibid.). Right to the end, Jinnah spent as much time with her as possible. When he was not beside her he wrote long letters urging his friends to spare no expense in attending to his wife's comfort. The last weeks were spent by her bedside in hospital.

The cause of Ruttie's early death in 1929 remains obscure. Some family friends believe it was cancer (M. A. H. Dossa, 'Roots of the Quaid', *Dawn*, 25 December 1994). Dina, however, maintained that Ruttie died of colitis, inflammation of the lining of the colon (also see Beg 1986: 312). It may have been colitis or something more complicated but it certainly involved some digestive disorder. The disease caused Ruttie excruciating pain towards the end and she was under constant medication. At one stage an overdose almost killed her and even suggested to some people that she had attempted suicide.

Ruttie's death 'devastated' Jinnah, according to Dina. When Ruttie's body was lowered into the grave, Jinnah wept like a child, his control collapsing; his last act in Bombay before leaving for Pakistan was to visit her grave. He would never be the same again; something died in him. 'A curtain fell over him,' said Dina, remembering her childhood. Once Jinnah's family life was over, this essentially private man poured his energy and his commitment into championing the Muslims. There is some psychological link between the two and it needs to be further explored.

Who's Afraid of Mr Jinnah?

Dina: Jinnah's daughter

Dina Wadia (see plates 2 and 4) has charm and vivacity but she is also brusque. She is clear in her thinking, strong in her likes and dislikes. She will not easily change her mind and can be obstinate. One can recognize her father in Dina. Even highly educated people in Pakistan have little idea about Dina. She was not his daughter, some will say. After all he married a *kafir* and therefore she does not count; he disowned her; he never gave her anything in his will. All these points are incorrect. Jinnah had made his will shortly after his displeasure with Dina for marrying against his wishes but he provided for her and never changed that will.

The partition of India split Dina from her father. It was a sword hanging over every Muslim home. Jinnah's was no exception. His one child Dina had to make a choice. She had either to accompany her father to Karachi and the new homeland he had created or to stay with her husband in Bombay. She chose to remain with her husband and children. She would not see her father again: he would be dead within a year.

The partition of father and daughter may have been overshadowed by the larger partition of India but in its tragedy it creates a powerful metaphor. It was made more poignant by the fact that the date of partition – midnight on 14–15 August – was her birthday. In her flat in Bombay she had put out two flags, Indian and Pakistani (Collins and Lapierre 1994: 269–70), symbolizing her dilemma. Dina's predicament must have weighed heavily on Jinnah and added to his sorrows as he saw the havoc caused by partition. The endless stream of Muslim refugees pouring into his capital city Karachi, bursting at the seams, short of everything, distressed and tormented him.

A decade earlier father and daughter had fallen out when Dina announced that she planned to marry Neville Wadia, a Christian who had once been a Parsee. At the time, Jinnah had just become the leader of the Muslims of India and was therefore highly conscious of his role. In an angry exchange between father and daughter, Jinnah 'told her that there were millions of Muslim boys in India, and she could have anyone she chose' (Wolpert 1984: 370). She replied that there were millions of Muslim girls and he could have married one of them, so why did he marry her mother? Inevitably there was a break in relations. Dina married Neville Wadia in 1938 and they had a daughter and a son, but the couple separated a few years after partition (Neville died at the age of 84 in August 1996).

Jinnah's relationship with his daughter is widely misunderstood. He is depicted as a cold and unfeeling father who ordered his daughter out of his house because she married against his will. Biographers like Wolpert have stated, for example, that 'Jinnah never spoke to his daughter after she married' (1984). This information is incorrect. Dina Wadia confirmed to me that when she heard her father had almost been assassinated in 1943 she telephoned to ask if he was safe and said she would like to see him. 'Of course,' he said. Immediately she rushed over to his house. Perhaps Jinnah had made a secret promise to his wife Ruttie – who was sensitive to not being a Muslim herself by birth – that he would never prevent Dina from marrying the man of her choice. Jinnah's disapproval as a South Asian parent was sociologically understandable (both Gandhi and Nehru were unforgiving when close members of the family wished to marry a Muslim). But Jinnah's reconciliation as a father was also naturally correct.

Now there is written evidence of the affection between Dina and her father in the

16

last years of Jinnah's life. A letter recently unearthed was sent by Dina from Bombay to her father on hearing the news about Pakistan on 28 April 1947 (Zaidi 1993: volume I, part I, 625–6):

> *My darling Papa,*
> *First of all I must congratulate you – we have got Pakistan, that is to say the principal [sic] has been accepted. I am so proud and happy for you – how hard you have worked for it....*
> *I do hope you are keeping well – I get lots of news of you from the newspapers. The children are just recovering from their whooping cough, it will take another month yet.*
> *I am taking them to Juhu on Thursday for a month or so. Are you coming back here? If so I hope you will drive out to Juhu and spend the day if you like. Anyway I have a phone so I will ring you up and drive in to see you if you don't feel like coming out.*
> *Take care of yourself Papa darling. Lots of love & kisses,*
> *Dina*

She wrote another letter early in June 1947 from Juhu, Bombay, after hearing of the announcement of the date for Pakistan (ibid.: 984–5):

> *Papa darling,*
> *At this minute you must be with the Viceroy. I must say that it is wonderful what you have achieved in these last few years and I feel so proud and happy for you. You have been the only man in India of late who has been a realist and a[n] honest and brilliant tactician – this letter is beginning to sound like fan-mail, isn't it?*

The letter had begun, 'It was really so sweet of you to write as I know how very busy you are', and ended: 'Take care of yourself. Lots of love and kisses and [a] big hug.' It is a typical letter from a daughter to her father and there is no hint of estrangement in it. There are many letters similarly refuting any idea that they parted and never reconciled.

In conversation Dina recalled her father with warm affection, describing him as 'a sweet man'. Of course he was austere, she said, like many other men born in the Victorian era, but she added that he used to take her to plays and pantomimes in London. She remembers sitting at the edge of his bed in the morning having tea while he read the papers, and recalls him as always having time for her. When I told her that Mountbatten had called her father a psychopath, she replied with spirit: 'Mountbatten was the psychopath.'

She dismissed the characterization of her father as cold, remarking that he would put his hand on people's shoulders while he was talking with them. He would interrupt his file work to speak to her, to explain things to her. But in the last years he was very sick and in any case he was reserved and brought up to be restrained and reticent. He often quoted Shakespeare to her and his favourite lines were from *Hamlet*: 'This above all: to thine own self be true, / And it must follow, as the night the day, / Thou canst not then be false to any man.'

One of the rare extant photos of Dina in the Pakistan archives was taken at her father's funeral in Karachi in 1948 (see plate 4). It is significant. She has her head covered

Plate 4 Fatima (to the right) and Dina (on the extreme left) weep at the grave of Jinnah, 12 September 1948

in a black veil. Although she had defied her father to marry a Christian, she was clearly making an effort to respect the modesty that Pakistanis would wish from the daughter of the Quaid. When Dina saw her father being buried he had already become the father of the nation and she had to stand in a long queue of admirers and those with a special affection for him.

While Dina and her daughter now live in New York, her son Nusli is a successful businessman in Bombay. She still keeps abreast of affairs in South Asia. 'They don't respect Gandhi in India, so why should they respect my father in Pakistan where they are more ignorant. No man is a prophet in his own country.' She also observed that there was a lot of what she termed 'sick thinking' in the subcontinent, that they were going in the 'wrong way towards fundamentalism', and that, like 'global warming', there was 'global fundamentalism'.

Relations between Dina and Jinnah's nation remained uncomfortable at best. Today she is bitter about Jinnah having given his life for Pakistan although doctors warned him that he was killing himself. She feels that the leaders of Pakistan have let down the high ideals of her father, and refers to the stories of corruption concerning Asif Zardari, husband of the former Prime Minister Benazir Bhutto. It was not worth the sacrifice, she repeats again and again. 'All Pakistanis want to know about my father is whether he drank whisky and ate ham.'

Dina Wadia is the one living link with her father. The nation of Pakistan claims her father as its own father of the nation. Surely there is a kinship with Dina, Jinnah's only child? Surely Pakistan's rulers could move towards a better relationship with her? Now, with Dina aged 78 and half a century since Pakistan was created, it is time for a reconciliation to take place.

Imagining Jinnah: why different people see different Jinnahs

We are living in a time of intrusive images – circulating, deceiving, seducing; confusing reality with illusion, conveying ideas that are part real, part fiction (Ahmed 1992a, 1993d; Baudrillard 1988a, 1988b, 1995; Giddens 1990, 1991; Robertson 1991, 1992; Turner 1994). Books, newspapers, television, the cinema, and so on, contribute to these all-pervasive images, which determine cultural as much as political discourse and influence public opinion and even foreign policy.

It is my contention that there is a two-way process which creates negative images of Muslims. The first process involves the conscious and instinctive reaction against them in the world media which is quick to depict them as fundamentalist, terrorist, fanatic and unworthy. The second process derives from Muslims' lack of comprehension of the importance of the world media and therefore indifference towards developing a strategy to deal with it.

By this two-way process, the image of Jinnah's life and achievements is in danger of becoming permanently distorted in and through the world media, and, further, his own people appear to know little about him. Within half a century of his death Jinnah is in danger of being not only forgotten but permanently misrepresented. However, the continuing relevance of his position as a Muslim leader is crucial to the global political debate on the nature of Muslim society and statehood.

Attenborough's Jinnah

In the 1980s a fresh assessment of the events of the 1940s was placed before the public in Richard Attenborough's film *Gandhi*, made in 1982. The film replaced and supplanted written accounts in the public mind. So Ben Kingsley became Gandhi; the actor Aleque Padamsee, representing Jinnah as a glowering, villainous figure, became Jinnah.

Gandhi, shot through a romantic Raj haze, was a powerful film because of its eponymous hero. On Mahatma Gandhi one can do no better than to quote Albert Einstein: 'Generations from now people will wonder that one such as he walked the earth.' The film won numerous Oscars and still remains popular over a decade after its release. In 1996 the Vatican issued a list of recommended movies. The *Guardian* newspaper then asked representatives of other denominations to nominate their top ten films and give reasons for their choice (*Guardian*, 13 April 1996). Eight of the major religions of Britain responded. Three – Catholics, Hindus and Jews – cited *Gandhi* in their list. For the Hindus and the Catholics *Gandhi* was the number one film in a section headed 'Values'.

In *Gandhi* the actor portraying Jinnah conveys one impression: menace. He never smiles. When he speaks he is sarcastic. A misanthropist, he seems to be scowling most of the time, battling with his own private demons. Attenborough's image of Jinnah as a villain had been fostered by Mountbatten and his associates and supported by the conventional portrayal of Jinnah in India. Jinnah became a metaphor for all that was terrible about Pakistan and the Pakistan movement.

The film gave the impression that Jinnah had created Pakistan because he was jealous of Gandhi. Jinnah's negative and inaccurate portrayal was not surprising in view of the fact that the film was dedicated to Nehru and Mountbatten, Jinnah's adversaries, and generously aided by Nehru's daughter, Indira Gandhi, then the Prime Minister of India. Yet it is surprising how even academics and Western experts on Islam swallowed Attenborough's *Gandhi*; for example, Professor Fred Halliday, 'endorsing Attenborough's portrayal in *Gandhi*', thought Jinnah was 'a thoroughly pernicious person', 'an appalling model' (*The Times Higher Education Supplement*, 31 May 1996). Demonizing Jinnah or reducing him to caricature represents a spectacular failure to explain not only one of the major players in the drama of India in the first half of this century but also the aspirations of the Muslims of South Asia.

Neither Dina Wadia nor her son Nusli agreed with the way in which Jinnah was portrayed, although they enjoyed the film. Dina saw it again in 1995, when, in the light of our meeting, she watched it carefully. She noted that her father appeared 'shifty-eyed' and 'furtive'; even his clothes were shabby, his collars too big. In reality her father was a 'dandy', she said, 'meticulous' in his dress. Besides, he had started wearing the *sherwani* and Attenborough shows Jinnah always in a Western suit. Nusli thought his grandfather had been 'much maligned'.

Although Attenborough's Jinnah never smiles, in Mountbatten's television series, *The Life and Times of Mountbatten*, the first time that Jinnah appears we see him with a broad grin standing close to Gandhi, Gandhi's hand on his shoulder. Later on, in several shots, he is smiling. In BBC2's *Enemy of Empire*, the documentary on the Indian nationalist Subhas Chandra Bose, shown in the UK on 13 August 1995, Jinnah is, in a rare archival shot, once again smiling broadly. Many of Jinnah's pictures in his biographies show him smiling (including the photographs on the covers of Bolitho 1954, Wolpert 1984 and Seervai 1990).

In a famous still photograph of Jinnah with Gandhi, both are looking at the camera with uninhibited smiles, Gandhi with his arm around Jinnah. The body language speaks for itself: these are two men who have a great deal of respect for each other. The two were obviously political opponents, with differences in their whole way of looking at the world. None the less Gandhi consistently showed Jinnah respect – even addressing him as the Quaid-i-Azam – and indeed at one point suggested that he become the Prime Minister of a united India, to the horror of the Congress leaders, Jawaharlal Nehru and Sardar Vallabhbhai Patel. Whatever Jinnah's personal opinion of Gandhi's politics, he too had high regard for him as a worthy opponent.

Richard Attenborough's film tells us none of these things. It was more convenient for Attenborough as a film-maker to cast Jinnah in the role of a villain opposite Gandhi. The black and white characters made for good cinema; it was also poor history. That is why S. S. Pirzada wrote a rejoinder to *Gandhi* and concluded: 'The film may be fabulous but it is factional. It may receive Oscars but it will leave scars' (1983: 40). In London, Rani Dubé, associate producer of *Gandhi*, told me that in retrospect she thought they had portrayed Jinnah incorrectly. 'Gandhi was a giant among giants,' she said. 'We made the mistake of making him a giant among pygmies.' Even Padamsee, the actor who played Jinnah, admitted that his characterization in the film was a distortion.

As a response to *Gandhi*, in the 1980s the government of Pakistan made a film on Jinnah, *Stand up from the Dust*. It was of such poor quality that it was discreetly hidden away in government vaults. It begins with the Arab soldiers of Muhammad bin Qasim galloping along the shores of Sind. It is the standard triumphalist version of the Pakistan story which simplifies and therefore misleads.

Recently Andrew Roberts wrote in the *Sunday Times*: 'In so far as western filmgoers know anything about Jinnah at all, it is as the glowering, sulking villain in Sir Richard Attenborough's *Gandhi*. The film reduced Jinnah's arguments for a separate Muslim state to a simple jealousy of the Mahatma and of Pandit Nehru. It was as insulting to Pakistanis as it was historically inaccurate' (18 August 1996). Roberts's article, 'Jinnah, Star of the East reborn', was a turning point. It was widely read and generated the predictable controversy and attracted the expected attention. Moved like many Pakistanis by Roberts's article, an associate of the Quaid living in London wrote to me. This was the first time he had read such a supportive and unequivocal statement in a major British newspaper praising Jinnah as he deserved.

Distorted scholarship

'History is mostly guessing; the rest is prejudice,' wrote Will and Ariel Durant. We will see how much guessing and how much prejudice are involved where Jinnah is concerned. Scholars, historians, polemicists and journalists imagine their heroes of 1947. Jinnah has perhaps been the greatest victim of this exercise. Swings in the imagination take us from one extreme to the other, from the unblemished triumphalist hero of Pakistan to the unmitigated villain of India. I shall try to identify the sources of this myth-making.

The academic editors of two standard volumes on India and Pakistan point out the paradoxes and nuances of South Asia:

> The Quaid-i-Azam's speech to the Constituent Assembly of Pakistan [on 11 August 1947; see chapter 7, pp. 173–5] is as secular a manifesto as any, yet he has passed in the political mythology of India as the master of intolerance. Jawaharlal Nehru was the personal embodiment of secularism, while Mahatma Gandhi's eldest son converted to Islam, yet the Congress movement and its leadership, including its own great Muslim leaders, have become branded in the political mythology of Pakistan as communalists. (James and Roy 1992: 27)

The serious scholars treat Jinnah simply as biography, their interest ending in 1948 with his death (R. Ahmad 1994; Jalal 1985; Mujahid 1981; Wolpert 1984; Zaidi 1976, 1993). No link is established between cause and effect, between founder and the state that he founded, between the creator and his creation. The contradictions and ambiguities surrounding the study of Jinnah can be removed if we are able to study his life as a whole in the context of his society and the country he created. We need also to trace currents in history that would influence Jinnah.

Who's Afraid of Mr Jinnah?

Some historians believe that great historical events are decided by economic or political factors beyond the control of individuals. For other historians, personal factors have an influence, sometimes decisively. (We do not have to discuss Caesar and Cleopatra in Egypt to drive home the point.) In this case, the Mountbattens got on famously with Nehru from their first meeting in Singapore in 1946. We also know that they did not hit it off at all with Jinnah from the moment they arrived in India in 1947. This personal interaction had an effect on how decisions were made in 1947. To pretend otherwise would be to leave out an important dimension of the story.

The British school of thought

We know that the British deliberately created an image of Jinnah (as for the influence of the British press, see, for instance, the role of the media, including the BBC and Fleet Street, in supporting the official line during the Suez crisis, in Shaw 1996). Lord Mountbatten and his staff gave this image the final seal (see chapter 5). It filtered into historical accounts and exists even today in the writings of the journalists on South Asia who are lazy in their analysis and research. It is the image of a cold, egotistical political leader who, for selfish reasons of vanity, refused to go along with the rational idea of unity and created a state so that he could be its leader; this was Attenborough's Jinnah, too.

Mountbatten, more than any Viceroy in history, was aware of the power of the media and used it effectively and ruthlessly after he was sent to India in 1947 to oversee the transition to independence. For the first time a public relations organization, headed by Alan Campbell-Johnson, was created to put a spin on the Viceroy's speeches and actions. But Mountbatten invariably was his own best publicist; his PR methods would make traditional empire-builders squirm. 'I dislike this modern craze for publicity,' said the soldier Lord Wavell, Mountbatten's predecessor as Viceroy (Wolpert 1984: 259).

Until recently Lord Mountbatten's widely accepted perspective on Jinnah and the events of 1947 appeared on several platforms. The definitive account came from Mountbatten in the twelve-part television series, *The Life and Times of Mountbatten*, filmed in the late 1960s and presented by Mountbatten himself. Yet we become uneasily aware of what Mountbatten was up to – the split between what he was saying and what he was doing – if we watch his television series carefully. He is out of sync. While Mountbatten remarks, 'My God, he was cold!', we see Jinnah smiling when he first meets Mountbatten. Mountbatten talks about being an impartial referee between Hindus and the Muslims, between Nehru and Jinnah; but he is doing everything in his power to damage Jinnah. In his long official meetings with Jinnah he speaks of giving him and the Muslims a fair deal but behind his back he abuses him as 'a bastard', 'psychopathic' and 'suffering from megalomania' (Seervai 1990: 132, n. 70).

The powerful Mountbatten school of thought influenced British attitudes for a generation. Mountbatten's views were supported by the standard British accounts, by the great and the good, Campbell-Johnson, Hodson and Ziegler. Popular accounts relied on the same sources. Janet Morgan's authoritative biography on Edwina Mountbatten (1991) mentions the usual names: Philip Ziegler, Mark Tully, Sir George Abell, Alan Campbell-Johnson. The author also thanks Rajiv Gandhi. Morgan relies entirely upon the British and the Indians for her account of Jinnah and the Muslims. In her acknowledgements (a long list of people, running to over four pages – Morgan 1991: 483–6) there is not a single Muslim or Pakistani name among the people interviewed. This is in spite of the fact that Jinnah features prominently in the book – not as prominently, obviously, as Nehru, but he is there as the villain of the drama. Once again, like other writers, Janet Morgan did not use any other source than those traditionally hostile to Jinnah.

The British historians of the last days of British India – David Page, Chris Bayly, Gordon Johnson, Francis Robinson – see Jinnah in the larger context of Indian history. Jinnah is a small piece on a chessboard dominated by the colonial players. Since these historians are unable to explore in any depth what Jinnah meant to the Muslims and why they reacted to him as they did, they fail to understand Jinnah, describing him in clichés such as 'enigmatic' and 'inscrutable' (Ian Talbot, 'Jinnah and the making of Pakistan', in *History Today* 34, 1984; see also Ahmed 1994, 1996a, 1997a, 1997b). For the British historian Jinnah is seen as a stereotype, as the 'Westernized lawyer' (Bayly 1990: 390). 'While others donned Indian dress and conducted politics in regional languages, Jinnah was prepared to make no compromises' (ibid.). This image is simply not correct, as I will demonstrate in chapter 4.

Most Western journalists continued to swallow the Mountbatten line unthinkingly (Collins and Lapierre 1994; Duncan 1989; Lamb 1991). Even their description of Jinnah as 'frigid', 'cold' and 'haughty' is Mountbatten's. The 'concept' of Pakistan for Christina Lamb was 'based on the hypocrisy of a few' (Lamb 1991: 23). Lamb then cites the Indian journalist M. J. Akbar, who appears to dislike Jinnah with passionate intensity (see below): 'Mohammad Ali Jinnah, a man with a weakness for a drop of whisky and a ham sandwich' (ibid.: 24). Lamb goes on to castigate the Quaid for being egotistical, concentrating power in his hands, loving pomp and denying democracy. Emma Duncan too quotes Jinnah as 'a whisky-drinking, ham sandwich-eating Muslim' (1989: 222). Duncan claims Jinnah 'wanted Pakistan to be a secular country' (ibid.; see discussion in chapter 7, pp. 193–202).

But those British officials who knew Jinnah spoke of him with respect. 'I got to know that I could trust him absolutely,' said Sir Francis Mudie, who had known Jinnah since 1936 and whom Jinnah selected as his Governor of the Punjab after the creation of Pakistan (Bolitho 1954: 208). Some ordinary people in Britain felt Jinnah had been neglected in history and spoke out. Gerry O'Neill, a soldier on duty in August 1947 in Karachi, had seen Jinnah and the Mountbattens pass by in their cavalcade:

> In the lead car were Mountbatten, looking every bit the 'El Supremo' in his naval uniform, with about one square foot of medals, and Jinnah. Behind them were Fatima Jinnah and Edwina Mountbatten. Edwina was looking dazzling, in Ascot's best, with a picture hat and, with a fixed *Tatler* smile, waving, just like the Queen, to the invisible hordes of spectators. Mountbatten was looking very dashing, with an all-over, almost *Chorus Girl* tan, and was obviously playing Errol Flynn, with a dash of John Wayne, or possibly Robert Mitchum.
>
> Mohammed Ali Jinnah was, on the other hand, playing himself, completely at ease and obviously enjoying, but not gloating in, his role as the

new Governor-General. His thin, aquiline features were not fixed in a smile, but showed emotion and concern for the occasion. To me, the Mountbattens, despite their plastic smiles, didn't even know we ordinary British soldiers were there. Jinnah, however, smiled at us and made a gesture of thanks with his hands, which to me spoke volumes. I was even more impressed with this when I read in the papers later what he said, in response to King George the Sixth's message, when it was read out, at the Constituent Assembly, 'We are parting as friends, and I hope that we shall remain friends. It is for this reason that I am pleased that so many British officials have volunteered for service in Pakistan. They will all be treated equally, as our own nationals.' I am not sure that Nehru ever made this sort of genuine promise....

After we returned to Napier Barracks, I heard of a further instance of Jinnah's humaneness and concern. We all used airmail letters, which were franked, for mail home. Apparently, no one high up had thought of what would happen regarding these when Pakistan came into being. Just before the official celebration, I think it was the night before, Jinnah was entertained at the Officer's Mess of the First Royal Scots, at Napier Barracks. One junior officer mentioned this problem to Jinnah and he made instant arrangements for the preparation of an official franking stamp, to be issued to our postal unit (and to other units, I presume), to make all our letters valid. This small attention to detail and regard for others spoke volumes, once more, to me regarding the character and sincerity of this great, but perhaps undervalued, man. (personal communication, 14 November 1996)

Wolpert's biography

Wolpert's *Jinnah of Pakistan* (1984) is probably the best book on Jinnah in its detail, sympathy and scholarship. What it lacks in its understanding of Muslim culture it makes up in the diligence of the biographical research.

But the American professor focuses on Jinnah alone, neglecting the context of Muslim history. The chain of ideas linking him with earlier Muslim history, which partly explains his fascination for Muslims, is not explored. Neither is Jinnah's relevance to Pakistan today discussed; nor is there comment on Pakistanis living in the West and what Jinnah means to them.

There is a tendency in Wolpert to project Jinnah in stereotypes not supported by evidence. Take his description of Jinnah: 'In London, the only round table left to him was one at which he and Fatima dined alone, rarely speaking to one another and never smiling' (Wolpert 1984: 123). How does Wolpert know this? The two people eating alone are dead and Wolpert interviewed neither. He did not even interview the third person who might have thrown light on Jinnah's London stay, Dina.

A major criticism is Wolpert's failure to explore in detail why Jinnah was converted from his role as ambassador of Muslim–Hindu unity to the champion of the Muslim cause. Wolpert asks, 'What made him decide to abandon hope of reconciliation with the Congress?' (1984: 162). His answer is their 'insults, stupidity, negligence etc.' What is not explored is Jinnah's rediscovery of his own roots, his own sense of identity, of culture and history, which would come increasingly to the fore in the last few years of his life. Besides, Jinnah was not alone in undergoing this transformation. Muslim activists such as Shaukat and Muhammad Ali, Yusuf Ali, Allama Iqbal, Ameer Ali and Sir Sayyed Ahmad Khan (see chapter 2) had all gone through a similar process of conversion. Therefore to reduce the Pakistan movement to insults by Congress, a standard enough explanation, will not do.

Because of his lack of detailed knowledge of South Asian society, Wolpert makes other mistakes. For example, when he describes Jinnah's Karachi school, the Christian Missionary Society High School, as 'exclusive' (1984: 6–7) he wrongly assumes it is one of the public schools established by the British for the Indian élite. He even gets its name wrong. He also describes the *choridar* pyjamas as 'traditional Punjabi garb' (ibid.: 180); in fact the *choridar* pyjama is worn in the United Provinces, and Punjabis not only do not wear it but look down upon it as effete. He incorrectly calls Kanji Dwarkadas a Parsee (ibid.: 70).

A generation earlier, Hector Bolitho, aided by the government of Pakistan, wrote a biography of Jinnah (1954). It is a straightforward hagiographical account; finely written and telling a good story well, it is neither deep nor analytic. We come away with the feeling that we know little about Jinnah; he remains an enigma.

Indians on Jinnah

The Indian Congress too had its own mythology. For them there was no conflict between the Muslims and the Hindus until the British arrived, bringing with them a policy of divide and rule. A split was created between the two major communities in order to weaken the Congress in its fight against the British. To further undermine Congress, the British supported Jinnah and his movement for Pakistan. This divided India.

After independence, pseudo-Marxist ideas emanating from Moscow further shaped Indian intellectual thinking. Jinnah now became a bourgeois leader followed by an exploiting feudal élite who created Pakistan for their own economic gain. The Muslim masses were regarded as having no will of their own. The Marxist perspective, which was dominant in the middle of this century, was espoused not only by many intellectuals in the West but by many in the subcontinent too. In India this was – and is still largely – the standard historical explanation. Congress, after all, was self-avowedly socialist and secular. It was logical for many Indian intellectuals to explain Pakistan in economic terms.

Here is the Indian version of the creation of Pakistan, the one many Pakistanis like Tariq Ali (1983, 1985) would echo:

> Neither was Jinnah's concept of Pakistan a theological one. He did not envisage an Islamic state. He dreamt of a secular bourgeoisie state for the Muslims. It clearly shows that those behind the Pakistan movement represented either feudal or middle-class interests. Hamza Alavi, a Pakistani sociologist, maintains that Pakistan was created by the Muslim 'salariat' (salaried) class. No wonder then that the Pakistani movement did not have a democratic and a mass base. The two-nation theory [which argued that

Muslims and Hindus were separate nations] resolution passed on 25 March 1940 in Lahore was opposed not only by the theologians but also by the Muslim masses. (Ali Asghar Engineer, in Gopal 1991: 186)

Indian analysis of Jinnah usually had a communal edge to it. Sharif al Mujahid explains: 'After all, he was the most maligned person in recent Indian history – probably the most except Aurangzeb (1618–1707) in all Indian history' (1981: xvii). In India, many see Jinnah as the demon who divided the land (for instance, see Arun Shourie, 'The man who broke up India', *Illustrated Weekly of India*, 20 and 28 October and 3 November 1985). In bazaar mythology Jinnah is equated to Ravana the demon who is vanquished by Ram, the most popular deity of Hindu mythology.

Some Indian Muslims, like Sheikh Abdullah (1993), M. J. Akbar (1985, 1988a) and Ansar Hussain Khan (1995), exaggerate their dislike of Jinnah, seeing him as the man who created Pakistan, the source of the misery for the Indian Muslims. Sheikh Abdullah, a friend of Nehru and Mountbatten, wrote of Jinnah: 'The entire subcontinent had to suffer the consequences of his inflated ego' (1993: 47). He blamed the Kashmir problem on the 'inflexible attitude of Jinnah' (ibid.: 61). Dr Rafiq Zakaria argued that a full-blooded civil war in India would have been preferable to Pakistan in 1947 (The Sardar Patel Memorial Lecture, 1996; see report in the *Asian Age*, 31 October 1996).

It is the negative image of Jinnah that many Indians nourish today, even outside the subcontinent. For example, a spokesman in Britain wrote that the only Jinnah acceptable to him was the one portrayed in Attenborough's film *Gandhi*, 'in which Jinnah was shown true to his colour and personality' (Randhir Singh Bains, in the *Asian Age*, 8 June 1994).

Yet some extraordinary Indian scholars have resisted the popular tide. S. K. Majumdar in *Jinnah and Gandhi: Their Role in India's Quest for Freedom* (1966) challenges the myth that Jinnah was the villain in 1947. According to his view, it was Gandhi's fuzziness and desire to create Gandhism in India that forced Muslims to separate. He believes that it was Gandhi and the Congress who made Jinnah change his mind in the late 1930s and pushed him towards the Pakistan position. But Jinnah does not get away lightly. He is criticized for Muslim communalism and for eventually laying the foundations of a state that would become anti-modern and illiberal in its politics.

Nirad Chaudhuri, for his part, commented on Jinnah and the other actors in the drama of 1947 thus:

> Jinnah is the only man who came out with success and honour from the ignoble end of the British Empire in India. He never made a secret of what he wanted, never prevaricated, never compromised, and yet succeeded in inflicting an unmitigated defeat on both the British Government and the Indian National Congress. He achieved something which not even he could have believed to be within reach in 1946. For this he can be compared to Weizmann who made a similar impossibility possible. (Chaudhuri 1990: 823)

Chaudhuri believes British and Hindu politicians and writers were unforgiving towards Jinnah because of his victory over them: 'But for this very thing he has been pursued with mean malice by British politicians, Hindu politicians, as also by writers of both the sides which had to admit defeat at his hands' (ibid.).

'Indian history needs to be rewritten. The revised version which exalts M. K. Gandhi must be scrapped.' So argues Krishna Gamre in a passionate piece published in the *Dalit Voice* (1–15 August 1995, Bangalore, India). He then puts forward the thesis that Jinnah, 'a great patriot', was the natural successor to Bal Gangadhar Tilak, who was then head of the Congress, that Tilak in fact wished Jinnah to succeed him and that Gandhi along with the 'socialist Brahmins' who controlled the Congress conspired against this. Gamre develops the argument that Jinnah remained honourable but was continually frustrated by Congress lies and perfidy. In the end, Pakistan was forced on him, though he was reluctant: 'when the documents were signed amputating Pakistan from India, Jinnah bowed his head in great sadness. Jinnah would have preferred a United States of India' with guarantees for Muslim human rights. Gamre argues that Nehru as a 'cunning Brahmin' wanted to be the first Prime Minister of an independent India, but feared Jinnah, whose popularity among all sections of the population was such that Jinnah might well have become the first executive president of the 'United States of India'. Gamre concludes with a question which implies his answer in the light of the argument: 'Who created Pakistan? Gandhi or Jinnah?'

Among South Asian authors, the Indian writers Rajmohan Gandhi (1986) and H. M. Seervai (1990) challenge and correct the tidal wave of the anti-Jinnah polemic in the Indian popular perception. Gandhi's sympathetic chapter on Jinnah in his study of eight Muslim leaders of the subcontinent is noteworthy considering he is the grandson of the Mahatma, one of Jinnah's main political opponents (see chapter 4, 'Gandhi and Ram Raj'). Both Gandhi and Seervai analyse him within the larger political context of the time, but they offer little explanation, and Seervai virtually none, of Jinnah's relationship with the Muslims – which was, in fact, the basis of his power.

In a carefully researched work Seervai reassesses the events of the summer of 1947 and reverses the accepted judgements in India. Jinnah emerges as the hero and Mountbatten as the villain. Nehru is knocked from his pedestal. 'Such an account cannot rest content with the popular view in India that the partition of India was brought about by the disappointed ambition, the vanity and the intransigence of one man, and one man only, Mohammed Ali Jinnah,' writes Seervai with admirable boldness (Seervai 1990: 4). 'This view receives no support from the materials now available to students of history. The fresh materials raise many questions which are not generally asked in India, for fear that the answers to them might involve criticism of the eminent men who at great personal sacrifice and suffering fought for our freedom, and whose memory is held in loving reverence throughout India' (ibid.).

Pakistani scholarship

Official Pakistani scholarship on Jinnah provides as orthodox an ideology as communist theory for Mao, the Long March and the struggle for power in China or for the revolution led by Lenin and consolidated by Stalin in the heyday of the Soviet Union, or indeed the political ideology unpinning the independence struggle led by Gandhi and Nehru against the British in India. Most nations – including Western ones – have their own mythology relating to their creation and to the founding fathers. Thus

Washington in America leads as he unites his nation in the fight against the colonial British. Jinnah for Pakistanis is Washington, Lenin and Gandhi rolled into one. In Pakistan we can identify several stages in the deification of Jinnah: from the Quaid-i-Azam of the 1940s to the 'Modern Moses' (Enver 1990) and the *Waliullah* (saintly 'friend of God') of the 1990s.

Because of Pakistan's political uncertainties the orthodox view has become ossified and rigid in its interpretation. At its centre is the figure of Jinnah, stern and forbidding. His official portraits confirm what the ideologues of Pakistan want from him: acceptance of Urdu as a national language, Islam as the official religion and belief in Kashmir as an integral part of Pakistan. Those who doubt risk being labelled traitor.

For most Pakistani scholars history is read as a linear progression which begins in the aftermath of the uprisings of 1857 and goes on to the creation of the Muslim educational centre at Aligarh, the nationalist writings of the Urdu poet Allama Iqbal and the political movement led by Jinnah in the 1930s. It terminates with the triumphant creation of Pakistan in 1947 by the invincible Jinnah. Jinnah would have been, according to this line of thinking, born with the idea of a Pakistan with its boundaries absolutely fixed, and we somehow skip over seventy years of Jinnah's life to emerge in 1947 when he vanquishes the enemies of Islam, creates Pakistan and then dies in a blaze of Islamic glory (see, for instance, the standard textbooks like *An Introduction to Pakistan Studies* by M. I. Rabbani and M. A. Sayyid, 1989; and *A New History of Indo-Pakistan since 1526* by K. Ali, 1990). This powerful cultural representation, accepted in Pakistan, disallows all the complexities of race, religion and caste. It ignores chance and character and the personal chemistry of and between leaders; and never more so than in Jinnah's case. It is scholarship at its simplest. It is what Muslim scholarship has been reduced to in the late twentieth century.

The general neglectful academic standard regarding Pakistan studies is reflected in the fact that there is still uncertainty even about key dates. Take the example of one of the most important dates of Pakistan history: Jinnah's swearing in as Governor-General on 15 August 1947. For Mujahid (1981: 642) and Rabbani and Sayyid (1989: 94) it is the 15th; for Bolitho (1954: photograph opposite p. 198) and Husain (1996: photograph 14) it is the 14th.

When Pakistani scholarship congeals, at the moment of triumph, in 1947, at the peak of Muslim history, we need to start the clock again. We need to point out that, although it was a great moment of triumph on one level, on another all hell had broken loose, that millions of people had been displaced and that the problems had just begun, not ended; that because complacency set in and a corrupt élite began to wander away from Jinnah's ideals it led to the disintegration in 1971. We must look at dates only as useful pegs; we must look beyond and behind them.

In the study of Jinnah a hagiographical perspective is officially encouraged; criticism, however mild, is severely discouraged. In the 1980s Sharif al Mujahid, director of the Quaid-i-Azam Academy, discovered this to his cost. A genuine admirer of the Quaid, he hinted at the mildest of criticisms in the most guarded of whispers in his book (1981). He was almost suspended from his job. The full weight of martial law regulations were prepared to be hurled at him. He was saved at the last minute by the intervention of S. S. Pirzada, another Jinnah devotee who was influential in General Zia's regime.

We must also not forget the flood of books on Jinnah in Urdu. Take, for example, Qazi

Sayyid Abdul Hannan's *Meer-e-Karwan Mohammad Ali Jinnah*, 1995). The book runs to 800 pages and is unadulterated hagiography. The tone of the approach is revealed by the title, which means 'the chief of the caravan'. In Urdu literature the caravan symbolizes the movement of a people from one destination to another; the *mir* is its chief, a man of unchallenged authority.

Books on Jinnah continue to tumble out in profusion, but most are neither good history nor good journalism; they continue to be unreadable and unread outside Pakistan. There is a regular Jinnah industry: Quaid-i-Azam study centres, Quaid-i-Azam chairs, Quaid-i-Azam posts at local universities and abroad all encourage work on Jinnah. There are several people who have devoted their lives to the study of Jinnah, so deep is their commitment to him: for example, Riaz Ahmad, Rizwan Ahmed, Sharif al Mujahid, S. S. Pirzada and Z. Zaidi (I have named them alphabetically to avoid the controversy of who takes priority in terms of the importance of their work).

The *Jinnah Papers*, which Z. Zaidi is editing (1993), form a primary source of information for Jinnah's multi-faceted personality. They help us to unravel the real Jinnah from the myths and images created by his opponents and devotees alike. The sheer bulk of the papers and the fact that they were often inaccessible has meant that no one has yet been able to read through the entire body; therefore no complete analytical and objective study of Jinnah and his times has been possible. For the first time what is available is the trivia. The anthropologist, the novelist, the journalist – these can now dig around and pick out the bits and pieces to complete their own jigsaw puzzle of the man and his movement. This helps us to see Jinnah not only as a towering political figure but also as an ordinary man dealing with ordinary, everyday matters.

The average reader must not be discouraged by the bulk of Zaidi's volumes, although he or she may need a stout heart and strong biceps: 1,015 pages make up the first book (volume I, part I); the second has 699 pages (volume I, part II). In 1976 Zaidi also edited the Jinnah–Ispahani correspondence which ran to over 718 pages. He has promised fifty more volumes of the *Jinnah Papers*.

But where the Jinnah scholars have failed – and failed spectacularly – is to produce between them one single book about him which would be popular, accessible and widely read. Even Jinnah's devoted sister Fatima could not help. There is a small, incomplete, scrappy book dictated by her called *My Brother* (1987). It too is hagiographic in tone and tells us little.

That Pakistan could not produce one standard international biography of Jinnah is a comment on Muslim scholarship. The last one, by Bolitho, was commissioned by Pakistan in the 1950s and Wolpert's biography was written over ten years ago. Nehru and Mountbatten had set the tone for the hostile perception of Jinnah. Then came the film *Gandhi* in the 1980s which sealed Jinnah's image in the popular mind. Poor Jinnah was doomed both by determined enemies and by indifferent friends. Biography is more than the life of an individual; it is also who your friends and who your enemies are.

Yahya Bakhtiar, the senator from Baluchistan and a disciple of Jinnah, is convinced that the leaders of Pakistan wished to sideline Jinnah so as not to be overshadowed by him. This sentiment is held by historians too. 'The Muslim League in Pakistan has done little or nothing substantial to counter the pernicious falsification of history, nor has it done much to vindicate the honour and sincerity of Quaid-i-Azam,' observed Riaz Ahmad (1994: 4). 'It has not published a definitive and authentic biography of the Quaid nor has it supported or encouraged scholars and historians to continue thorough research on Quaid-i-Azam'.

There is a Marxist perspective on Jinnah too (see also chapter 7, pp. 193–202). Tariq Ali blames the British for creating the two-nation theory that led to Pakistan and accuses the British of creating the Muslim sense of identity (1983: 27). The Muslim movement, for Tariq Ali, was bourgeois, representing only landlords and obscurantist religious figures (ibid.: 41). Ali, echoing the Indian line, accused Jinnah and Pakistan of being sponsored by the British (ibid.: 27). In a subsequent book on the Nehru dynasty he goes even further, condemning Jinnah as an 'opportunist' (1985: 74) and to be blamed for the crisis in Kashmir.

A generation of Pakistani writers, urban-based and English-speaking, would also repeat this view without much understanding of its implications for their own society. This tradition is apparent even today in the newspapers of Pakistan, where the hacks still churn out clichés about bourgeois élites, peasant struggles and exploitation of the masses, as if the collapse of the Soviet Union had never happened.

Jalal's RoboQuaid

Ayesha Jalal's book *The Sole Spokesman: Jinnah, the Muslim League and the Demand for Pakistan* (1985) is different in scope from that of Wolpert. Whereas Wolpert gives us a detailed picture of Jinnah, Jalal is more interested in the high-level negotiations in the last few years leading up to Pakistan. Writing as a historian, she presents a densely argued case for the thesis that Jinnah's Pakistan was vague – vague enough for people to construct their own version of it. It was powerful as an idea; Jinnah could bargain with it to maximize his weak hand when facing Mountbatten and Nehru. Jalal makes the point that Jinnah spoke not only for the Muslims of what became Pakistan but for all Indian Muslims, and that he was the sole spokesman for the Muslims of India; yet the Pakistan that was eventually created left as many Muslims outside the state as inside it. It is not clear whether Jalal is arguing that Jinnah did not want an independent Pakistan, that he wished to fight for the security of the Muslims of India but within an Indian frame.

Her book also gives us only the husk of a man. It does not explain how he linked up intellectually with Sir Sayyed and Iqbal in the quest for Muslim destiny, or how the changing situation in India from the 1920s onwards pushed Jinnah into altering his ideas and position. The passion he generated in the early 1940s, the cultural connection with his community and the dramatic increase in his following throughout the length and breadth of India are missing (see my chapters 4 and 7).

Ayesha Jalal's portrayal of Jinnah is not unlike that of the American film hero RoboCop, half machine, half man. Jalal's Jinnah is a robot, programmed to play poker for high stakes – her favourite analogy – and win in small committee rooms; and like a machine he does not even appear to believe in what he is doing. For Jalal he may be the Quaid but he is RoboQuaid.

Riaz Ahmad has criticized Jalal's work on the grounds that it was originally a PhD thesis 'completed under the supervision of Anil Seal, a historian born of a Hindu father and a British mother'. He goes on: 'It continues the old Congress propaganda supported by the skilful use of new records largely obtained from British sources.... Jalal's attitude has been most derogatory to Jinnah.... She has mainly relied upon the Congress and the British sources and paid little attention to the Muslim or other sources' (R. Ahmad 1994: 4–11; also see Shaikh 1989). Jalal does leave herself open on this flank since there is not a single Muslim academic in the list of acknowledgements.

Both Wolpert and Jalal have generated controversy over their work in Pakistan; Wolpert because he mentioned Jinnah's eating and drinking habits (see chapter 7), Jalal because she raised the question whether Jinnah wanted a Pakistan at all. This is a Pakistani caricature of their scholarly presentation. In fact Wolpert's book is as close to adulatory biography as you can get in academe, and Jalal speaks not with disbelief but with faith in Jinnah. Both have explored aspects of Jinnah's life which make him more, not less, impressive and interesting.

The official representation of Jinnah

Paradoxically the actions of the successive governments of Pakistan have reinforced the myth of a cold, distant Jinnah. Innocent of media theories and ignorant of the power of visual images, they have perpetuated their own notion of the Quaid. To start with, Jinnah is never shown as a normal husband, father or family man. As I have already mentioned, his wife and daughter appear to have been written out of history.

For the official Pakistani artists Jinnah is always formal, aloof, unsmiling and cold-eyed; with his jaw set he stares sternly at you. His clothes are dark, the colours behind him gloomy. This is the normative image of a grim father figure in a patriarchal society. At best he looks like a strict schoolmaster from Victorian times. (The *Guardian*, reporting from a court in Pakistan, observed that Jinnah's 'portrait, suspended above the court's proceedings, seemed to glare at the participants': 23 February 1995.) At worst, Jinnah looks like 'Christopher Lee in a horror film' (William Dalrymple in the *Sunday Times*, 12 June 1994).

Pakistani scholars have rarely understood Jinnah, who is a cardboard character to them. Typically Zaidi falls into the trap of projecting Jinnah as a stiff, formal lawyer. When Zaidi compares Jinnah to Nehru and Gandhi he reinforces the stereotype of Jinnah by pointing out that Gandhi and Nehru 'went native with a vengeance'. In contrast, 'Jinnah, however, stuck to his Western dress and Western ways. He made obeisance but rarely to populist symbols, shunned mass rallies and avoided the display of emotion in public. Even at those rare mass meetings, he spoke as though he were addressing a court room or a university audience. Logical and legal arguments were the hallmark of Jinnah's discourse. This is not the stuff of which popular leaders are made' (Zaidi 1993: volume I, part I, xxvi).

Yet Zaidi himself, in personal interviews with me, has recounted the excitement, the *frisson*, of seeing Jinnah at Aligarh, of his carriage being pulled by dozens of enthusiastic young students, after untying the horses, as a gesture of adulation. We have the statements of Yahya Bakhtiar, and evidence in his photographs, of star treatment given to Jinnah in the 1940s (see chapter 4), when he was seen as a charismatic figure. In the 1940s, with the growth in his celebrity status Jinnah noticed how people quickly became attracted to him (Menon 1957: 59). Muslim political leaders 'flocked to Jinnah's standard and he welcomed them like lost sheep' (ibid.: 221). Those who opposed him felt the intensity of his wrath: 'Fazli thinks he carries the Punjab in his pockets. I am going to smash Fazli' (*Pakistan Times*, magazine section, 13 September 1963). Disciples hero-worshipped him. Liaquat Ali Khan, who would become the first Prime Minister of Pakistan, 'revered Jinnah … with a schoolboy crush' (Moseley 1962: 70).

Jinnah's own belief in the Pakistan idea moved him passionately. 'Don't decry fanatics. If I hadn't been a fanatic there would never have been Pakistan,' Jinnah said to Mrs Casey, who was commenting about someone being 'a fanatic' at dinner in March 1948 (Bolitho 1954: 167). Even Jinnah's formal speeches are brimming with anger and passion, especially those made after Pakistan was created. Clearly Jinnah was an emotional man who wept easily – such as when he witnessed the plight of the refugees – and was capable of inspiring others with his strength of feeling.

Yet Jinnah seemed almost removed from the immediate hurly-burly of the here-and-now. In an interview with me Alan Campbell-Johnson remarked that Jinnah gave him the impression that he was almost in a 'reverie', and I wondered why he used that word. Of course, by the mid-1940s Jinnah was ill, and that might explain his apparent detachment. But it was something more. It was the example of a person fighting for a principle that was larger than the subject at issue. Zulfiqar Ali Bhutto had commented on 'his pure and virgin spirit' (Wolpert 1993: 29). The air of detachment suggested to many people that he was cold. But after talking to many who met him, particularly when they were young and he had no particular reason to be kind to them, I have come to the conclusion that he was formal but not cold, kindly but not effusive; rather he was correct and measured while attempting to keep his emotions under control.

Pakistan's failure to use modern images including cinema and television to project Jinnah in an interesting and accessible manner is spectacular. It is not for lack of resources. Pakistan has a talented artistic community and has made excellent productions, especially for television. What is urgently needed is for Pakistanis to create the image of a founding father whose values would echo those of the nation, whose aspirations and dreams would be the finest reflection of the nation's will. We need a human Jinnah, not a cadaverous one. By not having humanized images of Jinnah and utilized those in the media, Pakistan lost a chance to construct an idea of a national hero around which a national image could have formed. In its absence a vacuum remained, to be filled from time to time by a military dictator or demagogue. Such rulers caused society to become even more fragmented and rarely provided the unity that was so desperately required. Pakistan paid heavily for this: first by losing half of the country in 1971, then by being threatened with serious social disintegration.

Both Indian and Pakistani scholars study Jinnah as a Muslim nationalist. The Indians portray him as a fanatic who destroyed the unity of India; the Pakistanis portray him as a man who had no other idea in his mind except that of creating a Muslim homeland, exclusively for them. Both these perceptions deny Jinnah the man, the feeling, caring, breathing, living human being who transcends both national and religious categories. It is this Jinnah I am searching for in this book. By recovering this particular Jinnah I hope to place him in the context of larger South Asian history and culture and thereby make it easier to understand that region of the world, its history and its society.

Part II

Divide and Quit:
The Road to the
Partition and
Independence of India

CHAPTER 2

The Struggle for History

How unfortunate is Zafar for burial / he did not even get two yards of land in his beloved's lane.

(Urdu verses of the last Mughal emperor, Zafar)

Constructing the past

India has produced several world religions: Buddhism, Jainism, Hinduism and Sikhism are the more prominent ones. This fecundity is matched only by the Middle East, where, of course, Judaism, Christianity and Islam originated. But today societies in both areas are locked in confrontation, and religion itself has become a vehicle for turmoil.

Arriving

India seduced and attracted − a bit wistfully and a bit warily − Muslims from Persia, Afghanistan and Central Asia. It became a journey of adventure into a world full of phantasms and revelations: the climactic mystery, sequestered deep in the subconscious as the ultimate other which both repels and attracts simultaneously.

In the long millennium of Muslim history in India three figures stand out in popular literature and folk mythology: Mahmud of Ghazni (in modern Afghanistan), the last great Mughal emperor Aurangzeb and Jinnah. In Hindu mythology Mahmud is associated with raids into India from Afghanistan and the breaking of temples; Aurangzeb with harsh Muslim rule; and Jinnah with actually splitting Mother India. In the 1940s Hindu writers sarcastically called Jinnah another Aurangzeb (Mujahid

1981: xvii). Some people in India today more than ever employ these three figures as negative symbols of hatred against Muslims in general (see chapter 8, pp. 220–34). The BJP (Bharatiya Janata Party) make contemptuous allusions to Aurangzeb – and his ancestor Babar – and Jinnah; Bal Thackeray mentions Jinnah disparagingly. Ordinary people refer to Mahmud in everyday discourse as a representation of rapacity and tyranny (see letter under the heading 'Golddiggers' in *Outlook*, Delhi, January 1997). A Hindu academic describes the use of Mahmud as a symbol in recent anti-Muslim riots:

> After the riots of Ahmedabad many educated Hindu rioters felt that they had avenged the plundering of Somnath temple by Mahmud of Ghazni. An incident which had taken place ten centuries before was still fresh in the minds of the Hindus and in their perception, an attack on the present-day population of Muslims meant vindicating themselves against Mahmud of Ghazni. (Saxena 1991: 59)

Conversely, these three are shining heroes among the Muslims, for most of whom they symbolize an assertive, triumphant, positive Islam. The poet-philosopher Iqbal, his finger always on the pulse of his community, refers to both Aurangzeb and Mahmud as exemplary Muslim heroes in his poetry; in the letters he wrote to Jinnah just before he died he addressed Jinnah as 'the only Muslim' leader for the modern age (Malik 1971: 387; see below). At Jinnah's death one of the most prominent clerics of Karachi, the Sheikh-al-Islam, Allama Shabir Ahmed Usmani, in his funeral oration described Jinnah as 'the greatest Muslim after Aurangzeb' (Mujahid 1981: 659). The different perceptions sum up the problems of constructing history in South Asia.

Military commander versus saintly scholar

After the Arabs' initial incursion into Sind under their youthful commander Muhammad bin Qasim in AD 711, subsequent Muslim groups came to the subcontinent from the north and consisted of Central Asians, Afghans and Persians. The military commanders who set out to defeat the *kafir*, the non-believer, were responsible for breaking Hindu temples and committing atrocities against those who opposed them (who, of course, also included local Muslims). Of these Mahmud of Ghazni left his mark. Early in the eleventh century he conducted numerous raids into India, one of which resulted in the destruction of the Hindu temple at Somnath. His army carried the gates back in triumph. It was 800 years before they were taken back to India by a British general with a similar sense of triumph.

Muslims, especially in Pakistan, need to see the Muslim invasions through Hindu eyes: Muslims arriving from outside, threatening their temples, sacred animals, their very identity; reordering the world around their own notion of a monotheistic God, a defined truth, clear-cut rituals, thereby challenging the very hierarchy that sustained the caste system – and, worse, through intermarriage, penetrating into a system that had remained unique and distinct. The miracle for Hinduism was that it survived. Perhaps the Hindu notion of *maya* or illusion – the despair of economists and planners – provided a subtle but unending source of strength to a society facing the uncertainties of a changing world. The sense of transience, of changeability, gave Hinduism its characteristic resilience, which allowed it to withstand the centuries of Muslim domination – and a century of British rule.

The invader looking for plunder and military glory was one face of Islam. The more endearing – and eventually enduring – was that of the scholar and the saint. Al-Beruni in the eleventh century and Muinuddin Chisti in the twelfth are examples of the former and the latter respectively. Al-Beruni was the first major scholar of Hindu India, its customs, caste and culture, and his *Kitab Al-Hind,* 'The Book of India', remains a widely used classic. Chisti, called *Gharib Nawaz* or 'Blesser of the Poor', settled in Ajmer and his philosophy of *sulh-i-kul,* or peace with all, helped to convert vast numbers to Islam. His shrine at Ajmer remains one of the most popular in the subcontinent attracting hundreds of Muslims and non-Muslims daily. Another champion of harmony, Amir Khusro, who lived in the next century, believed that while he was a Muslim he was also an Indian and proud of it. For him India was undoubtedly one of the best places on earth to live and had all the blessings of flora and fauna.

Two faces of Islam in the subcontinent: the two poles in the Islamic character in South Asia, each opposed to the other and yet both, in an important sense, aspects of the same society. These two points would set parameters for Muslims within which they would respond to non-Muslims – sometimes aggressive and chauvinistic, sometimes talking of synthesis and harmony; but always swinging between one and the other.

Muslim history

Several dynasties, traditionally termed the Delhi Sultanate (1206–1526), preceded the Mughals, but it was left to the latter to provide the sense of continuity and unity in the subcontinent which left a historical impact. Mughal rule also saw impressive achievements in art, literature and calligraphy. The Taj Mahal perhaps best symbolizes the highest expression of Mughal thought and action.

The dynasty was founded by Babar in 1526 after he defeated the Muslim ruler of Delhi on the fields of Panipat. Although he died in India, Babar pined for his Central Asian homeland. Five rulers, each majestic in his own way, followed in straight genealogical succession, father to son. The last, Aurangzeb, died in 1707 when the empire, at least on the surface, was at its height. The exalted empire was a superpower of the age. In 1700 India had a population of 180 million people – about 20 per cent of the world population. Most of these were in one form or another under the hegemony of the Mughal emperor in Delhi. To have an idea of the scale of the empire we need to imagine present-day India (except the south), Afghanistan, Pakistan and Bangladesh as one entity.

After Aurangzeb a succession of incompetent or corrupt rulers hastened the decline of the Mughal empire. Mughal commanders sent from Delhi in the early eighteenth century to bring important provinces like Bengal, Avadh and Hyderabad into line broke away and established a rule which their successors would claim as their own. Their independence was further strengthened when Delhi was under the sway of Persian, Afghan and Maratha forces, although they continued to acknowledge the imperial court until the end of the century.

As the eighteenth century unfolded, Muslim rule in India slowly disintegrated. Saintly scholars like Shah Waliullah had become seriously alarmed and began to look round for Muslim saviours. Ahmad Shah Abdali in Afghanistan was in touch with Shah Waliullah and arrived in India to halt the Maratha advance with his victory at the Battle of Panipat in 1761. European powers battled for land and political control. Well-trained if small European units were able to vanquish large but ill-disciplined Muslim armies often racked by internal dissension and intrigue. General Robert Clive, defeating Sirajudallah, the ruler of Bengal, and thereby securing the rich province of Bengal for the British at the Battle of Plassey in 1757, is an example. Characteristically, Clive was aided by Hindu landlords and merchants as well as Muslim opponents of Sirajudallah. Surat on the west coast fell soon afterwards.

To make matters worse, even Muslims appeared to be hastening the process of Muslim collapse. In 1739 Nadir Shah came from Persia to defeat the Mughal armies, occupy Delhi, massacre about 20,000 citizens and loot the city. Not long afterwards Ahmad Shah Abdali invaded India three times, and in 1757 he repeated Nadir Shah's looting of Delhi. Three years later he returned once again and allowed his soldiers to plunder Delhi.

A Sikh kingdom established by Ranjit Singh with its capital at Lahore in 1799 added to the misery of the Muslim population. In the same year the British finally defeated Tipu Sultan, the ruler of Mysore, who died in battle sword in hand: the south of India now lay passive.

A new factor began to affect relations between Hindu and Muslim. Straightforward battles between dynasties or rulers started to give way to a communal element. Hindu–Muslim riots were recorded early on in the nineteenth century: in 1809 some fifty mosques were destroyed and several hundred people killed in communal riots in Benares (Pandey, in Das 1992: 96). Hindus and Muslims were beginning to view the world from different, increasingly opposed, perspectives.

In 1784 the Mughal emperor accepted the 'protection' of the Maratha warlords. With the defeat of the Marathas under Lord Lake in 1803, Delhi was occupied by the British East India Company. There were now two masters of Delhi. But, while the East India Company represented a growing and powerful empire with an eye on the river Indus and beyond, the Mughal emperor controlled little more than the Red Fort in which he lived. Indeed, there is an Urdu couplet which echoes the irony of the situation in which the authority of the emperor, Shah Alam (1788–1806), extended only up to Palam (which is now Delhi airport): 'From Delhi to Palam / Is the realm of Shah Alam.'

Muslims, however, continued to fight for freedom elsewhere in India. The most notable movements were those of Sayyed Ahmad Barelvi against the Sikhs in the northern areas of what would become West Pakistan and Haji Shariatullah and Dudu Mian (father and son) against Hindu landlords and European indigo estates in the early part of the eighteenth century in what would become East Pakistan.

The lesson of Muslim armed resistance was not lost on the British. Muslim state after state was captured. Afghanistan was invaded in 1839 and Kabul occupied. Although they were forced to leave, the British would be back in less than half a century. The states of Sind were invaded in the early 1840s. With the final conquest the triumphant general, Lord Napier, whose statue stands in Trafalgar Square, is said to have sent a telegram to Delhi containing the Latin word *peccavi* ('I have sinned'), hinting at

Victorian imperial irony. In 1846 the British sold the Muslim state of Kashmir to Gulab Singh. The sale was, according to the Treaty of Amritsar, 'for ever', and worked out at three rupees per Kashmiri head. In 1856 the Muslim kingdom of Avadh with its capital at Lucknow was finally annexed.

Delhi now remained. However much reduced to a mere symbol, it was still a reminder of past glory; and a Muslim king still sat on the throne. It could not be allowed to last.

The end of Muslim history in 1857

The immediate cause of the uprisings in 1857 was a cultural one. The spark came in the form of rumours about new bullets which offended both Hindu and Muslim soldiers in the East India Company army. To insert the bullets into their new Lee Enfield rifles, the soldiers had to tear the cartridge covering with their teeth. Rumour had it that it contained fat from either beef or pork. This caused offence to both communities: the cow was considered sacred by the Hindus, the pig unclean by the Muslims. It was an excuse, but it was a good excuse.

When the garrison in Meerut and other northern stations mutinied in May and June the British were taken off guard. Their forces were stationed in what was then their central base, the city of Calcutta, or deployed mainly in the Punjab to fill the vacuum caused by the collapse of Sikh power. The mutinous soldiers quickly gained support from the Mughal emperor, Bahadur Zafar Shah, in Delhi, from members of the dispossessed rulers of Avadh and from members of the Maratha court such as Nana Sahib at Kanpur. Some large landowners also joined in the uprisings. Hindu Jats also rallied to the Mughals, although they must have viewed the possible re-emergence of Muslim power in Delhi with mixed feelings.

However, the British were able to regroup swiftly and were aided by fresh troops from the Punjab and Bengal. In November 1857 Delhi was taken by a column from the Punjab after a ferocious battle and in the same month the uprising at Lucknow was finally quashed with great loss of life. Both communities had descended into uncharacteristic savagery. Kanpur (Cawnpore to the British), which boasted the second largest European community in the entire subcontinent, provides an example: only five men and two women had survived the massacre of the garrison by the end of 1857. As a direct consequence of the uprisings the East India Company was abolished and from 1858 the British Crown assumed responsibility for the administration of what became the Indian empire.

During the uprisings in 1857, race, religion and caste boundaries were blurred. With the Muslims fought the Hindu Rani of Jhansi; against the Muslims fought the freshly recruited Muslim Punjabi and Pathan soldiers of the north. The Muslim ruler of Hyderabad sent his soldiers to assist the British. The Sikhs also joined British troops in putting down the Delhi revolt. Like all uprisings on this scale, there was some confusion of objectives and some unlikely allies in the field.

The Sikhs, whose kingdom had recently been taken over by the British, were looking for fresh avenues of employment. As many as 16,000 Sikhs were soldiers in the East India Company army, anxious to prove their mettle and loyalty. Although glorified in the nationalist literature as a struggle that united Hindus and Muslims against the British, the actual events contained contradictions and lack of clarity on the part of the Indians.

Causes of the uprisings

The uprisings did not, as the British once believed, spontaneously take place simply because of the incident of the cartridges. Indian soldiers in the different British armies spread over the subcontinent had been rebelling since the last century. Contingents of the Madras army had revolted in the 1780s; in 1806 the garrison at Vellore had turned on its officers and was subdued only after a pitched battle in which several hundred men died; a company of the Bengal army had risen against its officers in Gwalior in 1834. Rebellion was also brewing in the ranks during the Afghan campaign in 1839–42. Another underlying cause was the feeling in the Bengal army that its special status was under threat from military reform. There was constant unrest among the Moplahs of the central Malabar coast, seen by the British as supporters of Tipu Sultan, as they rose against Hindu landlords and British officials in the early nineteenth century.

Lord Dalhousie, the Governor-General of India from 1848 to 1856, must share some of the blame too. He had quickened the pace of change throughout India, and his policy towards the princely states was aggressive. He introduced the 'doctrine of lapse' by which those Indian princely states in which the direct male line failed were absorbed into British India. Dalhousie annexed the Maratha state of Jhansi in 1853 on the pretext that there was no legitimate heir. Avadh was swallowed in 1856. Steamships, electricity, railway lines and trunk roads began to transform communications bringing the land and its people more and more tightly under control.

There were undercurrents of Islamic millenarianism. Muslim preachers were proclaiming the end of British rule in India a hundred years after it began with their victory at the Battle of Plassey in 1757. During the fighting several thousand devoted Muslim warriors came from different parts of India, some inspired by the Naqshbandi and Chisti Sufi orders, others by more orthodox schools; and *fatwas* declaring holy war were issued.

The task of the British was made easier in 1857 because they could find support from various elements within society: peasantry against landlords, Hindus against Muslims, or one ruler against another. Although 1857 was the culmination of an existing process, the reasons why people rose up varied: the Mughal emperor may have dreamt of restoring the authority of his ancestors but many of the Muslim warriors who arrived from outside Delhi to support him were hoping for an Islamic order. The ordinary soldiers reacted against the rumours about the cartridges as much as they expressed their resentment of a possible change in their status. Others were showing their dissatisfaction with the emerging order in which the Hindu money-lender and the British official appeared as tyrants. The aristocracy, both Hindu and Muslim, which had recently been deposed in Jhansi and Avadh, were resentful.

It is not altogether clear what the Hindus were fighting for in 1857. Muslims were, understandably, fighting for their own ruler, their own language and their own history. But many Hindus too had cause for resentment. In Kanpur, Nana Sahib represented the dispossessed Maratha court and its sense of grievance; that explains the vindictiveness with which the Europeans were killed. Similarly, the Rani of Jhansi was angry because her state had been taken over by the British. Ordinary Hindu soldiers in British regiments made common cause with their Muslim comrades in arms. Other Hindus, like the Jats, although supporting an uprising against the British, were ambivalent about restoring Mughal authority.

But would Hindus be happier under an alien ruler who would give them better chances in life than under the old dispensation? True, the Mughal empire had acquired legitimacy for all Indians over the centuries. Let us not forget that Aurangzeb's commanding general was a Hindu. The Marathas, the emerging power of the eighteenth century, assumed political control of North India in the name of the Mughal emperor. It was only after the removal of the last Mughal emperor and the visible destruction of the major symbols associated with the Mughals that a vacuum formed. Slowly but surely the idea of Hindu majority rule emerged.

Although there had been clashes between Hindus and Muslims, after 1857 they assumed a more vicious and organized pattern. They also adopted an ideological base with a focus on Muslims. The novel *Anandamath*, the activist Tilak, the religious Ganpati festivals, the socio-religious movement of the Arya Samaj – all these came after 1857. The Hindu notion of the Muslim as *mleccha* or 'unclean' began to gain currency shortly after the uprisings in Delhi.

Emerging European ideas on the nature of social order also had something to do with it. White Europeans assumed that their customs and thinking would be the successful model for the future of mankind; the rest were doomed to failure. This philosophy translated itself into ruthless military adventurism and political subjugation. In a minute of 1835 Lord Macaulay, then a member of the Supreme Council of India helping to formulate a penal code and introduce educational reforms, stated that the British needed to create an élite group of Indians who would be like the British in their tastes, morals and intellect and who would in turn help rule the natives on behalf of the white man. It was a more effective and sophisticated way of practising theories of racial superiority than colonial policies of genocide, as for example in America and Australia during the nineteenth century. In India entire tribes and groups were once again threatened, entire peoples were being marginalized. In 1857 came the explosion.

The Mughal emperor as symbol of the past

When we are told the Mughal emperor was at the head of the movement in 1857, we imagine a vigorous, youthful field commander, a true reflection of the founder of the dynasty, Babar the Tiger, a descendant of the ferocious conqueror Timur (Tamerlane). The truth was different. Old, frail, tired and out of touch, Zafar Shah, a man with little idea or experience of commanding an army on a battlefield, who spent his time writing verses in the decaying and isolated quarters assigned to him in the Red Fort in Delhi, typified the confusion and lack of purpose in the movement.

None the less, the most important symbol of Muslim rule – indeed history – was the Mughal emperor himself. He was addressed as Zil-i-Ilahi, God's representative on earth. For the Muslims of the subcontinent he was the highest authority representing Islam.

In practice this meant little: Muslim decline had begun after Aurangzeb's death in 1707. Muslims had not won any major battles for over a century. The major victory at Panipat belonged to Ahmad Shah Abdali, who had come with his Afghan troops from Kabul. Legitimacy, however, still rested with the Mughals, who provided a semblance of continuity and an illusion of authority. Even the hostile Sikhs, conscious that some of the holiest of their founding fathers had been killed by the Mughals, made ceremonial offerings to the emperor in 1783. The Mahadji Scindia, the greatest Maratha warlord, received the title of Regent Plenipotentiary of the Empire from the emperor in 1784.

The British understood this. In 1857–8 they quite deliberately set out to destroy the symbols of the Mughal dynasty. The emperor's sons and grandsons were herded together and shot unceremoniously in his presence by Major William Hodson. The emperor himself was shipped off to Rangoon to die in exile in a bamboo hut, pining for Delhi. Ordinary sepoys were encouraged to sit on the Mughal emperor's throne so that the message would be clear that the lowest in the British hierarchy was equal to the highest in India.

If Muslims complain of the British sacking of Delhi in 1857–8 they seem to forget that they themselves had sacked it several times during the previous century. The sacking by Nadir Shah and Abdali had been particularly brutal, weakening the foundations of Muslim power in North India. Muslims rarely talk about the Punjabi, Pathan and Muslim troops from Hyderabad who fought alongside the British. This was the reality of the nineteenth century. Muslim civilization appeared to be committing suicide. The events of 1857–8 remind Muslims of Muslim Spain all over again – extinction after centuries of glorious rule.

Retribution

The uprising of 1857–8 is romanticized by Indian and Pakistani nationalists, but it was a disastrous misadventure, an exercise in bluff and bravado. The response was confused, the strategy ineffective and there was no hope of victory. The massacre of not only the British soldiers but also women and children provided the justification for the savagery and retribution that followed, exemplified by Hodson's killing of the Mughal princes.

Entire regiments previously considered loyal going over to the other side; the ignominious surrender of the British garrison at Kanpur; the subsequent massacre after the promise of safe passage and the final indignity of the slaughter of defenceless British men and women in the Bibighar building in Kanpur: all this haunted the British for generations to come. Bibighar, where, rumour had it, white women were raped by natives, became a national shrine for the British (J. Robinson 1996; Ward 1996). Fresh recruits arriving in the subcontinent to join their regiment or the Civil Service were warned, 'Remember Cawnpore!'

The British responded with mechanistic fury and re-established order with brute force. In Kanpur, Indians were rounded up and made to lick up the blood on the Bibighar floor where the Europeans had been killed; then they were stuffed with pork and beef and sewn into pigskins. Finally they were blown from cannons, having been told that the Brahmins would be buried and the Muslims burned to ensure their eternal damnation. In Allahabad the sadistic Brigadier-General James Neill slaughtered 6,000

Indians, announcing that 'the Word of God gives no authority for the modern tenderness for human life' (for other such details of horrors, see J. Robinson 1996; Ward 1996; also, J. G. Farrell's excellent novel *The Siege of Krishnapur*, 1973). Yet few in Britain objected to the general's method: 'If our soldiers knock down every filthy idol they see and lay every mosque level with the ground, and if they pollute every shrine and plunder every one worth plundering, I shall not be sorry,' wrote a correspondent in *The Times*.

After 1857–8 Muslims were singled out for punishment by the British. As a letter from William Howard Russell in *The Times* stated in early 1858: 'The Mahommedan element in India is that which causes us most trouble and provokes the largest share of our hostility.... They are unquestionably more dangerous to our rule.... If we could eradicate the traditions and destroy the temples of Mahommed by one vigorous effort, it would indeed be well for the Christian faith and for the British rule' (Khairi 1995: 28–9). A British administrator called Lyall confided to his father in 1858: 'If the Musalman could by any means be entirely exterminated, it could be the greatest possible step towards civilizing and Christianizing Hindustan' (ibid.: 30). James Outram, Resident at Oudh, observed that the revolt was 'the fruit of the Musalman intrigue in the hope of gaining empire, and he must now pay the penalty for failure' (ibid.).

The city magistrate of Delhi, Philip Egerton, suggested that Shah Jahan's grand mosque in Delhi be converted to a Christian church. Others insisted that the Red Fort be destroyed and a new one, named Fort Victoria, built in its place. Yet others argued that all of Delhi must be razed to the ground. In fact almost one-third of Delhi, the most habitable parts especially around the fort, was destroyed in 'a frenzied vengeance of looting and destruction' (Evenson 1989: 99). In 1900 the Viceroy, Lord Curzon, regretted 'the horrors that have been perpetrated in the interests of regimental barracks and messes and canteens in the fairy-like pavilions and courts and gardens of the Shah Jahan' (ibid.).

A Muslim scholar looks back on that time in horror: 'As an act of sheer vindictiveness and vandalism, [the British] even destroyed and scattered the Imperial library, which contained thousands of rare manuscripts painstakingly collected by Mughal princes and princesses over a period of several centuries' (Khairi 1995: 30).

After the abortive uprisings, at one stroke the Muslims of India lost their kingdom, their Mughal empire, their emperor, their language, their culture, their capital city of Delhi and their sense of self. Politically and culturally the loss was totally devastating.

It was not simply the loss of Muslim political power – however symbolic. It was a fundamental reordering of the historical, political, social and economic map of India. In this new restructuring the Muslims found little space. Their language, Persian, already replaced as the official government language by English in 1835, now went out of fashion; the Indian establishment switched entirely to speaking English. Muslim ways – dress, style, food – were also put aside. Muslims now felt not only politically vulnerable but concerned for their very identity. By the 1870s W. W. Hunter had noted the plight of the Muslims. They were almost invisible in the services and nowhere to be seen in positions of influence (Hunter 1957; originally published in 1872). Seen as the troublemakers, as uppity natives, they would soon be squeezed out of history and sink into oblivion.

It is no coincidence that two seminal books for the two Indian communities were written within a few years of each other and not too long after the uprisings of 1857–8: Hali's *Mussaddas* in 1879 (*The Ebb and Flow of Islam*) and Chatterji's *Anandamath* ('The Abbey of Bliss') in 1882. Both were a clarion call to their respective communities to wake up, to rediscover pride in their culture and history and to work towards the achievement of their destiny.

Not only South Asia was in intellectual ferment. It was an extraordinary time for ideas that would transform the coming century. In 1848 Karl Marx and Friedrich Engels had published *The Communist Manifesto*, and in 1897 Theodor Herzl would lay down the charter of action for Zionism which would result in the creation of Israel half a century later and subsequently alter the political and cultural map of the Middle East.

Observing the collapse

'A single shelf of a good European library … [is] worth the whole native literature of India and Arabia,' wrote Lord Macaulay. Imperial arrogance or plain ignorance? Remember this man was writing in the age of Ghalib; just a short while after Mir, Sauda and Hassan, some of the brightest stars of Urdu literature. By the mid-nineteenth century, Muslim poetry, prose, humour and irony had all reached peaks of sophistication. Delhi and Lucknow were the main centres of excellence for Muslim culture. To understand the Muslim predicament in the eighteenth and nineteenth centuries we can learn from the Urdu poets Mir and Ghalib. The intensity is never more painful, the depth of gloom never more bleak, the shafts of light never more brilliant than in their poetry. Together they give us, Mir Taqi Mir for the eighteenth century and Mirza Ghalib for the nineteenth, a sensitive and authentic picture of what was taking place in Muslim society.

While Mir observed the rise of Maratha power and the decline of the Muslims, Ghalib saw the rise of the British and collapse of the Muslims. Mir and Ghalib both record the synthesis, interplay and cross-cutting of alliances and personal friendships between Hindus and Muslims. They describe the emerging political realities which affected them personally. In particular Mir loathed the Persian Nadir Shah and the Afghan Ahmad Shah Abdali, the two invaders of Delhi.

In despair Mir migrated from Delhi to Lucknow, the capital of the Muslim kingdom of Avadh. It was a depressing picture of decay and disintegration. Mir, asked about Delhi when he arrived in Lucknow, replies: 'Delhi, its name fairest among the fair. / Fate looted it and laid it desolate, and to that ravaged city I belong' (Russell and Islam 1969b: 260). Mir is, like Ghalib, a genuine humanist, a universal Muslim. His patron is a Hindu, Raja Nagarmal. A well-known verse asks: 'What does it mean to me? Call me "believer", / call me "infidel", I seek His threshold be it in the temple or the mosque' (ibid.: 173). In 1772, when he was an old man, he writes: 'I am usually in debt, and I live in great poverty' (ibid.: 257). The famine in 1782 laid waste half the population of Delhi, who died of starvation. Other cities were as bad. At Agra, Mir notes, 'I saw a scene of dreadful desolation, and grieved deeply' (ibid.: 36).

For Mir, Muslim culture, history and destiny were symbolized by the Mughals and the focal point of all civilization in India was Delhi. Mir yearned for the past, the golden age that had gone, lamented the fading of culture, friendship, loyalty (ibid.: 248–9), and despised the rich élite who had neither heart nor mind. In Mir we feel the decline, the obsession with past glory and the beginning of fear for the future. Both Mir and Ghalib describe scenes of despondency, of princesses begging in the streets, of mosques unlit, of houses dark, streets deserted and silent; they notice the absence of children.

When the Mughal structure finally collapsed, an entire way of life came to an end. Ghalib in an often quoted verse, perhaps one of the first political poems in Urdu literature, uses the Mughal king as a symbol of Muslim power: 'One candle left and that too is flickering and quiet.' Stunned at the scale of the loss, Ghalib vividly reveals the darkness of the Muslim mind confronting the disintegration: 'There is no hope in the future / once I could laugh at the human condition / now there is no laughter.' In this darkness Ghalib even challenges creation itself: 'If I did not exist it would not have mattered / I am sunk because of my creation.'

Ghalib's letters reveal the anguish of Muslims as the reality of the new order emerges. When he writes about Mughal princesses having to survive by becoming prostitutes he is saying something important (Russell with Islam 1969a; also see Russell 1972). Up to the present day, novels have used this theme as a metaphor for the collapse of Muslim power in India. Quratul Ain Haider's recent Urdu novel, *Gardish-i-rang-i-Chaman*, starts with two girls from the Mughal nobility who have to prostitute themselves after 1857.

Closing the chapter

The story of the Muslims was over. The history of India was no longer the history of Muslim princes, poets, saints and warriors. Muslims now became invisible, marginal characters. For Kipling the Muslim is a horse-trader, for Tagore a money-lender.

The final brutal termination of the Mughals by the British left the Muslims bitter and confused. The dynasty which had emerged from Central Asia and ruled India for over three centuries carrying with pride the name of the invincible warrior Timur, bursting with energy and vitality, now disintegrated. Overnight the Muslim ruling élite was neither ruling nor an élite. Their language, their way of life, their lands and their access to armed supporters were all under threat or had been taken from them. The next half-century would be one of uncertainty and awareness that their history was in danger of being lost for ever. The majority of Muslims now found themselves leaderless and rudderless. In spite of major figures like Sir Sayyed Khan, they would have neither a towering Muslim leader who would speak for them across the length and breadth of India, nor a clearly defined objective, until the emergence of Jinnah and the Pakistan movement late in the 1930s.

Gham, rona, ranj, dil tootna, verana, maut, hashar – sorrow, tears, broken heart, desolation, death, doomsday. These were the key notions of high Urdu literature set in and around Delhi. Growing up in the hills of northern Pakistan in the 1950s, I found them too pessimistic, unnecessarily gloomy. They did not correspond to the buoyant, assertive society of Punjab and the Frontier. Here the folk poetry was more confident, upbeat; the future looked positive, the outlook optimistic. And from this perspective it was easy to dismiss Urdu poetry and by extension the society that created it as decadent. It was easy to close the chapter on that part of Muslim history.

Hierarchy and purity: the clash of civilizations

If we examine the three major communities of India from the mid-nineteenth century onwards in terms of their relationship with history, then while the Muslims looked to the past the British and the Hindus looked to the future. Muslims wished to regain lost glory; the British wished to preserve and consolidate their rule; and the Hindus waited for a day when they would be in command once again of their land. Three peoples, three sets of history, three parallel destinies, sometimes overlapping, sometimes clashing but ultimately separate: there are, then, three perspectives.

The British way

The British as the dominant power consciously steered India towards the future; and the future belonged to them. Superstition, custom and tradition were things of the past especially when they came in the way of progress, science and Western education.

Lord Macaulay's minute written in 1835 became the basis for future intellectual and educational development in India (Ahmed 1990b). Macaulay's argument was simple: European languages and culture would bring enlightenment to Asians; Sanskrit and Arabic − and the culture they represented − were dismissed as something to be consigned to the dustbin of history. Macaulay condemned the entire edifice, with phrases like 'monstrous superstitions' and 'false religion'. The use of Persian was abolished in official correspondence and government weight thrown behind English education. Macaulay's Codes of Criminal and Civil Procedure (drafted in 1841−2 but not completed until the 1860s) sought to impose a Western legal system in British Indian courts.

The minute had many positive consequences. It released and opened India in many ways. English as a medium of instruction opened communication to the West and, more important, with India's own past, encouraging the growth of a new generation of Indians who interacted with the British. In 1857 the universities of Calcutta, Madras and Bombay were established on the model of London University.

For their part the British were able to play off the two Indian communities and thereby secure a firm foothold. This game was played on all levels − political, educational and economic. Its success depended on an appearance of British neutrality or at least pragmatism when tilting towards one or other of the two groups (we shall see in chapter 5 what havoc erupted when the British in the person of Lord Mountbatten tilted heavily against one).

Indian nationalist propaganda tended to depict an idealized land divided along simple religious lines: Hindus and Muslims, both versus the British. In fact this was never true. Shias and Sunnis clashed, especially during religious festivals. Caste Hindus dominated the untouchables and often made their lives a misery. Among the Hindus and Muslims, while many in a broad sense resented the British as their masters, others were happy to accept them.

In the nineteenth century attitudes to religion were sometimes hypocritical and intolerant. Naturally enough the British in India saw a heathen land ripe for conversion, where the one major obstacle that resisted them head-on was Islam. In contrast,

Hinduism in its multi-facetedness responded with greater subtlety, interacting with Christianity at one point, debating with it at another, imitating it here and resisting it there.

We need to separate Christianity from Christians in the subcontinent as far as the Muslims are concerned. With the former, Islam could be comfortable: both religions were distinctively monotheistic, the main prophets were similar and many of the values and rituals were mutually recognizable. Unlike Christianity, however, Christians posed problems for Muslims: they were rulers, conscious of their superior status; besides, neither community was likely to forget that until the arrival of the British it was the Muslims who ruled in Delhi, that Muslims saw themselves as the rightful élite of India.

Muslim attitudes included, at one extreme, those who regarded opposition to the British as a form of *jihad*, to a few who wished to imitate the British; but even those who adopted British ways would feel an underlying resentment. On the other hand, the British suspected that Muslims, as the former political rulers of the land, competed with them for power in India and could muster military force in the field. There was mistrust on both sides. Chaudhuri writes of Muslim feelings towards the British: 'The Muslim hatred for the British was very real and venomous, because it was they who had been supplanted in the enjoyment of political power by the British, and the deprivation was also recent' (1990: 50).

British policy was aimed at the Muslims from the start. In 1793 the Permanent Settlement of Bengal, one of the first and most far-reaching pieces of British legislation, had deliberately destroyed Muslim leadership based in agricultural land and resulted in their loss of power and status. When the Muslim language, Persian, was replaced as the official language by English, the Muslims were reduced to being deaf and dumb. 'I cannot close my eyes to the belief that that race [the Muslims] is fundamentally hostile to us and our true policy is to reconcile the Hindus,' wrote the Governor-General, Lord Ellenborough, to Lord Wellington not long afterwards (Sayeed 1968: 20).

The British in India taught local history on the basis that the primary duty of good government was to ensure law and order, otherwise there would be no stability, just plain anarchy. You have much, the subtext said, to be grateful for; without the British Raj there would be chaos. As if to prove the point, a well-oiled administrative engine of some 1,500 Indian Civil Service officers ran the lives of 300 million Indians early in the twentieth century. But underneath this simple logic lay the compulsions that formed European imperialism: white supremicism, financial aggrandizement, international prestige and strategic influence.

Some people like to look back on the British Raj in India with nostalgia. Others, like Trevor Royle in *Winds of Change* (1996), believed that 'British colonial rule was generally decent and fair, and invariably even-handed.' In *A Fighting Retreat* (1996) Robin Neillands also comes to the same conclusion, that 'the British rule, while sometimes oppressive, was generally benign.'

Despite the many atrocities committed by the British, particularly during the days of the East India Company (see, for example, the writing of Edmund Burke), it is possible to read Indian history in their imperial way. Through the ups and downs of Muslim rule in Delhi, especially during the Mughal empire, there had been long periods of continuity and stability. When Muslim power weakened in the eighteenth century chaos had ensued. The period from the mid-nineteenth to the mid-twentieth century –

when the British held India – was one of relative calm. In spite of uprisings in the North-West Frontier Province during the late nineteenth century, and the nationalist movement and the growing communal violence in the early part of the twentieth century, for the majority of people this was an era of relative stability. After independence in 1947, in the countries of the subcontinent there was a reversion to the chaos, with communal rioting bordering on genocide and large parts of several provinces in a state of anarchy and some even wanting to break away from the centre.

The attitude of the British to the Indians has changed several times over the three centuries during which they had a presence in India. Starting as straightforward traders, in the eighteenth century the British became, like so many in the land, conquerors on the battlefield. In the nineteenth century, after the British Crown took over from the East India Company and made India its colony, their attitude became paternalistic. By the turn of the century the attitude was less clear. The old Victorian paternalism persisted but from the 1920s onwards winds of change were blowing across the globe carrying ideas of socialist equality and universal brotherhood. In the late twentieth century, once again, the British assiduously cultivate India for its vast market. From trading to warfare, to colonization and back again to trading, there has been a full cycle, with changing corresponding relationships between the British and the Indians.

Today the traces of the British are difficult to locate. A few run-down buildings, some fast fading memories and a distorted, corrupted administrative structure are all that remains of the British; and, of course, the most important single legacy – the English language.

Hindus and Muslims

Hinduism and Islam provide a complex and fascinating history of shadow-boxing, conflict and synthesis in South Asia. On one level it is a straightforward opposition of two different systems; yet, on another, there is an overlap that convinces many philosophers on both sides that they are one and the same thing. On the surface no two more dissimilar systems could have evolved side by side – Islam believing in one God, Hinduism in many forms of the divine; Islam denouncing social hierarchy, Hinduism steeped in caste; Islam sharply and simply defined in its beliefs and attitudes, Hinduism always with shades of grey, understanding the world through the notions of purity and impurity, pollution and defilement.

Two different ways of life were locked together in one subcontinent, intermarrying, their blood flowing into each other. Culturally and linguistically, in their food and their clothes, they were similar; they were living with each other, yet withdrawing from each other. Synthesis yet distance, consensus but also confrontation: the relationship between Hindu and Muslim would be the greatest challenge to any leader in South Asia with a plan for unity.

Popular commentators talk of Muslim separatism, of weaning Muslims away from a united India, as if it had been created by Jinnah. But it was inherent from the time the first Muslims arrived in the subcontinent – from the eighth century, when Muhammad bin Qasim threatened to usher in a new order challenging Hindu customs, organization and beliefs. For centuries North India was under Muslim rule. The ruler of Delhi was

Muslim, the court spoke Persian, the judges consulted Arabic texts and pronounced Muslim law, most nobles and generals were Muslim and the battles were fought between them.

But the phyletic and political boundaries with Hinduism were more porous than this would suggest. From the Tughlaks to the Mughals many rulers had Hindu mothers, and Hindu blood brought with it Hindu custom and thought. Endogamy, that is men marrying women from outside and bringing them into the group, reflects social and political superiority and is widely discussed in anthropological literature. While Muslims married Hindu women when they were dominant, today the picture is reversed, with large numbers of Muslim women marrying non-Muslim men in India, or practising exogamy.

Cultural synthesis

What is of universal strength in Hinduism is the ability to absorb and synthesize other ideas and systems. Hinduism not only absorbed Buddhism, which began as a statement against it – in particular rejecting the caste system – but in the end almost obliterated it in India, its birthplace. Similarly many aspects of Jainism have been brought into Hinduism. Indeed, Gandhi's non-violence derives from Jainism and Buddhism and his testing of the sexual will by sleeping naked with women, it is said, from the former. This capacity to assimilate other cultures allows Hinduism to survive under difficult circumstances.

Simplistically put – and for millions of Hindus this is exactly how it is put – Muslims, and then the British, defiled Mother India. Purity was lost as temples were destroyed, women dishonoured and people converted. If history is to be corrected the wrongs of the past must be put right. The need to reintegrate Muslims into Hinduism is a move to close an unhappy chapter and once again develop a healthy, whole Hindu polity; purity would be regained, history redeemed.

While many leaders spoke of purity, the sociological reality was one of fluid borders between the communities. There were mutual cultural, political, social and even religious influences at work over the centuries all across India (there are several studies on this subject; see, for example, Roy 1983). Scholars like the Mughal prince, Dara Shikoh, influenced by Sufism, translated and respected Hindu religious texts. Perhaps the most dramatic example – one that strengthened the stability of Mughal rule – was the alliance with the Rajputs and their princely states. For most of Mughal rule they formed close personal relationships with the dynasty, providing it with wives and mothers of future kings.

Not all Muslims were pleased. Sheikh Ahmad Sirhindi, a leading religious figure in the late sixteenth century, complained about the Mughal emperor Akbar's tolerance too often in public. But the response of the rulers was characteristic. Sirhindi was locked up. Shah Waliullah in the eighteenth century also raised the alarm. If, he argued, Muslims continued as they were, they would soon be culturally absorbed into Hinduism. He was right. The criss-crossing of currents is evident even today. Kashmir, one of the largest Muslim states in the subcontinent, was ruled by a Hindu; Hyderabad in the south, a Hindu-majority state, was ruled by a Muslim. Many Muslim families – including

Jinnah's and Iqbal's – had Hindu influences, while many Hindu ones – like Nehru's – had Muslim influences. Indeed, these cultural interweavings would affect the main leaders of the independence movement: Jinnah's daughter married a Christian, Nehru's sister almost married a Muslim and Gandhi's son became a Muslim.

Rajendra Prasad, an eminent Congress leader, recalls a picture of harmony in rural India which was part imagined, part real:

> Religion permeated the village life and there was perfect harmony between Hindus and Muslims. Muslims would join Hindus in the boisterous festival of Holi. On the occasion of Dashara, Diwali and Holi the Maulvi [Muslim scholar] would compose special verses.... Hindus participated in Moharrum by taking out *Tazias* [bamboo and paper symbols of the tombs of the martyrs Hussain and Hassan]. The *Tazias* of the well-to-do Hindus ... were bigger and brighter than those of the poor Muslims. (Bonner et al. 1994: 45)

There was much in Hinduism which Muslims were comfortable with. Hindus were generally peaceful, accommodating, cultured and sophisticated. There was much to admire in Hindu philosophy and Hindus gave much to the world (for example, yoga). Over the centuries Muslims and Hindus had developed a common culture which included language, clothes and food.

Ordinary Muslims often missed what philosophers and poets saw: that Brahma, ultimate reality for many Hindu intellectuals, could well mirror their own notion of a universal God; indeed, Iqbal's poem to Ram refers to him as the 'Imam of Hind'. Such subtlety did not filter down to the village or street. Cultural synthesis at the popular level is something different. When Hindus hear the great Muslim singer, Mohammad Rafi, singing Hindu *bhajans*, devotional songs, they do not dismiss them because they are sung by a Muslim. The songs appeal to Hindus but also to Muslims. It is also incorrect to suggest that Urdu was only a Muslim language. Some of the most outstanding Urdu writers – Prem Chand, Rajinder Singh Bedi, Krishan Chandar, to cite some writing early this century (Russell 1992) – were Hindus.

To depict Muslims as struggling relentlessly against Hindus over the last thousand years is historically incorrect. The famous figures such as Babar and Jinnah often confronted their own community. Indeed Babar's great battle at Panipat which decided the fate of India was not fought against the Hindus but against the Muslim king of Delhi. Similarly Jinnah was several times the target of Muslim would-be assassins. He was called the *Kafir-i-Azam*, the great non-believer, by some orthodox Muslims. Nehru pointed out in his book *The Discovery of India* (1961) that the earliest Muslim invaders like Mahmud had Hindu commanders accompanying them, and neither the Muslim kings nor the Hindus regarded it as a straightforward religious war. Thus both Hindu and Muslim popular history is incorrect in depicting the relationship between them as one of unrelenting conflict.

Muslim rule

How did the Muslims rule over such a big Hindu majority? The answer lies partly in their military strength, partly in their stronger belief in a black-and-white solution to the problems of the world. We must also keep in mind that, while we think of Hindus as monolithic, in fact many different groups made up the large Hindu majority. These groups were divided by caste, and by ethnic, linguistic and regional boundaries. Thus a Muslim army would not face the Hindu population as a whole but only those sections of it which fought traditionally as warriors. The upper caste, like priests, did not generally fight in battle. Similarly members of the lower castes were not considered people of the sword and were traditionally allowed to perform only menial tasks. Besides, Muslims with their ideas of equality attracted Hindus, especially from the lower castes, and there were conversions. All this dilutes the somewhat simplistic idea of small victorious Muslim warrior groups taking on large Hindu armies that always lost.

By and large the Hindu population was left alone by the Muslims, but their rulers, in princely states where they were independent, were marginalized. The tolerant Muslim rulers treated Hindus well, but other rulers revived the idea of some kind of *jizya* or tax on non-Muslims. This was ironic because the majority population was always Hindu. It is a memory that rankles in the Hindu mind.

Muslim rule forced many ambitious Hindus to become master mimics, imitating their Muslim rulers – in language, in clothes, in the style of living. Europeans visiting India often found it difficult to distinguish between the two. Because of this experience, Hindus were more adaptable to the British when they replaced the Muslims, and many smoothly became successful mimics of the British.

Problems with caste

From the philosophers of Islam like Iqbal to the men of action like Jinnah, Muslims thought the caste system was at the root of many Indian problems and feared its impact if they should come under Hindu rule. 'If we fail to realize our duty today you will be reduced to the status of *sudras* (low castes) and Islam will be vanquished from India,' Jinnah warned the Muslim community (Sayeed 1968: 199).

How could men and women be tied down for ever to one caste which determined their status, wealth and marriage simply by accident of birth? As far as Muslims were concerned, their religion, Islam, constantly emphasized the equality of all human beings. The last address of the holy Prophet at Arafat had stressed that all, Arabs and non-Arabs, white and black, were equal in the eyes of God. All that mattered was good behaviour and anyone could aspire to that. There were thus major differences between Hinduism and Islam just as there were important common links.

Divisions in society are common in every civilization, but the rigidity and the rules that prop up the caste system in Hinduism potentially enforce misery on the millions who belong to the lower castes. The psychological, economic and social impact is enormous on those who are looked down upon with contempt as inferior beings.

In the ideal, members of the highest caste, Brahmins, cannot take food from the lower castes, eat with them, marry them or even, in the case of the lowest caste, let their shadow fall on them or touch them: hence 'untouchables' (Dumont 1970; Madan 1992; Mayer 1970; Srinivas 1952). Brahmins are usually vegetarian; in contrast the lower castes eat meat. A woman must marry only once in the upper caste, though some allow remarriage. Some of the upper-caste males are allowed to have more than one wife. The bride must be a virgin. What Srinivas clearly showed was that while rituals separate castes they also integrate the caste itself through marriage, death and birth ceremonies. In time Muslims themselves would be influenced by Hinduism. Anthropologists like the Indian scholar Imtiaz Ahmad have noted the high incidence of caste-like divisions and attitudes among the Muslims of South Asia. As already noted, family names in the upper class trace links outside the subcontinent which give them prestige and status. These names also indicate that they are not converted lower-caste Hindus.

The essence of Hinduism

Hindus are a quintessentially religious people. Because their sense of religion is so strongly sociological, it pervades every aspect of their lives and they can maintain their religion in the most unlikely social environment. The Vedas, ancient canonical hymns and texts, developed over the centuries to become a living, unified yet complex, religious, social and cultural point of view whose cornerstone is spiritual control over this world and eventual liberation. In contrast with the monotheism of Islam – or Judaism and Christianity – Hinduism is characterized by an apparent polytheism and pantheism, with many words and many voices. *Dharma* or duty irrespective of consequences is the key to correct behaviour. *Hindu* is actually the Persian word for India and comes from the word *hind*, the river Indus. The name has a geographical rather than religious connotation. Hindus, like Buddhists, seek enlightenment, although Buddhism does not accept the authority of the Vedas. For both, culture, myth, religion and philosophy constantly interact in a long historic tradition.

For an outsider, on the positive side, there is a remarkable balance in Hinduism between ideas of this life and the other, represented by the notion of the larger cycle of life which keeps things in proportion and never allows this world to dominate totally. There is also a concern with the discipline of the body and mind through the system of yogic thinking and practice. The four stages of life provide a sense of harmony and balance in the individual's life-span; the last two stages encourage contemplation, meditation and retreat.

But orthodox Hinduism also includes certain ideas which are difficult to reconcile with the late twentieth century. Its attitude to women in the old texts and practice is out of tune with the times. The ideal woman must be totally subservient to the male. She is suspect as a sexually ravenous and undisciplined creature. In the ideal, when her husband dies she is often encouraged to commit *sati* and burn herself on his funeral pyre. For her, *moksha* or spiritual attainment can be more difficult than for the male.

Holy men were often considered divine, that is a visible expression of God; 'gods' were also found in trees, in rivers, in animals, in mountains. God was everywhere and could take any shape. God was wealth, god was the husband in a home and god (or goddess) was the destruction of those who threatened the purity of the system. Kali, the goddess of destruction, sword in hand and purple painted over her body, a garland of human skulls hung around her neck and blood dripping from her fearsome mouth, was bloodcurdling. When faced with the manifestly bloodthirsty Kali, Muslims are baffled: 'The goddess is represented as a black female with four arms, standing on the breast of

Shivu [*sic*]. In one hand she carries a scimitar; in two others the heads of giants, which she holds by the hair; and the fourth hand supports giants' heads' (Suleri 1992: 95).

Muslims would find the stone or wooden images alien enough in themselves; after all, their notion of the one God who must not be depicted in visual images is a central tenet of the faith. But in their vengeful form these figures are unsettling. They are used to intimidate the Muslims by conveying an implicit if not explicit message of terror: 'Beware, the gods are out to get you.' (*Anandamath*, the late-nineteenth-century Hindu novel, would use the image of Kali to evoke nationalist feeling against the Muslims and the British.) Little wonder Muslims vainly yearn for a secular India that would push these threatening representations out of the public domain and back into private worship.

In the nineteenth and twentieth centuries Hinduism has produced some of the most universally admired figures like Mahatma Gandhi and the poet Rabindranath Tagore. It has produced great thinkers, writers and scientists. It can, with confidence, speak of itself as a modern world religion which has contributed significantly to the sum of things. Indeed, many in the West turn to Hinduism for solace – and not only rock musicians and hippies. Therefore to see Hinduism now reduced to mobs destroying Muslim, Sikh, Christian and Dalit religious places and attacking their property and lives is a tragedy: a universal religion reduced to communal urban thuggery. The philosophers of Hinduism need to clarify their thinking in the context of communal politics and in the light of their own traditions. The failure to do so will be the dilution of Hinduism and a distortion of its central teachings.

Bazaar stereotypes

A mythology was created around racial stereotypes popularized by the British in the subcontinent, a mythology that fed novels, poetry and the cinema. The stereotype of the northern Muslim, the noble warrior, straightforward and simple, who looked the imperialist in the eye, contrasted with the half-educated but cunning Hindu *babu*. The British even labelled certain groups the 'martial races' and recruited them for the army.

The edifice of the Raj culture and literature was based on these stereotypes. Writers such as Rudyard Kipling, M. M. Kaye, E. M. Forster, John Masters and Paul Scott all relied to some degree on such stereotypes. *A Passage to India* had an honest, impulsive, although flawed Dr Aziz; readers felt for him, sympathized with him, understood him. Forster clearly failed with Godbole, the Hindu, unable to fathom his supposedly inscrutable mind.

Village society in the north also looked on Hindus as money-grabbing *banias*, money-lenders. British officials like Malcolm Darling in the Punjab had created a whole literature around this social evil based on their experiences as district officers. One of the aims of the British officials in the Punjab was to relieve the financial burden of Muslim peasants under the yoke of Hindu money-lenders. In the popular myth this was depicted as a stark contrast between a wily, overfed, well-clothed money-lender and a plain, lean and honest peasant.

Stereotypes rooted in history helped to create further misunderstanding. Scholars who looked for an ancient past, philosophers who sought the meaning of life, mystics who searched for the otherworldly found satisfaction in Hinduism. Those who looked for more simple virtues of courage, companionship and honour on the battlefield discovered these in the Muslims. Muslim generals and Hindu warriors, one brave and stupid, the other cowardly and cunning: these were the stereotypes.

Muslim confidence in their martial prowess may be gauged by the fact that just after the First World War they were still considering inviting the King of Afghanistan to become the King of India with his capital in Delhi. They were reading history through Muslim eyes. This would be their undoing.

Gandhi himself confirmed this perception of history. If the British left, he warned his readers in several widely read articles, Muslims would very quickly re-establish their rule over the subcontinent. The Muslim, he said in several statements, is a 'bully', the Hindu a 'coward' (for example in *Young India*, 19 June 1924; also see Mujahid 1981: 192–3; also chapter 4 below).

Although these were stereotypes, particular groups in the subcontinent, like the Bengalis and the Madrasis, did well in the Civil Service examinations. At the turn of the century they were already making a mark where English mattered. In contrast Punjabi and Pathan Muslims made up the backbone of the British Indian army.

In bazaar stereotypes, for Hindus, Muslims were violent and lustful; for Muslims, Hindus were mean and cowardly. Of course, some Muslims were violent and lustful and not motivated by Islam; just as some Hindus were mean and cowardly. What is important is that these stereotypes filtered through to and permeated village society (Dube 1965). It was not surprising that where Hindus saw Muslims in terms of stereotypes and transposed these images on to the national stage the Muslims did the same. Very often Gandhi would be portrayed by Muslims as a *bania*, a money-lender, the embodiment of the entire Hindu nation. Jinnah would be depicted by the Hindus as a fanatic, again a stereotype for Muslims.

Muslim awakening

The shock effect of 1857–8 and the continuing blows of fortune perhaps acted as a catalyst and in the next half-century Muslim society gave birth to a new radical generation of writers and leaders. Unlike the previous generation, they would interact with British culture and their language would be English as much as Urdu or Persian. A strong sense of pride and self-esteem pervaded their work; although they adopted different strategies, they responded to Muslim misfortunes with an intellectual and political vigour which created a renaissance, an awakening. Iqbal typifies this response. Compare the unrestrained confidence of Iqbal's poetry to the unrelieved if resplendent gloom of Ghalib's verses.

Within a year or two of each other, around 1876, a remarkable Muslim triumvirate – the Aga Khan, Jinnah and Iqbal – was born (the first two in Karachi). The Aga Khan's financial acumen, Jinnah's leadership and Iqbal's poetic vision would change the map of South Asia in the next century.

Maulana Mohani, one of Jinnah's keenest supporters, was also born in 1876. Around this time, too, were born the scholar-activists, the brothers Shaukat and Muhammad Ali (see below). There was another important birth: in 1875 Sir Sayyed Ahmad Khan (also see below) laid the basis of what would become the Mohammedan Anglo-Oriental College (later the University) at Aligarh. Significantly, it was founded on Queen Victoria's birthday. Aligarh became the foundation of a Muslim educational and political reawakening. Muslims like Sayyed Ahmad wished for a synthesis between Muslim and British culture and education. The orthodox, rejecting the British altogether, would condemn Sayyed Ahmad as a heretic.

After the excesses of 1857–8 there had come a slow change of heart in the British. Sir Sayyed had written a pamphlet in 1858 on the causes of the uprisings in an attempt to remove the misunderstandings between the British and the Muslims, since the former had put the entire blame on the latter. Sir Sayyed explained the grievances of the Muslim community, including forcible conversion to Christianity and lack of political representation, and the fact that the Muslims expected high standards of justice from the British. In other works he pointed out the similarities between Islam and Christianity. W. W. Hunter had argued that the natural allies of the British were the Hindus, because Muslims were predisposed by their loss of power to oppose their interests. Sir Sayyed challenged this in his writings such as *An Account of the Loyal Mohammedans of India* (1860). The controversy set the scene for a rapprochement between the British and the Muslims later in the century.

Hunter's *The Indian Musalmans*, published in 1872, concluded that the British should ensure there were no legitimate grievances among the Muslims. This, he maintained, could be achieved only if Muslim hearts were won over. The book made a major impact. It was followed by *India Under Ripon: A Private Diary* by W. S. Blunt (1909), who argued along the same lines after visiting India in 1883–4.

Sir Sayyed Ahmad Khan

The autobiographical notes that Sir Sayyed left behind (see Lahori's biography based on these, 1993) reveal his devotion to the British. He genuinely believed that they were the masters of the age and that Muslims could do no better than to be their loyal followers. When Sir Sayyed Ahmad Khan in England, entranced by the white women he saw, called them *paries*, 'fairies', it was, I suspect, typical of his political position. It was more to do with the head than the heart. He was frightened out of his wits about what he saw happening to his community. They were on the verge of destruction. Everything, then, about the British was to be looked up to and admired.

Sir Sayyed's enthusiastic support of service in government encouraged the British, like Lord Minto, Viceroy in 1905–10, to declare, 'We have much to gain politically by our goodwill to Mussalman enlightenment.' What is also clear is Sayyed Ahmad's dedication to Muslim modernization and his aversion to the clerics, the mullahs, whom he regarded as crafty, hypocritical, ignorant and bigoted. Most important was his commitment to and belief in Islam's destiny, a chauvinist perception that appealed to Muslims: 'Our nation is of the blood of those who made not only Arabia, but Asia and Europe to tremble. It is our nation which conquered with its sword the whole of India' (Shaikh 1989: 116).

The desire to gain education and jobs in British India was linked to a larger awareness of a tacit competition with the majority community of India, the Hindus, who were already surging ahead. The thought of what would happen to them once the British left was not far from the minds of the Muslims. Indeed, Sayyed Ahmad located the problem precisely in a letter written to *The Times*: 'Now, suppose all the English were to leave India then who would be the rulers of India? It is necessary that one of them – Mohammedans and Hinduism – should conquer the other and thrust it down' (16 January 1888).

Although Sir Sayyed is credited with having originated and coined what is called the two-nation theory, in fact he constantly spoke of one India in which all the nations would belong to the same civilization. But he did plant the seeds for the two-nation theory. His writing lends itself to different interpretations, especially if seen over the course of his life.

Sir Sayyed's monumental achievement was the University at Aligarh, which played a central role in the Muslim renaissance. Take the example of Sirdar Shaukat Hyat Khan (1995). Like his father, Sir Sikander, Chief Minister of the Punjab from 1936 to 1942, Sirdar Shaukat Hyat Khan was educated at Aligarh University, which brought him into contact with Muslims from all over India – future Prime Ministers, presidents, generals, writers. From Liaquat Ali to Ayub Khan, so many leading figures studied there. It was a remarkable culture and it laid the foundations for what would become the Pakistan movement.

Aligarh had its critics. Akbar Allahabadi, the Urdu poet, captures the dilemma for the Muslims, torn between love of the community, *ummah* and the reality of the situation in India under the British (Russell 1992: 173): 'Our belly keeps us working with the clerks, / Our heart is with the Persians and the Turks.' Maulana Abul Kalam Azad, one of the leading lights of the Congress, claimed that Aligarh had paralysed the Muslims. He accused them of having become lifeless puppets dancing to the tune of the British government, and argued that it was the Hindus who were waging a *jihad*, God's battle, against the British while the Muslims were fast asleep (Sayeed 1968: 43–4).

A debate developed within Muslim society about how best to respond to the changing times. From the 1860s onwards Muslims had expressed their fears of the Hindu majority openly and in print. The Siddon's Union Club, which formed part of the Mohammedan Anglo-Oriental College at Aligarh, discussed the issue of representative institutions for India. In September 1887 the club resolved that religious divisions in India posed a formidable if not insuperable obstacle to the evolution of 'Western-style' representation in the subcontinent. In January 1888 the general consensus of the Siddon's Union Club members was that 'the complicated nature of the ethnological and religious differences' of India would substantially undermine any notion of common representative institutions.

Sayyed Hussain Bilgrami, who was among the small group of Western-educated Muslims associated with Sayyed Ahmad in the 1860s, and who was later to become one of Aligarh's 'elders', argued in an influential article that Western-style democracy or political representation in India was unsuitable because it ignored the hostility between India's 'races, castes and classes'. It was also unjust because it failed to acknowledge the unequal 'intellectual and moral development' of India's diverse communities. In 1890 the influential Mahomedan Literary Society, founded in 1863, submitted a memorandum to the government in which they 'prayed' for the withdrawal of political practices such as elections. Their arguments were more or less the same as those of Bilgrami. The fear of an unassailable Hindu majority would never fully leave Muslims. It would lead to the formation in 1906 of the Muslim League and eventually the demand for Pakistan.

Opposed to figures like Sir Sayyed and the jurist Ameer Ali were the 'nationalist' Muslims. Led by the first Muslim president of the Congress, Badruddin Tyabji from Bombay, they believed that for Muslims in India 'the proper course is to join the Congress and take part in its deliberations from our peculiar stand-point' (Sheikh 1989: 166). Many members of the *ulema*, the traditional Islamic scholars associated with the important religious centres at Deoband and Lucknow, believed that the survival of Indian Muslims depended less upon political than upon religious reform. Men like Maulana Hasrat Mohani and Saifuddin Kitchlew devoted their energies to Muslim proselytization in the late 1920s. Some *ulema* like Abdul Bari called for a withdrawal from politics, regarding it as an unworthy and unclean activity for good Muslims, while others like Maulana Azad opted to continue within the Indian Congress.

Making a mark

Muslims like Ameer Ali, Yusuf Ali, the Ali brothers, Rahmat Ali and Allama Iqbal clearly illustrated the synthesis between Islam and the modern world. They wrote of Islam with passion and commitment; all wrote in English. Their combined work forms a large part of the corpus of modern Muslim intellectual activity.

Ameer Ali's books, particularly *The Spirit of Islam*, first published in 1891, were the first Muslim attempt at explaining Muslim history rationally and specifically to a Western, English-speaking audience. One of the earliest and most distinguished Muslim jurists, Ameer Ali flourished under the British. He spoke with pride of the past and with hope for the future. His almost brash confidence can be gauged from his assessment of Indian history: 'It can hardly be disputed that the real history of India commences with the history of the Mussalmans' (Shaikh 1989: 95). Muslims were, without doubt, 'the paramount race in India' (ibid.: 116). Ali's work greatly influenced subsequent generations of Muslims. Jinnah himself was an admirer.

Yusuf Ali, like Ameer Ali a member of the British establishment until he left the Indian Civil Service, translated the Quran into English, and this became in itself a landmark event, the first English translation of the holy book by a Muslim. He demonstrated that it was possible to do so in good English and as a believer. In fact Iqbal's most significant intellectual essay, which first appeared in 1930, is in English – *The Reconstruction of Religious Thought in Islam* (1986).

The brothers Shaukat and Muhammad Ali – through their speeches, articles and appearance – did much to present the modern face of Islam in India. Scholar-activists, both were educated at Aligarh (Muhammad, the younger brother, went on to Oxford). By the 1920s their leadership qualities in challenging the British and rallying the Muslims were widely recognized. The Ali brothers founded the English weekly *Comrade* and the Urdu weekly *Hamdard*. They came to prominence in what was known as the Khilafat movement during the 1920s, the period when Muslim politics was not clearly defined (see chapter 3). Although Muhammad Ali died in 1931, Shaukat, along with the Aga Khan, would play a key role in the 1930s in getting Jinnah elected as president of the Muslim League and supporting him. Shaukat Ali talked about Islam on several lecture tours in the

Middle East and even in the USA. He could balance his Islamic learning with his love of cricket; he had been captain of cricket at Aligarh. He died in 1938.

Another notable scholar-activist, Maulana Hasrat Mohani, a graduate of Aligarh, almost singlehandedly launched anti-establishment political writing. It landed him in prison, but this did not discourage him. In 1921 at the All-India Congress meeting in Ahmedabad he proposed a resolution for the independence of India but was opposed by Gandhi, who preferred India to be given dominion status within the British Commonwealth. Maulana Mohani then took a leading part in the non-cooperation movement launched by the Congress and the Khilafat movement. He supported the Congress up until the 1920s, when, disillusioned, especially by Nehru and the Nehru Report (see chapter 3), he joined the Muslim League. After this he became an ardent supporter of Jinnah. Mohani was a writer and poet of note, popular in his day. After independence in 1947 he stayed behind in India rather than migrate to Pakistan in order to safeguard the interests of the Muslims there. He died in 1951.

Bahadur Yar Jung was another celebrated Muslim figure who has also faded from public memory and needs to be acknowledged. A favourite of Jinnah's, he died relatively young in 1944. He was considered one of the most powerful Urdu orators in India and would translate Jinnah's speeches into Urdu, making a powerful impact on the audience. A scholar of Islam, he had studied the Quran and the life of the Prophet. Sacrificing his estates he joined the radical Khaksar movement in 1938, but resigned after the attempt by a Khaksar on Jinnah's life in Bombay in 1943. His was a major public voice in the Muslim League and he was one of the stars surrounding Jinnah.

Chaudhry Rahmat Ali is one of the unsung heros of the Pakistan movement whose passion and motivation for the Muslim community, the *ummah*, are clearly reflected in his writing. Based in Cambridge, where he died in 1951, this Punjabi lawyer seems to have spent most of his life fighting for a Muslim identity and nation in South Asia in the last years of the British Raj (see, for instance, his *Pakistan: The Fatherland of the Pak Nation*, 1940; see map 2, p. xxvii). Rahmat Ali's pamphlets and writings still stir the blood and he is popular with large sections of the Muslim community. The word 'Pakistan' for a Muslim state is attributed to him. Rahmat Ali lived and died in obscurity. Few Muslims know him.

A discussion of the Muslim renaissance would not be complete without mention of one of the most remarkable yet saddest figures, Maulana Abul Kalam Azad. Born in 1889, he studied Arabic and Islamic studies and edited one of the most influential Urdu weeklies, *Al-Hilal*, which was suppressed in 1914 for its anti-British writing. Azad was a member of the Muslim League, took part in the Khilafat movement, was arrested several times and spent eleven years in jail. In the 1920s, however, he was converted to the Congress point of view and campaigned among Muslims on its behalf. He opposed Jinnah and his 'fourteen points' in 1928. He was President of the Indian National Congress from 1939 to 1946 and conducted the talks with Sir Stafford Cripps on behalf of the Congress in 1942, with Lord Wavell in 1945 and with the Cabinet Mission in 1946.

Azad consistently opposed the demand for Pakistan and advocated a united Indian nation. He wrote several books, perhaps the most important being his commentary on the Quran. His autobiography was first published with thirty pages missing; he had left instructions for these pages to be published thirty years after his death. When they eventually appeared, they reflected the sense of sorrow and disillusionment that he had felt after the creation of India (Azad 1988). A man of high ideals, he was shattered at the reality that emerged after 1947 and the fate of his community.

The Indian intellectual ferment was reflected in the larger Muslim world. Afghani, of Iranian origin, campaigned for a pan-Islamic vision in the Muslim world with a focus on the Caliph in Istanbul late in the nineteenth century and early in the twentieth. He was opposed to Sir Sayyed's method and strategy as too loyal to the British. (In the 1990s, the Hizb-ut-Tahrir in the UK, campaigning for the revival of the Khilafat, the caliphate, attacked Jinnah, who was the embodiment of Sir Sayyed's two-nation theory but seen by them as too pro-British; see also chapter 7). Afghani's disciple Abduh, and later Rida, in the Arab world, also responded to the challenges of the modern age. While pointing out the corruption of many of the traditional leaders, they also underlined the purity and vigour of Islam. All this helped to create a platform that would give Muslims a sense not only of pride but also of identity.

Muslim spite

We need to balance the rose-coloured account of the Muslim renaissance with a little-known aspect of Muslim society: the jealousy and malice which some of these Muslim leaders faced from fellow Muslims. Sir Sayyed Ahmad, Jinnah and Iqbal actually had *fatwas* delivered against them from religious scholars. Many Muslims considered them the worst kind of heretic. The rare personal glimpse we get of the hurt is from the writings of Ameer Ali.

The inability of the Muslims to honour their men of distinction contrasts strongly with the other main society in India, the Hindus. Whatever divisions and jealousies there are within Indian society – and there are many based on caste, language, region, and so on – none the less there is also recognition. The treatment of Gandhi and Nehru in Indian society contrasts strongly with the treatment given to outstanding Muslims. This is best summed up by the example of Yusuf Ali at 80, bewildered and frail, dying destitute and alone in London (Sherif 1994).

The emergence of Muslim women

In *Discovering Islam: Making Sense of Muslim History and Society* (1988) I suggested that when Muslim destiny is secure society is confident, the attitude of Muslim men towards women is more sensible and fair. Muslim women are therefore treated in a much more Islamic manner than when Muslims are colonized or subjugated.

The Mughals provide us with an example. Mughal society allowed women to play a leading role as poets, archers, artists and rulers; Nur Jehan virtually ran the empire as empress early in the seventeenth century. Central Asian tradition certainly played a part in this but so did Mughal ideas of Islamic rule. In other Indian states, too, Muslim women wielded power (for example in Bhopal in the west and Bijapur in the south). Muslim political decline meant the decline of women: 1857 was a low point for women too. As noted above, Ghalib wrote about princesses having to prostitute themselves to eat. Respectable women were locked out of sight. Women practically disappeared from public view for almost a century.

From the confident, assertive Muslim woman of the Mughal times to the unsure, rather lonely and sad figure symbolized by the eponymous heroine of *Umrao Jan Ada*, one of Urdu literature's most famous novels, the fortunes of Muslim women and their society have changed dramatically. We must not read too deeply into this comparison (after all, the Bhopal women did continue to dominate the state court), but it gives us pause for thought.

The Pakistan movement in the late 1930s and 1940s produced a completely new Muslim woman from different social and ethnic backgrounds – committed, nationalist, dynamic. She was out in the streets facing police charges and leading demonstrations; but also in the drawing-rooms and libraries. Begum Raana Liaquat Ali Khan and Begum Shaista Ikramullah (later to be governors and ambassadors in Pakistan) exemplify the renaissance of women. The latter wrote her popular autobiography, *From Purdah to Parliament* (1963), which reflected the optimism of Muslim women involved in the Pakistan movement. Even Begum Liaquat and Lady Noon, converts from other faiths, were committed Pakistanis. Most important was the formidable figure of Fatima Jinnah.

Jinnah's ideas on women need to be clearly brought out. He believed Islam gave women more rights than did the West. This generation of Muslim women had to take their place in history. On several occasions he defied traditional leaders by asking his sister to take the platform. Jinnah was clear about the role of women in Islam and his Pakistan movement:

> I am glad to see that not only Muslim men but Muslim women and children also have understood the Pakistan scheme. No nation can make any progress without the co-operation of its women. If Muslim women support their men, as they did in the days of the Prophet of Islam, we should soon realise our goal. (R. Ahmed 1993: 105)

The Pakistan movement created a new breed of women: in the 1960s and 1980s the greatest challenge to the military dictators General Ayub Khan and General Zia ul-Haq came from women – Fatima Jinnah and Benazir Bhutto respectively.

In the 1990s, however chaotic and corrupt Pakistan politics and whatever the general unsatisfactory situation of women, there are outstanding women succeeding through sheer merit and hard work in a traditional male chauvinist society. The list starts with the former Prime Minister Benazir Bhutto and includes ministers and ambassadors. A host of other Pakistanis including Asma Jahangir, the lawyer, Ameena Saiyid, the managing director of the Oxford University Press in Pakistan, Anjum Niaz, one of Pakistan's best-known columnists, Mona Kasuri, head of the Beacon House Schools and Sehyr Saigol, editor of *Libas*, have made a name for themselves. Of several women editors, Jugnu Mohsin, who runs the *Friday Times* with her husband and sister Mohni, is noteworthy for introducing political satire in Pakistan with her column *Ikhtelaf Nama*.

Compare this to other Muslim societies in the region – in Afghanistan and even in India. Only perhaps in Iran have women, both before and after the revolution, played a comparably substantial role in social and political life. Although Bangladesh has a woman Prime Minister and a woman leader of the opposition, it is well to recall that it was once part of Pakistan and the Pakistan movement.

CHAPTER 3

Jinnah's Conversion

You are the only Muslim in India today to whom the community has a right to look
up for safe guidance through the storm which is coming.

(Iqbal's letter to Jinnah, 21 June 1937)

What caused Jinnah's conversion from a belief in the unity of India to a commitment
to a movement to shatter it? How much should be attributed to Gandhi's increasing use
of religion in politics from the 1920s onwards? Is there any link between the death of
Jinnah's young wife and his subsequent unrestrained support for the Muslim community? What was the influence of thinkers like Iqbal on Jinnah? Was the Pakistan
movement in the 1930s and 1940s a reflex reaction to the steady and inexorable rise of
Hindu power, or was it the culmination of the Muslim awakening that had begun in the
second half of the nineteenth century? How influential was Jinnah's leadership? Would
the outcome in 1947 have been different if Congress had had a more mature and wiser
leadership? I shall explore these questions in this chapter and the next one.

The causes of Jinnah's conversion

M. J. Akbar blames Jinnah for his disillusionment with Congress. He asks: 'Why had
Jinnah sung that song [swan-song to Indian nationalism] so early? Nothing had
happened till 1928' (1988a: 211). *Nothing*? The death of Indian liberals like G. K. Gokhale
and others, the subsequent rise of Hindu nationalism and its transformation of
Congress, the resignation of Jinnah in protest from the Imperial Legislative Council, the
Home Rule League and the Congress, the emergence of Gandhi, the collapse of the
Khilafat movement, the birth of the Rashtriya Swayamsevak Sangh (RSS) and organized communalism, the extraordinary communal riots as at Nagpur which set a trend,

the Nehru Report, which antagonized a large section of Muslim opinion – all these had happened over the decade which changed the course of Indian history.

What continues to baffle people is the transformation of Jinnah from a liberal, Anglicized, seemingly secular politician, whose proudest title was ambassador of Hindu–Muslim unity and whose early political life was spent fighting for a united India, into the champion of an exclusive Muslim identity. It is one of the most intriguing yet least explored areas of modern South Asian history.

In discussing it I do not suggest a sudden conversion; there is no single dramatic event or turning point. I shall, however, examine the general cultural and political changes occurring in the subcontinent and in his personal life after 1920 which help explain the conversion. In December that year, when he first became president of the Muslim League, his position was expressed in a conversation with Durga Das, a prominent writer, after rejecting Gandhi's call for non-cooperation: 'Well, young man – I will have nothing to do with this pseudo-religious approach to politics. I part company with the Congress and Gandhi. I do not believe in working up mob hysteria. Politics is a gentleman's game' (Razi Wasti, 'The genius of Jinnah', *Friday Times*, Lahore, 17–23 March 1994).

Jinnah and Gandhi were already disagreeing in their approach to national questions. While condemning the Amritsar massacre at Jalianwala Bagh in April 1919 when British troops fired on a crowd of Indian nationalists – those 'celebrated crimes ... which neither the words of men nor the tears of women can wash away' – Jinnah did not support Gandhi's call for a nationwide Satyagraha, a campaign of passive resistance (Wolpert 1996: 42).

Many other influential Muslim leaders would also change their position at the end of the decade. Take the brothers Shaukat and Muhammad Ali. Making common cause with Gandhi during the Khilafat movement and the struggle for Indian independence, they became so close to him that after visiting their home Gandhi wrote, 'I have never received warmer or better treatment than under Muhammad Ali's roof' (Gandhi 1986: 111–12). A cow was purchased from a butcher and escorted to the safety of a cow-home, a *pinjrapole*. 'What love has prompted the act!' wrote a gratified Gandhi (ibid.). It was a feast of love during Gandhi's stay – a vegetarian feast, since the entire household gave up eating meat for the duration of his visit.

Muhammad Ali was elected president of the Congress in 1923–4; but shortly before he died in 1931 Muhammad Ali had changed his opinion of Gandhi. He wrote that Gandhi's aim was not independence but making '70 million Muslims dependents of the Hindu Mahasabha [Great Assembly, the name of the main right-wing Hindu nationalist party]' (ibid.: 120). Muhammad's brother Shaukat wrote, 'For any honourable peace and pact we are always ready but not for the slavery of the Hindus ... the Congress ... has ceased to be National now. It has become an adjunct of the Hindu Mahasabha' (Mujahid 1988: 244–5).

In 1920 the rising stars of Muslim India, like Iqbal and the Ali brothers, were opposed to Jinnah. In the Nagpur Congress session that year, Maulana Shaukat Ali was outraged when Jinnah opposed Gandhi's policies on the grounds that they were leading to disunity, and he attempted to assault Jinnah while hurling abuse at him. A decade later, the same stars would be proclaiming that Jinnah was the only hope for the Muslims. They had arrived at the same conclusion as Jinnah and abandoned the attempt to work on one platform with the Hindus, although they took different routes.

Some of the developments I discuss below explain Jinnah's conversion (and that of other Muslims too) and the background to the creation of Pakistan; other developments led to a new cultural and political climate which influenced his thinking.

The end of the old guard

First, the Anglicized liberal-humanist politics advocated by a few wealthy individuals which prevailed until the First World War were now out of fashion and becoming obsolete. A vacuum formed after the deaths within a few years of G. K. Gokhale, P. Mehta, Dadabhai Naoroji and B. G. Tilak, influential figures of the earlier kind of politics who wished to discover a *modus vivendi* to enable people to coexist; men with respect for Jinnah. The vacuum was filled spectacularly by Gandhi after he captured the Congress in 1920, the year that Tilak died. The most dramatic manifestation of the new mass politics was Gandhi himself, who directly appealed to those previously neglected – the villagers, the untouchables, the poor. It was a radical strategy which would lead to freedom from the British. The colonial masters would never again be able fully to take the initiative or be entirely in control.

The Indian nationalist movement led by the Congress in India was one of the most powerful indigenous movements in twentieth-century colonial history. It swept through the religions, sects and castes of India; and many Muslims took part in it. A genuine Indian personality absorbing the different cultures was encouraged in which caste and community were submerged, although they were never far from the surface.

By the time Gandhi emerged after the First World War to give a lead to the Congress, for the first time in history Hindu society was unifying around something beyond immediate caste and village politics. A national consensus was forming. At first it focused on the vague idea of independence from the British, but as it evolved it increasingly concentrated on questions of identity. Gandhi's own struggle with his identity interwoven with questions of morality enraptured millions of Hindus. To them the freedom struggle became the attempt to rediscover a lost Hindu identity. One strand of this discovery led to increasingly virulent communal politics, as we see below. Many of the Congress old guard like Jinnah now felt they could not fit in. Jinnah resigned from the Congress in 1920.

Muslim leadership too was changing. The traditional leaders, the *ashraf*, like the Sayyeds and the learned clergy or religious scholars, the *ulema*, were no longer able to provide the answers to the politics forming after the First World War. As early as 1920 Jinnah had already denounced the participation of the *ulema* in politics. He had appealed to 'the intellectual and reasonable section' of Muslim opinion to regain the initiative. This line of thinking allowed Jinnah, and the Muslim League, to speak with confidence on behalf of the Muslim community as a whole. Other Muslim leaders aligned to the Congress, like the Ali brothers, also expressed their doubts about the role of the *ulema* in politics.

The matter did not end there: there was a vigorous response from the *ulema*. In 1921, the Jamiyyat al-Ulema-i-Hind, under the influence of Maulana Azad, supported the idea of an Amir-i-Hind, or supreme Muslim leader, selected from the *ulema*. The Amir would provide guidance to the Muslim community according to the *sharia*, the Islamic law. The idea was to restore the *ulema* to their traditional role as the chief custodians of the law and as exemplars and organizers of Muslim life.

There was another incipient leadership visible from the 1920s onwards which would grow in strength. It had little time for the sycophants who looked to the British, the landed aristocracy who exploited their tenants or the obscurantism of the clerics. These were the professionals, the lawyers and doctors, trained in the British manner, independent and yet working the system. They were going to recreate history but with a sharp eye on the future. Their position was eclectic. They borrowed from ideas previously circulating but infused them with an Islamic vision. Iqbal is a good example of this category. His poems are filled with references to the Sufi master Rumi as much as to Lenin. His greatest hero was the holy Prophet of Islam yet he also wrote poems to Lord Ram, the Hindu deity.

Jinnah, the Ali brothers and Iqbal did not come from the upper echelons of traditional Muslim society; indeed, the fading upper class resented them as upstarts. People like Sayyed Hussain Bilgrami, echoing Sir Sayyed, complained that this new leadership was represented by men of 'very low birth' (Shaikh 1989: 171). Yet members of the old aristocracy were dying out; Ameer Ali, admired by Jinnah, died in 1928.

In time, Jinnah would draw his most loyal supporters from the younger sons, the lesser nobility, the often neglected and less influential members of the élite. Liaquat Ali Khan, his chief lieutenant, is a good example. Abdur Rab Nishtar from the North-West Frontier Province and Qazi Isa from Baluchistan belonged to respectable but ordinary families. They were not the tribal chieftains of their provinces. The same was true of Sir G. H. Hidayatullah and Sir Abdullah Haroon in the Sind. In the Punjab the established feudal aristocracy opposed Jinnah and only came in to support him when the creation of Pakistan was upon them. Bahadur Yar Jung did not represent the family of the Nizam of Hyderabad.

The growth of Indian representation

Second, the Montagu–Chelmsford Report of 1918 led to significant political shifts in British India. Named after the Secretary of State for India, Edwin Montagu, and the Viceroy of 1916–21, Lord Chelmsford, the report led to the Government of India Act of 1919 which significantly altered the framework of decision-making and gave Indians a wider role in government. An all-Indian parliament of two houses was established, with certain limited powers. To some extent, control moved away from élite, urban-based politicians to representatives of the provinces backed by large rural populations – from the United Provinces and Bombay to the Punjab and Bengal in terms of Muslim politics. New groups began to emerge, with far-reaching consequences for political leadership among the Muslims (for examples, see David Gilmartin 1988 and David Page 1982).

We note how the Punjabi agriculturalist group, the Arains, traditionally small farmers and tenants, emerged socially and economically to articulate their demands and identity in specifically Islamic terms. In time they would be ardent supporters of Jinnah and the Pakistan movement. One of them – General Zia ul-Haq – would become President of Pakistan, as a military dictator enforcing a radical programme of

Islamization. Without the Punjab, the biggest and most powerful province of Pakistan, there would have been no Pakistan.

The stirring of Muslim resistance

Third, Muslims responded with anger to the punishment of the vanquished Turks and humbling of the caliphate (from the Islamic notion of the Caliph, the Muslim chief civil and religious ruler, who was the head of the Ottoman empire) at the Treaty of Sèvres in 1920 with what became known as the Khilafat movement. Gandhi championed the Khilafat movement but Jinnah, though sympathetic to the Turks, was not convinced. In July 1921 the Khilafat Conference held in Karachi adopted a resolution which declared the 'allegiance of the Muslim population to His Majesty the Sultan of Turkey'. The Hindus present at the conference were, understandably, not amused.

The caliphate was abolished in Turkey in 1924 by the Turks themselves, who wished for a modern identity. The Muslims of India, however, saw this as yet another British plot to undermine Islam. Their leaders advised them to march out of British India and migrate to Afghanistan and other Muslim countries in protest. A glow of communal harmony surrounded the early stages of the Khilafat movement. But when hundreds of thousands of Muslims attempted to march out of India and found no refuge in Afghanistan they returned to their homes and fields to find them occupied by Hindu neighbours. They were outraged. Maulana Muhammad Ali expressed his disillusionment with Gandhi. The Khilafat movement caused a flutter of excitement in the community but also much hardship and in the end led nowhere.

Other Muslim expressions of disquiet included the Moplah rebellion in Malabar in South India in 1921 (see also chapter 2). The Moplahs set about establishing an Islamic kingdom and in the uprisings Hindu money-lenders and landowners were killed. There were also stories of forced conversions to Islam. The British responded with ferocity: 2,339 Moplahs were killed as a result of the military action and about 25,000 convicted of rebellion; but the figures were withheld from the public. These movements illustrate that the Muslims of India were leaderless, without a grand strategy and devoid of a viable objective. Jinnah and the idea of Pakistan would give them all this in the next decade.

The rise of Hindu nationalism

Fourth, Hindu fundamentalist organizations came into being in the 1920s with a specific in-built bias against the minorities, especially Muslims – which set the alarm bells ringing. Recent academic work has established the link between present-day communal violence and the rise of Hindu nationalism in the 1920s (see, for example, Basu et al. 1993; Jaffrelot 1996). Nirad Chaudhuri sums up the situation of the three communities in the early 1920s: 'In 1923 three spectral hatreds were skulking on the Indian political stage: the hatred of all Indians for British rule; the same hatred on the part of the Muslims; and the mutual hatred of the Hindus and the Muslims, which was ineradicable' (1990: 50).

I believe that the 1920s bore the fruit of communal seeds planted during the previous half-century. Let us pause and consider the seminal novel *Anandamath* ('The Abbey of Bliss', 1882) by Bankim Chandra Chatterji. This novel was the first Hindu nationalist tract, which not only expressed an explicit aversion to Muslims but indicated a way of challenging them – through a military campaign in alliance with the British. *Anandamath* itself was a turning point for Hindus and a charter for political action, echoing the Hindu dilemma over the next century: fascination with the West and its ways, and revulsion against it. The sub-theme is clear too: Hindu pride and anger against the Muslims as 'foreign' invaders and destroyers. Once the British leave they will hand India back to the Hindus and the purity of the past can be restored. This became the broad Congress theme, however much it was couched in secular, modern rhetoric.

Anandamath had a major impact on the minds of young Bengali Hindus and set a trend in Bengali literature. The plot revolves round the revolt of the sannyasis (Hindu ascetics) in the 1760s and 1770s, which is depicted as a national rising. The sannyasis, worshippers of the Hindu goddess Kali, who symbolizes Mother India, have one aim: the destruction of every trace of Muslim rule. They attack Muslim rulers and go about massacring Muslim communities, plundering and burning Muslim villages. The story ends with a supernatural figure telling the sannyasi leader that he has already completed his task by defeating the Muslims.

The song 'Vande Mataram' ('Hail to thee, Mother') was taken from *Anandamath*. It is an intensely passionate devotional hymn to the mother figure of India and to goddesses like Durga and Lakshmi. The association of the mother with India and in turn with Hinduism fired a passionate sense of Hindu nationalism. (Gandhi constantly referred to a loving, nurturing, self-sacrificing mother and Madhav Sadashiv Golwalkar signed his letters 'Yours in the Service of the Mother' and 'Yours in the Love of the Mother', 1969: 5, 20.)

Understandably Jinnah and the Muslims complained when in 1937 'Vande Mataram' was declared a national anthem to be sung by all schoolchildren in every school. Today Muslims at schools in India have to sing it. The Dalit author V. T. Rajshekar complains that the present Muslims 'said nothing and did nothing even though the song is outrightly used to hate and debar Muslims' (1993: 79). He notes the Muslim response from 'stiff opposition' to 'silent accommodation'.

Bankim Chatterji bristled against the common South Asian stereotypes. He hotly challenged the myth of Muslim martial prowess. In his novel *Mrinali* (1869) he refuses to accept the story that seventeen Pathan horsemen conquered his homeland, Bengal. In his darkest novel, *Kapalkundala* (1866), the Kali cult broods menacingly in the background waiting to reassert its triumph after the British have left India.

Bankim's work was a milestone in the cultural and intellectual landscape of Bengal. He was an important forebear of the famous Bengali *bhadrolok* – Westernized, middle-class writers and artists affecting sophisticated British thought and manners and providing India with an intellectual and political lead. One of them, Rabindranath Tagore, would win the Nobel Prize for literature in 1913 and place Bengal on the world map in the next century.

Many of those who followed Chatterji achieved fame and glory. Rangalal's *Ode to Liberty*, for instance, comes from the mouth of a Rajput fighting against Muslims. Even Rabindranath Tagore, as a Muslim scholar points out, wrote poems glorifying those who fought Muslims, like Sivaji and the Sikh heroes Guru Govind Singh and Banda (Khairi 1995: 66).

Nirad Chaudhuri, who called Chatterji 'the greatest novelist in the Bengali language' (Chaudhuri 1990: 150), has observed that the author of *Anandamath* 'was positively and fiercely anti-Muslim' (Bonner et al. 1994: 91). Chaudhuri recounts his own earliest memories of childhood reflecting the hostility to Muslims: 'Even before we could read we had been told that the Muslims had once ruled and oppressed us, that they had spread their religion in India with the Koran in one hand and the sword in the other, that the Muslim rulers had abducted our women, destroyed our temples, polluted our sacred places' (1988: 226).

There were two births among the Hindus in 1889 which would have an influence on the course of events in India from the 1920s onwards. Jawaharlal Nehru and Keshnav Baliram Hedgewar were born in that year; two men from different social backgrounds who would be educated in different ways, possess different temperaments and symbolize two distinct approaches to political life. By the 1920s Nehru, back from Cambridge, was already marked as the up-and-coming man of India, the darling of the Congress. In 1925 Hedgewar organized the Hindu communal party, the RSS, in Nagpur at the festival of Lord Ram's triumph over Ravana, the Vijaydashami.

The middle of the century would see Nehru's zenith as India's first Prime Minister. Many Hindus saw him as a prophet, a yogi with divine powers (Akbar 1988a: ix). In contrast, Hedgewar's fortunes reached a low ebb in the middle of the century when his aide, Nathuram Godse, would assassinate Gandhi for being too sympathetic to the Muslims. His party would be banned. But by the end of the century Nehru would have almost faded from public memory and Hedgewar's party, the RSS, which in turn would feed and spawn another party, the Bharatiya Janata Party (BJP), would attain political power in Delhi and one of its members become a Prime Minister in 1996, even if only for a few days.

Several right-wing Hindu organizations that came into being from the 1920s onwards – the Mahasabha, the Jana Sangha, the Vishva Hindu Parishad (VHP), the RSS (and later the BJP) – had a close ideological relationship, one spawning the other. Hindu communalism grew rapidly from the 1920s onwards. Leaders like Hedgewar were angry at the Khilafat movement which, to them, expressed Muslim disloyalty to India. The Hindu–Muslim riot in Nagpur in 1923 was not the first of its kind but it helped to promote organized and regular communal rioting, and it was followed by the setting up of the RSS. Physical exercises, cabalistic oath ceremonies, flags, secret funds and disciplined cadres soon characterized it. A militant Hindu philosophy motivated the RSS.

Madhav Sadashiv Golwalkar, who followed Hedgewar to become one of the major ideologues of this form of Hinduism, in *We or our Nationhood Defined* (1938), compared the situation of the Muslims of India to that of the Jews in Germany. If, he argued, the German Jews could be exterminated by Hitler, so could the Indian Muslims by the Hindus. Hitler's attempt at 'purity' was 'a good lesson for us in Hindustan to learn and profit by', he wrote (Golwalkar 1938: 27). Golwalkar labelled non-Hindus 'traitors', 'enemies to the National cause', 'or to take a charitable view, idiots'. He clearly spells out the Indian implications of what he had learnt from Nazism:

> From this standpoint sanctioned by the experience of shrewd old nations, the non-Hindu people in Hindustan must either adopt the Hindu culture

and language, must learn to respect and revere Hindu religion, must entertain no idea but the glorification of the Hindu nation, i.e. they must not only give up their attitude of intolerance and ingratitude towards this land and its age-long traditions, but must also cultivate the positive attitude of love and devotion instead; in one word, they must cease to be foreigners or may stay in the country wholly subordinated to the Hindu nation claiming nothing, deserving no privileges, far less any preferential treatment, not even citizen's rights. (ibid.: 52)

Since the 1920s, therefore, those Hindus who wished to preserve Hinduism as peaceful, universal and non-violent faced a growing challenge within their own house. In the 1920s members of the Hindu Mahasabha advocated the re-conversion of Muslims to Hinduism because they argued that most of India's Muslim population had originally been Hindus and forced to convert to Islam during the centuries of Muslim rule. The 're-conversion' was called the Shuddi movement. One of the most popular communal leaders of this movement, Swami Shraddhanand, was assassinated in Delhi in 1926 by a Muslim. The Swami had belonged to another fundamentalist Hindu society, the Arya Samaj, which wished to push India's history back 3,000 years to when Brahmins and cows were treated as gods on earth (Wolpert 1996: 72). The Nehrus stood up to the Mahasabha and for his pains Motilal Nehru (Jawaharlal's father) was accused of being a beef-eater and a supporter of the Muslims wishing to legalize cow slaughter.

The internal crisis in Hinduism informed an increasingly bitter confrontation which reached a climax in the 1990s. Figures like Gandhi and Nehru have, in retrospect, been openly criticized for being too soft on the minorities (especially the Muslims), and for ultimately having betrayed Hinduism by advocating a secular India.

Jinnah recognized that while Hindu leaders like Gandhi and Nehru were not enemies of the Muslims (on the death of Gandhi he acknowledged the loss for the Muslims of India) Hindu extremists would make life difficult if not impossible for Muslims. Living in Bombay, the main RSS centre, Jinnah understood and commented on the implications of treating Muslims 'like Jews in Germany' (Wolpert 1984: 189). He voiced Muslim sentiment, alarmed at the growing Hindu communalism, when he declared that British Raj would be succeeded by Hindu or Ram Raj. Jinnah's prediction would be echoed in the slogan of the BJP, one of the major parties of the Indian Parliament in the 1990s.

The confidence of Congress

Fifth, it was becoming clear in the 1920s that the British would be sharing power with Indians, sooner rather than later. The Congress was emerging as the authentic voice of India after Gandhi gave it fresh confidence through his high media profile and wide popular appeal. It was already planning for a strongly centralized India. Its leadership – which would take India to independence – was beginning to fall into place: Gandhi the saintly politician, the personification of renascent India; Nehru the cultivated, charismatic spokesman for the Congress; Sardar Vallabhbhai Patel, the committed Hindu nationalist and party boss, always a strong contender for Nehru's position; and

Maulana Abul Kalam Azad, the scholarly and gentle Muslim presence in the Congress (many Muslims dismissed Congress Muslims as a token presence; for Jinnah, Azad was a mere 'show-boy').

Muslims complained that Congress, sensing power in the 1920s, was becoming arrogant. It dismissed their demands, ignored their sense of insecurity and preferred to speak on their behalf. Many Muslims felt they would become second-class citizens with not only their religion but also their culture under threat. For instance, the Urdu language, generally – though not exclusively – associated with Muslims, was increasingly a 'foreign' target of communal Hindu groups. In time its script would be changed and in many places it would cease to be taught altogether.

By the end of the 1920s Muslims were alert to the sense of crisis. The Nehrus – father and son – did not help matters. They dominated the 1928 Congress Committee which prepared a report to determine the principles of the constitution for India. It rejected not only separate electorates but also weighting for minorities. Jinnah and Motilal Nehru were also 'attacking each other in the press' over policy issues (R. Ahmad 1994: 186). The antagonism would carry over to the next generation: Jawaharlal Nehru would always harbour a sense of animosity towards his father's rival (see below).

Rethinking Muslim identity

Sixth, throughout the Muslim world extraordinary events were taking place and nationalist leaders were redefining and discovering nationalism. Muslims were challenging tradition and inventing a new sense of identity, more in consonance with Western culture and ideas. Kemal Atatürk in Turkey, King Reza Pahlevi in Iran and King Amanullah in Afghanistan, for example, were openly encouraging women to discard their veils, men to shave their beards and give up their traditional clothes and ways.

But Muslims in India had few clear ideas about modern nationhood. Indeed, they were still harking back to the past. This Muslim ignorance of world trends and their tendency to be out of touch with reality indicated that a deep crisis was looming for the community. The sense of unreality would continue to mark Muslim behaviour. Right up to the independence of India the Nizam of Hyderabad would cling on to his dream of an independent Hyderabad which he would rule as an independent state within India. He ignored the warning signs from Britain insisting on a united India; he set aside the trends in the Congress thinking for a united India; and he did not get on with Jinnah and his Muslim League which could have perhaps provided an alternative.

Although there were compelling reasons in the 1920s for Muslims to rethink their identity and their future, the idea of India divided into two nations, Hindu and Muslim, had been around, however ill defined, for half a century. When Muslim scholars talk of a direct link from Sir Sayyed to Iqbal and then Jinnah in the creation of Pakistan, they are being simplistic. The early Muslim leaders had little idea of a modern nation-state. Indeed, when Sir Sayyed began to talk of two distinct communities in India, Britain was in the process of securing her colonial grip on the subcontinent more firmly than ever before. It would be two generations before Muslims dreamed of separation, as Iqbal did in 1930, and then only within some kind of loose configuration in India. But what these

Muslims were pointing towards is important: the awareness of a growing assertiveness of Muslim identity. Without this, Jinnah's Pakistan movement would not have been possible.

The nationalism that became a major force in the self-definition of most African and Asian societies from the 1920s onwards created the momentum that would lead to independence from the European colonial powers. It would be sustained by a mixture of expectations, of pride in the past and faith in the future; it would mean a harmonious balance between tradition and modernism. It would mean all things to all men. By the end of the century it would have run its course and there would be a general disillusionment with the idea of nationalism. Indeed, nationalism – as expressed through the nation-state – would create a general sense of disillusionment. It would mean horrendous forms of torture (backed by sophisticated machinery imported from the West) of those who opposed the state; it would mean a policy of persecution towards the minorities, often expressed in ways that can only be described as genocide; it would mean corruption, mismanagement and cynicism disguised under the figleaf of modernity, democracy and modern nationalism. It would also mean the growing gap between the rich and the poor, between the urban and the rural – a gap that many saw as dangerously increasing and, as most economists felt, unbridgeable in the near future. Nationalism has run out of steam by the end of the twentieth century. It was a short-lived, powerful, exciting idea and its collapse has now created a vacuum, which allows traditional ideas of ethnicity and religious identity to emerge.

Jinnah's mid-life crisis

Finally, while the India he knew and loved was changing so dramatically, after 1920 Jinnah's own personal life was also changing. There was a pause in Jinnah's life in the 1920s, when he was well into his forties. His life appeared to be on hold. His marriage had turned sour by the mid-1920s and his wife was dead by the end of the decade.

By the 1920s it was also clear that Jinnah was out of step with his community. Still wearing his Western clothes, speaking English, not pandering to the values and rhetoric of the Muslims, not even responding to the most important political crisis of the decade, that of the Khilafat, he seemed to be increasingly isolated from his community. Most important of all, he continued to talk of a united India, one in which all communities would live in peace and harmony. The common enemy was British imperialism.

Little wonder that Iqbal during the 1920s was critical of Jinnah. Many Muslims were beginning to express their distrust of the majority community, now talking increasingly of an aggressive new Hinduism. When Jinnah left for London in 1930 and decided to stay on, it appeared that his career in India was over. He would not be missed by the Muslims. Indeed, a member of the Muslim League who was removed from the All-India Muslim League Council criticized Jinnah's distance from popular Muslim causes thus: 'No national or religious crisis, however stupendous, can move him. Jalianwala Bagh [the Amritsar massacre] does not affect him. The great clash of Khilafat of the heart-rending disintegration of the Islamic brotherhood does not move him' (Sayeed 1968: 87).

Others disagreed. In 1930 Maulana Muhammad Ali predicted that Jinnah was the man to lead the Muslims in the future. Jinnah's departure for London at the end of the decade had deprived the Muslims of a major voice:

> In this situation, a feeling of despondency and helplessness pervaded the
> ranks of Muslims. They had no leader of calibre to guide them. Hakim Ajmal
> Khan, Maulana Mohammad Ali, Maharajah of Mahmoodabad and Sir
> Mohammad Shafi had gone the way of all mortals. In spite of their
> limitations, they could have given some lead. The only leader in whom the
> Muslims reposed trust and who could guide them fearlessly was in self-
> imposed exile in London. They desperately wished that he could put an end
> to his exile and return to his homeland in the hour of crisis. The League
> Council, when it met at Delhi on March 12, 1933, devoted most of its time in
> discussing as to what steps it should take to persuade the Quaid to return
> home. It toyed with the idea of sending a deputation to England to meet him
> and press him to come back. (Hasan 1976: 54)

In 1934 Jinnah returned and was elected unanimously as president of a reunited
Muslim League. The Aga Khan was behind this move. Jinnah was held in high esteem
and several Muslim members of the Central Assembly offered to vacate their seats for
him at the time of his election (Mujahid 1981: 23).

Jinnah soon discovered he had inherited the leadership of diverse Muslim groups
spread over a continent with only a loose link through Islam. They did not have a
common language, dress, political organization or territory that they could call their
own. Even their Islam was divided into sects which often fought with each other. So his
genius was, apart from his recognized talents as a political strategist and constitutional
lawyer, to encourage the development of a modern Muslim persona, one which would
represent a modern Muslim nation and reflect its spirit while providing identity and
unity. It heralded the dawn of modern Muslim mass politics, a new awakening, the
emergence of political images and symbols which we shall discuss in the next chapter.
But before then let us consider the influence on Jinnah of Iqbal.

The passing of the flame: Iqbal and Jinnah

Dr Z. Zaidi, working on the Jinnah papers, confirms the story of the delegation that
came to pray for Iqbal when he lay on his deathbed. Do not pray for me, Iqbal told them.
I have done my job; I have accomplished my mission. Now pray for Jinnah; he has yet
to accomplish his. What was Jinnah's mission? And what was the relationship between
the two men?

Iqbal and the challenge of modernity

Allama Iqbal, like Jinnah, came from a modest social background. He was the son of a
tailor, from the respectable lower middle class in the Punjab. His Kashmiri forefathers had
recently converted from Hinduism. There is considerable uncertainty about his year of
birth; scholars have placed it somewhere between 1873 and 1877. As a mature student he
arrived in Cambridge in 1905, and went on to complete his PhD at Heidelberg; throughout

his life he retained a penchant for intellectual synthesis and innovation.

Iqbal was closely connected with the Anjuman-i-Himayat-i-Islam (Society for the Support of Islam), which had been created with the direct participation of the Mohammedan Education Conference headed by Sir Sayyed Ahmad Khan. In 1899, at the annual session of the society, Iqbal made his début as a poet. Sayyed Ahmad's philosophy of Muslim nationalism containing an implicit anti-imperial message sat comfortably together with pro-British ideology in the Punjab; many Muslims were unaware of the inherent contradictions. Punjabis approved of Sayyed Ahmad because they did not share the bitterness against the British felt by many in and around Delhi as a result of the uprisings of 1857–8. Indeed, to Muslims in the Punjab, British rule from 1849 onwards was an act of providence that liberated them from the Sikhs.

Iqbal applied for and was rather ignominiously rejected by the lower branches of the Civil Service. This not only gave him a chip on his shoulder but kept him in a precarious financial position for most of his life. Only after his literary reputation had been established and he became a member of the Legislative Council in the Punjab in the 1920s did he achieve some economic stability. But had he succeeded as a bureaucrat it might have meant the death of Iqbal's intellect; it certainly would have muffled his poetic genius. The bureaucracy of the subcontinent is not a safe place to house literary talent.

As the death of Jinnah's wife in 1929 was a turning point for him, so was Iqbal's failing the provincial Civil Service examination in 1901. Each man found he had nowhere to turn to except his community. Thus personal tragedies can often inadvertently affect the course of someone's life. Although both were drawn by the love of their community, during the 1920s Iqbal was often pitted against Jinnah, since each took a separate path. Iqbal's response to what became known as the Delhi Proposals after the meetings held in Delhi on 20 March 1927, which achieved an agreement for the future constitutional development of India, is an example (Malik 1971: 88): Jinnah as president of the League was denounced by Iqbal and his colleagues from the Punjab.

Iqbal's ideas

Ralph Russell, the British expert on Urdu, begins a chapter on Iqbal by quoting a Pakistani friend: 'Pakistanis have three articles of faith – Islam, the Quaid-i-Azam and Iqbal' (Russell 1992: 176). Iqbal himself developed the teachings of Shah Waliullah, Sir Sayyed and Afghani. Sir Sayyed's philosophy offered, in his words, 'a new orientation of Islam' (Malik 1971: 126). Sir Sayyed, in turn, had developed Shah Waliullah's ideas.

Iqbal's own position shifted from that of an ambassador of Hindu–Muslim unity, like Jinnah, to that of championing his own community, the Muslims. It is significant that one of his most famous poems *Tarana-e-Hindi* ('Indian Anthem'), which begins, 'Our Hindustan is the best place in the world', is still a popular song in India although it was written in the early twentieth century. He later wrote *Tarana-e-Milli* ('Anthem for the Muslim Community') for the Muslims.

Iqbal's popularity rests in the fact that he wrote from the heart and made a direct emotional appeal. For him, the warriors of Afghanistan could still decisively influence the destiny of India – as had Ahmad Shah Abdali in the eighteenth century. Although

Iqbal did slide into sentimentality and a crude Muslim chauvinism, his work became the epitome of the Muslim nostalgic sense of history. Ralph Russell comments: 'In short, Iqbal all too often shares, and appeals to, the deplorable chauvinism that affects the Muslim community no less powerfully than Hindu chauvinism affects the Hindus and British chauvinism the British' (1992: 187).

Iqbal's well-known demotic poems, the *Shikwa* ('Complaint' to God) and the *Jawab-e-Shikwa* ('The Reply of God'), capture the essence of the modern Muslim malaise and mood. Anyone interested in broad Muslim responses to modernity regardless of nationality need look no further than Iqbal's poems. That is why when the Sabri Qawal group sang the *Shikwa* and *Jawab-e-Shikwa* on cassette the songs became instant bestsellers in South Asia in spite of competing with Westernized pop songs. The two poems reflect the best of Muslim thinking and the worst of Muslim prejudices, appealing not so much to the mind as to the heart, for they were written in anger. It is this radical anger which still appeals to Muslims today. Yet Iqbal's poems are directly inspired by the *Mussaddas* of Hali written late in the last century. In the form of a long poem, the *Mussaddas* is a lament and a charter of action for the Muslims. In it the triumphs of the past are glorified, and through this pride Muslims can face the adversities of the age in which they live. Only in discovering their own identity can they survive – or they will be extinguished.

It is a theme that would be picked up and repeated by later Muslims. There is the loss of power, of glory (Andalusia is often mentioned), the exposure of the hypocrisy of the men of religion, the emphasis on *ilm* or knowledge and finally the attempt to recreate glory, a call to arms. These are eternal Muslim themes. Sir Sayyed is supposed to have said that when he will be asked in heaven about his achievements on earth he would reply that he had assisted Hali in writing the *Mussaddas*. What Iqbal did was to inject a new vigour and passion into popular Urdu poetry. Furthermore, he took the ideals in the *Mussaddas*, the reading of which was largely restricted to the middle-class urban intellectuals and Urdu-reading circles of Delhi, and spread them to the widest possible audience of Muslims throughout India. Because the colours are so brightly painted and the emotions are so raw the appeal is far greater. The Muslim masses found in them a cultural rallying point.

Iqbal and Jinnah

'For a thousand years the lily mourns its misfortune. / A person who appreciates it is born with great difficulty.' Scholars in Pakistan have agreed that in these verses Iqbal was referring to Jinnah and his relationship with the community.

In the last years of Iqbal's life, just before his death in 1938, there was a fascinating interaction between him and Jinnah. Iqbal seemed to be drawing Jinnah into his world, and Jinnah seemed to be moving almost inexorably towards it. I am not suggesting that Iqbal converted Jinnah into a mystic or a Sufi, but that Iqbal gave Jinnah an entirely new dimension to his understanding of Islam. There seems to have formed between them a spiritual connection that resulted in the passing of the flame from one to the other.

Henceforth Jinnah would acknowledge Iqbal as his mentor. He went on to use the rhetoric, imagery and language that Iqbal had perfected over the preceding decades; in doing so he utilized them correctly, with a sure instinct. Although he may not have reached this point entirely through his own intellectual reasoning, struggle or anguish, once he eventually arrived he was unerring in grasp of Iqbal's position.

Jinnah took up Iqbal's notions of a separate Muslim homeland, of the discovery of an Islamic identity, of the construction of an Islamic destiny and of pride in Muslim tradition and culture. He thus not only embraced Iqbal's political philosophy but consciously absorbed his conceptual framework. Now he was at one with the poet and through him with the powerful mainstream of Muslim thought and culture. After this time Jinnah would not put a foot wrong as far as the Muslim community was concerned. His speeches, his behaviour, his statements, his gestures, his clothes – all would be in harmony with his community. He had finally, unequivocally, arrived home.

Iqbal's letters to Jinnah

The eight letters Iqbal wrote to Jinnah between 1936 and 1937 and Jinnah's foreword to them help us to understand the relationship (Malik 1971: 383). In his foreword Jinnah calls Iqbal 'the sage, philosopher and national poet of Islam', acknowledging his role as a spiritual mentor.

It is symptomatic of the turbulence of the times and the relative unimportance given to literature in modern Muslim society that the correspondence between Jinnah and Iqbal is incomplete. Jinnah was a meticulous man who would certainly have filed Iqbal's letters to him, but Jinnah's letters to Iqbal are lost for ever. Iqbal's house, a poet's home, was no doubt somewhat disorganized, so letters even from one of the most important leaders of India might have been thrown together with piles of unimportant papers or destroyed. They might have been dispersed in the chaos that ensues at the death of a Muslim and the struggle for property, in which families often ignore books and letters. Jinnah sensed this loss and expressed it as 'much to be regretted' (Malik 1971: 384) He himself had no copies of his own letters because 'During the period under reference I worked alone, unassisted by the benefit of a personal staff and so did not retain duplicate copies of the numerous letters that I had to dispose of' (ibid.).

On 21 June 1937, shortly before he died, Iqbal wrote the famous letter in which he identified Jinnah as the leader Muslims had been waiting for: 'You are the only Muslim in India today to whom the community has a right to look up for safe guidance through the storm which is coming to North-West India, and perhaps to the whole of India' (Malik 1971: 387). Pointing out that there 'is a civil war which as a matter of fact has been going on for some time in the shape of Hindu–Muslim riots' (ibid.: 386), Iqbal added: 'I fear that in certain parts of the country, for example North-West India, Palestine may be repeated.'

Earlier, in 1930, Iqbal had not proposed a separate sovereign state but expressed the two-nation theory. However, in these letters to Jinnah he now advocated a sovereign Muslim state. Iqbal asked Jinnah: 'Why should not the Muslims of North-West India and Bengal be considered as nations entitled to self-determination just as other nations in India and outside India are?' (ibid.: 388).

Jinnah's Conversion

The flame passes

Inner secrets of the self, esoteric mysticism, hidden meanings, definitions of divinity – these were all outside Jinnah's intellectual domain and held little real interest for him. He was a pragmatist, the lawyer preparing his brief thoroughly and presenting it with skill. Yet Jinnah in his foreword to the correspondence expressed his unanimity with Iqbal: 'His views were substantially in consonance with my own and had finally led me to the same conclusions as a result of careful examination and study of the constitutional problems facing India' (Malik 1971: 384).

Jinnah was usually precise in his choice of words: he was after all a top constitutionalist lawyer and words were the tools of his trade. Even his quotations from Shakespeare – remembered from his London days and his infatuation with the theatre – were used to reinforce a political point. But when Jinnah said he was in agreement with Iqbal did he mean what he said? Two words in the sentence – 'finally', which acknowledges that at the end he was at one with Iqbal, and 'constitutional' – give us an important clue to Jinnah's thinking during that transitional period of his life.

Iqbal's letters clearly are not concerned simply with 'constitutional' matters. They discuss culture, society and, of course, politics – in fact the destiny of his people, the Muslims. Iqbal's links with Sufism need to be stressed. After the holy Prophet, his hero was Rumi, one of the greatest Sufi masters. Significantly, before he left to study in the United Kingdom, he went to Delhi to visit the shrine of Nizamuddin, the celebrated Sufi saint, companion and role model for that other noted Sufi figure, Amir Khusro.

So when Jinnah stated that his own views were in 'consonance' with Iqbal's he was referring not only to Iqbal's constitutional ideas but to Iqbal's general convictions. One cannot be accepted without the other, as indeed Iqbal was at pains to point out in everything he said and wrote. Clearly Jinnah was conceding far more than perhaps even he realized.

Spreading the message

Iqbal's ideas on the Islamic nature of the community, the need to focus on the poor and the dispossessed (again derived from Islam), the passionate reverence for the holy Prophet, misgivings about the 'atheistic socialism' of Congress leaders like Nehru, the continuing Hindu–Muslim riots, the emphasis on Muslim identity and destiny – all these would become essential components of Jinnah's thinking.

Iqbal's influence on Jinnah is revealed in Jinnah's speeches from 1937 onwards. It is no coincidence that later in the same year Jinnah referred to the 'magic power' of the Muslims in his presidential address to the All-India Muslim League at Lucknow (Kaura 1977: 192). The word 'magic' is redolent of mysticism; it is poetic. It is not a word that we associate with Jinnah, whose speeches were usually constructed on the basis of rational arguments and legalistic references. Until now he had spoken of separate electorates, minority representation and constitutional safeguards. Now he would use Islamic symbolism to represent Pakistan. The moon of Pakistan is rising, he would say. He would choose the crescent for the flag of Pakistan. Something had clearly changed in the way that Jinnah was looking at the world.

Consider the bravura speech he made when presiding at the historic meeting in 1940 at Lahore. Jinnah's fresh orientation is made crystal clear. Tracing the history of the two communities as mutually separate cultural and religious entities, he emphasized the point by using a cultural rather than legalistic argument: the cow that the Hindus worship, Jinnah says, Muslims eat, the villains that Hindus malign, Muslims idolize – and so on. 'The Hindus and the Muslims belong to two different religious philosophies, social customs, literatures,' he concluded. (Jinnah now talked like an anthropologist, echoing society. Here is a European anthropologist with expertise on Hinduism: 'Hindus and Muslims form two distinct societies from the point of view of ultimate values' – Dumont 1970: 211.)

Jinnah's speech contains the essence of Iqbal's cultural arguments for a separate state. When Pakistan was created and he delivered his first two speeches to the Constituent Assembly in 1947, he once again echoed the themes of a tolerant, compassionate, honest, caring society, one reflecting the time of the holy Prophet of Islam (see chapter 7, 'Jinnah's Gettysburg address').

In a hard-hitting letter to Jinnah written on 28 May 1937, Iqbal pointed out: 'The problem of bread is becoming more and more acute. The Muslim has begun to feel that he has been going down and down during the last 200 years.... The question therefore is: how is it possible to solve the problem of Muslim poverty?... And the whole future of the League depends on the League's activity to solve this question. If the League can give no such promises I am sure the Muslim masses will remain indifferent to it as before' (Malik 1971: 385). So the issue of bread was another plank of Iqbal's political platform. Now listen to Jinnah echo Iqbal in his presidential address at the thirtieth session of the All-India Muslim League at Delhi, on 24 April 1943:

> Here I should like to give a warning to the landlords and capitalists who have flourished at our expense by a system which is so vicious, which is so wicked and which makes them so selfish, that it is difficult to reason with them. The exploitation of the masses has gone into their blood. They have forgotten the lesson of Islam.... There are millions and millions of our people who hardly get one meal a day. Is this civilization? Is this the aim of Pakistan? (Cries of 'No, No') ... If that is the idea of Pakistan, I would not have it.... The minorities are entitled to get a definite assurance or to ask 'Where do we stand in the Pakistan that you visualize?' (Merchant 1990: 10–11)

In 1946 he repeated the same theme in Calcutta: 'I am an old man. God has given me enough to live comfortably at this age. Why would I turn my blood into water, run about and take so much trouble? Not for the capitalists surely, but for you, the poor people.... I feel it and, in Pakistan, we will do all in our power to see that everybody can get a decent living' (R. Ahmed 1993: 62).

Jinnah spoke to the underprivileged in society, the young, the dispossessed. He talked about the economic needs of the community, he spoke of their victorious past, and he promised a future for them. For the first time the Muslims outside the closed circle of the élite were being addressed. He was probably the first All-India Muslim leader who was specifically referring to economic issues, as Iqbal had advised him.

Yet another plank is what Iqbal called 'the atheistic socialism of Jawaharlal' (Malik

1971: 385). Iqbal was clearly suspicious of Hindu socialism. In 1944 Jinnah declared: 'We do not want any flag excepting the League flag of the Crescent and Star. Islam is our guide and the complete code of our life. We do not want any red or yellow flag. We do not want any isms, Socialisms, Communisms or National Socialisms' (R. Ahmed 1993: 153).

Iqbal believed that an Islamic renaissance would save Muslims. He said in his address as president of the 1930 session of the All-India Muslim League: 'One lesson I have learnt from the history of Muslims. At critical moments in their history it is Islam that has saved Muslims and not vice versa.'

Iqbal proposed the creation of 'an assembly of *ulema* to protect, expand and, if necessary, to reinterpret the laws of Islam in the light of modern conditions' (Malik 1971: 94). In keeping with his thinking in 1938 just before he died Iqbal invited Maulana Maududi, the founder of the Islamic party, the Jamat-i-Islami, to establish an Islamic Research Institute in the Punjab (ibid.: 398). He was already wishing to give an Islamic character to the *ummah* – something that Jinnah would pick up and express in speeches such as the following:

> The injunctions of the Qur'an are not confined to religious and moral duties. The Qur'an is a complete code for the Muslims – a religious, social, civil, commercial, military, judicial, criminal, and penal code. It regulates every-thing, from religious ceremonies to the affairs of daily life; from salvation of the soul to health of the body; from the rights of all to the rights of each individual; from morality to crime; from punishment here to that in the life to come. Our Prophet has enjoined on us that every Mussalman should possess a copy of the Qur'an and be his own priest. (Merchant 1990: x)

It is significant that in his poetry and in his prose Iqbal defended Turkey and the idea of pan-Islamism, the universal Muslim brotherhood. He regarded it as the duty of Muslims to support the Turks, whether the Ottoman or the modern Turkish state. In his book of poetry, *Payam-i-Mashriq*, published in Lahore in 1923, Iqbal dedicated one of his poems to Mustapha Kemal Pasha (Kemal Atatürk). Jinnah would fervently repeat the refrain of pan-Islamic action. In his presidential address at Lucknow in 1937, Jinnah stated: 'The Muslims of India will stand solidly and will help the Arabs in every way they can in their brave and just struggle that they are carrying on against all odds' (R. Ahmed 1993: 91). Jinnah was predicting – and promoting – an Islamic bloc years before it became a reality, promising to liberate first the Muslims of India and then the Muslims of the world.

Notwithstanding the Muslim extremists, Jinnah's statements after his conversion to the Muslim cause like 'I shall never allow Muslims to be slaves of Hindus' (Sayeed 1968: 199) became a battle-cry, a philosophical utterance and a call for political action. This would find an immediate echo in Muslims throughout India. It explains why, in spite of all the orthodox Muslim propaganda against him – that he was not sufficiently a practising Muslim, that he could not even say his prayers properly in Arabic, that his actions were un-Islamic, that he could not speak Urdu, the language he claimed was the national language of the Muslims – Jinnah came to be acknowledged by his followers as the Quaid-i-Azam.

At the height of the Pakistan movement, in the middle of a hectic schedule, in

December 1944 Jinnah paused to pay tribute to Iqbal. His words sum up his deep feelings and what to him was an intensely close relationship:

> To the cherished memory of our National Poet Iqbal, I pay my homage on this day, which is being celebrated in commemoration of that great poet, sage, philosopher and thinker, and I pray to God Almighty that his soul may rest in eternal peace. *Amen!*
>
> Though he is not amongst us, his verse, immortal as it is, is always there to guide us and to inspire us.... He was a true and faithful follower of the Holy Prophet (peace be upon him) – a Muslim first and a Muslim last. He was the interpreter and voice of Islam. (J. Ahmad 1976: 146)

Iqbal the thinker had passed the flame to Jinnah the man of action. The result was a formidable combination of ideas and action. Nothing would stop the Muslims now.

Crossing the Rubicon

If there was a watershed in Jinnah's life and the Pakistan movement, it was 1937. It was the year not only when Iqbal exchanged those letters with him shortly before he died, but when several other crucial personal and political events took place. As the year began, Jinnah had just completed sixty years of his life a week earlier on 25 December. It was the year in which Jinnah's health began to fail, adding to his sense of urgency in fulfilling his mission; it was now or never, whatever the personal cost. Jinnah's daughter Dina had announced her intention to marry against her father's wishes. With his wife dead and relations with his only child broken down, Jinnah had no family life left. His personal energies were now diverted to the Muslim cause.

It was also the year of the historic Muslim League session in Lucknow in October. There was great excitement among the 5,000 delegates who had travelled from every part of India. Jinnah in his speech talked about the 'magic power' of the Muslims. Indeed, the gathering was aware that something extraordinary was happening. The political heavyweights of British India – the chief ministers of the Punjab, Bengal and Assam – joined the League and accepted Jinnah's leadership. Only a few years earlier the Punjab leadership had warned Jinnah 'to keep his finger out of the Punjab pie'. Their support was of immense significance, quite apart from the prestige it brought him, as Jinnah now had, at last, the Muslim-majority provinces open to him. The League was now a genuine all-India party.

Jinnah arrived wearing full Muslim dress for the first time in public. He adopted it with pride and it became the Muslim national dress (see chapter 4, 'Seeing Saladin: what Muslims saw in Jinnah'). In the time leading up to the creation of Pakistan and afterwards, Jinnah would wear it on major state occasions. Just before the meeting Jinnah had borrowed from Nawab Ismail Khan a black *karakuli* sheepskin cap, of the type worn by Muslims in the north-west of India. After the meeting it became known as the 'Jinnah cap' and a recognized symbol of the Muslim League, just as the 'Gandhi cap' identified members of the Congress. For the first time a green flag with an Islamic crescent and star was unfurled – which eventually became the national flag of Pakistan. The features of a future Pakistan were becoming visible.

Jinnah's Conversion

Many in the gathering would have recalled the conference here, two decades before, which had brought together the Congress and the League; they would have considered how far apart the two parties had drifted. Others would have gone back even further in history. There would have been men whose fathers had witnessed the British annexation of Avadh in 1856. No one present would have missed the significance of what was now happening in Lucknow, the capital city of Avadh which evoked bittersweet memories of the past. After Avadh had been annexed by the British, it disappeared from the map. Lucknow was evocative of a certain period of Muslim rule in India. It was a place of high culture; the city of Mir, the Urdu poet. Lucknow: the word itself was redolent of nostalgia. Less than a century after the British annexation, the Muslims were once again resurgent.

In his speech for the first time Jinnah challenged the national character of the Congress, casting doubt on its capacity to speak for the minorities. Jinnah also developed a pan-Islamic vision. This was in marked contrast to the previous decade, when he had appeared almost indifferent to the Khilafat movement. At Lucknow he promised to help Muslims wherever they were oppressed; he mentioned the Arabs in particular.

Jinnah roused Muslim spirits thus: 'I want the Mussalmans to believe in themselves and to take their destiny in their own hands. We want men of faith and resolution' (Kaura 1977: 187). He advised Muslims that they 'must first recapture their own souls', and ended his speech by saying that the 80 million Muslims of India 'have their destiny in their hands' (ibid.: 192). Belief, destiny, magic, faith, soul – Jinnah was no longer speaking like a lawyer but using the language of a visionary.

However, the success of the meeting in 1937 is not to be explained only in terms of magic and mystery. As Jinnah explained in his presidential address, he had spent the previous year reorganizing the Muslim League. For the first time the party had tried to reach out beyond the élite and down to the district level throughout India. Discouraged by their first experience of Congress rule (see next section), Muslims were now looking at the League with renewed interest. One resolution at Lucknow mentioned 'full independence' of a federation within India to safeguard the interests of minorities. Jinnah singled out Gandhi as 'the one man responsible for turning the Congress into an instrument for the revival of Hinduism and for the establishment of Hindu Raj in India' (Gandhi 1986: 150).

This was the year in which the Muslim League consciously set out to transform itself from a small group of concerned and influential Muslims into a genuine mass movement. From 1937 onwards, Jinnah *became* the Muslim League. He would relinquish the presidency of the Muslim League only after it had achieved Pakistan ten years later.

Congress rule

Jinnah was helped, paradoxically, by the first taste of life under Congress rule in India. On 1 April 1937 some sections of the Government of India Act of 1935 became effective. Franchise had been given to 30 million voters. In the elections held for provincial assemblies in 1937 Congress captured 711 out of 1,585 seats and seven – later eight – out of the total of eleven provincial governments. The Muslim League managed only 104 of the 489 Muslim seats. Undeterred, Jinnah took the offensive in Lucknow:

> Hindi is to be the national language of all India, and 'Bande Mataram' [the Hindu nationalist song from *Anandamath*] is to be the national song, and is to be forced upon all. The Congress flag is to be obeyed and revered by all and sundry. On the very threshold of what little power and responsibility is given, the majority community have clearly shown their hand that Hindustan is for the Hindus; only the Congress masquerades under the name of nationalism, whereas the Hindu Mahasabha does not mince words. (Kaura 1977: 186)

Confirmation of Jinnah's comments is supplied in Beverley Nichols's description of life under the Congress after the elections:

> The Act received the royal assent on August 2nd, 1935; elections for the new legislatures were held in the winter of 1936–7; Congress found itself in a large majority in seven out of the eleven provinces. As soon as it was in power in these provinces, it dropped the mask. Instead of inviting the Muslims to share the fruits of office, instead of attempting any form of coalition, it rigidly excluded them from all responsibility. But it did not confine its autocracy to political matters; it proceeded to attack the Muslims in every branch of their material and spiritual life. A great campaign was launched to enforce the use of Sanskritized Hindi at the expense of the Persianized Urdu; the schools were dominated in a manner so ruthless that it would have aroused the admiration of the Nazis, Muslim children being compelled to stand up and salute Gandhi's picture; the Congress flag was treated as the flag of the whole nation; justice was universally corrupted and in some provinces the police were so perverted that to this day the Muslims refer to them as 'the Gestapo'; and in business matters the discrimination against Muslims, from the great landowners and merchants to the humblest tillers of the soil, was persistent and pitiless. (Nichols 1944: 182–3)

These and other facts were published in the Pirpur Report, commissioned by the Muslim League and entitled *The Report of the Inquiry Committee Appointed by the Council of the All-India Muslim League to Inquire into Muslim Grievances in Congress Provinces* (Delhi: All India Muslim League, 1938). It contained a long list of complaints. Thirty-two articles listing Muslim grievances were also published in *Dawn* and *Manshoor* under the series entitled *It Shall Never Happen Again* (Sayeed 1968: 201).

It became clear that the Muslims and Hindus aimed at very different goals. For the Hindus, independence would mean the reversion to a land dominated by them, in which their culture and traditions could be revived; it was encapsulated in the Vedic word *swaraj* (self-rule, implying revival of the ancient Hindu Ram Raj). Hindu politics was thus suffused with a mystical aura. India for the Hindus was literally Mother India, the mother deity.

All these developments thrust on Muslims disturbing questions. If they were Muslims what kind of Muslims? Were they to be traditionalist or modern? Or did they need to create some kind of synthesis between the two positions? Were they Indians first, prepared to drop their Muslimness, or would they still wish to preserve their exclusive identity while living in India? Or did they need to create their own separate country?

Parting of the ways

The Congress governments resigned in October 1939 in protest against the policies of the British government in declaring war on Germany on behalf of India without a promise of independence. The Muslim League was overjoyed: 22 December 1939 was declared 'Deliverance Day' throughout India by Jinnah; deliverance from 'tyranny, oppression, and injustice during the last two and a half years' (Sayeed 1968: 99–100). Jinnah's action was bitterly resented by the Congress.

Nehru was livid with anger: 'I would have to repudiate all my past, my nationalism and my self-respect to resume the talks with Mr Jinnah in the face of his appeal to the Muslims to observe "a day of deliverance"' (Wolpert 1996: 266). 'Nehru is either utterly ignorant of what is going on in his own province or he has lost all sense of fairness and justice when he characterises the charges against the Congress government as baseless,' Jinnah responded (ibid.: 250). Gandhi, sensing what Nehru missed, fretted about the growing distance between Hindus and Muslims: 'No other unity is worth having. And without that unity there is no real freedom for India' (ibid.).

Nehru never understood the fears of the Muslims. Some of Nehru's best friends were Muslims from his own province, the UP, and he could point to other Muslim leaders like the Khan brothers in the North-West Frontier Province who were dedicated to the Congress cause. Indeed one of their leaders, Khan Abdul Ghafar Khan, was termed 'the Frontier Gandhi'. Besides, the young Nehru saw the growing confrontation in terms of class conflict and imperial British rule, the divide and rule policy. Nehru's blindness to the reality would cause India to be divided.

It is important to differentiate the politics of the Congress from the Hindus as a community. At the height of the Pakistan movement, Jinnah assured the Hindus: 'I have expressed many times that whatever differences there are, they do not, from my side, arise from the slightest ill-will against the great community of Hindus or any other community' (Mujahid 1981: 205). On another occasion he declared: 'The Muslim League is fighting the British and not the Hindus' (ibid.). Gandhi acknowledged Jinnah's position: 'I observe from Quaid-e-Azam's speeches that he has no quarrel with the Hindus. He wants to live at peace with them' (ibid.).

Not everyone wanted peace. By the early 1940s Hindu communalists were openly aggressive about their objectives, as observed by Beverley Nichols:

> Here, for example, is the typical viewpoint of Hindu orthodoxy as represented by the Mahasabha.... In a recent presidential address, Mr V. D. Savarkar aroused great applause by asserting: 'Oh yes,' they say, 'the Muslims are a nation, just as much as we are, but we don't propose to grant them anywhere to live. Oh yes, they are *in* India, and unfortunately there are 100 million of them – heretics and outcasts to a man – but India is *ours*, and we intend to keep it so. Oh yes, it is true that they were the dominant power for many centuries, and that they were the only people apart from

the British who ever gave India even the semblance of unity, but all that happened in the past and we have no intention of allowing it to happen again. Thanks to the British we are now top dog. We are three to one in numbers and twenty to one in cash. And when the British have gone we shall be even more top dog. *And* how!' (Nichols 1944: 184–5)

Jinnah was responding to this aspect of Hinduism, dismayed at the loss of the genuine Indian nationalism that he believed in, and his response came in the form of Pakistan. It was an attempt to salvage something for the Muslims, an attempt at survival. It was as much a response as an initiative. Pakistan would not have been possible without the tidal wave of Hindu communalism that had swelled up in the 1920s and now surged forward. In the clashes the Muslims found themselves outnumbered and outgunned: 'Here and there the worm did turn and not all the conflicts were one-sided. But so indeed could the German historian accuse the Poles for turning upon the aggressive and death-dealing Nazi hordes!' (Sayeed 1968: 202). A poem recited at a Muslim League conference in the district of Mymensingh in March 1941, published later in the Bengali daily, *Azad*, indicated the Muslim attitude. In the context of our discussion of Muslim heroes it is revealing for its reference to Somnath, the Hindu temple smashed by Mahmud of Ghazni (ibid.):

> The oppressed remain silent by seeing the hypocrisy
> Of the idolatrous Hindus – oh death-like eddy!
> Where are the Muslim youths? We shall attain
> The desire of their hearts by tying down the wild tiger.
> Come quickly – break down Somnath.

'Quit India' became a universal slogan by the 1940s. But while the Congress wanted the British out quickly, the Muslim League wanted the British to divide India first and then leave, since they knew that if the British did not give them their Pakistan they would in all probability never get it from the Congress. Their slogan was 'Divide and Quit'.

After 1937 Jinnah was everywhere – encouraging, advising, uplifting Muslim spirits. In speech after speech, on platform after platform, Jinnah unfurled and waved the Islamic flag. The following speech, delivered in Peshawar in November 1945, is typical:

> The Congress has chosen me as the main target of their attack.... Why? Because I am organising Muslims on one platform. Let me declare from this platform that Muslims are a thousandfold more keen to get their independence than Hindus. But what do the Hindus want? They want to remain the slave of the English but at the same time want us to become their slaves. They want the Muslims to be doubly enslaved....
>
> We want the Hindus to be free and we want freedom for ourselves. But the Hindus want to rule in Akhand Hindustan [undivided India].... Remember, Muslims can never be crushed. They have not been crushed during the last 1,000 years by any power.... Our religion, our culture and our Islamic ideals are our driving force to achieve independence. (Shouts of Allah-o-Akbar.) (J. Ahmad 1976: 241–2)

Jinnah's Conversion

Although Jinnah increasingly talked about a Muslim identity he would also emphasize Islamic tolerance, as the following incident, recounted by Yayha Bakhtiar, illustrates. Yahya, as a young supporter of Jinnah, was present at a Muslim League session in 1943 in Karachi when members voted to impose prohibition in the province. A final decision was postponed. Sir Ghulam Hidayatullah, the Chief Minister, was dismayed. He had several Hindu members. Besides, prohibition had been tried by Congress in Bombay and failed; it had resulted in bootlegging, violence and crime. But he could not stop the powerful emotions generated by the debate. Although Liaquat Ali Khan, secretary-general of the Muslim League, was present, the meeting referred the matter to Jinnah at the evening session. If you impose prohibition, Jinnah asked the delegates, would you also prevent Christians, Hindus and Parsees from drinking, some for religious reasons, and some for health reasons? The holy Prophet banned drinking 1,300 years ago, he said, so why do we need to reinforce this ban? We need to do the positive things in Islam, to pay *zakat*, to say our prayers, to be good citizens, not to impose hardship on other people. (When Yahya Bakhtiar later included this anecdote in an article sent to the national press in Pakistan it was censored out.)

Divisions in Muslim society

While almost all Hindus were unanimous on the issue of independence not all Muslims wanted Pakistan. Muslims may have felt threatened by the growing communal violence but were not entirely convinced of the Pakistan solution. In the end as many remained in India as became Pakistanis.

Many people felt that the idea of a separate Muslim state posed questions that were not easily answerable. For example, would the interests of the Muslims of India be better served by an Indian federation or by an all-Muslim state which would leave almost half the Muslims in India? How would the new state work and could it survive in the long run? Would it be democratic or organized on Islamic lines by religious figures?

Jinnah had to convince two kinds of Muslims about the need for Pakistan: those living as a minority in their province and those living as a majority. The Pakistan movement contained many Muslims who lived as a minority, for example in the United Provinces (UP), Bombay, and so on, as well as those in the Muslim-majority provinces like Bengal, Punjab, Sind, Frontier, the provinces that eventually formed Pakistan. Significantly, a large proportion of the leadership of the Muslim League came from the provinces that would not in fact go to Pakistan. In the Council of the All-India Muslim League in 1942, out of a total membership of 503 there were 245 members from the Muslim-minority provinces, outnumbered by the 258 members from Muslim-majority provinces. During 1945–7 there were only ten members from the Muslim-majority provinces in a working committee of twenty-three members.

Paradoxically, it was the Muslims living as minorities who were most vocal in demanding a Pakistan – those in the UP, in particular. Yet Muslims here were aware that although some of them might escape to the new Pakistan many of them would remain behind. Those who remained would in a sense become hostages to their Pakistan. Hindus were bound to look on them with disfavour for having broken the unity of India. It was a risk they were prepared to take. Subsequently they had to pay a heavy price for Pakistan in the riots that regularly exposed their lives and property to danger and the general prejudice against them in official and unofficial circles.

Muslims living in the Muslim-majority provinces were at first not only indifferent but in some cases hostile to the idea of Pakistan. They were secure in their own homes and did not perceive the Hindus as a threat. Culturally, politically and economically Muslims dominated these areas, although there were signs of an emerging Hindu professional class in cities such as Peshawar and Lahore. In Bengal, many Hindus owned lands in the rural areas, some of them notorious absentee landlords living in Calcutta off the lands tilled by Muslims. In provinces like the North-West Frontier Province the Congress had a stronghold. Its ally Ghafar Khan, 'the Frontier Gandhi', led the Khudai Khidmatgar social and political movement (Korejo 1994). The mythology of a tolerant, humanist, passive Gandhi had caught the imagination of the warlike Pathans. In the Punjab until the end the ruling Unionist party opposed Pakistan.

Lack of support for the Pakistan movement in areas that now form Pakistan is regarded by many commentators as a rejection of the idea of a Muslim state. This is incorrect. As we have seen, during the previous century there had been regular and sustained attempts by Muslims to move towards an Islamic identity: in the 1890s the entire Frontier Province along the tribal belt was in flames as religious leaders raised the banner of revolt against the British; the Islamic revivalism from the 1920s contributed to a high awareness of Muslim identity in the Punjab; and by the 1930s the Sind already had one of the earliest movements for a Pakistan.

However, many Muslims in India had little idea of Pakistan and did not wish to be part of it. Among these were such eminent Muslims as the scholar-statesman Maulana Azad who became head of the Congress in the 1940s. It is significant in the context of the Pakistan argument that Azad was later increasingly critical of how things turned out for the Muslims of India after independence; indeed, he blamed Jawaharlal Nehru and Vallabhbhai Patel for mishandling Jinnah and making Pakistan inevitable.

The Pakistan idea was attacked by Muslims in the Congress who argued that a Western-educated modern person like Jinnah did not have the credentials to make Pakistan a Muslim state because he was too secular and not religious enough. From the other end of the spectrum, and paradoxically, Hindus in the Congress accused Jinnah of being a 'communalist' and a 'fanatic'.

Jinnah's building blocks

Looking back to events half a century ago, we imagine a three-way struggle between the British, the Indian Congress and the Muslim League. We tend to visualize a rough balance between the adversaries in terms of resources, organization and expertise; but this is a grossly misleading picture.

What Jinnah faced was an attack on two flanks, the British and the Congress. Both were backed by enormous financial and administrative resources; they were organized down to the subdivisional level of administration in India, even in the remote areas; and both were backed by some of the brightest and most committed people in the subcontinent. Without newspapers or television or radio Jinnah found it difficult to convey his message and convert his Muslim constituency to his cause. It is well to recall that only a decade before the Pakistan movement the Muslim League was almost defunct.

If the Muslims were not all united on one platform, the Hindus were definitely united on one issue: Pakistan. From secular Hindus like Nehru, to communal ones like Patel, to the saintly ones like Gandhi, all Hindus opposed the idea of Pakistan.

Besides, until the early 1940s many in the Muslim élite – aristocrats, feudal landlords, businessmen – maintained a discreet distance from Jinnah. Many who flirted with the idea of a Pakistan let him down politically and economically (see the personal letters in Wasti 1994; also in Zaidi 1976, 1993, volume I, parts I and II). They made promises of financial assistance and then did not deliver. They conspired behind his back, linking up with either the Congress or the British. The scale of his achievement can only be understood in the context of what he was up against in the 1940s. Jinnah's statement that he created Pakistan with a typewriter and a secretary is to be viewed in this light.

If his followers could not provide Jinnah with finances and influence they compensated with commitment and passion: from the north came Abdur Rab Nishtar, from Baluchistan Qazi Isa, from Sind Sir Abdullah Haroon and G. H. Hidayatullah, from the Punjab many stalwarts such as Shaukat Hyat, Nawab Iftikhar Hussain Mamdot and Mumtaz Daultana, from the UP the Rajah of Mahmudabad and Nawab Ismail Khan, from Bengal Khwaja Nazimuddin and Hussain Shaheed Suhrawardy and, from Hyderabad, Nawab Yar Jang. Furthermore, from the heart of the UP, Aligarh students fanned out to propagate the idea of Pakistan. Among Jinnah's admirers were young intellectuals who would subsequently become well-known academics with an international reputation like Dr Z. Zaidi from the UP, Sharif al Mujahid from Madras and Khalid bin Sayeed from Hyderabad in the south. Through his supporters, Muslim thinking and Muslim action at last came together. Jinnah had created a genuine all-India movement.

CHAPTER 4

Jinnah and the Pakistan Movement

The two things that made the greatest impression on me were seeing the Taj Mahal and Mr Jinnah for the first time. These overwhelmed me as nothing had done in the whole of my life.

(Yahya Bakhtiar)

He was like God – although we Muslims can't say God. He was on a pedestal; he was our salvation.

(Zeenat Rashid)

In this chapter I shall discuss the cultural symbols which made Jinnah and his movement popular with the Muslim masses; I shall also examine Jinnah's relationship with Gandhi and the idea of Ram Raj; and finally I shall explore the road to Pakistan.

I will show how grossly Nehru misread Jinnah and the Muslims when he wrote: 'What a poor lonely figure he has been ... living a starved life of isolation, lacking friendship and affection' (Morgan 1991: 436). I shall challenge this stereotype of Jinnah in the demonology around him by showing the adulation and affection Muslims gave him.

Seeing Saladin: what Muslims saw in Jinnah

In 1857 the Muslims, desperate for a leader in their fight against the British, rallied round the Mughal emperor, Bahadur Zafar Shah. A tired old man, he was quickly picked up and packed off to die in Rangoon. This was no Saladin. Nevertheless Muslims still looked for traditional leaders – as, for example, with the abortive plan after the First World War to invite the King of Afghanistan to Delhi as their ruler, or the failed Khilafat movement in the 1920s.

When they accepted Jinnah in the late 1930s and 1940s, Muslims still viewed him in the traditional manner. It is significant that to many his leadership was seen in military terms: Iqbal said he was a simple soldier in the army led by Jinnah; Yahya Bakhtiar observed that Jinnah reminded him of the Muslim generals who conquered India (see below).

Jinnah himself was using the military metaphor by the end of his life: 'Have you ever heard of a General take a holiday, when his army is fighting for its very survival on a battlefield?' he said to Fatima when, alarmed at his health, she insisted he take time off to rest (F. Jinnah 1987: 2). On 9 June 1947, after Pakistan was announced, he contemplated retirement in these terms: 'I have done my job. When the Field Marshal leads his army into victory it is for the civil authority to take over' (Sayeed 1968: 223).

Other supporters used religious titles for him such as Maulana; some called him Shah-in-Shah, the King of Kings. Sahibzada Yaqub Khan, who was on his staff when Jinnah became Governor-General of Pakistan in 1947, told me that he was with him in Delhi when some people in a crowd shouted, 'Shah-in-Shah of Pakistan!' Jinnah stopped dead in his tracks and ticked them off for using a term like Shah-in-Shah. He would have none of it. But this did not discourage his admirers. 'Here indeed', noted one of Mountbatten's staff, 'is Pakistan's King Emperor, Archbishop of Canterbury, Speaker and Prime Minister concentrated into one formidable Quaid-e-Azam' (Campbell-Johnson 1985: 156). By the end he would be compared to archetypical Muslim heroes like Aurangzeb. The Muslims of India had found their Saladin.

The feel-good, look-good factor

When historians like Dr Zaidi argue that if Jinnah had died even after the announcement of partition in June 1947 there would have been no Pakistan, what do they mean? Jinnah's charisma added to his central role in the momentum that built up towards the creation of Pakistan in the 1940s but what were the defining characteristics of that role?

In Jinnah we are looking not at biography but at the definition of a people. During the last few years of Jinnah's life, in his clothes, aspirations, rhetoric and speeches he expressed Muslim identity and the future of Islam. It was as if Jinnah was finally coming home, as if after a long journey of discovery he had returned to his roots. He had come to terms with his identity and culture.

By the early 1940s Jinnah had become the symbol of Muslim pride in India. His arrogant reputation, his elegant clothes, his deliberate wearing of Muslim dress, his defiant stand against the British, the Indian National Congress and Muslims who were not in the League – all contributed to the growing confidence of the Muslim community. He was telling the world: I am a Muslim and proud of it; I represent a historical tradition that combines the best of several cultures – of Islam, of India and indeed of Europe. Jinnah was inspired by his supporters and he in turn inspired them; it was a symbiotic relationship in which each encouraged the other and both flourished. At one of the lowest ebbs in their affairs, in a century of decline, Jinnah made the Muslims feel good.

They came out of curiosity, admiration and interest. Although Jinnah spoke in English and most of the audience could not understand the language they heard him with 'rapt attention' (G. H. Khan 1993: 80). The gap between the speaker and the audience was bridged by a mutual affection and understanding. It was an act of faith on both sides.

Jinnah's Muslim League won virtually every Muslim seat in India after the 1937 elections. It was an astonishing political achievement. It is also a sociological comment on the notion of pride and the sense of purpose it can inject in order to transform a community into a coherent political body and an idea into a movement. The Muslims had not felt like this for a long time. Sir Sayyed's position had been apologetic, too accommodating, making many Muslims feel uncomfortable. Jinnah was saying: we are now of age; we can look the colonial master in the eye; talk back. All his anecdotes, his scraps with British officialdom which sometimes earned him a penalty, fed his reputation as a champion.

Stories circulated about how he had clashed with Lord Minto in the Legislative Council, how he had walked out of Lord Willingdon's dinner party, or how he strode alongside Mountbatten instead of behind him, or how he was – notoriously – deliberately a few minutes late for appointments with senior British officials. The Muslims thrilled to these stories; they loved this assertiveness. They had been used to their fawning, grovelling feudal lords and officials whose privileges depended on the good humour of their colonial masters. Jinnah was defying all that. His refusal of a knighthood, something both Sir Sayyed Ahmad Khan and Allama Iqbal had accepted, was culturally most significant. Like his switch from wearing British clothes to Muslim ones, it was a symbolic gesture but none the less a powerful one for his community. For Indian subjects of the British empire perhaps the greatest honour was the knighthood. It was regarded as the culmination of service to the British or as an acknowledgement of an individual's worth, particulary since only a few Indians were actually granted this honour. Even those who were fighting for the nationalist cause of eventual independence from the British would still happily receive such baubles from them. This contradiction and ambiguity marked most nationalists, whether in the Congress or in the Muslim League.

None of the Muslim leaders matched the stature of Jinnah on the national level. There were many outstanding figures but in spite of their political power bases, in spite of their family background, in spite of their status and wealth, they remained local provincial leaders. It was Jinnah and Jinnah alone who was in the same league as the big boys. It was Jinnah and Jinnah alone who was able to cross swords with Nehru and Gandhi. It was difficult to envisage any of the others contemplating a fight in that category of heavyweights.

Another reason why Muslims responded to Jinnah by the time the movement for Pakistan was growing in the 1940s was the obvious respect accorded him by his adversaries, the British and the Indian National Congress. He was now being treated as the third major player in the subcontinent. Jinnah himself was aware of this change in attitude both among his own following and outside it. 'Suddenly there came a change in the attitude towards me. I was treated on the same basis as Mr Gandhi' (Menon 1957: 59).

Significantly, in his book on India, Beverley Nichols titles his long interview with Jinnah in 1943 'Dialogue with a giant' (Nichols 1944). 'And now, let us pay a call on the potential emperor – Mr M. A. Jinnah,' he wrote. 'In view of the strategic position which he occupies, it is hardly an exaggeration to describe him as the most important man in

Asia' (ibid.: 187). Nichols summed up Jinnah's hold over the Muslims of South Asia in these words: 'His hundred million Muslims will march to the left, to the right, to the front, to the rear at his bidding and *at nobody else's*' (ibid.)

Biographers and scholars give the impression that Jinnah was fighting for 'constitutional' rights for the Muslims, that he was a detached lawyer who would be satisfied with an extra seat in one province or an extra place on a central committee in Delhi. What they miss is the cultural and social dimension. Jinnah responded directly to what he perceived were cultural threats to Muslim society. He was sensitive to the novel *Anandamath* and insisted that it be withdrawn. He picked up Madhav Sadashiv Golwalkar's threats to exterminate Muslims as the Nazis did to the Jews in Germany, and mentioned this in his speeches. He championed the cause of Urdu because he rightly regarded it as the one unifying language, a symbol of culture and history; he championed this in spite of the fact that Urdu was not his mother tongue. Further he commissioned the Pirpur Report of 1938 which documented the grievances of the Muslim community. Jinnah was echoing the fears and hopes of his community while emerging as its sole spokesman.

Bringing integrity and order

'You Mussulmans, either you are up in the sky or down in the dumps. You cannot adopt a steady course' (Hamid 1986: 219). Jinnah had shrewdly identified a central weakness in the Muslim character: in general Muslims were capable of strong emotion and commitment but not of consistency. Therefore he set out to create consistency among his followers.

Yahya Bakhtiar recounted an incident he witnessed when Jinnah was in an argument with a renowned Maulana, a religious figure. The Maulana, berating Jinnah about some point, said 'You are all brain', and tapped his own head. 'But', he continued, 'you have nothing in the heart', and thumped his chest. Jinnah immediately replied, 'You are all heart', punching his chest, 'but you have nothing in the head', and rapped his head.

By rejecting certain Muslim characteristics Jinnah was challenging the established social norms but, paradoxically, in the process gaining even greater respect: it increased his reputation for integrity. He would not listen to *sifarish*, that cancerous word meaning influence, usually based on the nepotism of family, clan or tribe, or simply plain bribery. A typical example of Jinnah's attitude towards *sifarish* occurred in his response to a letter written in November 1938 in Calcutta by Hassan Ispahani, a close friend and confidant of Jinnah, requesting help for the great-grandson of Sir Sayyed Ahmad Khan. 'Sir Sayyed rendered a service to the Musalmans of India that will remain unequalled so long as civilization remains,' Hassan reminded Jinnah, and added: 'You will therefore agree with me that a young and worthy descendant of his who is willing to work for his living should not be allowed to knock from pillar to post searching desperately for employment' (Zaidi 1976: 119). It was a case worthy of help, and Jinnah himself had benefited from Sir Sayyed's work. But his answer was characteristic. Jinnah replied in a note from Delhi the following month. A brief line in a brief letter dismissed the *sifarish*: 'I think I did drop you a line from Bombay with regard to Anwar Masood saying that I could not help in the matter' (ibid.: 120).

Nepotism favouring a spouse, offspring, son-in-law or daughter-in-law has blackened many political figures in South Asia. The Nehrus in India, the Ayubs and the Bhuttos in Pakistan, the Bandarnaikes in Sri Lanka are now into their third or fourth generation of political influence and office. In contrast Jinnah did not found a political dynasty to tarnish his name. It is significant that he made Lady Haroon, Sir Abdullah Haroon's wife, and not his sister Fatima, the head of the women's wing of the All-India Muslim League. He prohibited his own brother from misusing his name after the creation of Pakistan, as his ADC informs us (G. H. Khan 1993: 76). Jinnah took a red pen and drew a line through the words 'brother of Quaid-i-Azam, Governor-General of Pakistan' on his brother's calling card which the ADC presented. The brother took the hint, for the ADC never saw him again. Jinnah wished for no nepotism.

Even his beloved Aligarh students received no favours from Jinnah. Dr Zaidi told me that when he turned up with a large number of students to meet Jinnah at the railway station without having made an appointment Jinnah reprimanded them. He insisted that they should not waste his time and their own and that they would do better to spend their time in class, but the students refused to move until he came out of the train. The train started slowly. Dr Zaidi recalls sitting in between two carriages on the bumpers for almost two miles; but still Jinnah did not appear.

When in 1946 one Muslim complained that he had waited with his supporters by the roadside and Jinnah had not even deigned to stop, Jinnah wrote him a lengthy reply (Jinnah to Ghulam Bhik Nairang, 3 June 1946, *Shamsul Hasan Collection*). 'I am extremely sorry that you should have felt hurt,' Jinnah began. He then went on to explain that he had merely been keeping to a fixed itinerary and would have been late for his other meetings if he had stopped. Muslim society, he reflected, had declined because the Muslim's 'temper is uncontrollable and he does not make any allowance from the point of view of the other side ... but condemns him without any explanation, unheard and in the strongest terms'.

Makhdoom Qureshi, ex-Governor of the Punjab, recalls how Jinnah's authority was unchallenged even by the most eminent figures. As a boy, the son of a friend and colleague, the Makhdoom had been present in Jinnah's Simla house on the second floor, where Jinnah was working on a file. Suddenly a black Rolls-Royce drove up outside and halted. A smart ADC jumped out of the car to open the door and an elegantly trousered leg appeared. At this moment Jinnah, who had been watching all this with interest, said in a loud voice, 'Hamidullah!' 'Hamidullah,' repeated Jinnah, 'I am extremely busy today. Try your luck tomorrow.' The elegant leg withdrew; the ADC jumped back in the car; the Rolls reversed. Hamidullah was gone. The young Makhdoom was astonished.

Hamidullah was Nawab Sir Muhammad Hamidullah Khan, the Nawab of Bhopal and Chancellor of the Chamber of Princes. He was from one of the most distinguished ruling houses of India. Here was Jinnah treating one of the grandest figures in the subcontinent with a casualness that bordered on rudeness. He had not only dismissed him but also not arranged a meeting for the next day: 'Try your luck.' This was real authority, and what was instructive was the response of Sir Hamidullah, who left without a murmur.

Jinnah played by the book, by a strict moral code. When handed compromising letters that had passed between Nehru and Edwina Mountbatten and advised to get them splashed across the papers, thus killing two birds with one stone, he refused (see chapter 6). He would not fight his opponents with such dirty tricks, he said. When I discussed this with several Pakistani leaders they were critical of Jinnah; they felt he should have used this knowledge to the advantage of his party by publishing the letters.

That Jinnah constantly kept his integrity at the cost of his political position was again confirmed for me by Zeenat Rashid, daughter of his host and friend, Sir Abdullah Haroon. According to her, Jinnah was furious when she told him that she and her friends had been voting several times for the Muslim League in the name of the future Pakistan in Karachi. They did this by wearing the Muslim black *burkha* so that the polling agents did not recognize them when they went back to vote again. Jinnah ordered them to return immediately and declare the votes invalid. 'I will not have Pakistan on this basis,' he said angrily to Zeenat Rashid, who should have known that vote-rigging was hardly Jinnah's style.

Yahya Bakhtiar told me a similar story. Jinnah was in Quetta, and Yahya, his young disciple, was beside him with a camera. Jinnah had been reading a book of the sayings of the holy Prophet, and Yahya said he would like to take a photograph of him with the book. Immediately Jinnah put the book down and picked up another one. Yahya insisted that he would prefer him to be reading the book on the Prophet, whereupon Jinnah replied that he did not want to have such a photograph taken, since it could easily be misconstrued as a propaganda exercise.

Jinnah as superstar

In the 1940s the young men and women were not only challenging the British establishment but also taking on their traditional opponents, the Hindus. They were also aware that they were fighting the feudal vested interests among Muslims; indeed, many were defying their own parents' values. Those who lived through that experience and those who supported Jinnah impress you with their commitment. Ultimately the achievements of Pakistan will not have lived up to their expectations but their devotion to the Quaid shines through even today, half a century after his death. Even the title they gave him – the Quaid-i-Azam – echoed that of their greatest dynasty, Mughal-i-Azam or the Great Mughal. For them, Jinnah was the superstar of their age, the one Muslim who could take on the Hindu superstar, Gandhi.

'You have mesmerized the Muslims,' Gandhi had told Jinnah. He was right. 'I was mesmerized,' said Moeen Qureshi, who was Prime Minister of Pakistan in 1993, thinking back to the first time he saw Jinnah just before the creation of Pakistan. Students almost hero-worshipped Jinnah, 'such was Mohammed Ali Jinnah's magic' (Khurshid 1990: 4). They would even pick up pieces of paper after a meeting in the hope he might have scribbled something down and they could then auction their find (ibid.; see also Wasti 1994, 1996, for the story of young Rafi Butt, a Punjabi industrialist devoted to Jinnah, and his son Imtiaz who carries on the tradition). Mrs Almas Chinoy recalls a handshake with Jinnah when she was a young girl in Karachi. She remembers her sense of near ecstasy; for days afterwards she refused to wash her hand. She became famous among her friends, who would point to 'the hand that shook the hand'.

Young people were prepared to change their lives after hearing Jinnah. Sartaj Aziz, the Pakistani statesman, was a student at Lahore in the mid-1940s, when he heard Jinnah telling students to join commerce and business. Until then Muslims were traditionally agriculturalists or joined the army. There and then he decided to change his career and went to enrol in the Commerce College of Lahore. He took a few friends with him. He was shocked to learn that there were hardly any Muslims at college. He has remained a committed Jinnah and Muslim League supporter since then.

According to Zeenat Rashid, when her father Sir Abdullah Haroon heard that Jinnah's death was rumoured in 1941 he was so shaken that he prayed that his life might be taken instead of Jinnah's; without him there would be no Pakistan. A few months later Sir Abdullah died, and his wife until the end of her days believed it was because he had wished ill to himself at that time.

Colonel S. G. Mehdi, 75 years old in 1996 when he visited me in Cambridge, recounted how he wrote to Jinnah offering him the land he had received from the British government after winning the Military Cross for valour. In his letter he had prayed, 'May Allah grant you the lifespan of Noah', and added: 'May the day come when you unfurl the crescent flag on the land of independent Pakistan by your own sacred hands.' The letter ended: 'I wish to see the day when you lead not only the Muslims of Pakistan but the entire Islam world.' Jinnah was moved but refused the offer. Colonel Mehdi wrote again to his 'admired leader', and declared: 'May you live long enough to see a *parchame hilali* [green flag] being unfurled over the holy land – Pakistan.' Already Jinnah was being cast in prophetic mould and Pakistan seen as a sacred mission, as a 'holy land'.

Dr Sadia Chisti, member of the Council of Islamic Ideology of Pakistan and at one stage a Member of Parliament, is working on a thesis to establish that Jinnah was a *vali* – a saintly figure. She has met Jinnah and remains spiritually in awe of him; she has recounted stories of people seeing him in their dreams sitting by the holy Prophet, whose hand rests on him. Dr Chisti reported that the Governor of Baluchistan's family told her there was propaganda to depict Jinnah as an irreligious man. Yet those who attended him in his last days confirmed that he used to pray by himself at night.

In these Urdu verses Jinnah is cast as Moses (Zaidi 1993: volume I, part I, 683):

> May you live until the Day of Judgement
> and may the Day of Judgement never dawn.
> There frequently have been, and there are even now,
> many Pharaohs lying in ambush for you but don't you worry about them,
> as you have in your sleeve that dazzling light that will sear them out of existence.

Even the letters to Jinnah sent by the most exalted of the Indian princely rulers, the Nizam of Hyderabad, express an exaggerated adulation. Jinnah is 'the life-giver of the whole community' and 'the cynosure of all eyes throughout India and also beyond the seas'. But the Nizam also made it quite clear that Hyderabad was not 'joining any Unit in British India'. If he requested Jinnah to come to Hyderabad and advise him, it was only in connection with his claim over the neighbouring area of Berar and his intention 'to announce my Independence the day the British leave the shore(s) of India' (Zaidi 1993: volume I, part I, xxxv).

A fan letter was sent from Cairo on 5 May 1947 (ibid.: volume I, part I, 684–5). Even making allowances for hyperbole in Arabic it is strong stuff:

My Lord, Orator of the Nations, the Great Leader of Islam and India, My Lord, emerging from a heart which holds you in the highest position in itself, I express loyalty, because I hold you in high esteem in the heart, similar to the mother of the entire earth. And this is God's Grace on you, which He has ordained on the people, towards you. And love with true loyalty, love of the Prophet in the Quran, pride like the pride of the eye for its light and like the sincerity of the body towards the spirit God willed to order His creatures to obey you. You, therefore, proceed, and behind you are millions in the world, following in your footsteps divinely guided towards freedom and glory.

What is often overlooked is that the responses to Jinnah are not restricted to Muslims. Many Hindus and Christians supported him (Zaidi 1993). A Mr L. Lobo, a Christian, wrote to Jinnah on 18 March 1947 from Bombay:

I believe implicitly in Pakistan, the idea has possessed me and it is the only plan bearing practical operating value.... We shall not consent to remain serfs of Hindu dictators for they stand for the indefinite promotion of Hindus alone with utter disregard to our welfare. Pakistan is the only defence against any designs of the Congress aimed at the destruction of the Muslims and Minorities.... Pakistan is our destiny.... We have therefore no choice but to fight to keep the flag of Pakistan flying over the Citadel.... My mission is to unite the Minority elements, to collaborate with you.... May Providence grant you unbroken health to witness the birth and functioning of Pakistan is my prayer. (Zaidi 1993: volume I, part I, 281–2)

The camera never lies

Three extraordinary photographs given to me by Yahya Bakhtiar, unpublished and taken with the simple camera he had when he was a student, help us understand Jinnah and his relations with the Muslims (see plates 5, 6 and 7). They show how far Jinnah had become the sole spokesman of the Muslims and the visible symbol of their self-esteem.

The first was taken in April 1943 in Delhi, where Jinnah had arrived to attend the Muslim League session (plate 5). Yahya Bakhtiar, half a century later in the summer of 1995, dining in the neo-colonial rooms of the Oriental Club in London, recounted with increasing excitement his emotions on seeing Jinnah arriving, seated on a dais, which was mounted on a truck covered in flowers, surrounded by thousands and thousands of people in a grand procession through Delhi. The atmosphere was electric, Yahya said, bringing out all the Muslims of Delhi. The Hindus had just melted away. 'He was like the conqueror of Delhi; like Nadir Shah.'

Behind Jinnah is one of the most magnificent examples of Mughal architecture, the central mosque built by Shah Jahan. Opposite it is the Red Fort; together the two symbolize Muslim rule in India. Here Jinnah is finally in complete harmony with North Indian Muslim culture. It is not surprising that many Muslims regard him as the heir to the Mughals, their own Mughal emperor. People were on top of the mosque itself, high up, precariously perched. They must have waited hours for the slow-moving procession to arrive. There is a

Plate 5 Jinnah in Delhi with the central Mughal mosque in the background, April 1943; photograph courtesy of Yahya Bakhtiar

sea of humanity as far as the eye can see – hundreds and hundreds of little dots. Here Jinnah, his clothes, his persona, his words make sense. This is not kitsch, it is culture, and it is revivalist culture. It is a triumphalist procession, an irresistible march.

Jinnah sits coolly, one leg crossed over the other as if he is sitting in his study. He is unperturbed, controlled, the centre of a vast, shifting, amorphous, excited crowd. He is at the heart of a magic moment in history. Both he and the crowd know that something special is happening, that history is coming alive.

The other two photographs were taken by Yahya in November 1942 at the Jullundur railway station, where Jinnah's supporters greeted him (see plates 6 and 7). The pictures tell us several things: that adoring crowds wanted to be near him, to touch him; that he was uncomfortable when the order around him broke, when he was jostled or pushed; also, that Jinnah was attracting a large variety of Muslims from different social and cultural backgrounds. This we see through the dress they are wearing in the pictures – from the man wearing the Western tie, jacket and felt hat to the man wearing *salim shahi* shoes curling up at the feet and traditionally worn in Delhi. Behind Jinnah is a flag, which bears the words 'Allah-ho-Akbar', 'God is great'. So Islam was clearly a central motif in the Pakistan movement.

We also observe how Jinnah travelled. He is standing outside the railway station at Jullundur by the 'entrance first, second and interclass'. He is not coming out of the third-class exit/entrance which Gandhi used. He bristled with indignation when someone suggested he too should imitate Gandhi for public appearances. Not only was it hypocritical but he earned his money honestly and wished to spend it as he saw fit.

Yahya Bakhtiar described the pop-star reception and adulation. The crowds surged around Jinnah, wanting to touch him and embrace him. One impulsive young man even planted a kiss on Jinnah's cheek. 'A slobbery kiss,' recalled Yahya Bakhtiar with some indignation. 'Please get back, get back,' admonished Jinnah, not pleased by the chaos.

One of the photographs shows him looking uncomfortable and with his hand at his throat (plate 7). For once, at least in a photograph, he has lost his cool. He looks preoccupied and, unusually for him, even flustered. The reason is not difficult to guess. Around him, too close for comfort, is a pushing, heaving, undisciplined crowd.

Clothes maketh the community leader

The difference between Jinnah and the last Mughal emperor, Bahadur Zafar Shah, in terms of dress, the language they spoke, styles, values and temperament could not have been greater. They could have been from two different planets. They were two different people representing different cultures. One was a medieval Mughal, descended from Timur and the Muslims of Central Asia, to whom dynasty and ritual meant everything, to whom the preservation of the past was paramount; the other an Anglicized, Indian lawyer educated in London who spoke and thought in English and was determined to play a part in leading his country into the future.

With his monocle, clipped accent and his Savile Row suit, Jinnah was the perfect upper-class English gentleman of his day. His tall thin body, his lean features and his liking for good clothes enabled him to wear English clothes with flair, confidence and conviction. His mimicry of the upper-class Englishman in India was so accurate it made the English uncomfortable. He was that most dangerous of natives, the credible mimic. The British could only respond in two ways: they could hate him or admire him; they could not ignore him.

There was no loincloth or *dhoti* for Jinnah. We think of Gandhi as a young Anglicized dandy with gold watch and chain, Gladstone collar and gloves, taking speech lessons from Beryl's *Standard Elocutionist* so he could pronounce English like a sahib, and know that he gave this dress up for the *dhoti*. Nehru had sarcastically remarked that there was as much difference between Jinnah and the Indian masses as between Savile Row and Bond Street and an Indian village with mud huts (Sayeed 1968: 87).

'He carried it off, including the solar topee and monocle,' declared the Royal Air Force group captain who was the officer commanding the Peshawar base in 1946 deputed to accompany Jinnah (personal communication). Wearing Western suits was not unusual among the Indian élite. What was unusual was the authenticity and exaggeration of Jinnah's aristocratic English appearance, down to the monocle. The monocle was the icing on the cake. Very few natives would have had the nerve to

Plate 6 Jinnah being received at Jullundur railway station; photograph courtesy of
Yayha Bakhtiar

attempt it. A monocle required confidence. Not getting it right would be disastrous,
comical; it would be a Peter Sellers caricature of an Indian.

As anyone living in the subcontinent will confirm, to look clean and neat in
formal Western clothes requires a great deal of physical effort, since the weather
is often hot and humid. Jinnah changed two or three times a day, according to Yahya
Bakhtiar. This was hygienic and sensible, but it also served to make a point. Every
time he was photographed or appeared in public he appeared freshly dressed, which
not only projected a positive image but helped to conceal the effects of his failing
health.

Those who disparage Jinnah's expensive public habits − in use of hotels, cars, clothes,

Plate 7 Close-up photograph at Jullundur station showing Jinnah uncomfortable when surrounded by an unruly mob; photograph courtesy of Yayha Bakhtiar

and so on – have little idea of Muslim society, whose members would have responded negatively to Jinnah's attempts to do a Gandhi. There is no tradition of a half-clad *faqir* leading the Muslims to a great victory. Muslims dismiss Gandhi's dress as empty posturing, citing the remark by his colleagues about it costing them a lot to keep the old man in poverty. Had Jinnah discarded his expensive Western clothes for homespun or Sufi garments he would have killed his political career and the Pakistan movement. The influential power-brokers, the feudal lords, the industrialists, even ordinary Muslims, would have responded differently had he appeared in ordinary garb. They may well have closed their doors to him.

Muslims look up to a person of substance, a leader whose dress and deportment proclaim his or her *shan* – glory. Muslims want their commanders and leaders to look like commanders and leaders: proud, dignified, head held high. This is exactly what Jinnah personified: his expensive suits and elegant *sherwanis* spoke to the British of a man of sophistication and substance and to the Muslims of a man of worth and importance.

Clothes as a diacritical cultural symbol

In the early twentieth century, Muslims were spread over a continent with only a loose link through Islam. They had no common language, dress, political organization or territory; even their Islam was divided into sects. When Jinnah began to lead the movement in the late 1930s there was no popular radio or television and newspapers were not widely read. Indeed Muslims did not have their own press until Jinnah helped to start *Dawn* in Delhi in the early 1940s. The *Dawn* would become the main English newspaper of the Muslims (and later of Pakistan).

Jinnah created a united platform for all Muslims. When asked by a heckler in a meeting whether he was a Shia or a Sunni he answered with a question: 'What was the holy Prophet?' 'Neither,' said his critic; 'he was a simple Muslim.' 'Then I too am neither Shia nor Sunni but just a simple Muslim,' replied Jinnah.

So Jinnah's genius was, apart from his recognized skills as a political strategist and constitutional lawyer, to create the modern Muslim persona, one which would represent a modern Muslim nation and reflect its spirit while providing identity and unity. It heralded the dawn of modern Muslim mass politics and political symbols.

During the 1930s Jinnah set about creating an all-India Muslim persona. It was based on a common language, Urdu, common clothes, and a common notion of identity and destiny. Nothing like this had been attempted since the Arabs entered India through Sind in the eighth century with their non-Indian language, Arabic. His cultural use of language and clothes could not have been bettered by Madison Avenue media experts.

Jinnah was not parochial in this exercise. He spoke Gujarati, since he came from that linguistic group in western India. Yet he supported Urdu as the language which would unite the Muslims of India and thus gave them a lingua franca. To the masses his accented and sometimes grammatically incorrect Urdu would be delightful; instead of criticizing him they appreciated his attempt to use it.

By the late 1930s Jinnah had adopted Muslim dress although he did not entirely give up his Western clothes. The *sherwani* (knee-length black coat) he got from Aligarh. The students of Aligarh wore the *sherwani*: it was their trademark. After the Pakistan movement picked up in the 1930s it would soon become the trademark of the Muslim League throughout India. Even those people who did not wear the *sherwani* adopted it. The *shalwar* or baggy trousers that he wore came from the people of the river Indus, the lands that would form West Pakistan.

As headgear Jinnah preferred the *karakuli*, which was already worn by many Muslims in North India. It was neater and more modern than either the turban or the traditional fez worn by people of the older generation. The fez was associated with the Ottomans and had been rejected by Kemal Atatürk as symbolic of the old order. Jinnah did not accept either the fez or the turban. He wished to make a statement about headdress which reflected his modern yet cultural position: the *karakuli* cap suited all this.

A semiotic examination of the photographs of the time will tell us much. Take the historic photograph recording the arrival of Jinnah on the soil of an independent Pakistan in August 1947 (see plate 8). It shows him with Fatima Jinnah stepping out of the plane, wearing a *sherwani, shalwar* and *karakuli*. After the creation of Pakistan he was seen in national dress on all the major occasions – the address to the Constituent Assembly, the swearing in ceremony as Governor-General, the opening of the State Bank. With that single gesture he stamped the idea of the national dress on the new nation. It is still the official dress of Pakistan.

Jinnah was making several points through his clothes: he was creating a modern Muslim identity while at the same time representing all the Muslims, not just one particular group. In doing so he rose above a provincial or ethnic identity. Any other Muslim leader in contrast looked local or rooted in his particular area or group. He was also signalling that the Muslim dress was in opposition to the one worn by Gandhi, Nehru and the Hindus – the Gandhi cap, the *dhoti*, the Nehru jacket, and so on. Muslims were visibly rejecting Hindu identity and underlining their own. But by continuing also to wear his elegant English suits – often, as depicted in official pictures, with a *karakuli* – he was suggesting that this was the identity of a Muslim proud of his past and yet at ease with the present, part of Eastern as well as Western tradition.

Jinnah had an instinct for choosing the right clothes to make a cultural and political point. When Pakistan was created, he stopped wearing the *choridar* or tight *tang* pyjamas worn in the UP and in and around Delhi, and adopted the loose-fitting *shalwar* worn

Plate 8   Jinnah arriving on the soil of Pakistan for the first time with Fatima Jinnah, Karachi, 7 August 1947; photograph courtesy of Douglas Crook

in the area that became West Pakistan. (According to Yahya Bakhtiar, Jinnah wore the *tang* pyjamas until a few years before the creation of Pakistan, after which he wore the *shalwar*, which was more common in what became Pakistan.) At the age of 70 he was flexible enough to accommodate and respond to local cultural practices.

When we analyse Jinnah's clothes, let us not forget Fatima Jinnah. When the Pakistan movement was in full flow, photographs show her appearing in public wearing Muslim dress. What is remarkable is that she covers her hair with the *dupatta*, a light veil which is symbolic of modesty in Islam. This is important because it became an issue in Pakistan politics decades after the creation of Pakistan. When Benazir Bhutto became Prime Minister of Pakistan in 1988, people began to discuss how 'Islamic' she was. She responded by covering her hair with a *dupatta*. Of course this was symbolic but it was also an acceptance of the Islamic idea of a woman covering her hair. Fatima Jinnah was, like Jinnah, responding to the expectations of the Muslim community in India half a century before the debate began in Pakistan. She too, like her brother, was underlining her Islamic identity. Like him, she was consciously prepared to take on and interact with the challenges of the modern world, but with her Muslim identity firmly in place.

Gandhi and Ram Raj

As we saw in chapter 3, Gandhi's emergence in the 1920s was an important factor influencing Jinnah's conversion, eventually resulting in his support for the Pakistan movement. Yet the relationship between Jinnah and Gandhi was never one of enmity (as depicted in Attenborough's film). On Gandhi's death Jinnah 'acknowledged how great was the loss for the Moslems' (Gandhi 1986: 183).

Jinnah treated Gandhi with affectionate exasperation, taking his politics with a pinch of salt. Commenting on Gandhi's spells in jail, he observed:

> I do not believe in starting a movement for the sake of jail-going. Believe me it will not be difficult for me to go to jail for six months or so. After all nothing happened to Mr Gandhi. He was safely lodged in the Aga Khan's Palace. He had his private secretary. In fact his whole family was with him.
> (J. Ahmad 1976: 244)

Jinnah's daughter, Dina Wadia, confirmed that there was little 'personal animosity' between her father and Gandhi, only 'political animosity'. Gandhi was 'charming', 'sweet', 'enchanting' and had a 'sense of humour' as well as an eye for pretty girls, Dina laughed, recalling she was young and pretty when she first met him.

Western and Indian commentators are inclined to compare Jinnah unfavourably with both Gandhi and Nehru. They point to Gandhi's humility, austerity and palpable human warmth, to Nehru's charm and learning. What they miss is how Muslims saw Jinnah; I have attempted to provide this perspective.

For the West, Gandhi was a man of extraordinary charisma. He had everything that the West was looking for in an Oriental saint-hero: inner spiritual struggle, a philosophy of non-violence, a universal message. Besides, he dressed, talked and looked like a genuine Asian sage. There was also a deeper, atavistic need to support Gandhi against Jinnah. Tony Benn, the Labour MP, compared the response of most British people –

especially left-wing people and politicians traditionally sympathetic, like him, to minorities – to the different personalities of Gandhi and Jinnah. Gandhi represented the romance of the East, the exotic, the affection for and the flirtation with a completely different 'Asian' culture. On the other hand, Jinnah represented Islam, always antagonistic, combatant, knocking on the doors of Vienna or actually occupying Spain for centuries: Islam alive and a forceful neighbour, a cousin, both friend and enemy. Islam was too close to the bone. The West could not be neutral to it. These responses to Indian Muslims and Indian Hindus in turn would have consequences for the creation of Pakistan (as we see in chapters 5 and 6).

Interestingly enough Gandhi and Jinnah had much in common. They were about the same age, came from the same region and linguistic group, had a similar social background and died in the same year. They were worthy opponents, but had a healthy respect for each other, and remained slightly aloof from day-to-day politics. Indeed, for the Interim Government of 1946 Jinnah nominated his lieutenants rather than himself; Gandhi stayed away from government both before and after independence.

The two real giants of South Asia, Jinnah and Gandhi, have come to symbolize their respective communities. In their lifetime they were the target of assassins. But the serious attempts came not from their non-Muslim or non-Hindu enemies but from members of their own community – the extremists who found their leaders' broad-based, accommodating, tolerant position threatening. They had to be removed by death.

Ram Raj

The idea of Ram Raj or the rule of Ram was central to Gandhi – he died with Ram's name on his lips. It was central to larger Hindu historical mythology as an ideal, a golden age. But Gandhi helped convert the notion from culture to politics, from private belief to public policy. To him independence meant *swaraj,* a Vedic term implying a reversion to Ram Raj (see also chapter 8, 'From British Raj to Ram Raj').

Lord Ram in Hindu mythology is a noble figure embodying bravery, generosity and compassion (for a discussion of the impact of Ram on the politics of contemporary India through the media, see chapter 8, 'Lord Ram as media superstar'). In the stories he vanquishes Ravana, the symbol of evil. So popular is Ram that even Iqbal dedicated a poem to him. His reign – Ram Raj – meant a time of justice and prosperity. It was an attractive idea to strive towards and it provided a strong rallying point for modern Hindu nationalism.

But it had a dark side. It also meant the suppression of both the non-Hindu minorities and the lower castes. Ram ultimately symbolized the rule of the upper castes in Hindu society. This was a paradox, as there are episodes in the *Ramayana* in which Ram transcends caste discrimination, indeed pointedly embracing those of the lower castes. However, his critics relate the story of his killing Sambhok, a member of a lower caste, to show him his place in society. In the south of India, where there is a developed consciousness against caste, Ram is not seen as a heroic figure. Many tribals and Dalits have taken up Ravana's cause. He, not Ram, is their hero. Indeed, in many areas they burn effigies of Ram (*Times of India,* 21 October 1989; Bonner et al. 1994: 199; for the Dalit position, see Rajshekar 1993: 81).

The suppressed castes of India – the so-called 'untouchables' – saw Ram and the entire caste structure as designed to keep them chained to slavery and misery. Regular but futile attempts at challenging the Hindu hierarchy and structure were made over the centuries by the low castes. The challenge was symbolized in the first half of this century by the leader of the 'untouchables' Dr Baba Saheb Ambedkar himself. For Dr Ambedkar, Ram is a figure of villainy accused of, among other things, incest with his putative wife Sita (Ambedkar 1987: 325).

By the 1980s communal parties in India were using Ram as the symbol of a revivalist, threatening and disruptive Hinduism. Their immediate target was the mosque at Ayodhya, their larger objective – power in Delhi. They succeeded in both. The conversion of Ram from a universal Indian to an exclusively upper-caste Hindu figure is a comment on the manipulation of Hindu mythology by modern politicians.

It was Gandhi who had let the genie out of the bottle. In retrospect Jinnah had been right. In 1920 Gandhi clearly expressed his philosophy of bringing religion into politics: 'The politician in me has never dominated a single decision of mine, and if I seem to take part in politics, it is only because politics encircle us today like the coil of a snake from which one cannot go out, no matter how much one tries. I wish therefore to wrestle with the snake' (*Young India*, 12 May 1920).

Nehru had examined religion and found it lacking (Nehru 1961: 26); it had not attracted him, he said, because 'behind it lay a method of approach to life's problems which was certainly not that of science' (ibid.). He believed that religion was a hindrance to 'the tendency to change and progress inherent in human society' (ibid.: 543). Nehru was also critical of caste: he blamed neither the Muslim conquerors, as Hindu chauvinists would, nor British colonialism for India's backwardness, but the caste system. Most important, he publicly stood by the idea of secularism, even criticizing Gandhi's use of 'Ram Raj' (Nehru 1941: 72).

Nehru voiced his alarm in his autobiography: 'I used to be troubled sometimes at the growth of this religious element in our politics, both on the Hindu and the Muslim side.... Even some of Gandhiji's phrases sometimes jarred upon me – thus his frequent reference to *Ram Raj* as a golden age which was to return' (Sayeed 1968: 96).

By the 1920s, Ram Raj had become a slogan and a central idea in Hindu politics. It was accompanied by the introduction of several other Hindu rituals and ideas into public life. Muslims like Jinnah, as indeed leaders of other minorities, were becoming apprehensive. They were not sure where it would all end.

Gandhi and the myth of non-violence

There are several myths about the Indian nationalist movement that need to be reassessed by scholars. According to one myth in the common demonology, Jinnah is supposed to have stoked the communal fires which Gandhi, the saint, attempted to stamp out. Once again the reality is more complex. Jinnah never disputed the national character of the Congress until the Lucknow Muslim League session in October 1937 and often referred to Gandhi as Mahatma Gandhi until the 1930s.

The image of Gandhi perpetuated by Attenborough's film is a distortion. Gandhi struggled with himself and that was his greatness; but there were times when he was determined to implement Hindu belief in India even at the point of a knife. In an exchange with Jinnah in New Delhi on 28 September 1944 Gandhi lost his temper. 'Pakistan', said Gandhi, 'means war to the knife' (Mujahid 1981: 101; Seervai 1990: xx). Immediately Jinnah exclaimed, 'Here is an apostle and a devotee of non-violence threatening us with a fight to the knife' (Seervai 1990: xx).

On Pakistan Gandhi was capable of showing a militant side. Gandhi thumped the table at a meeting, reported the Viceroy Lord Wavell, and cried, 'If a bloodbath was necessary, it would come about in spite of non-violence' (Mujahid 1981: 219). In a prayer meeting on 31 May 1947, Gandhi had said: 'Even if the whole of India burns we shall not concede Pakistan, even if the Muslims demanded it at the point of the sword' (*New York Herald Tribune*, 2 June 1947). Jinnah never used threats of violence against Hindus in his struggle for Pakistan. Instead he focused on the need for unity among members of the Muslim community, as Seervai points out: 'Jinnah rarely made the kind of religious appeals which were usual with Gandhi, although Jinnah's followers did so. Jinnah harped on the theme of Muslims organizing themselves economically, socially and politically in order to stand on their own feet' (Seervai 1990: xv).

Nirad Chaudhuri pointed out how Bengalis saw Gandhi: 'I always heard most Bengalis of my class saying that all of Mahatma Gandhi's non-violence was a political ruse, and they rather admired him for the duplicity they attributed to him' (1990: 43). Chaudhuri adds: 'Gandhi's non-violence was conceived in London from Tolstoy's interpretation of the New Testament' (ibid.: 44). We know of Rabindranath Tagore's trenchant opposition to Gandhi's non-cooperation movement, recorded in his 1925 essay 'The cult of the Charka' (see Dutta and Robinson 1995). A gentle literary mystic, Tagore was uneasy with some of Gandhi's political thinking, and this made him unforgiving enemies. He soon dropped out of fashion in India, though he remained a popular figure in his native Bengal.

Gandhi and the mythical Muslims

Gandhi contributed significantly, if inadvertently, to the growing rift with the Muslims. For all his saintliness, Gandhi considered Muslims as Hindus who had converted to Islam from Hinduism. He found it difficult to see them as a distinct Indian community. For the Muslims of India, as Omar Khalidi, an Indian commentator, observes, Gandhi's impact was ultimately not dissimilar to that of the communal parties like the BJP (1995). Both wished to incorporate the Muslims into Hinduism – Gandhi through peaceful means, by arguing that they were lapsed Hindus, the BJP through force and terror. Paradoxically, Gandhi's moral message of tolerance was diluted, indeed perverted.

Professor Bhiku Parekh, one of the best-known authorities on Gandhi, pointed out Gandhi's weak spot in looking at Muslims:

> For him India's history began with the arrival of the Aryans and continued for several thousand years during which it developed a rich spiritual culture. It was rudely interrupted by the arrival of the Muslims and then the British, and was to be resumed at Independence. The Muslim and British periods were largely aberrations made possible by Hindu decadence, and

had little impact on India. The Muslims were little more than converted Hindus or ex-Hindus whose religion was but an icing on their essentially Hindu cultural cake. (Parekh 1985: 308)

Parekh's conclusion shows how Gandhi responded to the Muslims:

> Gandhi and many in the Congress then had great difficulty in coming to terms with the Muslim past. Even as he could only see the Muslims as ex-Hindus and could not fully appreciate their distinctive place in India, he could only see the Muslim past as an historical aberration, a regrettable episode brought about by Hindu degeneration. (ibid.: 309).

Gandhi was partly right. Although the Muslims paraded a myth that they were all foreigners, 'pure' Muslims, this was not racially accurate. The stream of Muslim immigrants had dried up centuries ago. By the later period of the Mughal empire there were no fresh waves coming from the northern passes into India. Power and authority had consolidated in Delhi and this discouraged any fresh adventurers. Over the centuries intermarriages, conversions and social mobility had diluted whatever purity there remained among the Muslims. Nevertheless it was obviously irrational for Gandhi to fail to recognize the existence of a genuine Muslim identity with a long Muslim past.

Gandhi and the Muslim stereotype

What would happen, Gandhi asked, if India became independent and Muslims from outside invaded India? Would the Indian Muslims join them if a *jihad* was declared? Surely the lessons of the past were to be heeded, especially with rulers like Mahmud of Ghazni? Surely the Hindus would be enslaved once again and India would become a Muslim empire? This was his response:

> Consider for one moment what can happen if the English were to withdraw all of a sudden and there was no foreign usurper to rule. It may be said that the Punjabis, be they Muslims, Sikhs or others, will overrun India.... Thus if anybody has cause to keep the British rule for protection from the stronger element, it is the Congressmen and those Hindus and others who are represented by the Congress. (*The Collected Works of Mahatma Gandhi*, volume LXX: 260).

Gandhi's assumptions were based on stereotypes: 'The Mussulmans take less interest (in the internal political life and advancement of the country) ... because they do not yet regard India as their home of which they must feel proud' (*Young India*, 2 April 1925). With regard to the communal riots he wrote that 'the Mussulman as a rule is a bully and the Hindu as a rule is a coward' (ibid.). Muslims were 'too free with the knife and the pistol' (*Young India*, 30 December 1926). The Muslim was a 'bull-terrier', the Hindu a 'rabbit' (*Young India*, 29 May 1924 and 15 October 1925). The same observation was made by him in another article in *Young India* on 19 June 1924:

> the Mussalman, being generally in a minority, has as a class developed into a bully ... the thirteen hundred years of imperialist expansion have made

the Mussalmans fighters as a body. The Hindu has an age-old civilization. He is essentially non-violent.... The Hindus have become docile to the point of timidity or cowardice.

Gandhi exhorted Hindus to retaliate and 'to learn to die' (Mujahid 1981: 192).

Gandhi's attitude towards lower castes and minorities

Gandhi's views on caste evolved somewhat sporadically towards accepting the lower castes. In South Africa he still insisted on a colour bar between black Africans and brown Indians. On his return to India he supported caste prohibitions on intermarrying and interdining until the eve of the Second Round Table Conference. It was only a few months before his assassination that he reluctantly agreed to intermarriage between castes.

Gandhi opposed separate electorates for the lower castes:

Gandhi fiercely opposed this scheme. 'Give the untouchables separate electorates', he cried, 'and you only perpetuate their status for all time.' It was a queer argument, and those who were not bemused by the Mahatma's charm considered it a phoney one. They suspected that Gandhi was a little afraid that 60 million untouchables might join up with the 100 million Muslims – (as they nearly did) – and challenge the dictatorship of the 180 million orthodox Hindus. (Nichols 1944: 39)

Not surprisingly, Dr Ambedkar, leader of the so-called untouchables, or Dalit of today, repeated again and again: 'Gandhi is the greatest enemy the Untouchables [60 million then] have ever had in India' (ibid.: 38).

Dr Ambedkar, who had through sheer courage and willpower obtained a PhD from Columbia University, almost converted to Islam in 1935. Had he done so, the history of India might well have been different. He was prevented by massive Hindu pressure led by Gandhi. But this did not stop him from converting to Buddhism just before he died in 1956. He had few illusions about Hinduism, as he makes clear in his book, *Riddles in Hinduism* (1987). Ambedkar was one of the few vocal supporters of Pakistan, constantly explaining why Jinnah did what he did. To his Dalit followers even today, Jinnah is far closer to their position than Gandhi or Nehru (see Krishna Gamre in *Dalit Voice*, 1–15 August 1995).

According to Krishna Gamre, a prominent spokesman for the Dalit movement, Jinnah was a supporter of Dr Ambedkar. The Dalits are about 200 million strong in India, and their perception of Pakistan is very different from the negative one of the establishment, the media and the politicians in India, dominated by the upper castes. Most Dalits, even today, blame Gandhi and Nehru for the creation of Pakistan. Jinnah to them was leading a similar struggle to their own for the preservation of their security and rights as a minority.

This theme is reflected in several letters sent from Lahore by Mrs K. L. Rallia Ram to M. A. Jinnah, such as one written in March 1947:

Look how the Hindu press always wants to hide the murderous assaults by Sikhs and Hindus on the Muslims. They do not even want to publish the fact when the Sikh is a culprit, whereas when a Muslim attacks for defence of his life, he is presented as the aggressor.... As I wrote, this is all a conspiracy of Brahman plus the 'Bania' to make the Muslim nation surrender to the Hindu 'Raj'. But thank God that you are there to withstand their most violent onslaughts on the honour and dignity of the Muslims and minorities. (Zaidi 1993: volume I, part I, 419)

The myth of monolithic nationalism

The nationalist movement in India has falsely been portrayed as monolithic, with all Hindu Indians united behind it. But in fact each region pulled in a different direction. Whereas the Maharashtrans produced a fiercely parochial nationalism, the Bengalis had a more sophisticated, Westernized approach. Those in the south were more concerned with asserting themselves against the north – especially the hold of the Brahmins and the United Provinces – than against the British.

We associate the Indian nationalist movement and Hindu revivalism with Gandhi after the 1920s, but in fact it had begun much earlier, in the last century. The writings of Bankim Chandra Chatterji and Raj Mohan Roy clearly testify to this. Early in the nineteenth century Raj Mohan Roy had already established a strong intellectual movement for Hinduism. His problem was that there was no such term as a Hindu religion, no such word as religion. In 1828 he founded what was later called the Brahmo Samaj.

Even the use of the Hindu scriptures has been employed differently by different Hindus. For Gandhi the *Bhagavad Gita*, which was not translated into the modern Indian languages until the 1880s, was a path to spiritual harmony. For Bankim Chatterji and Tilak it was a call to arms. Golwalkar used it to encourage the shedding of blood, and cited Krishna telling Arjuna that he must not leave the battlefield merely because he had to kill friends and teachers: 'Sri Krishna tells Arjuna, "I am the power of destruction, come to slay these men here. Even without thee, all the warriors standing arrayed in hostile ranks, shall be destroyed." It only means that death and destruction are in the very nature of this world' (Golwalkar 1966: 232).

Gandhi's experiments with sex

In accordance with his honesty in dealing with the most sensitive of matters, as part of his search for truth, Gandhi recorded his sense of sexual frustration whenever he met Jinnah. Parekh has pointed out these connections:

On 14 April, 1938, he [Gandhi] had a 'bad dream' involving a 'desire to see a woman' and an ejaculation. Evidently, he was completely shattered.... He was in a 'well of despair', 'obsessed by a feeling of self-guilt' and did not know what had gone wrong. He lost all self-confidence, became moody and his political work began to suffer. He had to see Jinnah for long and difficult negotiations, and he did not feel up to it. Although he met him and worked out important proposals, he felt unsure of himself and looked to Nehru to provide the lead. (Parekh 1989: 188)

Gandhi's sexual experiments failed to create the moral superiority he wished to develop over his adversaries:

> Gandhi embarked upon the sexual experiments in order to, among other things, acquire the kind of moral and spiritual power he thought he needed to arrest the tidal wave of violence raging all around him and to control political events. Judged by this test, they must be considered a failure. Jinnah, the Muslim League and the Muslim masses remained implacable; the Hindus, who might have been expected to respond better, were not won over to the path of *ahimsa* either; inter-communal carnage went on unabated; three attempts were made on his life during the period of his experiments; he gained no privileged insight into the messy political situation; his lifelong friends, including Nehru and Maulana Azad, deserted and even deceived him; and none of his close associates or any of the women involved in the experiments showed unusual courage and prescience. (ibid.: 201)

From magnificent Mahatma to 'bastard bania'

Gandhi had been evolving in public perception, visibly, into sainthood, step by step, stage by stage, in the full glare of history, on his return to India from South Africa. By the 1920s and early 1930s he had almost singlehandedly changed the political map of India. He had used his international standing to great effect in projecting his cause. It was difficult for local district magistrates – mostly young British officials of the élite Indian Civil Service cadre and aware of larger developments taking place around them – to deal with a man whose admirers included Leo Tolstoy, George Bernard Shaw and Albert Einstein.

Gandhi also democratized politics, bringing it directly to the ordinary person in the village and in the shanty towns; he had made politics indigenous by equating the fight against the British with a national Indian effort of self-expression; by rejecting Western clothes he had provided a symbolic challenge to Western civilization while at the same time creating pride in things Indian. Most important, he brought religion directly into politics. There was no going back on this score.

By the time Mountbatten arrived in India, in 1947, Gandhi had been elevated to a saint but he had been made almost irrelevant to the structure of politics in Delhi with its machinations and back-door decisions. Indeed he was being seen as a nuisance. The Congress high command was pleased to encourage his visit to Pakistan, the trip he was planning just before he was killed; Gandhi would be Jinnah's headache and not theirs. Gandhi's humanism, religious tolerance, search for truth and tendency to speak out against injustice and opposition to Western materialism did not suit all Hindus. He was politically dead well before Nathuram Godse, representing the hardline extremists among Hindus, shot him.

If Jinnah was the towering giant on the Muslim side then his counterpart was Gandhi, although it is fashionable in contemporary India to knock Gandhi, to blame him for many of the ills of the land (there is a vast literature on Gandhi; for a recent authoritative study, see Dalton 1993). They blame him, above all, for partition. Yet Gandhi's name gives India its international lustre and his example is one that constantly inspires people, not only Hindus. Throughout his life he maintained a sympathy for those outside his faith. His prayer meetings were noted for recitations of the holy books of the Muslims and the Christians. But his finest hour came in his death. He had just finished a fast in protest against the killing of Muslims and India's refusal to pay the agreed share of assets to Pakistan. He was preparing to visit Pakistan to create brotherly relations between the newly formed country and India. His life had made him a great man; his death made him a saint. Even Jinnah, his old adversary, conceded the loss to the Muslims.

In the end he was devoured by the tiger: a member of the RSS – the extreme wing of Hinduism, which Gandhi had compared to 'Hitler's Nazis' – assassinated him. When it was first formed, the RSS had the full support of the president of the Congress and the Hindu Mahasabha, Madan Mohan Malaviya (Bonner et al. 1994: 101). These links were never publicly exposed. Today, he can be called a 'bastard *bania*' on Indian television with impunity (see the *Guardian*, 5 July 1995; also chapter 8, 'From *Anandamath* to Ayodhya').

If Jinnah is seen as a villain in India, in Pakistan the compliment is reversed. There is a demonology surrounding Gandhi, who manipulates and guides his two equally villainous but stupid assistants, Nehru and Mountbatten. He is determined not to grant Pakistan independence, and threatens the Muslims of India with bloodshed. Even the fasts that he undertook for the Muslims are ignored. In Pakistan history there is only one towering hero and that is Jinnah.

Yet Gandhi represented the best of modern India. A pious man with a mischievous sense of humour, he was genuinely kind and compassionate. What Gandhi was to the world as a symbol by the 1940s, Nelson Mandela was to become in the 1980s and 1990s. For all his critics Gandhi is a moral giant and I believe an acknowledgement is long overdue from Muslims in Pakistan.

The path to Pakistan

Until the middle of the nineteenth century India was very much the home of the Muslims. In perhaps his most poignant verses Bahadur Zafar Shah, the last emperor of Delhi, lamented from his exile in Rangoon, 'How unfortunate is Zafar for burial/he did not even get two yards of land in his beloved's lane.'

Delhi was still a metaphor for the beloved's lane to the Muslims of India. It was their city and it was their land. In the next generation this sense of certainty would be lost. After the First World War, during the Khilafat movement, Muslims would seek a home outside India. By the end of the Second World War Muslims would be wondering whether India indeed was the beloved's lane any longer. They would soon be creating their own homeland.

Jinnah and the Pakistan Movement

On the downward graph of history

In 1857–8, as we have seen, Muslims touched a low point in their history; a few decades later, in the 1890s, Muslim uprisings failed in the Frontier Province; at the turn of the century Bengal was partitioned and then, in 1911, reunited – making Muslims complain of Hindu domination. In 1912 the government refused to support a Muslim university at Aligarh. In 1913 part of a mosque was demolished at Kanpur; riots followed and Muslims lost lives.

Muslim fortunes were on a downward curve on the graph and Muslims were acutely aware of it. The feeling was summed up by the president of the Muslim League. In his presidential address at Bombay, in 1918, Fazl ul-Haq voiced his fears: 'To me the future of Islam in India seems to be wrapped in gloom and anxiety. Every instance of the collapse of the Muslim powers of the world is bound to have an adverse influence on the political importance of our community in India' (Sayeed 1968: 45). His pessimism was justified. In the 1920s the Ottoman empire and the Khilafat movement in India collapsed. It was a century of defeat and despair (for the Muslim trajectory, see the four maps, 'The Shrinking World of the Muslims').

To make matters worse for the Muslims, significant developments were taking place in the Hindu community. Most important of all, by the 1920s the Hindus had found in Gandhi a major voice, a symbol of their culture and religion. In the 1920s they had also discovered a sense of unity and purpose through the rapidly growing and aggressive communal parties. The two fed into each other, always maintaining an uneasy relationship.

Muslims were usually behind the Hindus in terms of a larger idea of a united land, of planning, of organization, of locating and recruiting expert personnel. While Hindus had produced a number of all-India-level leaders, Muslims, while producing first-rate provincial leaders, had few at the national level. It was a race between a larger, more determined, better organized partner and a weaker, less organized, smaller one. And if the bigger partner turned his rivalry into physical violence then the smaller partner would find it impossible to live under the same roof. It was this sense of imbalance and the unease generated by the race with the Hindus that helped to fuel the Muslim renaissance late in the nineteenth and early in the twentieth century. Running parallel to the Muslim awakening was the continuing series of political setbacks, the two providing a dynamic interactive tension in Muslim society.

The Pakistan movement

Pakistan meant all things to all people. For some it was theology – *Pakistan ka matlab kia La'illaha illallah*, 'What is the meaning of Pakistan? "There is one God [and Muhammad is his Prophet]".' To others it was sociology. Many Muslims, including those who had little time for orthodox practice, were concerned about preserving their culture and language. Yet for others it meant economics; it meant escape from the powerful Hindu commercial and entrepreneurial presence emerging all over India. Yet to others it was an expression of the Hindu–Muslim confrontation that had been taking place for centuries; it was a challenge to those Hindus who believed they could dominate

Muslims and impose Ram Raj on them. But for everyone Pakistan meant something in terms of their identity. This is what made the movement work.

Many scholars trace the Pakistan movement to the two-nation theory Sir Sayyed had espoused which held that the Hindus and Muslims of India were separate people and needed to live separately. I would suggest we go back even earlier to look for the first stirrings of a Muslim nationalist movement. Haji Shariatullah and Dudu Mian in Bengal and Sayyed Ahmad Barelvi in northern India led movements in the first half of the nineteenth century based in the peasantry in the two areas that would become Pakistan.

Barelvi, who led a movement against the Sikhs, was a follower of Abdul Aziz, Shah Waliullah's son. Shah Waliullah had helped shape an alliance between Ahmad Shah Abdali – who had just forged the tribes of Afghanistan into a nation – and Indian Muslims to resist the tide of Hinduism. Shah Waliullah had written: 'If, God forbid, domination by infidels continues, Muslims will forget Islam and within a short time become such a nation that there will be nothing left to distinguish them from non-Muslims' (Sayeed 1968: 4). Shah Waliullah had made his thinking on Muslims in India clear: 'We are an Arab people whose fathers have fallen in exile in the country of Hindustan, and Arabic genealogy and Arabic language are our pride' (James and Roy 1992: 36). Sayyed Ahmad Barelvi echoed him a century later: 'We must repudiate all those Indian, Persian and Roman customs which are contrary to the Prophet's teaching' (ibid.).

Barelvi's attempt to impose an Islamic vision on and create an Islamic state in tribal society did not last long. He came to Peshawar with the fire of religion burning in his breast. He could not conceive of the tribal passions that he would run into, of other loyalties, of different identities. Tribal leadership, tribal organization and tribal values reasserted themselves after the initial enthusiasm for his Islamic *jihad* had abated. It was not long before he was on the run. Up in the Kaghan valley in northern Hazara he was struck down and killed. He remains a celebrated martyr in Pakistan.

Reformers like Waliullah, Barelvi and Shariatullah were not demanding a Pakistan in the modern sense of nationhood. They were, however, instrumental in creating an awareness of the crisis looming for the Muslims and the need to create their own political organization. What Sir Sayyed did was to provide a modern idiom in which to express the quest for Islamic identity.

Partly as a response to the success of Congress, partly to consolidate the Muslim position, the Muslim League was formed. It met for the first session in Dhaka in December 1906. Nawab Salimullah of Dhaka drew attention to this meeting composed of 'Mussalmans from all parts of India' dedicated to 'protect and advance the political rights and interests of the Mussalmans of India'. In 1906 a Muslim delegation visited the Viceroy, Lord Minto, with a statement of intent: 'The representative institutions of the European type ... place our national interests at the mercy of an unsympathetic majority ... we Mohommadans are a distinct community with additional interests of our own which are not shared with other communities' (Enver 1990: 13). Already the arguments for Pakistan were being rehearsed. But at first Jinnah stayed away from the League.

During and after the First World War leaders of the League attempted to make common cause with the Congress against the British. This became more difficult in the 1920s as Congress dismissed Muslim demands and Hindu revivalist parties were formed which encouraged communal riots. Memories of the events of 1857–8 also influenced developments. It is not surprising that the same area in which the uprisings took place – roughly confined to the boundaries of the UP with a few outbreaks in Bihar and central India – would provide the earliest and most enthusiastic expression of support for the Pakistan movement. Indeed it is notable that many of the influential leaders of the Muslim League came from this area.

The Muslims saw the Nehru Report, the guiding spirits of which had been Motilal and Jawaharlal Nehru, as an attempt to placate the Hindu Mahasabha (Kaura 1977: 165). Besides, Muslims were disunited and therefore could more easily be ignored by the Congress. Muslims met in Lucknow in August 1928, to consider the Nehru Report. Shaukat Ali expressed what many Muslims felt. As a young man, he said, he had been a keen owner of greyhounds, but he had never seen greyhounds deal with a hare as the Hindus proposed to deal with the Muslims. Jinnah, who had been president of the Muslim League since 1920, put forward his 'fourteen points' – amendments to the Nehru Report – on 28 December 1928. But the Muslims were disunited. Muslim leaders like Dr Ansari, Abul Kalam Azad and Abdul Kadir Kasuri (from Punjab) were in wholehearted agreement with the proposals of the Nehru Report.

When the Congress escalated resistance against the British, the Muslims were again divided. As 26 January 1930 was declared Independence Day, the resolution circulated by the Congress working committee noted: 'We hold it to be a crime against man and God to submit any longer to a rule that has caused this four-fold disaster (economic, political, cultural and spiritual) to our country' (Sayeed 1968: 76). Indians were called upon to prepare for civil disobedience, including non-payment of taxes. The campaign of civil disobedience began in March and April 1930. Significantly Muhammad Ali called upon Muslims to remain aloof from the Congress movement at a meeting of the All-India Muslim Conference at Bombay in April 1930. He denounced the Congress and Gandhi: 'Mr Gandhi is working under the influence of the communalist Hindu Mahasabha. He is fighting for the supremacy of Hinduism and the submergence of Muslims' (ibid.).

On the Muslim side, the first call for a separate political entity came from Iqbal in 1930 at the League session in Allahabad. He talked of a Muslim homeland to be formed in the north-west of India. It would, however, still be within a united India. Other thinkers were more adventurous. Chaudhry Rahmat Ali in Cambridge outlined a plan for ten Muslim states that would be part of a federation (see map 2, p. xxvii). The biggest of these would be formed by the Muslims of north-west India. He even coined a name for the state: Pakistan, an acronym for Punjab, Afghanistan, Kashmir and Baluchistan. Pakistan also meant the land of the pure from the word *pak*, pure. But the Pakistan idea still lacked a champion.

Jinnah was finally persuaded to return to India from England in 1935 and unite then lead the League. The state of the Muslim League was unimpressive until Jinnah transformed it in the late 1930s. Wajid Shamsul Hasan, the son of Shamsul Hasan, a secretary of the Muslim League, recounted how his father had often to remove the Muslim League board from outside the office so that the bailiffs would not be able to locate him for the unpaid rent. No wonder opponents like Nehru did not take it seriously. The total membership of the Muslim League in 1926 was just over a thousand. When Iqbal gave his historic address in 1930 the League did not even have its quorum of seventy-five members. The League discreetly reduced the quorum to fifty. In the early 1930s its annual expenditure did not exceed 3,000 rupees.

Jinnah hardly had time to organize his party when the elections of 1937 were on him. Predictably, the League did badly at the polls, winning only 4.6 per cent of the total Muslim vote. In the Punjab, the League won two out of 84 seats reserved for Muslims (and one of its two members soon crossed the floor to another party); in Sind, 3 out of 33; in Bengal, 39 out of 117; and in the North-West Frontier it won no seats at all. At this stage Jinnah could well have used another quote from *Hamlet*: 'The time is out of joint; O cursed spite, / That ever I was born to set it right!'

By 1940 the lines were drawn in India: a Muslim League resolution in Lahore that year demanded a separate homeland for Muslims; the Congress was determined to hold on to the idea of a strong, socialist and united India. But the Congress made a tactical error by challenging the British when their backs were against the wall during the Second World War. The Congress leadership was jailed, leaving the field wide open for Jinnah. In the 1940s the popularity of Jinnah and his League increased daily among the Muslims, and the Pakistan movement gathered pace (see plate 9).

By 1944 the Muslim League officially claimed a membership of some two million. In the 1945–6 general election it won about 4.5 million or 75 per cent of the Muslim vote (it had won only 4.6 per cent of the Muslim vote in the previous elections). It took 460 out of 533 Muslim seats in the central and provincial elections (Sayeed 1968: 178). The League was now a force in India representing a large part of the population and could not be ignored. Around this time the Muslim population reached a hundred million (it

Plate 9 Map of a projected Pakistan in the mid-1940s which includes Punjab and Bengal as full provinces in Pakistan

had been 94.4 million in the 1941 census). An impressed observer wrote:

> For those who like statistics, the figures are overwhelmingly convincing.
> With only one exception, EVERY SINGLE BY-ELECTION FOUGHT BY THE MUSLIMS
> ANYWHERE IN INDIA DURING THE LAST SEVEN YEARS HAS BEEN WON BY LEAGUE
> CANDIDATES. They were cent per cent pro-Pakistan, their programmes
> contained not the faintest shadow of the suggestion of compromise or
> prevarication, and they swept the board, every time, everywhere, in Bengal,
> in Assam, in the North-West Frontier, in Sind, in all the provinces, in fact,
> which Pakistan will eventually absorb. In the Central Legislature itself, out
> of 30 Muslim seats, 28 are held by vehement Leaguers. (Nichols 1944: 196–7)

The Muslim League won every Muslim seat in the Central Legislative Assembly and those Muslims who opposed it lost their deposits in many cases. The success of the Congress was equally impressive. The overall position in the Central Legislative Assembly was as follows: out of the 102 seats, Congress won 57 seats, Muslim League 30; independents, Sikhs and others made up the rest.

But the position in the provinces was complicated. The Muslim League could form governments only in Bengal and Sind. In the Punjab the Muslim League had won 79 out of a total of 86 Muslim seats but it still did not have a clear majority in a house of 175. The opposition along with Congress and Sikh support formed the government. Similarly Congress formed the government in the North-West Frontier Province, since it had won 19 Muslim seats as against the 17 won by the Muslim League.

It is noteworthy that the successes of the Muslim League were a result of the Muslims seeing it as a *Muslim* movement. Although many of the religious figures were indifferent to the Pakistan movement many others supported it vigorously. According to a prominent religious leader, Maulana Zafar Ahmad Usmani, Jinnah had himself requested the *ulema* to help the League in these campaigns. Another religious figure, Maulana Niazi, in his speeches captured the essence of the Muslim position: 'We have got two alternatives before us, whether to join or rather accept the slavery of *bania* Brahman Raj in Hindustan or join the Muslim fraternity, the federation of Muslim provinces. Every Pathan takes it as an insult to prostrate before Hindu Raj and will gladly sit with his brethren in Islam in the Pakistan Constituent Assembly' (Sayeed 1968: 205).

Putting Pakistan on hold

If there were three histories – British, Hindu and Muslim – running simultaneously, unresolved and problematic, by 1947 the Muslims had forced a separation. They had demanded and established a separate history of their own. The Pakistan idea appeared irresistible and widespread among Muslims, Pakistan itself inevitable. But the road to Pakistan was not as straight as Pakistanis like to think. In 1946 Jinnah accepted what was known as the Cabinet Mission Plan, which proposed a federation of Indian provinces for the future. Many Leaguers, including influential figures like Maulana Hasrat Mohani, opposed Jinnah.

Was this not risky, considering Muslims are notorious for their short attention span and brief bursts of action? Muslim movements are invariably quick, sharp, furious affairs. Once the momentum has been lost, a leader often finds himself looking in vain for his dispersed followers. By 1946 the Pakistan movement was reaching a climax. Had Pakistan not happened soon, the probability is that it would have never happened. The momentum would have dissipated and no other political leader in India could have stepped into Jinnah's shoes and regenerated it. Besides, the inevitable strong centre in Delhi after 1947 would have ensured that no such Pakistan movement would grow. Jinnah would have probably been arrested and sent to a rest-house in southern India to spend his last days in isolation. For those who think this improbable, the example of Sheikh Abdullah, Nehru's friend who helped him get Kashmir for India, is salutary. Unhappy with the fate of his people, Sheikh Abdullah protested and was put under house arrest to languish far from his home in northern India for years.

On the face of it Jinnah had given up the demand for a separate Pakistan. What was he thinking? Several answers suggest themselves. The dramatic one is that he knew by then that he was dying and that the new state of Pakistan would not be able to survive without him and therefore he needed to put it off. But then why did he accept Pakistan a year later?

Another answer is that he continued to think of the Muslims of the subcontinent as a whole and by accepting the Cabinet Mission Plan he would not only secure the rights of those living as a majority in some provinces but also those living as a minority. As a lawyer, he had noted the escape clause in the plan which allowed the Muslims to leave the Indian union if they wished to do so in the decennial review of the constitution. Besides, the Cabinet Mission Plan envisaged that the provinces would not be divided – something that Mountbatten would do the following year and thereby cause so much bloodshed.

Or perhaps it was just a bluff. Jinnah knew Nehru well. He had called him 'Peter Pan', the boy who never grew up (Wolpert 1996: 44). He knew that Nehru would not stomach the continued presence of the Muslim League in his India. Nehru would get rid of the headache by cutting off the head. When, predictably, Nehru rejected the Cabinet Mission Plan, it was the last straw.

In the middle of 1946 Jinnah supported an act which violated his known principles of upholding the law. Frustrated at what he saw as British and Congress perfidy, he called for a meeting of the Muslim League Council on 28 July in Bombay. He made his exasperation clear: 'All efforts of the Muslim League at fair-play, justice, even supplication and prayers have had no response of any kind from the Congress ... the Cabinet Mission have played into the hands of the Congress.... Pandit Jawaharlal Nehru as the elected President made the policy and attitude of the Congress clear.... Congress was committed to nothing' (Wolpert 1996: 370). The next day the League Council voted for direct action to achieve Pakistan, and 16 August was chosen by the League as 'Direct Action' day. A civil war situation developed, with Hindus and Muslims fighting each other in many parts of India; Calcutta was the scene of horrific rioting. Nehru saw the situation as a direct challenge to the Interim Government which he headed as Vice-President. Although the campaign for direct action was called off, Bengal and Bihar experienced rioting in the following months (Gandhi's efforts to bring communal peace and comfort to the victims were magnificent). Influential members of the Congress were coming round to the view that perhaps there was no realistic solution but the parting of the ways; that Jinnah was right. Pakistan, it appeared, was the solution.

Jinnah and the Pakistan Movement

Sahibzada Yaqub Khan, adjutant of the Viceroy's bodyguard and later commandant of the Governor-General's bodyguard in Pakistan, recounted the conversation at a private dinner in 1947 with Lord Ismay, then Mountbatten's Chief of Staff, who had just returned from a meeting with Jinnah. Ismay told the guests that his impression was that if Jinnah was offered even a matchbox with the word Pakistan on it he would accept it.

When partition was announced, the major provinces of Bengal and Punjab were to be divided between India and Pakistan; the Sind province came complete to Pakistan. In addition a referendum was to be held in June–July 1947, to decide the future of the North-West Frontier Province, Baluchistan and the Sylhet district. In each case the majority voted for joining Pakistan. There were question marks over some decisions. For instance, Gurdaspur and Ferozepur – Muslim-majority districts which were also contiguous to what would become Pakistan – were inexplicably transferred to India (see next chapter).

Jinnah's choice

Like the eponymous heroine of the novel and film *Sophie's Choice* who was forced to choose one of her two children to take to safety from the horrors of the Nazi camps, Jinnah was faced with a similar decision. Ideally he would have liked to save both the Muslims in the minority provinces who would be left behind in India and those in the majority provinces who would become Pakistanis. As late as 1946 he avoided making Sophie's choice by accepting the Cabinet Mission Plan, which allowed both to stay within India and therefore united. After Nehru rejected the plan there was no way out for Jinnah and he was forced to make a decision. Jinnah therefore had to make that most terrible of choices, and he decided to opt for the safety of at least half of the Muslims of South Asia.

In concluding this chapter we note the increasing numbers of people attending key meetings of the Muslim League to illustrate the support Jinnah was gathering from 1937 onwards. In 1930 at Lucknow, fewer than 75 people had turned up to hear Iqbal's presidential address. From 1937, when Jinnah presided, the attendance figures show the changing picture:

1937   Lucknow: 5,000
1940   Lahore: almost 100,000
1941   Madras: over 100,000
1948   Dhaka: 300,000

In 1948, in Karachi, an estimated one million people accompanied Jinnah's funeral cortege.

Contrary to Nehru's remarks quoted at the beginning of this chapter, Jinnah was far from being lonely or isolated. The increasing numbers of people he attracted and the different venues contradict two points in the propaganda against Jinnah: that Jinnah's was never a mass movement and that it was restricted to one or two areas. The expansion from 50 people, when the Muslim League in 1930 could not gather its quorum of 75, to the million who attended Jinnah's last journey in 1948 demonstrates the enthusiasm for Jinnah and the Pakistan movement.

CHAPTER 5

Mountbatten: Last Viceroy and First Paki-Basher

> Nothing we could do. After three hundred years of India we have made this whole, damned, bloody, senseless mess.
>
> (from *The Jewel in the Crown*, Granada television, 1984)

At the climax of *The Jewel in the Crown*, it is the summer of 1947. The heroine of the British television dramatization of Paul Scott's novel is standing at a railway station when she makes her statement about 'three hundred years of India'. She is surrounded by bleeding, dead and dying Muslims. Their train has just been attacked by Hindus. It is a scene of carnage.

What a disgraceful end to what the British boasted was the greatest prize in their colonial empire, India. The scale of the killings, the disorderly transfer of populations, the setting of the arguments for constant wars between neighbours in South Asia are all directly related to the events of 1947. How it could have ended differently will continue to be debated. The fact of the matter is that the British added India to the list of their possessions in 1858 in blood and chaos, and less than a hundred years later handed it back to the Indians in the same way – with about two million killed and almost fifteen million permanently displaced. It was a shameful epitaph to their colonial and administrative skills. British rule became a short-lived but powerful indictment of imperialism.

There had been many good things. There was the British educational system, the schools and universities in India. There was the English language, which enabled South Asians to interact with the West, even to make an international mark – Ved Mehta, Salman Rushdie, Vikram Seth. There was the sport: cricket and hockey. There was, above all, the Indian Civil Service as well as the military services which were, thanks to the training and the *esprit de corps* in the regiments, among the finest in the world. Indeed, after independence, at their best the defence institutions vied with the mother country itself – the Staff College in Quetta, the Defence College in Islamabad, the Pakistan Military Academy in Kakul, the Indian Military Academy in Dera Doon. This was part of the Anglo-Indian encounter.

But the bitter legacy of partition remains to haunt the land. The British, having been in control for a full century, their regiments always ready to march to maintain order and their efficiently organized Civil Service in place, were, in a few weeks, reduced to helpless bystanders, their empire unravelling before their eyes. The makers of history had been reduced to the observers of history. The anguish of the girl in *The Jewel in the Crown* came from the fact that it need not have ended like this. There could have been a more orderly, a more dignified, withdrawal, a more lasting relationship between India and Pakistan if there had been a less impetuous, emotional and partisan Viceroy in Delhi than Lord Mountbatten.

Mountbatten's mission

In the twelve-part television series filmed in 1967, *The Life and Times of Lord Mountbatten*, Mountbatten recounted how he was selected as the last Viceroy to hand over a united India to Indians peacefully. He was given plenipotentiary powers, a *carte blanche* to deal with India as he saw fit, the only time such powers were given this century. The King-Emperor George VI, in an audience, expected him to save the day, do the British proud. Mountbatten said it was a difficult task and the chances of failure were high. Yes, retorted the King, but if you succeed it will redound to the glory of the monarchy. Everything henceforth would be done for maximum public effect, to project the idea behind Mountbatten's appointment. This became Mountbatten's mission.

Fifty years ago Britain, for so long the world's leading imperial power, could no longer sustain its empire. After India was granted independence, the British empire would gradually disintegrate over the next two decades. In 1947 Lord Mountbatten, a great-grandson of Queen Victoria and a cousin of George VI, would have appeared an ideal choice to be the last Viceroy of India. Whether or not he was well qualified for the job, he symbolized the British monarchy and empire, and this would be immensely reassuring not only to the British establishment but to the Indian aristocracy.

However, although Churchill had given him considerable responsibilities during the war, appointing him Chief of Combined Operations and then Supreme Allied Commander of South-East Asia, Mountbatten's background was mainly in military matters. He may have found himself virtual ruler of the disordered countries of South-East Asia for a few months after the Japanese surrender in 1945, but he had no experience whatsoever of complex political administration in peacetime. Yet in 1947 he arrived as imperial ruler of India with plenipotentiary powers – full authority to act at his own discretion and make decisions affecting the lives of millions of people. In contrast, when the last vestiges of empire were being shed in the 1990s, an experienced former government minister in the very unaristocratic person of Chris Patten was appointed Governor of Hong Kong, to oversee the process of decolonization there. No matter how popular a figure Mountbatten might have been, the responsibility he was being given in India was far in excess of his competence.

In a nutshell this was the problem that faced Mountbatten on his arrival: India's princely states (over 500 in number), 3,000 castes divided into 400 million people (including 250 million Hindus, 90 million Muslims and 6 million Sikhs) speaking twenty-three languages were somehow to be given independence peacefully and, if possible, kept within one country. The diversity ranged from isolated tribal groups untouched by modern ways to the 2 million soldiers who had fought on the side of the British during the Second World War. They had seen something of the world, witnessed comrades fall, and many had won the Victoria Cross for extraordinary courage; 200,000 had been wounded and 25,000 had died for the King. They were, like their countrymen, ready for independence.

The appeal of the idea of unity is greater than that of disunity: India as one united nation from the Khyber Pass to the southernmost tip of the peninsula. For those rulers of the subcontinent with an imperial vision, from Asoka to Akbar to Curzon, the unity of the land had been a cardinal principle of central government.

Mountbatten's historic mission was to transfer power to the Indians as peacefully and swiftly as possible. The British could then say with pride that they had ruled India for a full century and had been able to hand back India honourably and efficiently. Mountbatten, upon his arrival, seriously negotiated with the Congress and the Muslim League. When it became clear to him that the Muslim League would not be convinced of a united India he conceded a Pakistan.

Once out of South Asia, the British would be able to say that they granted independence in the most friendly manner possible. Britain had handed over power and legitimacy to two sovereign states with functioning administrative structures fully in place. Significantly, both countries, after independence, had friendly relations with Britain and became members of the Commonwealth. A vital consideration for Britain would be continuing trade and diplomatic relations with India and Pakistan, which were successfully safeguarded.

One has to compare the British achievement to the experience of the French in Algeria or South-East Asia or indeed the Dutch in Indonesia. These European imperial powers prolonged the inevitable as they hung on to their colonies as long as possible with terror and violence mounting. The legacy of hatred for the colonial power remained for decades in their ex-colonies. In South Asia, in spite of the actual bloody transfer of power, this was rarely true.

The last imperial action hero

Mountbatten always imagined himself as a Hollywood hero, the last imperial action hero. He certainly had all the Hollywood ingredients including star-quality good looks, in contrast to the homely and plain-looking Viceroy he replaced, Lord Archibald Wavell. In addition he was energetic, charming, bold, and not yet forty-seven years old. During the Second World War, in 1942 he had become Chief of Combined Operations and the next year was appointed Supreme Allied Commander in South-East Asia, responsible for the recapture of Burma from Japan. Under his command, the Japanese invasion of India had been halted and Japanese troops driven out of Burma.

Earl Mountbatten of Burma (as he became in 1947) had received the surrender of the Japanese in Singapore. To the sound of trumpets and fanfare of bugles he now arrived in India to save the situation for the British. He was the one man who could lead them out of their declining empire. He was already casting an eye on the immortals in the imperial hall of fame and comparing himself to Lord Clive, an eighteenth-century founder of the empire. Mountbatten even died as a representative of empire when in 1979 he was blown up by a bomb planted on his fishing boat in Donegal Bay, near his home in County Sligo in Ireland; the IRA claimed responsibility for the bombing, stating that Mountbatten had been 'executed' in order to draw attention to Britain's imperialist tradition.

Earl Mountbatten's father, Prince Louis Alexander of Battenburg, had married Queen Victoria's granddaughter Princess Victoria of Hesse and was First Sea Lord from 1912 to 1914, having entered the Royal Navy in 1868 after being naturalized as a British citizen. Yet when Britain entered the First World War he was forced to resign from the Admiralty, and at the request of King George V anglicized his family's German name to Mountbatten. Young Lord Louis, who looked up to his father, would always have an ambition to make good in the navy, to succeed at all costs. The treatment meted out to his father as a German, the thinly disguised prejudice, would never be forgotten. He would become the champion of the British empire, more English than the English. There was a hankering for medals and honours which displayed itself to the last.

Mountbatten often dressed in full naval regalia, all the medals displayed on his chest. He so obviously wanted to do good, to be loved and remembered. The Indians could hardly be expected to resist his formidable arsenal of glitter and glamour, cajoling and coercing. If he failed it would reflect not only on him but also on the British. He saw himself as a man of crisis, the man of the hour.

Edwina, Lady Mountbatten, was as much of a star as her husband (see also chapter 6). Lord Attlee in his memoirs mentions that one of Lord Mountbatten's greatest assets was his wife Edwina: 'In these personal relations Lord Mountbatten was immensely assisted by his wife' (Hodson 1985: 206). The Indian perception of the Mountbattens was similar: 'Mountbatten had, of course, great personal assets: good looks, links with royalty, a dazzling war reputation, a wife of charm and intelligence' (Gopal 1975: 342). If in his mind he was the dashing hero and Lady Mountbatten, whom he called the 'divine Edwina', the gracious heroine, then he also had, in his impetuous boyish way, identified the good guys and the villain. Gandhi and Nehru were the amiable sidekicks, the hero's companions; the evil villain, sinister and forbidding, was Jinnah.

I am not criticizing Mountbatten's intentions or instincts or indeed his objectives. They were by and large correct. Like very few English people before him, certainly very few of his predecessors, he had a gut understanding of India. Like no previous British administrator he could mingle with Indians and be one of them and, above all, be accepted as one of them. Mountbatten brought a fresh approach. One of his first actions on arrival in India was to appoint six ADCs, three British and three Indian, to the Viceroy's staff. The Indian appointments were a break with British Indian tradition. It was also a good sign, a happy omen of how the new Viceroy would deal with Indians.

What I am objecting to is not Mountbatten's intentions but the implementation of his objectives. These are to be seriously challenged and faulted. He was there as an impartial Viceroy, a neutral referee, between two opposed parties. By becoming closely involved with one party he compromised his neutrality. He thus became not only ineffective but morally vulnerable. The deaths and the subsequent unending confrontation between

India and Pakistan are in that sense traceable to his poor implementation of what were solid and sensible ideas.

Instead of remaining neutral, Lord and Lady Mountbatten were decidedly pro-Hindu. From the first meetings with Nehru they had declared their hand. The staff around Lord Mountbatten took their cue from their master. Not only was there a natural bias towards the Hindus in Delhi but the personal relationships we discuss in chapter 6 ensured that Jinnah was permanently cut off from access to the heart of power. Important British officials had picked up the signs. Field Marshal Claude Auchinleck, commander-in-chief of the Indian army, observed that 'Mountbatten was already a partisan before he arrived' (Hamid 1986: 139).

Mountbatten's assignment to try to preserve the unity of India and hand over power peacefully to the Indians was difficult enough, but within days of his arrival Mountbatten made his task almost impossible by compromising the neutrality of his high office. He remarked that the idea of Pakistan was 'mad', even though it was supported by the second largest political party in India, the Muslim League (Zaidi 1993: volume I, part II, 654).

To be fair to him Mountbatten had been appointed to a near-hopeless enterprise. We know it was a zero-sum situation between the two parties and two communities. Every time one gained the other lost, and vice-versa. No Viceroy could be totally impartial. The more the Indians won, the more the Pakistanis would lose; every subdivision, every district was the same. Mountbatten's game was to keep chipping down the original idea of Pakistan, down from the two full provinces to two half-provinces, to cut out Calcutta, to remove the districts of Gurdaspur and Ferozepur from the Pakistan borders, to ensure that Kashmir and Hyderabad would fall into the lap of India. There was no certainty in the middle of 1947 where these areas would go. The argument to join them to Pakistan was as strong as the argument to remove them from it. But Mountbatten had made up his mind.

A suitable Viceroy

Mountbatten had been identified as a suitable Viceroy to lead India to independence, not only because he was a cousin of the King-Emperor but because he had also got the stamp of approval of Nehru.

Nehru had met the Mountbattens in Singapore in 1946 and the three had hit it off. Mountbatten made a genuine effort to win over the nationalist leader. When Lord Wavell proved a difficult Viceroy to manipulate, the Congress high command used its powerful links in London to pass the word round that a new Viceroy would be desirable. Indians like Krishna Menon, Nehru's trusted friend and roving ambassador, had important connections in the British Labour Party, having even been a Labour councillor for St Pancras in London in 1934–47. Among his friends were Bertrand Russell and Aneurin Bevan. Mountbatten was 'Krishna Menon's first choice to be the last British Viceroy of India' (Wolpert 1996: 361) and had met him in London before he flew out to India as Viceroy in March.

In 1945 Labour came to power, with Clement Attlee as Prime Minister. Attlee, like his colleagues, was determined to give India honourable independence. But he also sympathized with the Congress leadership, which had many links with the Labour Party. Some of the key Congress players – Nehru as well as Krishna Menon – were accepted by the Labour Party as fellow socialists. Labour promised a new world for Britain, a world based on equality, a fairer distribution of wealth, an end to the old class system and exploitation of the working class. The Congress had a similar vision for India.

A conversation with Tony Benn confirmed for me that Attlee was a typical Labour leader in the 1940s. Part of his programme was to grant independence to the imperial colonies. Already several British government representatives, including Sir Stafford Cripps, had tried but failed to negotiate an agreement with the Indian leaders. Attlee was sincere in wanting to hand over power to the Indians in India, but India to him meant the Indian Congress. Jinnah not only demanded the break-up of India but represented a mainstream Muslim movement. In February 1947 Attlee announced that his government would relinquish power in India no later than 30 June 1948. Once Attlee had appointed Mountbatten, India's fate was sealed as far as Pakistan was concerned. It was more than bad luck for Pakistan; everything would be stacked against it.

Attlee's appointment of Mountbatten as Viceroy was not seen as curious at the time. After all, it was not generally known that Mountbatten had taken a ship out to sea and virtually invited the Germans to sink it and then followed this disaster with his planning of the Dieppe raid which resulted in the slaughter of thousands of allied troops. Wartime secrecy enabled him to conceal such fiascos at first, and the post-war British establishment tended to gloss over its members' misdemeanours in the interest of keeping up appearances. In any case Attlee himself had been educated at public school and Oxford and was no anti-establishment rebel.

When the BBC journalist Mark Tully asked Attlee who was the most difficult man he had ever dealt with in his life, the name Jinnah sprang to Attlee's lips without a moment's hesitation (Mark Tully interviewing me for BBC Radio 4, 23 February 1995, Cambridge). Jinnah had ruined Attlee's plans for a neat and tidy end to British history in India. Jinnah was proving that there are no neat and tidy solutions when religious passions are roused and injustice is in the air, a lesson very clear to us in the 1990s.

Meeting the Mountbattens

But how could I hope to understand Jinnah if I did not understand his main adversary, Mountbatten? In an attempt to gain some insight, in the summer of 1994 I wrote to Patricia, Countess Mountbatten of Burma, the elder daughter of Lord Mountbatten and, during his life, a close confidante. She invited me to her London home. Later, I met her sister, Lady Pamela Hicks.

If I could not condone or sympathize with Mountbatten's actions in 1947 I certainly understood him better after meeting his daughters at the family home of Lady Pamela Hicks, The Grove, at Brightwell Baldwin, near Oxford (see plate 10). The Mountbatten family genealogy going back a thousand years, the dazzling full-length portraits, the trophies and treasures were overpowering. Meeting his daughters enabled me to envisage Mountbatten for the first time. Here was a man of monumental ego, a man convinced of his destiny, a man not prepared to respond to any other vision but his own – not necessarily a bad or evil man but a man of dangerous vanity.

Plate 10   The author with Countess Mountbatten and Lady Pamela Hicks in 1994

The daughters fully accepted their father's interpretation of Indian history. All the main figures were characterized in the expected way: Gandhi was a saint, Nehru a charmer, Mr Jinnah ... well, 'awe-inspiring', 'like a schoolmaster', 'not warm'. They were courteous, but firm, in an aristocratic manner.

Mountbatten came to India with strong, clear-cut notions of how to deal with the situation. He would perform the task quickly, hand over power, leave in a blaze of glory, for he was anxious to return to his naval career. What he did not see was how deep the chasm had become between Hindus and Muslims. He was not prepared to accept the alternative view of reality on the ground. To him Jinnah represented the forces of disunity and had to be opposed. His dislike of Jinnah was partly determined by his attempt to impose his own vision of the world on Jinnah.

I learned much of this through my conversations with Mountbatten's daughters. Almost half a century later they still did not appreciate why Pakistan had been necessary, why Jinnah had fought for a Pakistan, why the Muslims had felt threatened. They, like their father, had an idealistic notion of a non-violent land, of peaceful natives coexisting with each other. I found it difficult to convey the deep differences between the communities.

The Viceroy and decision-making in British India

Great events in history are sometimes shaped by economic and political factors, sometimes by the direct intervention of people at the helm of affairs. In the summer of

1947 decisions which would affect millions of people and set the pattern for history in the entire region were being made by one or two people. The Viceroy of India, aided by a handful of personnel, had spread the map of India on a table and with a pen demarcated what were to become the two states of India and Pakistan. Seldom in history was there such a concentration of power.

Theirs was an almost impossible task. Tribes and communities and villages were sometimes cut in two; people who had lived together for centuries were suddenly on the other side of an international border. In East Pakistan the platform of a railway station fell in one country, the ticket office in another.

The Congress high command was clear about the future. They wanted power and they wanted it quickly. They wished to administer India through a strong centre and set about building a modern nation. They had fought long and hard to take independence from the British and they were not to be stopped at the finishing post by Jinnah and the Muslim League. They gave in to the Pakistan demand however reluctantly, but it was done with bad grace. The high command expressed its doubts about Pakistan in public. It was a temporary concession and sooner rather than later Pakistan would return to the fold.

The final outcome of partition, the final shape of the two countries, depended as much on what political support the leaders could muster and the strength of the argument as, ultimately, on the capacity of the leaders to convince the Viceroy. In this Jinnah and the Muslims were unlucky.

In the late twentieth century we are accustomed to major decisions being made democratically in a public manner after debates in Parliament or other elected political assemblies and against a background of public discussion. It is increasingly difficult for one individual to make a major decision affecting millions of people on the basis of his or her own opinion without expert consultation.

The Viceroy of India could do precisely that. The power of the Viceroy to make rapid decisions on the basis of experience, judgement and advice was the greatest asset of the British Indian empire. It allowed one individual to react swiftly to events taking place far away from London: there were no bureaucratic interferences or delays. The system worked particularly well in a crisis when there was greater need for an immediate unified response. The Viceroy was virtually unaccountable to anyone; furthermore, Mountbatten came to India with plenipotentiary powers. He was perhaps one of the most powerful Viceroys in the history of the subcontinent. With such immense authority the Viceroy had no difficulty in getting his point of view across; a suggestion, a hint, was enough.

In the summer of 1947 there were no public debates, there was no consultation with a body of experts, there were no discussions in the press. Mountbatten, aided by his personal staff, made the decisions that would affect the future of India and Pakistan. That is why access to and friendship with the Viceroy became crucial.

People who do not know the structure of British India and are too remote from events half a century away will argue that so much power vested in one individual is unlikely. Unfortunately in 1947 this is exactly what happened. Besides, Mountbatten rode roughshod over wiser opinions offered to him. He was notorious for ignoring the recommendations of many of the experienced officers; there are records of numerous experienced administrators advising him and being snubbed. As Noel Coward, playing Mountbatten's character as a war hero in the film *In Which We Serve*, said, 'I like things done quickly.' Philip Ziegler, Mountbatten's official biographer, said in the Channel 4 television documentary on Mountbatten: 'He was going much too fast quite often in the wrong direction and as a result ended up in the wrong place at the wrong time' (*Secret Lives*, March 1995). Mountbatten believed in hunches, in instinct, in his own judgement and in those whom he trusted. In 1947 Lady Mountbatten and Nehru were two of his closest advisers, with disastrous results for the subcontinent.

The Viceroy had a large staff of ADCs and so on, some of whom were Muslim. Muhammad Ahsan, who would later become commander-in-chief of the Pakistan Navy, and Sahibzada Yaqub, who would be a general in the Pakistan Army and then Foreign Minister, were on the Viceroy's staff. The Mountbattens liked them and years later when I interviewed their daughters they spoke of them with warmth. Indeed, they quoted their father explaining his fairness and even-handedness: he even gave up Ahsan, his ADC, to Pakistan.

Real decision-making on matters relating to partition, however, rested with Mountbatten's kitchen cabinet and members of the newly formed Boundary Commission. In that select number were two Hindus, V. P. Menon in the former and V. D. Iyer in the latter. Both were committed, well-informed, highly intelligent Indian nationalists. After the departure of the British they would continue to shine in the Indian government. Indeed, Menon would ruthlessly and efficiently spearhead the absorption of the princely states of India into the Indian union. They were in close touch with the Congress high command, especially Nehru and Patel. In the summer of 1947, Menon and Iyer manipulated and organized the partition of the subcontinent along lines that would favour the future Indian government, even at the cost of not giving Pakistan its just share, as we shall see below.

To aid Mountbatten in the task of dividing India, the British government had sent out Sir Cyril Radcliffe, a distinguished lawyer who was appointed the head of the Boundary Commission to plan the partition of Punjab and Bengal. As he had never been east of Suez before, had only been in India for six weeks and knew practically nothing about India, Sir Cyril was totally out of his depth. According to his secretary, Christopher Beaumont, he was amenable to pressure from Mountbatten. Indeed Mountbatten himself was later to muse to Lapierre and Collins, 'I'll tell you something ghastly. The reasons behind his Awards weren't very deep-seated at all' (Roberts 1994a: 97).

Of course common sense dictated most of the decisions. Those states contiguous to or in India or Pakistan joined that nation; similarly those along the borders with the majority of that particular religion joined that particular state. But Mountbatten altered this process in several cases: in the Muslim-majority districts of Ferozepur and Gurdaspur and, most fatally for the subcontinent, in the Muslim state of Kashmir.

How Mountbatten persuaded the Indian states to join India or Pakistan was illustrated in an anecdote recounted in his television series. Is this history, the record of events that actually took place, or simply Mountbatten's version? If the former it also reflects badly on the Indians princes, who appear gullible and spineless – the idiot natives of colonial caricature.

Mountbatten was pushing the rulers of the princely states of India to opt for India or Pakistan in the Chamber of Princes. With one stroke he was going to terminate centuries of history, social obligations and legal treaties. The princes were demanding their own independent grouping – neither India nor Pakistan – on the basis of strong legal, cultural and historical arguments. Some states were as big as European countries and had histories of independent rule at least as old as theirs. Then the Chief Minister to one of the princes announced that his master was on the high seas and could not be consulted. Picking up a crystal paperweight, Mountbatten peered at it. 'A picture is forming,' he murmured. 'Yes, I can see the ruler. He wishes you to sign the agreement.' Upon hearing this the Chief Minister signed. Others followed suit. The Viceroy played the Pied Piper for the Indian princes.

The steel frame

An understanding of the British administrative structure in India is important to an appreciation of the role, status and authority of the Viceroy. The philosophy of Plato's guardians permeated the élite British administration. Indeed, a member of the élite corps, the Indian Civil Service, the famed ICS, looking back, called his book *The Guardians* (Woodruff 1965).

The secret of the British in India was straightforward: clarity of organization and unity of purpose. Neither was to be affected over the century they were there. The British ruled India not through military force nor through investing vast resources in it. They ruled through an administrative structure that was breathtaking in its simplicity and effectiveness. Authority and power were concentrated in a few hundred members of the ICS. They headed the districts, and each district in turn formed part of a division which, in turn, formed part of a province, all of which were under the Viceroy. It was perhaps the most effective administrative system in the entire colonial world, superior to anything the Germans, the French or the Dutch had evolved.

The general level of intelligence, competence and dedication of the ICS was acknowledged even by its critics. These civil servants were expected to be the ideal administrator/scholar/judge/executive; the virtues of action and thought fused in them. They were the best representatives of the Raj, benign father figures, the steel frame that propped up the entire structure. That is how they saw themselves and that is how many natives saw them. Indeed, they called them *mai-baap*, 'mother-father', in rural India. If imperial administrators were considered *mai-baap* by Indians then the Viceroy was the Big Daddy of them all. Yet the last Viceroy by his actions set in motion a sequence of events which would cost millions of lives and disrupt millions more in the most traumatic manner possible. This was infanticide on a scale that would make Nero a model father.

The district administrative structure explains why the British could so effectively control the subcontinent. The question of how a few thousand British controlled an entire world is thus resolved. Indian nationalists caricature the ICS in terms of divide and rule, arguing that the British created the divisions in order to rule. In fact the rifts were already there in society. Leaders of both communities had begun to recognize that the only solution was to have a relationship with the British to secure their own future. For the Hindus the struggle was not so simple. Although they wanted independence from the British they did not want a reversion to the old order; they wanted a new order.

The Muslims on the other hand wanted nothing but a reversion to the old order where they would once again dominate India as they had in the past. So they had two different objectives. There was an inherent structure of conflict between the two which the British could easily exploit; they did not have to create it.

The clash of the titans

The British and the Congress were united on one point: they were determined to preserve the unity of India; the former for reasons of the past, as a parting tribute and monument to their empire; the latter to create their own empire in the future. India's diversity and the political realities on the ground with the mounting violence between Hindus and Muslims were ignored in this perspective. Both saw one man forming an obstacle to the unity of India: Mohammed Ali Jinnah.

To nearly all the British in India 'the idea of partition was horrifying' (see Raj comments in, for example, Allen 1975). Many saw it as 'the biggest disaster of the whole of British rule' which 'undid the greatest thing we had done during the Raj, which was to unify India'. Few had any doubts as to who was responsible. Ian Stephens, editor of the *Statesman*, noted how hostile Lord Mountbatten and his staff were to Jinnah (1963: 174). This is confirmed by Sahibzada Yaqub. British statesmen, administrators and writers opposed Pakistan because it meant the end of their Raj dreams as well as the break-up of the institutions that they prided themselves on – the army and the Civil Service (ibid.: 15). The idea of dividing the army was 'particularly distressing' (ibid.). 'British governing circles' therefore had a 'distaste' for Pakistan (ibid.). Christopher Beaumont informed me that most civil servants were against Jinnah's idea of dividing India. However, he admitted that now, looking back, Jinnah was 'probably right'. A British official in India who observed political developments leading up to partition had no illusions about the forces ranged against Jinnah:

> In judging Jinnah, we must remember what he was up against. He had against him not only the wealth and brains of the Hindus, but also nearly the whole of British officialdom, and most of the Home politicians, who made the great mistake of refusing to take Pakistan seriously. Never was his position really examined. (Sir Francis Mudie, in Bolitho 1954: 208)

Mountbatten's relationship with Nehru must also be clarified. Pakistani passion must not cloud the fact that he was, on arrival, dealing with Nehru primarily because he represented the Indian Congress. Indeed, Nehru was already, for all practical purposes, the acting Prime Minister of India, the Prime Minister designate of independent India. The close working relationship of Nehru and Mountbatten cannot be faulted. But informal personal links between the Mountbattens and Nehru reinforced the latter's official position and helped further his cause, most notably during the partition, as we shall see in chapter 6. Matters of state were influenced by the personal chemistry of friendship and dislike.

Mountbatten: Viceroy and Paki-Basher

Personal chemistry

In his television programme Mountbatten explained his view of statecraft. He had said at the start of the programme that he felt 'everything was going to depend on personal relationships'. Gandhi had called him and Edwina 'dear friends'. It meant a lot to him. Mountbatten repeated this twice in the film. His admiration of Gandhi appeared to be genuine (although he later changed his opinion). Gandhi in Bengal, Mountbatten said, was equal to four divisions of soldiers. Gandhi was 'a modern-day saint'. 'Nehru was already a friend,' declared Mountbatten, even before he became Viceroy. But 'he was more than a friend'; there was 'complete mutual trust'. Mountbatten confessed that Jinnah was 'the man who I had the greatest difficulty in getting through to'. Mountbatten always 'hated' the idea of partition.

After the first official meeting between Mountbatten and Nehru the Viceroy wrote: 'Pandit Nehru struck me as most sincere' (Ziegler 1985: 367). On this occasion 'they talked as much as anything of Jinnah, of whom Nehru spoke with mingled respect and loathing' (ibid.). Mountbatten, it seems, had already made up his mind about Jinnah before they had even become acquainted. After his first meeting with Jinnah on 5 April 1947 Mountbatten noted, 'My God, he was cold!' Not long afterwards he compared Nehru ('a really great man') and Jinnah ('a megalomaniac'). For Mountbatten Gandhi was 'an old poppet' (ibid.: 369). Every other Indian leader except for Jinnah was given a first name or bare surname but throughout his private and informal diary Mountbatten refers to Jinnah as Mr Jinnah. 'Time and again carrots were dangled for Nehru, whereas Jinnah only ever experienced the stick,' observed the British historian Andrew Roberts (1994a: 87).

In contrast Chaudhri Muhammad Ali refers to Jinnah speaking of Mountbatten in 'unusually warm terms' about the Viceroy's integrity and goodwill on his arrival (Ziegler 1985: 369). But towards the end of June Jinnah expressed his antipathy towards Mountbatten, who he claimed was in the pocket of Nehru (ibid.).

The tensions between the Mountbattens and Jinnah often degenerated into farce. One story about Jinnah's supposed *faux pas* with the Mountbattens was recounted by Edwina Mountbatten's biographer (critics rarely miss it; see, for example, Akbar 1988a: 397; Collins and Lapierre 1994: 100):

> Photographers had assembled in the garden to take pictures of the meeting and Jinnah, expecting that Edwina would stand between himself and Dickie [Mountbatten], had prepared an appropriate remark. 'A rose between two thorns!' he exclaimed gallantly – too late, for he found that he was in the middle himself, with a Mountbatten on either side. (Morgan 1991: 394–5)

When the British tell this story there is the implicit suggestion of the native muddling his English. But was Jinnah confusing his English, the language of Shakespeare, the author he loved so well and often cited? Was this Jinnah the masterly and razor-sharp lawyer who spoke English so well? Or was this a Freudian slip? To Jinnah the Mountbattens were indeed thorns; to the Muslims of India he was the rose.

Making fun of Jinnah's English exposes Mountbatten as it draws attention to his own carelessness. He had written to Edwina, 'You happen to be my first, principle [*sic*] and truest friend' (Morgan 1991: 199). Nehru wrote to Edwina after a suitably inscribed silver cigarette box was given to him by Mountbatten: 'For your private ear I might tell you, provided you do not tell Dickie, that the spelling of my name was all wrong. I make no grievance of it. Indeed in a way I like this mistake which makes the inscription characteristic of Dickie; who has thus far failed to grasp completely how my name should be written or pronounced' (Ziegler 1985: 473).

Jinnah and Mountbatten seem to have adopted opposite methods of approaching a problem. Recall Mountbatten in the Chamber of Princes treating the Indian princes like fools. Jinnah on the other hand was never condescending towards his opponents. He stuck to his rational arguments, as this assessment illustrates:

> Jinnah had been almost brutally critical of British policy ... but his criticism had been clear and creative. It was not merely a medley of wild words, a hotchpotch of hatred and hallucination, in the Hindu manner. It was more like a diagnosis. The difference between Jinnah and the typical Hindu politician was the difference between a surgeon and a witch doctor. Moreover, he was a surgeon you could trust, even though his verdict was harsh. (Nichols 1944: 191)

The images of the two that stay in the mind are of Mountbatten attempting to charm Jinnah and then, once he has said goodbye, turning to his aide to describe him in foul language: 'bastard', 'psychopath', 'egomaniac'. A related image is of Jinnah returning from his meetings with Mountbatten and being advised and warned not to trust the Viceroy. Jinnah replied that they must give him a chance; they must presume a person innocent before he was proven guilty; they must not go by rumour and hearsay.

Edward Said points out in *Orientalism* (1978) how the Oriental in the Western stereotype is supposed to be capricious, emotional, egotistical and underhand, given to changing moods. Yet Mountbatten behaved like the classic Oriental. Jinnah on the other hand was like Said's stereotypical Western gentleman – consistent, correct and fair, appealing to reason and logic.

The arguments over partition

The now published minutes of the top secret meetings between Mountbatten and Jinnah reveal the strategy, character and objectives of the two men (Zaidi 1993). Mountbatten is, as we see below, blustering, changeable, frivolous. He does not hold his position but keeps moving the goalposts. It all appears as a game to him, a pastime.

Jinnah has set his sights on Pakistan and nothing will deter him. Every charm that Mountbatten tries is rebuffed, every argument, every inducement, every threat resisted. Mountbatten will cut Jinnah's two most important provinces, Punjab and Bengal, in half; Mountbatten will not give Jinnah an army; Mountbatten offers Jinnah the prime ministership of a united India; Mountbatten, finally, exasperated when everything else fails, bares his teeth. Jinnah must accept the mutilated Pakistan or Mountbatten will offer him nothing. He will hand over power to the Congress and leave India. It is crude but time is running out for Jinnah. It is a choice between what Jinnah calls a 'truncated' and 'moth-eaten' Pakistan and no Pakistan. The choice is an obvious one and Jinnah takes it.

Jinnah, wrote Mountbatten, 'offered no counter-arguments. He gave the impression that he was not listening' (Ziegler 1985: 368). It was more than an impression; to all intents and purposes he was *not* listening; he had made up his mind, concludes Ziegler. (Campbell-Johnson in his meeting with me talked of Jinnah with respect but also said that he was in a 'reverie' most of the time. Like his chief he did not know Jinnah was dying.)

Years later Mountbatten recounted his meetings with Jinnah to Larry Collins and Dominique Lapierre. With a hint of sadistic pleasure he recalled: 'I drove the old gentleman quite mad' (1994: 104). In fact it was the other way round: Jinnah was driving Mountbatten mad. After receiving a letter from Jinnah, Mountbatten exploded: 'This is the type of a letter which I would not tolerate from my King nor would write to my *chaprassi* [peon]' (Raza 1982: 36). Jinnah would be to Mountbatten what Nasser was to Anthony Eden, the native who would not give ground, who would not be browbeaten, who had the support of his own people solidly behind him.

An exasperated Mountbatten confessed later to Collins and Lapierre: 'I was trying every trick I could play on him' (1982: 39). He was determined 'to shake Jinnah's resolve to have partition. Nothing would. There was no argument that could move him from his consuming determination to realize the impossible dream of Pakistan.... The Moslems of India, Jinnah insisted, were a nation with a "distinctive culture and civilization, language and literature, art and architecture, laws and moral codes, customs and calendar, history and traditions".' Mountbatten repeated Jinnah's explanation to him: '"India has never been a true nation," Jinnah asserted. "It only looks that way on the map. The cows I want to eat, the Hindu stops me from killing. Every time a Hindu shakes hands with me he has to wash his hands. The only thing the Moslem has in common with the Hindu is his slavery to the British."' (Collins and Lapierre 1994: 103–4). Jinnah pleaded for a Pakistan that would not be formed out of shattered provinces. Mountbatten recorded:

> Once more he appealed to me not to give him a moth-eaten Pakistan; and once more I pointed out that although I had not made up my mind in any way whether to agree to partition or not, I simply could not visualise being so inconsistent as to agree to the partition of India without also agreeing to partition within any Provinces in which the same problem arose. (Zaidi 1993: volume I, part II, 645)

Jinnah's arguments for not dividing the provinces were weighty. When Mountbatten explained in his television series how he had threatened to divide Jinnah's two main provinces, Punjab and Bengal, he claimed to be using the same argument as Jinnah – that minorities must have protection, so the Hindu-dominated areas in these two provinces must be separated from Pakistan and joined to India. The argument would almost certainly have been fed by Nehru and Menon. It reduced the meaning of partition to absurdity.

According to this logic the large Muslim estates in the United Provinces should have been separated and joined to Pakistan. According to Mountbatten's logic, provinces would have been divided down to district and subdivisional level. This is *reductio ad absurdum*. The province was the basic unit of administration. It was also an easily identified, distinct ethnic, cultural, linguistic and in many cases geographical area. Many

Indian provinces were as large as European countries. They contained large cities and a common history. The provinces created their own ethnicity. Thus a Bengali or Punjabi, even if Muslim or Hindu, would also have a defined ethnic identity as a Bengali or Punjabi. Early in the century an attempt had been made to divide the province of Bengal into two and had failed. Dividing provinces would be disastrous, argued Jinnah. It would be like drawing a knife through the heart. For this reason the unity of the provinces needed to be maintained. But Mountbatten was deaf to Jinnah.

After being offered a malformed Pakistan, Jinnah returned late on 2 June, an hour before the deadline at midnight, to try to persuade Mountbatten to reconsider. Mountbatten threatened Jinnah, saying, 'You will lose Pakistan probably for good' (Jalal 1985: 284). 'What must be, must be,' replied Jinnah stoically (ibid.). Next day, at the moment when Jinnah agreed to partition itself, the tension for Mountbatten was almost unbearable:

> At that instant Mountbatten had absolutely no idea what the Moslem leader was going to do ... [he] would always look back on that instant as 'the most hair-raising moment of my entire life'. For an endless second, he stared into Jinnah's impassive, expressionless face. Then, slowly, reluctance crying from every pore, Jinnah indicated his agreement with the faintest, most begrudging nod he could make. (Collins and Lapierre 1994: 160)

Although neither the Congress, nor the Muslim League, nor the Sikhs, were happy about the final shape of things, the meeting held on 3 June in New Delhi confirmed the arrangements: 15 August 1947 was fixed as the date for independence. Subsequently, 14 and 15 August became Independence Day for Pakistan and India respectively so that the two countries could have their own separate celebrations.

Jinnah, who flew from Delhi to Karachi on 7 August with Fatima, was sworn in as Governor-General of Pakistan on 15 August in Karachi. Mountbatten took oath as the first Governor-General of India in New Delhi on the same day, thus ceasing to be Viceroy of India. Nehru's friendship – as Prime Minister of India – and the general high regard of the Congress leadership for Mountbatten ensured his appointment for a one-year term. Indeed, the Congress in their zeal had proposed Mountbatten as joint Governor-General of India and Pakistan.

The post of Governor-General was more than symbolic. The Governor-General was the representative of the Crown in a Commonwealth country which regarded the King as the head of state and hence was called a dominion. Not long afterwards India and Pakistan replaced the post of Governor-General with that of President and became republics. However, they continued to remain in the Commonwealth.

The Governor-General controversy

Perhaps the turning point in the relationship between Mountbatten and Jinnah was Jinnah's refusal to offer the Governor-Generalship of Pakistan to Mountbatten. Mountbatten's ego was wounded: this was the one blow he could not accept. His career too was on the line and as a result of Jinnah's decision both he and Edwina thought seriously of returning to England. There was no point in staying on as Governor-

General of part of India, that is, taking a demotion from the post of Viceroy of all of India. After this incident the antagonism of the Mountbattens appeared openly to increase.

On 2 July 1947 Jinnah took the advice of the Muslim League and proposed himself to the Viceroy as the Governor-General of Pakistan. Mountbatten had tried straight-forward strong-arm tactics to discourage Jinnah:

> Mountbatten argued against this decision and suggested a compromise under which Jinnah would be Officiating Governor-General in Pakistan when Mountbatten was in Delhi. Jinnah did not accept the compromise. Thereupon, Mountbatten recorded: I asked him 'Do you realise what this will cost you?' He said sadly 'It may cost me several crores of rupees in assets,' to which I replied somewhat acidly 'It may well cost you the whole of your assets and the future of Pakistan.' (Seervai 1990: 130–1)

Having thrown this threat at Jinnah, Mountbatten stormed out of the room. His report to London of 4 July showed his anger and disappointment. Jinnah is 'suffering from megalomania in its worst form' (Ziegler 1985: 397). Ziegler notes:

> According to Chaudhuri Muhammad Ali, who was present at this encounter, the Viceroy 'belaboured Jinnah with arguments and appeals and bluster.... Jinnah bore this onslaught with great dignity and patience.' The account is not unconvincing; Mountbatten clearly lost his temper and Jinnah's impassivity would only have fuelled his indignation. (ibid.: 398)

Jinnah's refusal remains a source of controversy to this day. People, including Pakistanis, argue that, had Jinnah given this prize to Mountbatten, Mountbatten might have been mollified and treated Pakistan more fairly (S. S. H. Khan 1995). This is a misreading of both history and psychology. Who else could have been Governor-General of Pakistan? Liaquat Ali Khan, Jinnah's disciple, was perhaps the most eminent person in the Muslim League after Jinnah. But Jinnah had become aware of Liaquat's limitations. Although a man of many qualities, Liaquat was a stranger to the lands that were forming Pakistan and was not of sufficient stature to hold the new country together. There was no other figure remotely equivalent to Jinnah who could take over as head of state. What Pakistan needed desperately in those early months was a symbol of the state, one that would unify people and give them the courage and resolve to succeed. Had Jinnah not assumed the Governor-Generalship, Nehru's prediction that Pakistan would not last for six months might well have come true.

In any case, after independence Mountbatten had little real power and, although he still retained the prestige that had gone with his job, in effect power had been transferred to the elected government. Men like Vallabhbhai Patel now controlled India. Mountbatten would have had only a limited say in relations between India and Pakistan. He was increasingly marginalized even over Kashmir. Besides, Mountbatten and Jinnah barely saw eye to eye on most issues from the serious to the trivial. Almost every meeting was marked by some petty hostility and misunderstanding.

Even the last meeting, when the Mountbattens flew out to Karachi on 13 August to join in the Pakistan Day celebrations, had its little dramatic moments. Many British officials felt that Jinnah had insulted Mountbatten by not receiving him at the airport.

Instead, Jinnah waited to receive Mountbatten at the Governor-General's house (Campbell-Johnson 1985: 154). The next day Mountbatten insisted on taking the chair in the Assembly. He claimed that the Viceroyalty still had a few hours to run. This was breaking protocol because Jinnah as the president of the Constituent Assembly – not as the Governor-General designate – should have been in the chair (Hodson 1985: 386). Had Jinnah been less of a gentleman and more of an egotist he would have refused Mountbatten. Mountbatten not only would have been disgraced but could have done practically nothing about it. Feelings against him were high in Karachi because of his actions over Pakistan, which I shall describe in the next section. It was Jinnah's graciousness, setting aside his prickliness where the British were concerned, that saved the day for Mountbatten.

Had Jinnah allowed Mountbatten to become Governor-General there would have been the real fear that Mountbatten might have accelerated the unravelling of Pakistan, something which he had always predicted and indeed hoped for. States such as Kalat in Baluchistan, already restless, could have been encouraged to break away from Pakistan and its viability seriously threatened. Mountbatten could also have frustrated the formation of the Pakistan army as an independent fighting machine. He had vigorously argued that the Indian army had to remain united as one force and not divided.

Later, Mountbatten confessed that the Governor-General affair was badly handled by him: 'I do not want to conceal from you that I consider the whole of this situation to be my fault. I should have foreseen it' (in a letter to Lord Attlee; later to Stafford Cripps also; Zaidi 1993: volume I, part I, xliii–xliv). In a subsequent personal report Mountbatten admitted: 'Jinnah scores an undoubted victory over Congress from a psychological point of view in having an Indian Governor-General for Pakistan' (ibid.: xliv).

Most Pakistanis supported Jinnah's decision for the reasons mentioned in the following *Dawn* editorial:

> In the first place, a common Governor-General would have created the impression abroad that this subcontinent still somehow retained its oneness. Such an impression would have been fatal to the dignity and prestige of Pakistan. In the second place, no Briton, however eminent, if placed at the head of the new Muslim State, would have given to that State the character that it was essential for it to acquire from the very start. Nor could his presence have contributed to the satisfaction of that psychological urge of its people to see their independence emerge as a visible reality. In the third place, Pakistan's prestige in the eyes of the world as an independent State would have doubtless suffered if its people chose to install a foreigner as the head of its administration. (A. Husain 1996: 63; also see Chaudhri Muhammad Ali, who attended some of the Mountbatten–Jinnah meetings; 1967)

The historian Khalid bin Sayeed, after a judicious sifting of the facts in the controversy, concludes that 'it is difficult to see how Jinnah could have put forward any name other than his own for Governor-Generalship' (Sayeed 1968: 229). Yahya Bakhtiar rejects Sirdar Shaukat Hyat Khan's argument that Jinnah made a mistake by not allowing Mountbatten to become joint Governor-General (S. S. H. Khan 1995). He wrote:

'We know that at that time there were numerous pending disputes between India and Pakistan to be settled including the division of assets, sterling balances, accession of Indian states, transfer of Pakistani troops who had been left in India etc. By refusing to allow Mountbatten to become common Governor-General, Quaid saved Pakistan from getting destroyed at inception' (*The News*, 1 July, 1995). Yahya also mentioned that 'Nehru in those days was having a roaring love affair with Lady Mountbatten, said to be with the tacit approval of Mountbatten.' How could the Mountbattens be neutral to Pakistan, he concludes.

In retrospect and on balance Jinnah was correct to assume the top job himself. By taking on the post he gave a clear message to the world not only that Muslims were taking over their own destiny, but also that they had to find their own way into the future. Muslims who are critical of this decision do not fully appreciate the complexities of the relationship between the British and the 'natives'. They simply parrot the empty ideals that the British themselves propagated of justice, truth and brotherhood, ideals that have consistently been violated by not only the British but the West generally in numerous examples at that time and subsequently in the last half-century since the creation of Pakistan.

In the 1990s Muslims seem wiser. They point to the double standards of the West in Bosnia and Palestine and the continuing problems from 1947 in Kashmir. They point to how the West behaved when it gathered half a million troops to hammer Iraq and destroy its enemy. They also point to how it remains indifferent to the suppression of Muslims in Bosnia, Chechniya, Palestine and Kashmir. Double standards, they are able to say now.

But Jinnah's role as Governor-General did create one significant and enduring problem for Pakistan. Jinnah was not only Governor-General but also President of the Muslim League and head of the Constituent Assembly – although he soon gave up the League office. (The trend has been in reverse in Pakistan: when General Ayub Khan became President and Chief Martial Law Administrator he also took on the title of President of the Muslim League.) With the adulation for Jinnah it became axiomatic that real power and status lay in the office of the Governor-General – later converted to President – rather than that of the Prime Minister. In recent decades the tension between the two offices has created serious political and constitutional problems. Some politicians, like Zulfiqar Ali Bhutto, have tried both jobs to see which suits them better. But the matter had not been resolved and the relationship remains an uneasy one. The mould of Jinnah's Governor-Generalship made it easy for generals imposing martial law to assume authority beyond the office. The elected Prime Minister, as in General Zia ul-Haq's time, was reduced to little more than a cipher.

Paki-bashing

If Jinnah is the first Pakistani, Mountbatten is the first Paki-basher. In contemporary Britain this is a term denoting racial abuse of Asians generally, not just of Pakistanis. We are not implying that Mountbatten was motivated by a racist hatred of Pakistanis like a young skinhead in the UK out looking for Asians to beat up. On the contrary, Mountbatten belonged to that generation of British who genuinely believed that it was time that Asians were given independence and treated with respect. His actions, his friendships and his attitude confirm this. But for Pakistanis, because of his undisputed bias towards Hindus and India during partition, it is difficult not to conclude that he was hostile to them and intent on 'bashing' them, if only in a metaphorical sense. He was accused even by his own officers of seeing the world through 'Hindu eyes'.

Because Jinnah and the Muslims were represented as the awkward faction that had caused the ancient Indian empire to be broken up and because the eventual shape of the Muslim state was truncated, Pakistan was seen from the outset as inferior to India by many in Britain. If Pakistan was treated with contempt by the British, is it hardly surprising that the word 'Pakistani', itself truncated to 'Paki', became a term of abuse?

Mountbatten's behaviour towards Jinnah, Nehru's open contempt of him and the constant double-dealing and deception that Jinnah faced convinced Muslims that they were achieving Pakistan against the wishes of both the British and the Indian National Congress. It left them bitter and suspicious. It would become part of their character. It was a bad start and it coloured future dealings with both the British and the Indians.

When Mountbatten was asked by Collins and Lapierre if he would have sabotaged Pakistan if he had known that Jinnah was dying of tuberculosis, his answer was instructive. There was no doubt in his mind about the legality or morality of his position on Pakistan. 'Most probably,' he said (1982: 39).

Wolpert points out that Jinnah, in acute physical pain and towards the end dying, still put on a public show of normality so that no one would have any idea of his physical condition (1984). It was a strategy aimed at achieving Pakistan. Had Mountbatten got a hint of his condition there would have been no Pakistan; Mountbatten would have simply let the original date stand, in 1948, by which time Jinnah would be gravely ill or even dead.

How did Mountbatten damage Pakistan? The list is a long one, ranging from psychological to political charges. In one way or another Mountbatten is involved in each case and must take some of the blame.

Hostile progaganda

The first charge, and perhaps the gravest of all (especially for Pakistanis), is that Mountbatten consciously manipulated and propagated a negative image of Jinnah, thus damaging the Pakistan cause. Andrew Roberts wrote recently:

> Mountbatten contributed to the slander against Jinnah, calling him vain, megalomaniacal, an evil genius, a lunatic, a psychotic case and a bastard, while publicly claiming he was entirely impartial between Jinnah's Pakistan and Nehru's India. Jinnah rose magisterially above Mountbatten's blatant bias, not even attacking the former Viceroy when, as Governor-General of India after partition, Mountbatten tacitly condoned India's shameful invasion of Kashmir in October 1947. (*Sunday Times*, 18 August 1996)

Because Jinnah was a 'psychopath', 'lunatic' and 'obstinate', he refused to respond to my charms, Mountbatten seemed to be saying. Yet the fact that Jinnah represented the authentic aspirations of millions of Muslims and struck a chord like few in their history was never seriously considered. Mountbatten reduced political dialogue and negotiation to personal relationships.

'Megalomaniac', 'pathological case', 'bastard', 'cold': where have we heard these words before? They reflected the standard Ministry of Information propaganda that the European powers were employing against each other. Mountbatten represented what had been the highest echelons of the British war effort directed against Germany. The propaganda strategy was to focus on Hitler and depict him as a 'megalomaniac', a 'pathological case'. Depicting the enemy as megalomaniac and as emotionally frigid was one way of justifying hatred for him. It simplified matters. Mountbatten picked up both the technique and the vocabulary and applied it to Jinnah.

In Karachi Jinnah and Mountbatten were the target of a suspected assassination attempt. After arriving at the Governor-General's residence, Jinnah, according to Mountbatten in his television programme, leaned across to touch him on the knee and said, 'Thank God I've brought you back safely.' Mountbatten describes this as 'a moment of rare emotion' – once again seeing Jinnah as a stereotype, a robot, lacking in human feelings.

The same impression of Jinnah prevailed with the Countess Mountbatten and Lady Pamela Hicks, the daughters of Mountbatten. Lady Pamela contrasted the warmth of Gandhi and Nehru, who would 'hug and kiss' them, with the formality of Jinnah, who was 'awe-inspiring'. 'One just sort of said, How do you do, and then tried to escape out of the room.' Her 'mother who normally had a great success in unfreezing people tried the same with Jinnah and had very little success.' The Countess added, 'Mr Jinnah was a cold personality.'

In turn, those influenced by Mountbatten propagated the same image, often using the same words. For example, Alan Campbell-Johnson, Mountbatten's press attaché and author of *Mission with Mountbatten*, wrote: 'Jinnah's personality is cold' (1985: 156; Collins and Lapierre also employ the image of a 'cold' Jinnah after their lengthy sessions with Mountbatten, 1994).

Not everyone in Britain was influenced by Mountbatten. In the mid-1990s several British people wrote to me about Jinnah, people who had either seen him or met him briefly in the last years. All of them confirmed that he was kindly and courteous and that the enthusiasm for him among the Muslims was unrestrained; their views contrasted with Nehru's and Mountbatten's assertions that Jinnah was cold and isolated from his people. Typical is the anecdote of the retired squadron leader who flew him on his last journey to Karachi. He entered the cabin to check on his important passenger. Jinnah, only hours from his death, looked up and gave him 'the sweetest smile I have ever seen in my life'. 'It has remained with me all my life,' said the officer, plainly moved by the memory of half a century ago. He also spoke of the vast enthusiastic crowds that greeted Jinnah wherever he went.

Unfortunately for Jinnah, Mountbatten's opinions became the official version of the people and leaders of India. Mountbatten alone had the resources to write history and propagate it on any scale. He had the entire archives, the secret minutes, the access to the records in London. Indeed he was responsible for briefings at the highest level about the situation in India and wrote many of the top secret minutes. Above all he was aware of the power of the media and made full use of it. We note the time and energy he put into the making of the television series which was seen worldwide. Mountbatten's version of history thus prevailed.

Few people could challenge Mountbatten; some did. But their individual voices were not enough. In time his views fed into the journalistic writings of the second generation (like Christina Lamb and Emma Duncan) writing about the subcontinent. What Mountbatten had begun in 1947, and what still colours perceptions of Jinnah, convinces Pakistanis that Jinnah was deliberately misrepresented. As Roberts writes, 'Because Jinnah is Pakistan's equivalent of Churchill, de Gaulle or George Washington, such unfair and often deliberately vicious criticism is bound to infuriate Pakistanis' (1996).

Mountbatten never missed an opportunity to gloat over anything he thought would discomfort Jinnah. When Gandhi announced his plans to leave for Pakistan, Mountbatten was delighted: 'Gandhi has announced his decision to spend the rest of his life in Pakistan looking after the minorities. This will infuriate Jinnah, but will be a great relief to Congress for, as I have said before, his influence is largely negative or even destructive' (Mountbatten's personal report no. 16, 8 August 1947: 228).

Lord Wavell saw Mountbatten in London on 20 November 1947 and noted: 'He has very much gone over to the Congress side, as was, I suppose, inevitable' (Ziegler 1985: 461). Ian Stephens confirms this after his meetings with Mountbatten in Delhi: 'I was startled by their one-sided verdicts on affairs. They seemed to have become wholly pro-Hindu. The atmosphere at Government House that night was almost one of war. Pakistan, the Muslim League, and Mr Jinnah were the enemy' (A. Husain 1996: 72).

Mountbatten's partiality was apparent in his own statements. He tilted openly and heavily towards Congress. While doing so he clearly expressed his lack of support and faith in the Muslim League and its Pakistan idea: 'Administratively it is the difference between putting up a permanent building, and a Nissen hut or a tent. As far as Pakistan is concerned we are putting up a tent. We can do no more' (Campbell-Johnson 1985: 87).

The Nehru/Menon Plan for partition

In Simla, a few weeks before partition, Mountbatten broke all official protocol and precedence by giving in to a 'hunch': he showed his house guests, Nehru and V. P. Menon, the plans for the future division of India because they were 'good friends' and had 'complete mutual trust'. Nehru reacted badly, lost his temper and objected in writing. Mountbatten was stunned by the 'Nehru bombshell'. With the help of Nehru, Menon, Mountbatten tells us, 'came to the rescue' by drafting what came to be known as the Menon Plan. Nehru now gave his approval to Mountbatten. These plans were the basis for partition. The same Menon, Reforms Commissioner and the only Indian adviser to Mountbatten, had already expressed his loyalties and kept a direct channel of communication throughout those critical days with the Congress, especially with Patel and Nehru.

Giving Nehru access to top secret documents containing draft plans for the future of the subcontinent and then allowing him to change them with the help of his own staff was totally improper. Jinnah, on the other hand, was kept in the dark, and plans were made to counter him in case he balked at the Menon Plan, which offered a truncated Pakistan. The strategy henceforth was to keep chopping down the original idea of

Pakistan at all levels – provincial (Punjab and Bengal), district (Gurdaspur and Ferozepur) and state (Kashmir).

The shifting of key districts: Ferozepur and Gurdaspur

Ferozepur and Gurdaspur, both Muslim-majority border districts, were initially earmarked for Pakistan. The district of Ferozepur was important for Pakistan. (Ziegler in his recent attempt to defend Mountbatten missed the fact that two subdivisions of Ferozepur, Zira and Ferozepur, a large area with over half a million people, not just the 'headwaters', were shifted from Pakistan to India; Ziegler 1995.) Ferozepur housed a major arsenal, which was to be the only one in Pakistan territory, and was to ensure supplies to the future Pakistan army. Mountbatten was determined that Ferozepur would not go to Pakistan.

Beaumont, secretary to the Boundary Commission, relates the scandalous manner in which Mountbatten ordered the changing of the boundary that was to divide the two countries ensuring that Ferozepur was shifted from Pakistan to India (personal interview). It is a cloak-and-dagger story as told by Beaumont. Menon visited Beaumont and Sir Cyril Radcliffe, the head of the Boundary Commission, late at night with an invitation from the Viceroy for lunch the next day. Beaumont was told not to attend and a flimsy excuse given. After lunch, an agitated Radcliffe returned to readjust the borders in order to give Ferozepur to India.

The killings in Ferozepur in 1947 were especially brutal, since the district was thereby purged of Muslims, who until then had been in the majority. The refugees from Ferozepur who came to Pakistan still harbour a deep-seated hatred for Mountbatten.

If Mountbatten was capable of such fraud in the Ferozepur case surely he could have done exactly the same in other instances? Gurdaspur, also a Muslim-majority district, is another example. Gurdaspur was even more important than Ferozepur because it provided the only land route to Kashmir from India. Mountbatten's Hindu staff were quick to perceive this strategic factor and were determined the district should go to India. Mountbatten could hardly feign ignorance of Gurdaspur's ultimate and real significance. The shifting of Gurdaspur to India sealed the fate of Kashmir.

One year before Mountbatten came to India V. P. Menon was already pointing out the significance of Gurdaspur as the only land route to Kashmir in case of a division between a future Pakistan and India. He had already earmarked the district for India. The problem was that it was a Muslim-majority district. If and when Gurdaspur was shifted from a possible Pakistan to India it would have to be done by underhand means and by violating the principles upon which a possible division could take place. Mountbatten's acquiescence in the summer of 1947 resulted in pressure on Radcliffe to shift the district.

Kashmir

Kashmir was one of the biggest and most important states of India (also see Epilogue for a discussion on Kashmir). About 80 per cent of its population was Muslim. Apart from its religious composition, the basis of the partition, Kashmir was geographically, economically and strategically part of the areas that would form Pakistan. Seeing it as a prize, the Congress was determined to keep it. Besides, Nehru, whose ancestors came from Kashmir, was passionately attached to it. He found the Mountbattens strong allies in his fight to ensure Kashmir came to India (see next chapter).

Mountbatten recounted the sequence of events leading to the tragedy of Kashmir in his television series. He blamed Pakistani tribesmen for invading Kashmir and marching on Srinagar on 24 October. This justified the use of Indian troops. Three days later India flew in troops, since the Maharajah had agreed to sign the Accession Instrument, thus joining India. 'Just in time,' added Mountbatten. All this is now challenged by scholars (see, for example, Alastair Lamb 1991, 1994; Schofield 1996). In the last meeting between Jinnah and Mountbatten on 1 November Jinnah accused India of seizing Kashmir by 'fraud and violence' (Wolpert 1996: 420).

In fact Mountbatten ensured that Indian troops were sent to Kashmir *before* the state declared its intention to join India or Pakistan, thus technically ordering an invasion of foreign territory. He assisted in supervising the backdating of the ruler's signature so that the accession to India would appear legal. The ruler was crudely threatened and found it difficult to resist the combined pressure put on him by Mountbatten and Nehru. Mountbatten even ensured that the RAF, neutral between the two new dominions, would fly secret sorties to Kashmir at a time when there were hardly any planes available to India and virtually none to Pakistan, thereby violating international law (Alastair Lamb, personal interview).

An emergency meeting was organized at Lahore between Mountbatten, Nehru and Jinnah to resolve the Kashmir problem. Nehru feigned illness, much to Mountbatten's embarrassment and Jinnah's ire. Both Mountbatten and Nehru promised to implement several United Nations resolutions to allow Kashmir to choose her own fate through a plebiscite but reneged each time. The continuing Kashmir problem is another Mount-batten legacy.

Churchill treated Mountbatten roughly over Kashmir. 'He accused me of having planned and organised the first victory of Hindustan (he refused to call it India) against Pakistan by sending in British trained soldiers and British equipment to crush and oppress the Muslims in Kashmir,' Mountbatten complained (Ziegler 1985: 461). Church-ill had warned Mountbatten 'to get out quickly and not involve the King and my country in further backing traitors' (ibid.).

Even Indian authors, known for their frank impartiality, fault Mountbatten over Kashmir: 'His partisanship of the Congress, which was due to his infatuation with Nehru, was blatant, and it was shown most blatantly after independence when he actually supported Nehru over the Kashmir question. He collaborated in giving help to the Maharajah of Kashmir, which was to make the British dishonesty over the princely states even worse' (Chaudhuri 1990: 831). 'Lord Mountbatten's complicity in the Kashmir affair created a permanent sense of injury in Pakistan,' wrote Chaudhuri (ibid).

Feelings on Kashmir and Britain's role in its woes have remained consistently high over the last half-century, as this report, which quotes an earlier report, 'Pakistan's distrust of Britain' (*Guardian*, 'Past notes', 15 March 1995) shows:

Bitterness was to grow into outrage in October when East Gurdaspur, by providing India with its only land-link with Jammu, made it possible for Delhi to come to the rescue of Kashmir. Since then everyone in Pakistan believes that Lord Radcliffe was made to change the boundary line in the last minute because Lord Mountbatten wanted to do Pakistan down. (Taya Zinkin, 15 March 1958)

The invisibility of Muslims on the Viceroy's team

In the charged political and communal atmosphere of 1947 the lack of Muslim staff on the Viceroy's team working on partition and the influence of its Hindu members became a significant issue. Muslims were quick to point out that there was no Muslim of influence on Mountbatten's staff. Mountbatten revealed his contempt for Muslims when he asked 'whether there were likely to be sufficiently intelligent Muslim officials to administer Pakistan' (Roberts 1994a: 85). In contrast several important posts were held by Hindus. Hamid confirms that it was common knowledge that they were leaking sensitive information (1986). Yet Mountbatten turned a blind eye to what was a gross dereliction of duty and ignored its enormous consequences.

Menon became the Viceroy's link to the Congress high command. It was only 'when V. P. Menon ... confidant of Sardar Patel, joined the group that any real insight into day-to-day Indian thinking was vouchsafed its members,' notes Ziegler (1985: 371). Ziegler goes on to admit, 'The price that was paid for Menon's inclusion was the conviction of the Muslims that the Viceroy's staff was prejudiced against their cause' (ibid.). Thus a close ally and disciple of Patel, the hardline Hindu in the Congress leadership, was now the trusted confidant of the Viceroy on all matters relating to the partition of the country. A partisan Hindu was placed in a position where he could influence plans for Jinnah's Muslim state. The irony escaped the Viceroy.

Another key appointment involving partition was given to a Hindu: that of Iyer as assistant secretary to Radcliffe. Beaumont has written: 'It was a serious mistake to appoint a Hindu (the same would have been true for a Muslim) to the confidential post of Assistant Secretary to the Boundary Commission' (Beaumont 1989; also in Hamid 1986: xiv). Beaumont adds: 'I have not the slightest doubt that Iyer kept Nehru and V. P. Menon informed of progress.'

Beaumont was correct. Sensitive matters were leaking. Take the case of Nehru voicing alarm about the Chittagong Hill Tracts which were earmarked for Pakistan (as part of its eastern province) *before* Beaumont actually presented the Commission's report to the Viceroy. Beaumont later pointed out that Nehru could have known of the secret decision only if Iyer had told him.

Supreme Headquarters, Field Marshal Auchinleck's office, regarded as sympathetic to the Muslims, was closed, and this again was seen as evidence of Mountbatten's partiality (Hamid 1986: 258). Hamid, private secretary to Auchinleck, blamed the machinations of the Congress: 'So the Congress has succeeded in getting rid of the Auk' (ibid.). Accusing Mountbatten, he described the closure as 'a degrading and dirty trick'. 'Mountbatten', he concluded, 'has become a tool in the hands of the Congressmen.'

The Partition and Independence of India

Influencing the princely states

Mountbatten vigorously encouraged the hesitating Indian princely states to join India. The problem of the princely states was potentially explosive. Some had Hindu rulers but Muslim subjects – or vice versa; others wished to remain independent. For example, the Nawab of Junagadh, a Muslim ruler with a majority Hindu population, declared his intention to opt for Pakistan, although his state would have no land access to Pakistan. The Indians simply ignored his wishes and sent in a strong paramilitary force to absorb the state; that was the end of Junagadh.

Hyderabad (in central and southern India) and Kashmir were different from Junagadh. These were two of the largest, most powerful states of India. Both had long histories of independence, both had distinct cultural, geographical and ethnic identities, and both had a strong argument for an independent political identity of their own in the future. Hyderabad even had its own army, its own railways and its own postal system. The Nizam of Hyderabad was one of the richest men in the world.

The problem of course was that while Hyderabad had a majority-Hindu population it was ruled by a Muslim. The situation was reversed in Kashmir, which had a Muslim population ruled by a Hindu. It was assumed automatically that on the basis of this principle, and that of contiguity, Kashmir would go to Pakistan and Hyderabad would go to India. This did not deter League and Congress leaders from attempting to claim both states. In the end Pakistan ended up by losing both.

In both cases the Hindus on Mountbatten's staff played their part. We saw above how the Maharajah of Kashmir was 'persuaded' to join India. Hyderabad was simpler. The Indians played a waiting game. The day after Jinnah died, on 11 September 1948, waiting troops marched into Hyderabad and occupied it. To provide a figleaf Delhi called it a 'police action'. The history of one of the most important Muslim states of India was abruptly over.

Calcutta

Mountbatten's removal of Calcutta from the projected plans for Pakistan is not widely known. Had Calcutta gone to Pakistan, at least one of the major cities of India would have been given to Pakistan, but Patel objected so strongly that Mountbatten dropped the idea. Instead of Calcutta, Mountbatten would offer Chittagong, a small fishing village near Burma, to Pakistan.

In Assam too, in the north-east of India, similar ploys ensured that Pakistan would not be given its fair share of territory. Assam had a similar problem to that of Junagadh but in reverse. Its area was Hindu but it had no land access to India. Culturally and ethnically it belonged more to South-East Asia than to South Asia. It had always been considered part of the Bengal area. Logically, it was part of Pakistan. But Menon ensured that a corridor would be given to India north of East Pakistan so that Assam could plausibly be brought into the Indian union (Zaidi 1993: volume I, part II, xliv). Therefore a thin sliver of land beyond East Pakistan was allocated to India, connecting India to Assam; that ensured Assam could be given to India.

Mountbatten: Viceroy and Paki-Basher

The division of assets

Pakistanis also blame Mountbatten for India's refusal to honour the payments to Pakistan under the Division of Assets Agreement. Under the agreement one-sixth of the assets of the government of India (about £30 million at exchange rates then prevailing or 55 crore rupees) was to go to Pakistan. It was withheld from Pakistan, almost strangling it at birth, and only partly released after Gandhi fasted in protest. Mountbatten did not mention this in his television series. After all, he was then the Governor-General of India which had reneged. But, to be fair, it is not clear how much say Mountbatten had in this; he claimed later to have encouraged the Indian government to honour their commitment. In December 1947 he enlisted Gandhi in the battle to release the assets.

The bloodshed of partition

Finally, many Pakistanis – and Indians – blame Mountbatten directly for the killings in the summer of 1947. After promising that British troops would be in place to ensure law and order he withdrew them when they were most needed. The Punjab Boundary Force, small enough for the task with only 35,000 soldiers, Muslim, Sikh and Hindu, and officered mainly by the British and commanded by a British general, was disbanded after thirty-two days of service. The abrupt withdrawal made the communal slaughter inevitable. Seeing the chaos in the summer of 1947 Nehru said in despair, 'My country has gone mad!' (Ziegler 1985: 438).

Yet Mountbatten had given 'complete assurance' to Maulana Azad, representing the Congress, that once partition was accepted there would be no bloodshed and that as a soldier he would put down violence by calling out the army and by using tanks and aircraft if necessary (Seervai 1990). Indian authors like Seervai damn Mountbatten; indeed Seervai's criticism occupies an entire chapter: 'Mountbatten's responsibility for the massacres and the migrations in Punjab' (ibid.: chapter 10). Andrew Roberts would go further: if it was possible he would impeach Mountbatten (1994b).

Mountbatten further worsened the situation by suppressing the actual decision of the Boundary Commission dividing Punjab or what was called the Punjab Awards. The Viceroy received the Awards on 12 August but kept it a secret until they were announced on 17 August, yet every hour increased the tension. Seervai calls Mountbatten's suppression a 'great betrayal' (Seervai 1990: 163). He argues that Mountbatten betrayed not only the British, not only the leaders of the Congress and the Muslim League, but the hundreds of thousands who suffered and died in consequence. Mountbatten suppressed the information and stood by for five days, while rumour and accusations fuelled the hatred of the communities against each other, forcing hundreds of thousands to flee in haste to the country of their choice.

Mountbatten had already set the stage for disaster. Although he had arrived with a date for independence and partition set in 1948 he impulsively brought it forward by one year. In spite of the fact that nothing was prepared and no one was ready London agreed. The ten weeks' time given for independence was 'madness', a countdown to disaster (Roberts in Channel 4's *Secret Lives*, March 1995). Beaumont called it a

141

'disgraceful scurry'. The mass killings and mass migration were almost inevitable in the chaos and confusion that followed. Mountbatten, perhaps anxious to return to the Royal Navy and resume his career, wished to rush through the partition of India regardless of the cost to human life.

Dickie-bashing

Mountbatten remains a hate figure for Pakistanis (see, for example, the cover of the 1993 edition of Shahid Hamid's autobiography, *Disastrous Twilight*, 1986, which proclaims: 'Includes new evidence proving Mountbatten's biased role and how Pakistan was cheated of Kashmir'). Mountbatten may have been guilty of many sins against Jinnah, but Pakistanis sometimes interpret Mountbatten's dislike of Jinnah unfairly. Zaidi, for instance, claimed that he had come across evidence that Mountbatten had planned a physical assault on Jinnah.

Zaidi quotes Mountbatten from the *Transfer of Power Documents* (volume 12: 339, dated July 1947). Mountbatten wrote of Jinnah: 'He was only saved from being struck by the arrival of the other members of the Partition Council at this moment. However, I sent Ismay round to beat him up as soon as possible, and Jinnah claimed that I must have misunderstood him.' Zaidi takes this literally: Mountbatten would have 'struck' Jinnah. He then sent Ismay to 'beat him up'. All this is hardly likely in the context of discussions at the Viceroy's palace with literally hundreds of staff on hand to witness the coming and going. Any such incident would have been picked up and blown out of all proportion – particularly in view of Mountbatten's dislike of Jinnah.

Whatever I had studied of Mountbatten I could not believe he would be rash or foolish enough to do something like this. Besides, this was out of character in terms of both Mountbatten's temperament and his social background. It was a serious misreading. Mountbatten would have hardly put down in black and white, in the personal report which was sent regularly to London and circulated to key officials including the Prime Minister, his intention to have Jinnah beaten up. In any case, Ismay was Mountbatten's Chief of Staff. A refined aristocrat, he would have been the last person to organize the kind of thuggery that Zaidi's gloss puts on these words, however much the prima facie evidence.

No Viceroy could have left India satisfying both of the two new countries after the decision to divide it. Both sides complained. Patel objected thus: 'They may think they are acting impartially but as they are all mentally completely pro-Pakistan, they are in fact out to help Pakistan at every turn' (Ziegler 1985: 463). But by his personal responses to problems that demanded the coolest of heads and the largest of hearts Mountbatten ensured continuing bitterness and hatred. To this day Pakistanis feel cheated, that justice was not done, that the British neither gave Pakistan what it deserved nor wished to see it prosper.

CHAPTER 6

Partition: In the Heat of Passion

Edwina lay on her back, raised her lovely lissome legs high above her head on the surrounding lawn and, grinning, said [to Nehru] in her inimitable sweet frank way, 'Not bad for fifty, is it?'

(Hough 1983: 209)

If historians can be blamed for distortion by suggesting Jinnah created Pakistan because he was a cold, egotistical megalomaniac, they are equally guilty of deception for drawing a veil over the love affair between Edwina Mountbatten and Jawaharlal Nehru, as we will see in this chapter. Yet the published letters and photographs speak of a joyful and intense friendship. In discussing Nehru and the Mountbattens we are not interested in the prurient tabloid obsession with 'sleaze'. Stories about Mountbatten's alleged homosexuality and Edwina's promiscuity are a red herring. Whether the friendship was sexual or platonic barely matters. What is most significant is the impact of this close relationship.

Romancing the Vicereine

However fascinating the issue of adultery in high places, we must not be distracted. Edwina Mountbatten becomes important to our story only if we are able to establish two facts: one, that her opinions mattered with her husband and that she was able to influence him (both Lord and Lady Mountbatten describe Jinnah in *exactly* the same words – 'pathological case', 'megalomaniac', etc. (Morgan 1991: 408); who is influencing whom?); and, secondly, that this influence affected, however indirectly, the politics of partition, affairs of state and public policy. We can confirm both with confidence after reading the published letters, minutes, diaries and notes of that period.

The close friendship between Edwina and Nehru seems to have developed soon after the arrival of the Mountbattens in 1947. By the summer people in Delhi were talking about it. 'Nehru's relationship with Lady Mountbatten is sufficiently close to have raised many eyebrows' (Hamid 1986: 153). This was a unique and extraordinary situation. Never before in the history of British colonial rule in India had an Indian, however high-born, had this access to and authority with British officialdom at this level. Nehru appeared to command the Viceroy's office through his bedroom.

This was also the first time in the history of the British Raj that a woman at that level of administration was actually a player and not just a decoration. The Raj was characterized by masculinity. The Great Game was played by men. It was physically punishing and played on the high plateaux of Central Asia and the passes along the Durand line, with tribesmen, bullets, swords and lances. But the nature of the game changed: it was no longer being played in ravines and mountains but in drawing-rooms and in summer retreats up in the hills.

Jinnah had already pointed out the harmful impact of the friendship on the politics of partition (see, for example, Akbar 1988a: 391–2). But he was ignored by the scholars and journalists of the time. Only recently have British scholars begun to appreciate the existence of an alternative view: 'Nothing will persuade the Pakistanis today that the relationship between Nehru and Mountbatten's wife, Edwina, was not an important element in the links that bound Viceroy's House to the Congress leadership' (Ziegler 1995: 14).

The affair affected Jinnah and his Pakistan in several ways. Had the Mountbattens not been besotted by Nehru, Nehru would not have been able to convince them so completely on the subject of Jinnah. Nehru would also not so easily have been able to obtain vital information pertaining to the partition plans of the future states of India and Pakistan and influence decisions being made by the complaisant Viceroy. When Nehru insisted on changing the future projected boundaries, after a secret and private viewing, Mountbatten had them redrawn. When Nehru complained about Sir Olaf Caroe, Governor of the North-West Frontier Province, Mountbatten immediately prepared to remove him.

In the case of Kashmir, not only did Edwina applaud the illegal transportation of troops to the state but visited it with Nehru. Her visit caused comment in the British press, who saw it as compromising the neutrality of the Mountbattens. Nehru was using Edwina in his fight to win Kashmir. 'The fact that the last Viceroy's wife went to Kashmir with Nehru will be taken to mean that Lord Mountbatten favours India's claim and backs Nehru in his defiance of the United Nations' resolution,' remarked one London newspaper (Hough 1983: 209).

When India invaded Hyderabad the day after Jinnah's death Edwina expressed her full support by saying: 'Right is right and wrong is wrong' (Morgan 1991: 436). Edwina passed on her opinions to top British officials: 'When Edwina herself saw Horace Alexander three days later, she said straight out, "Of course we think that Gandhi and his friends are absolutely right. We must try to fit in with what they want us to do"' (ibid.: 395). Edwina's influence worked both ways. In the following example she influenced Nehru on behalf of the British Crown: 'V. P. Menon told his daughter afterwards that Lady Louis' conversations with Nehru played a significant part in helping him to make up his mind to go for Commonwealth membership. By the time

Nehru left on the Sunday evening, a new formula had been agreed' (ibid.: 400).

The position of Edwina and Dickie Mountbatten was clear. Their charm, power and authority would be used whenever possible on behalf of their Indian friends. Here is Edwina on the 'neutral' Viceroy helping the Indian states decide between India and Pakistan:

> It took all Dickie's energy and ingenuity to coax and bully the rulers into accepting Patel's terms. The two who gave the most difficulty were the Nizam of Hyderabad and the Maharajah of Kashmir. The Nizam was a Muslim, his state, India's largest (it was the size of France and had a population of sixteen million), mainly Hindu. The Nizam was being manipulated by a powerful Muslim faction, in close touch with Jinnah. (Morgan 1991: 404)

Old habits die hard and faithful lovers remain steadfast. Back in England Edwina was reporting to Nehru the goings-on in the British cabinet (ibid.: 468). She sent scores of letters sympathizing with Nehru over Kashmir, over Pakistan, over his other problems. Between 1950 and 1960 she went to Delhi every year. 'Her visits, Nehru told her, were the pivot upon which everything else revolved' (ibid.: 470).

Lobbying for friends

I had asked Mountbatten's daughters if Nehru's access to their parents, the intimate relationship and his influence over them, justified what critics had said of Mountbatten – that he saw the world through 'Hindu eyes'. 'No,' they answered firmly, and to prove their point they recalled that one day they had overheard their father actually admonishing their mother in the bedroom as she argued on behalf of Nehru, telling her she must never be influenced by Jawaharlal on the Kashmir issue. 'He's very emotional, very emotional about Kashmir,' their father had said. In denying influence, however, they had hinted at the possibility.

Edwina lobbied strongly for Nehru and his causes and communicated her feelings to her influential friends in London. Equally important, these feelings were picked up by the administration in India. In turn, all this affected an already prejudiced Viceroy. Her unkind remarks about Jinnah and her glowing affection for Nehru and Gandhi reinforced the monolithic hostility towards Jinnah in the Viceroy's office and home (as also noted by, for instance, Ian Stephens 1963):

> Mountbatten's deep-seated dislike of Jinnah has been confirmed recently by the revelations in *Mountbatten and the Partition of India* by Larry Collins and Dominique Lapierre. Edwina shared his distaste and suspicion, and while she worked with equal vigour to ease the sufferings of Sikhs, Hindus and Moslems alike in the bloody riots of 1947–8, she laid the blame for the massacres firmly at the feet of Jinnah and the Moslems. (Hough 1983: 209)

There was no denying in Edwina the humanity, the energy, the frantic desperation to do something about the suffering as thousands and thousands of refugees poured into Delhi in 1947. But it was one-sided and therefore flawed. She had done what no person in her position ought to ever have done: by taking sides she had crossed over and personally become part of the Indian political confrontation. 'Her relationship with Nehru has been of immense help to Congress' (Hamid 1986: 172).

A platonic or physical affair?

Was the affair with Nehru a passing flirtation, something to occupy Edwina's Indian summer, one in the long series of liaisons she had had before? Was it platonic or was the passion physical?

The last question appears to interest people most. The affair was being conducted by a notoriously promiscuous Vicereine and an established philanderer. There is sufficient material in the letters Edwina and Jawaharlal wrote to each other to suggest there was a physical aspect to the relationship. After their return to England, Edwina confessed to Dickie: 'Others are love letters in a sense, though you yourself will realize the strange relationship – most of it spiritual – which exists between us. J. has obviously meant a very great deal in my life in these last years and I think I in his' (Morgan 1991: 476). Mountbatten just wished to be told and kept in the picture: 'That is why I've always made your visits to each other easy and been faintly hurt when at times ... you didn't take me into your confidence right away' (Ziegler 1985: 474). 'Certainly Mountbatten himself knew that they were lovers,' concludes a study of the Mountbattens (Hough 1983: 182).

Nehru's own letters to Edwina reveal an intense relationship: 'Suddenly I realised (and perhaps you did also) that there was a deeper attachment between us, that some uncontrollable force, of which I was only dimly aware, drew us to one another. I was overwhelmed and at the same time exhilarated by this new discovery. We talked more intimately, as if some veil had been removed, and we could look into each other's eyes without fear or embarrassment' (Ziegler 1985: 473). Nehru's letters show a man in love:

> 'What did you tell me and what did I say to you...?' he asked, in a letter written after one of their late-night conversations at Government House. 'The more one talks, the more there is to say and there is so much that it is difficult to put into words.' ... Edwina was alarmed: 'The thought of any reservations... between us rather frightens me.' (Morgan 1991: 429)

The lovers spent hours talking late into the night: there was 'Delightful gossip with Jawaharlal at his house' (Morgan 1991: 427). '"A perfect evening," Edwina wrote in her diary, and, when the others had left, "... a fascinating heart to heart with J.N."' (ibid.: 428). 'Early in the morning they met in the garden, late in the day they sat together. Nehru's holiday was nearly over. Next morning Edwina rose at half past six to say goodbye. She sent a letter after him. "I hated seeing you drive away this morning... you have left me with a strange sense of peace and happiness. Perhaps I have brought you the same?"' (ibid.).

S. S. Pirzada, former Foreign Minister of Pakistan, told me that Jinnah had been given three or four letters that had passed between Edwina and Nehru. They had been intercepted by an opponent of Nehru who wished to embarrass him. The tone of the letters may be gathered from some of the remarks. One noted that 'Dickie will be out tonight – come after 10.00 o'clock'. Another said, 'You forgot your handkerchief and before Dickie could spot it I covered it up.' A third note contained the line 'I have fond memories of Simla – riding and your touch.' After Nehru discovered that this correspondence had gone missing, he and Edwina numbered their letters so they could check them.

These letters were discussed between Jinnah and Fatima, I. I. Chundrigar and Nishtar. Jinnah had the letters sent back to the source after stating: 'Caesar's wife should be above suspicion.' This, he said, was not his kind of politics.

The content of the letters was conveyed to Pirzada by Nishtar, Fatima and I. I. Chundrigar a few years after Jinnah's death. In 1967 Pirzada met Lord Mountbatten for dinner at Buckingham Palace, and Mountbatten asked him about the letters that had gone astray and enquired what Jinnah's response was. Pirzada quoted Jinnah's line about Caesar's wife, and explained that Jinnah would not have capitalized on the discovery because he was a man of principle. If this correspondence is to be believed – and Pirzada retains a sharp memory – then we have further strong proof of a close relationship. However, since there is no other evidence of these particular letters, we have to rely on the oral testimony of Pirzada.

Indians close to power in Delhi, like Krishna Menon, suggested that the affair was 'more than' [friendship] (Hamid 1986: 172). M. J. Akbar asks 'The Great Question': 'Was the affair platonic or not?' (1988a: chapter 36; see also *Edwina and Nehru: A Novel*, Clément 1996). He concludes that the affair was physical and cites an anecdote involving Russi Mody, the son of the Governor of the UP, Sir Homi Mody, to support his contention. Up in the hill-station of Nainital, Russi, when asked by his father to bring Lady Mountbatten and Nehru down for dinner, walked up to Nehru's room, knocked on the door and opened it to see them 'in a clinch' (Akbar 1988a: 391).

Akbar then goes on proudly to point out and justify Nehru's other affairs (Hamid 1986 names names: 172). Our hero, Akbar seems to imply, is a satyr unleashed, a hot-blooded Romeo who will not be denied. Even Gandhi, Akbar suggests, seems to acquiesce at Nehru's antics with a schoolboy's chuckle. Rushdie too notes the affair's 'intimate details' were 'much-observed … though little-commented-on' (1995: 175).

Nehru's clues

Rushdie was right. The affair was 'little-commented-on' and 'much-observed'. But where were the clues? When Nehru kissed Edwina at New Delhi airport in front of the press it sent shock-waves throughout British India (Trench 1987: 341). In India men did not kiss in public even their wives. People were not sure how to interpret Nehru's kiss. By violating social taboo was he deliberately providing them with a clue to something important? Some thought that Nehru's kiss had a message for Jinnah and the world: that the Mountbattens 'belonged' to him and the Congress. Similarly, was Nehru kissing Edwina with his bedroom door open another deliberate ploy (Akbar 1988a: 391)? In India people are more informal than in Britain and walk into rooms without announcement. Besides, servants were always about.

We have other clues. There is a photograph of the Mountbattens and Nehru which hints at a close relationship (see plate 11). It speaks of intimacy, joy, affection and

Plate 11   Nehru with the Mountbattens in a photograph which hints at their intimacy

genuine warmth between the trio. We do not need the whisperings of *ayahs*, cooks and servants to elaborate all this for us.

The three are standing, framed by the massive columns at the entrance to the Viceroy's palace in Delhi. The body language in the picture speaks volumes. Mountbatten is pleasantly aware of the other two but is looking away from them with a faint smile on his lips; he is dressed in formal naval uniform. In contrast, Nehru's jacket and shirt are open and crumpled, and Edwina wears a summer dress and sandals.

Nehru is bent over laughing, his face turned towards Edwina and lit up with merriment. He is standing close behind Edwina, who appears to be sharing a joke with him. The atmosphere appears electric, the hilarity barely containable. This is popular imperial theatre. And the people at that time, tired of the hatred and violence and uncertainty, were fascinated by these three glamorous figures so much in love with each other.

Contrast this picture to those of the earlier Viceroys. The thought of an Indian native being so familiar with the Viceroy and his wife would have shocked the empire. The photographs of Jinnah with the Mountbattens are a study in formality by comparison. They are cordial, the main figures smiling, but none the less they are formal affairs.

The love triangle

Philip Ziegler dismissed the love affair thus: 'To call it a triangle, or Mountbatten a complaisant husband, would be to belittle a relationship that was enriching to all concerned' (Ziegler 1985: 475). Without wishing to belittle the relationship I will call it a triangle and point out why Mountbatten was 'complaisant'. It may have been enriching to the Mountbattens and Nehru, but millions of people, Muslim and Hindus, were directly or indirectly made to suffer on account of their friendship.

The Mountbattens first met Nehru in Singapore in 1946. It was love at first sight. Edwina stumbled and Nehru picked her up. Wolpert describes the encounter thus: 'Nehru lifted her up ... and fell just as swiftly in love with her' (Wolpert 1996: 361). Clearly the Mountbattens and Nehru were 'bewitched' by one another, under each other's 'spell'. 'As one mutual friend, who saw them together many times, defines Mountbatten–Nehru relations, "I can't think of any three people who had such a natural and uninhibited affinity with each other"' (Hough 1983: 181).

Wolpert's suggestion of Nehru's homosexuality and Mountbatten's own alleged homosexuality adds a new dimension to the relationship (Wolpert 1996). Clearly Mountbatten and Nehru were fascinated with one another; both were upper-class public schoolboys and there is little doubt that they amused each other in 1947. I suspect, however, that the relationship did not develop beyond a mutual fascination. After Mountbatten left India it soon faded. The relationship with Edwina was different. It was deep, permanent and intense.

For this cosy triangle Jinnah was the outsider. In the context of the relationships it is significant that both Nehru and the Mountbattens describe Jinnah in emotional terms. Without following up the implications of what they are saying, several writers give us clues to the nature of Mountbatten's political strategy. Here is a description of Mountbatten attempting to win over Jinnah: 'With his legendary charm and verve,

Mountbatten turned the focus of Operation Seduction on the Moslem leader. Jinnah froze' (Collins and Lapierre 1994: 100). 'Operation Seduction', 'charm', 'froze' – these are terms used in emotional relationships. For Mountbatten the division of the subcontinent was also an intensely personal and emotional exercise.

What did the three people see in each other? How did the *ménage à trois* come about? What does each relationship tell us about the lover and the loved one? Three different sets of answers need to be constructed. Let us start with Lady Mountbatten, who adored and was adored by Nehru at first sight. In the words of a former Labour MP she 'became bewitched by Nehru' (Roberts 1994a: 108).

Edwina: magnificent obsession

Like many Western women Edwina had gone to the East searching for spiritual solace. The fascination with gurus is a permanent and universal feature of society whether in the East or the West (Storr 1996). In Nehru Edwina had found her Oriental guru; her friend, philosopher and guide. Gazing on Nehru she dreamed up an ideal, an androgyne, a man with a bisexual nature and an almost mythical capacity to transcend history and culture. Nehru was no longer situated in an Indian context. He was her demon lover. She gave herself to him as to no other man. 'Edwina had no will where he was concerned,' remarked a friend who observed them closely (Hough 1983: 182). 'Just like water.'

What a contrast between Mountbatten and Nehru. For Mountbatten sex was hydraulics, for Nehru it was part of a total relationship in which two beings fused, in which literature, politics, art and culture became part of the fusion. The difference was between an empty-headed English schoolboy and a sophisticated guru from India. There was no match.

Nehru had persuaded Edwina that Jinnah and his Muslims were like the Nazis. This was a shrewd move. Edwina was Jewish and was convinced that in the Hindus she saw the Jews, because they appeared 'down-trodden slaves of the imperial tradition and Muslim cruelty, as the Jews had been persecuted through history' (Hough 1983: 195). At one stroke Nehru had adroitly consolidated her hatred of Jinnah and the Muslims through the metaphor of the Nazis. Paradoxically it was the Hindu leader Golwalkar and his supporters who had started talking and writing about the Nazis, and they had discussed applying Hitler's solution for the Jews to the Muslims of India (as we saw above).

Through Nehru Edwina had also found the big cause of her life: India. For the rest of her life she would be the most passionate advocate of things Indian. The evidence shows that the Indian affair was like nothing Edwina had experienced before. The last quarter of Morgan's biography is devoted to it. Clearly this was no brief flirtation but a lifelong relationship. Indeed it resembles an old-fashioned, stable, long-lasting engagement between two devoted people: detailed letters written by her every day when they part; annual visits to India and, in return, Nehru's annual visits to Broadlands; and expressions of love and irritability in equal measure (for instance, complaints from Edwina that the letters were becoming less frequent and less voluminous towards the end).

Right to the end Edwina was loyal: Nehru's letters, her nightly reading, were by her bed when she died in 1960. When Edwina was buried at sea according to her wishes, Nehru, breaking all protocol, sent an Indian warship, the *Trishul*, to strew a wreath of marigolds on the waves.

The love of Nehru's life

In order not to belittle or caricature Nehru it is important to point out that ours is a snapshot view of one angle of him in the summer of 1947. Nehru's spells in prison, facing baton charges and standing up to authority, combined with his good looks and high caste, made him a celebrity long before he became Prime Minister of India. Members of the British élite were particularly susceptible to Nehru's charms. When Woodrow Wyatt, who had also been at Harrow, first met him on a cabinet mission he felt instinctively at ease with him, seeing Nehru as 'an English public schoolboy' (Wolpert 1996: 22). Yet Nehru was a complex man, evolving and changing visibly over time. The exuberant, impetuous Nehru of the 1940s is not the wiser and sadder Nehru of the 1960s. By the time of his death in 1964 he was a widely respected elder statesman on the international stage, an authentic Third World spokesman, a major leader of the Non-Aligned Movement. A cult figure in his lifetime, Nehru inspired an entire genre of hagiographic writing. It was even given a name, 'Nehru-ana'. (See, for example, *The Gentle Colossus: A Study of Jawaharlal Nehru* (Mukerjee 1964), the typical hagiography of the time; also see Edwardes 1962; Nehru 1941; Nehru 1961; see the three-volume Gopal biography and the 1980 volume; for an exuberantly contemporary if hagiographic Indian account of Nehru read Akbar 1988a, especially chapter 47, *Greater than His Deeds*. He compares Nehru to Caesar (ibid.: 562), to emperors and kings (ibid.: 571). Nehru is a prophet reincarnate, a divine yogi with miraculous powers (ibid.: ix); 'Nehru was, truly, a king of hearts' (ibid.: 571). He was 'virtuous and truthful', 'his generosity was legendary' (ibid.: 575). 'Nehru was born high enough: a Kashmiri Pandit and wealthy to boot.' 'He was certainly very moral, if not quite godly', etc. etc. For a more recent, if darker, picture, see Wolpert 1996.)

The literary and sensitive nature of the man shone through his writings. Take the eloquent speech delivered by him on the eve of Indian independence in August 1947:

> Long years ago we made a tryst with destiny, and now the time comes when we shall redeem our pledge, not wholly or in full measure, but very substantially. At the stroke of the midnight hour, when the world sleeps, India will awake to life and freedom. A moment comes, which comes but rarely in history, when we step out from the old to the new, when an age ends, and when the soul of a nation, long suppressed, finds utterance. (Wolpert 1996: 406)

Nehru was the up-and-coming man of India, an undeclared king, the anointed future Prime Minister, when Edwina fell in love with him. Unlike any other Indian politician he also had sexual glamour and was known and adored by millions. Nehru was the quintessential Indian representing the finest of both Eastern and Western cultures. As befitted his noble birth (as a Brahmin), he received a typically upper-class education in England (at Harrow and Cambridge).

Edwina, who like Nehru was born into the upper class, was an energetic and passionate socialite. As pictures make clear, she was no beauty. Yet something electric, something special, was taking place between the two. 'Our meetings have been rare and always fleeting but I think I understand him, and perhaps he me, as well as any human being *can* ever understand each other' (Morgan 1991: 476). It would be easy to say cynically that Nehru became involved with her only to gain direct access to and influence with the Viceroy, to find out exactly what was going on at the highest level of government; indeed, Nehru was able to use this information and manipulate it to his cause with deadly effect on several occasions, not least in the case of Kashmir. However, in 1947 Nehru would have found Edwina a sympathetic and cultured friend offering a shoulder to lean on in a difficult and trying time. His wife Kamala had died ten years before and he had not remarried.

Like Jinnah, Nehru too had an unhappy married life. Nehru's feelings towards his wife could be those of Jinnah contemplating Ruttie: 'I seemed to be losing her – she was slipping away and I resented this and felt miserable. Many of our little tiffs … were due to this background of conflict…. In politics I was an unhappy, lonely figure, and now even my home life was ending for me. Loneliness everywhere. Nothing to hold on to, no lifeboats or planks to clutch while I struggled with the rising waters' (Wolpert 1996: 175). The difference was that after Ruttie's death Jinnah turned his energies into the politics of his people, the Muslims. Nehru did the same but also found comfort in the company of other women.

We know from the extensive anthropological literature that those of Brahmin background, like Nehru, where Brahmin women were models of purity, would hold adulterous women in contempt. In Edwina's case Nehru was crossing sacred barriers: he was touching an untouchable. But Edwina had several important qualifications – she had power through her husband, she was white, a memsahib and she was an aristocrat.

There is a more complex reason for Nehru's fascination with Edwina. To seduce the memsahib was the ultimate taboo, the no-go area for Indians. Only a man of Nehru's immense charm and chutzpah could have pulled it off. Sex with the memsahib was the ultimate racial and colonial metaphor for power, providing the ultimate emotional *frisson*. Nehru was reversing the roles: he had conquered the white woman, in the person of the Vicereine herself; it was the ultimate victory, the planting of the flag on top of Everest. The crudity of the metaphor would not have been lost in India where society was so sensitive to the issues of sex, race and empire.

There could also be sociological reasons for Nehru's infatuation with Edwina. Nehru's family originally came from Kashmir but lived in Allahabad in the United Provinces. It was a family priding itself on service to the Mughal court, predisposed to looking up to the ruling aristocracy. Nehru's own Brahmin caste, although he was not orthodox, would have made him especially conscious of hierarchy in society. Indian society is intensely class and caste conscious and Nehru would have acquired tremendous social mystique by associating with the highest in the land, the ruling couple of India, the Viceroy and his wife, and a Viceroy related to royalty.

Wolpert in his biography of Nehru observes that 'Jawahar tried to talk Edwina into staying on with him after Dickie flew home, for he knew by now that her heart belonged to him alone.' Mountbatten, of course, also 'knew that they were lovers', as did all of their close friends. Edwina's sister Mary hated Nehru for it, blaming him for having 'hypnotized' her (Wolpert 1996: 435). Nehru came close to a public confession of the love affair at the farewell banquet given for the departing Mountbattens on 20 June 1948. Seated next to Edwina, he said in his speech: 'To you Madam ... the gods or some good fairy gave ... beauty and high intelligence, and grace and charm and vitality, great gifts, and she who possesses them is a great lady wherever she goes. ... Wherever you have gone, you have brought solace, you have brought hope and encouragement. Is it surprising, therefore, that the people of India should love you and look up to you as one of themselves and should grieve that you are going?' (ibid.: 436). Nehru's question would continue to echo until the end of their lives. This was more than a polite, diplomatic farewell. 'Very sad and lost,' Edwina noted in her diary as she headed home with her husband.

The lovers continued to meet whenever they had the opportunity. On 6 October 1948 Nehru flew into London late in the evening, was picked up by Menon and driven straight to Dickie and Edwina's house, where 'Dickie discreetly left the reunited lovers alone for their first midnight rendezvous in months' (Wolpert 1996: 439). 'Too lovely,' Edwina noted in her diary (ibid.). Nehru and Edwina then spent four nights in Broadlands alone while Dickie stayed away in London. 'A heavenly weekend,' Edwina called it (ibid.).

But only a few days after Edwina left him Nehru was exchanging warm letters with Clare Boothe Luce, reminding each other of their 'passionate interlude' (Wolpert 1996: 436). Up to the end Nehru could not resist flirting with attractive women. The US President John F. Kennedy declared Nehru's '"the worst State visit" he had ever experienced and found infuriating Nehru's focus on his wife and his inability to keep his hands from touching her' (ibid.: 480; for visual evidence of Nehru not being able to keep his hands off Jackie Kennedy, see the photograph of the two walking arm in arm in Wolpert 1996 between pages 260 and 261).

Mountbatten the cuckold

Those Indians who knew about Edwina's affair felt that 'Mountbatten seems quite happy about it', the private secretary to Auchinleck, commander-in-chief of the Indian army, noted in his diary (Hamid 1986: 172). Mountbatten 'had fallen under Nehru's spell at Singapore at the end of the war,' stated Brendan Bracken (Roberts 1994a: 81). He 'was soon bewitched by Nehru's personality. He saw Nehru as an aristocratic, radical leader in his own mould' (ibid.: 82). As Mountbatten was alleged to be bisexual, it is possible that he was sexually attracted to Nehru (Wolpert 1996). His desire for Noel Coward to play him in the film *In Which We Serve* and his infatuation with Michael Redgrave give clues to Mountbatten's sexual preferences, as indicated in the Channel 4 *Secret Lives* programme. It may explain his ambiguity about Edwina's affairs. (Pirzada told me of what Nishtar had said to him. Had Jinnah given them an *ishara*, a simple sign, they would have dealt with Mountbatten. Two virile men from the north would have been sufficient and changed his attitude to Pakistan, he chuckled.)

Throughout his life Mountbatten manipulated people, forcing them into situations with a predetermined objective (as Philip Ziegler acknowledged on TV in *Secret Lives*). He famously encouraged the courtship between his nephew Prince Philip and the heir to the throne Princess Elizabeth which would lead to their marriage in November 1947.

Through Edwina he now had direct access to the most important man in the Congress party, the future Prime Minister of India. As much as Nehru thought he was manipulating the Mountbattens, Mountbatten knew that he was manipulating Nehru. It is not surprising that he manipulated an image of Jinnah.

Mountbatten and Nehru may have been well matched in charm and ego but there was no comparing their command of literature and culture. Nehru was the true Renaissance man, a cultured intellectual whose reading was wide and deep and who had written influential books, the autobiography (1941) and *The Discovery of India* (1961). It was said of him that had he not been the first Prime Minister of India he would have made an outstanding Cambridge don. Mountbatten, in contrast, was an intellectual lightweight. In general he preferred sport, especially polo, to reading or other cultural activity.

The friendship with Nehru fitted neatly into Mountbatten's scheme of things. He had access to and influence with the Congress, the most important political party in India. Because of Nehru he could genuinely report back to England that the Indians loved him, so much so that they had offered him the post of the first Governor-General of an independent India.

But the complaisance regarding Edwina concealed pain. The Mountbattens had a troubled marriage, Mountbatten quickly becoming aware of her love affairs. Both his daughters on camera in *Secret Lives* declared that 'it broke his heart'. In other circumstances they would have separated, confirmed another member of the family. The more frustrated he became with his wife, the more he threw himself into his job and the more aggressive and brash he was in it, according to his biographer Ziegler.

Mountbatten's affair with Yola Letellier, the French woman who inspired Colette's 1940s novel *Gigi* (later to become a successful film) – an affair which began in the 1920s, and lasted over forty years – was recounted by the present Countess Mountbatten (in *Secret Lives*). 'But everybody remained good friends,' said the Countess. In fact Yola and her husband had both become friends with both Lord and Lady Mountbatten. Philip Ziegler confirmed (in the same programme) that Edwina had 'indulged herself in other directions' and claimed that Mountbatten always felt a sense of 'inadequacy': 'He put up with all her excesses' and 'condoned if not abated her relationships'. Mountbatten transferred Lieutenant-Colonel Harold 'Bunny' Phillips, Edwina's lover, to his staff and seriously contemplated divorce so that the lovers could be happy.

Right from the start Mountbatten was out of his depth with Edwina. When she allowed him to sleep with her he triumphantly recorded in his diary: 'Slept with Edwina!!' (Morgan 1991: 191). He was then rebuffed. 'Edwina and I ever so nearly had a row,' he complained. The most recent birthday present to his wife had been a portrait of himself (ibid.).

After independence the friendship between Mountbatten and Nehru cooled. Although Mountbatten continued to give advice, he became increasingly isolated from events in India. He was living in the past, still offering his opinion as if he were Viceroy. Nehru resented Mountbatten's interference. On global events such as the rise of the Soviet Union and its influence on India, and the emergence of the Non-Aligned Movement, Mountbatten found it increasingly difficult to comment with any meaning.

Again and again Mountbatten repeated in his television programme that he and his family 'loved India'. I believe that the Mountbattens had a genuine love of India which included Pakistan, although that was a bit of an afterthought and contradicted their actions. But they were not, as their critics claim, pro-Hindu or anti-Muslim in any deeply thought-out way. It is clear from listening to Mountbatten and reading him; it is clear from talking to his daughters. It is significant that Countess Mountbatten, then visiting her parents, in the Indian scenes of her father's television programme greets Indians in the Hindu manner: holding both palms to each other in the *namaste* salutations. It is a genuine cultural gesture, the kind that made the Mountbattens so popular in Delhi. At last, says an Indian in the series, the British have conquered India. But, Muslims will point out, the salutations are specific to Hindu culture. Muslims use *salaam*, peace. Once again the Mountbattens are partisan, they will say. It was difficult, if not impossible, to maintain total neutrality and please all Indians.

Shielding the Vicereine

Why have historians blacked out the affair between Nehru and Edwina Mountbatten? Philip Ziegler, H. V. Hodson, Larry Collins and Dominique Lapierre, Alan Campbell-Johnson – none of these standard writers delves into this most sensitive and important matter.

Were these observers blind? Hardly. They picked up every wart, every quirk, every foible of the main actors. Even Jinnah's 'bad teeth' were commented upon; 'good-looking' Nehru – fit through yoga – was praised in comparison (Morgan 1991: 395). Collins and Lapierre too write of Jinnah's 'mouthful of rotting yellow teeth' (1994: 103). Bearing in mind that there are no colour photographs of Jinnah, how did these authors know his teeth were yellow? Given that he was 70 years of age and a heavy smoker, his teeth in the black-and-white photographs appear in reasonable condition; at least he had them. Someone who knew Jinnah at the time would disagree with the repellent description of Morgan and Collins and Lapierre. Lady Wavell, surrounded by fresh-faced and good-looking ADCs, still said of him, 'Mr Jinnah was one of the handsomest men I have ever seen', going on to wax lyrical about his 'clear-cut, almost Grecian, features' (Bolitho 1954: 213). Who is right? And where did the three authors, who never set eyes on Jinnah, obtain such intimate information?

In the immediate aftermath of partition a protective shield was erected. Any criticism of Lord and Lady Mountbatten would have reflected badly on the core institutions of the British establishment – indeed, even the monarchy itself. After all, Mountbatten was related to royalty and his nephew had married the Queen. Mountbatten was also a glamorous imperial war hero. In the 1940s and 1950s the private conduct of the British upper class, however well known and even condoned by members of the inner circle, was hidden from the rest of the British public. At that time the media would not have revealed the misdemeanours of the monarchy and aristocracy to the lower orders. It was simply not done. By the 1960s reverence towards the British establishment had begun to crumble, so that today the media publish every intimate detail they can discover. Forty or fifty years ago, however, adultery in high places was concealed from the public and it is only relatively recently that most people are beginning to discover hidden aspects of respected public figures in such programmes as Channel 4's *Secret Lives* series.

Although the general respect for and fear of the authority of the ruling classes discouraged gossip in British India, some people knew of the affair. In general the British – those who knew – concealed the affair as conscious policy; the Indians – understanding its implications, and enjoying the metaphorical reversion of the colonial encounter, an Indian atop a British woman – none the less covered it up out of respect for Nehru; the Pakistanis failed to disclose the scandal out of trepidation, diffidence or plain ignorance.

British historians in general have either ignored or glossed over the affair. Even Ziegler in his 786-page official biography dealt with the friendship in a few paragraphs, pausing only to emphasize its beauty (1985). He talked about the 'intensely loving, romantic, trusting, generous, idealistic, even spiritual' relationship between the two (ibid.: 473) and was dismissive about the sexual side of the affair: 'If there was any physical element it can only have been of minor importance to either party' (ibid.). Ten years later he conceded the affair but denied its impact on partition (1995).

Hodson in his authoritative study (1985) has several entries in the index on Nehru's relations with important people, including 'Relations with Lord Mountbatten', 'Relations with Patel', and so on. Not surprisingly there is no 'Relations with Edwina'. Edwardes in his popular biography takes the same approach (Edwardes 1962). Understandably, orthodox British historians have discreetly written out Edwina's role in the politics of the subcontinent (for example in the exhaustive *Cambridge Encyclopedia of India: Pakistan, Bangladesh, Sri Lanka*, edited by F. Robinson, 1989, or *The Raj: India and the British 1600–1947*, edited by C. Bayly, 1990). They blacked out Edwina's affair with Nehru, simply mentioning that 'her interest in welfare ... endeared them to the Indian people and eased political tensions' (Bayly 1990: 415).

Not even the self-conscious investigative bloodhounds Larry Collins and Dominique Lapierre tell us what was going on (in either their 1982 or their 1994 book). Claiming to give us new information never before published, they gloss over one of the central moments in the drama of 1947, the love affair between Edwina and Nehru, and see nothing there.

I do not entirely blame the historians, since the affair was a well-kept secret. Even someone as close to the action as Yaqub Khan, then a cavalry officer and adjutant of the Viceroy's bodyguard, did not suspect it – though he knew Edwina and Nehru were close friends.

Alan Campbell-Johnson, Mountbatten's press attaché, had rejected my view that in the summer of 1947 Edwina influenced decisions, especially those of her husband Mountbatten and her lover Nehru. As the last living member of Mountbatten's staff, he explained that his objection was not on moral grounds but because Edwina had lesbian tendencies. Mountbatten, he suspected, was bisexual. No, he felt Edwina did not have that kind of influence on Mountbatten.

The Countess Mountbatten told me she thought the friendship was on a high spiritual plane. Ending letters with 'love' and beginning them with 'darling', she pointed out, were expressions of affection used regularly by the upper class. Indeed, she knew that even her father loved Nehru. It was all very proper and correct. The Mountbatten family's love of India has prevented the publication of other letters between Nehru and Edwina in their possession. The Indian government had requested that these letters not be published or Nehru's reputation might be tarnished. When I told her about the letters between Edwina and Nehru that Jinnah had been given and refused to publish, the Countess was interested and asked where the letters were. She remarked that her father was 'sad' that he was misrepresented in Pakistan.

When I discussed the affair with Mountbatten's grandson, the Hon. Philip Knatchbull, he asked me why Edwina would not have disclosed her affair with Nehru to the family when they had evidence of the other affairs; she was after all generous with her affections. The answer may be simple. Her affair with Nehru, unlike the other lovers, lasted right until the end, up until her death in Borneo in 1960. The significance of their relationship is revealed by the presence of his letters by her bedside when she was dying. Nehru was an international statesman, and any such scandal would have hurt him. Perhaps also because this affair was more serious than any in the past, she may have wanted to treasure it by keeping it to herself: she would never say or write anything that would hurt Nehru or embarrass him; she would not let him down.

Philip Knatchbull related an incident when Edwina, his grandmother, flew to Paris to meet and befriend his grandfather's mistress, Yola Letellier. This was typical, he said, and Mountbatten too turned his wife's lovers into friends. But Nehru was not her lover, he insisted. I found all this confusing. How the affair was being interpreted by the family conflicted with what common sense and research told us.

An attempt was made in India to conceal the affair – a mirror image of the British position. The standard three-volume study of Nehru by Gopal, the son of Radhakrishnan, a President of India, ignores the relationship. Gopal's third volume (1984), which covers Nehru's last decades, the time of the affair with Edwina, does not even carry a reference to her in the index. It is as if he had wished away the one blemish he needed to hide regarding Panditji.

Nirad Chaudhuri has written: 'I can understand Mountbatten's infatuation with Nehru, which amounted to moral hypnotism' (1990: 831). Chaudhuri goes on to mention Edwina's involvement with Nehru: 'His wife felt that even more strongly ... but she showed her admiration so indiscreetly that even a private secretary of Nehru has used her letters to him to give the most slanderous interpretation to the friendship' (ibid.: 832). The normally irrepressible and voluble Chaudhuri leaves it at that. Once again a curtain is drawn over the affair; it becomes one of the unwritten rules of the subcontinent in studying history.

While pointing out the strange reluctance of past writers to discuss the love affair, Akbar seems to do the same (1988a). The Edwina–Nehru love affair is cast in a lighthearted manner. Jinnah's objection that it had a direct bearing on political decisions is not explored, although it is raised.

We can understand the amnesia or failure of vision in British and Indian historians. Less explicable is the timidity of the Pakistani ones. What is perhaps most surprising is the Pakistani lack of serious interest in the affair – if for nothing else than its impact on partition itself. Yet Pakistani scholars ignore it. There is no mention of Lady Mountbatten or Edwina in the index to Mujahid's magnum opus on Jinnah (1981). Perhaps it is a cultural imperative not to pry too deeply into people's private lives; perhaps pusillanimity that prevents scholars from entering such dangerous waters or perhaps lack of access to relevant documents. None of the established historians – Zaidi, Jalal, Riaz Ahmad or Mujahid – talks about Edwina and the implications of her role in 1947.

Pakistanis were making a standard mistake. They were placing the affair in their own cultural context. A Pakistani husband would have reacted with outraged jealousy and been tempted to a violent act involving his wife and perhaps her lover. Half a century after it shook their world, many Pakistanis still do not believe the affair took place. If Nehru had indeed been involved with Edwina it would have gone in Jinnah's favour if Mountbatten, the jealous husband, had sought revenge against Nehru, remarked an indignant M. H. Askari in the *Dawn* (10 January 1996), reacting to my Longman/*History Today* lecture in which I discuss the affair (reprinted in *History Today*, March 1996). Besides, suspecting Edwina and Nehru of an affair was in 'bad taste'. Pakistanis respond, as Jinnah had observed, emotionally and, most dangerously, on the basis of poor information.

Sex and the British empire

The British empire rested on an indiscriminate military acquisition of territories, one area leading to another. It was not the rapacious conquest of an Alexander the Great marching about Asia and Africa, nor of the ruthless Spanish Conquistadors in Latin America, sword in one hand, Bible in the other, and the lust for gold in their eyes. The British empire was more haphazard and more casually acquired. The British perception of its own benevolence, justice and evolutionary politics was part of its chosen imperial method.

The notion of the superiority of the white race in India was underlined by an aloofness and segregation which ensured authority and the preservation of dignity (Ballhatchet 1980; Barr 1976; Kiernan 1972; MacMillan 1988; J. Robinson 1996; Scott 1983; Young 1994; for a recent popular account, see Gill 1995; the matter is further explored in *Ruling Passions: Sex, Race and Empire*, the BBC2 documentary series shown early in March 1995 in the UK). All this made sense in a society divided hierarchically into a caste structure based on power, status, wealth and authority (Dube 1965; Dumont 1970; Mayer 1970). The British fitted neatly into the top slot, becoming the new ruling caste, in the schema of Indian society.

At the core of this imperial philosophy was the belief that the imperial system was highly moral and that men and especially women were its exemplars. Whatever went on in private, the outward appearance of strict moral conduct thus became an imperial imperative.

British rule was seen by Indians as imposed by force of arms. Yet Indian rulers and native officials were regarded by the British as venal, easily corruptible, leading a life of sensuality, capricious in their judgements (the Orientals of Edward Said (1978)). In contrast, Europeans maintained that they made their decisions on the basis of rational choice, after balancing the pros and cons; they were reflecting a superior civilization. Far more than individual reputations was involved in the glaring impropriety of what was going on in the Viceroy's office and home in the summer of 1947.

As the Viceroy embodied imperial values – and, moreover, was a cousin of the King – the British were obliged to treat him as beyond reproach. To challenge the honesty or character of the Viceroy and his wife was to challenge the very core of British self-esteem. It was unimaginable.

For a Vicereine, the wife of the most important figure in all the British colonies, to be actually involved in an affair with a native was not only revolutionary but only possible at the close of that period of history. It could not have happened in quite this manner a few years before. Although there were rumours about Queen Victoria and her domestic assistant, they were discreetly kept within the household. The veil of morality that hung over the British aristocracy was little more than Victorian hypocrisy; yet the sense of moral superiority, the sheer untouchability of the women at the top, gave the empire its self-perception of its own importance.

The conduct of the Mountbattens and Nehru no longer seems shocking today. Stories that would have appeared unbelievable a generation ago are now commonplace in a society where members of British royalty admit publicly to adultery and members of the British government and MPs are regularly exposed in the media for acts of 'sleaze'.

The Mountbattens' relationship with Nehru cannot be understood without reference to changes taking place globally or in a certain social class of people. From the 1920s onwards – the decade that would form both the Mountbattens and Nehru – a new international élite emerged. Rich, powerful, spoilt and capricious, this élite saw the world as its oyster. It would seek its pleasures where it found them but its backyard was the south of France, the east coast of the USA and California. This was the new international jet-set, for whose members it was the era of ostentatious love affairs, of conspicuous consumption, of extravagant parties.

Until the First World War, members of the European or American élite remained separate in their own social and cultural environment. If they travelled to the East it was often self-consciously, to write a book, or take up a temporary posting. Interaction with the native population was limited and not encouraged. This began to change dramatically from the 1920s. International travel increased; the British empire was weakened after the First World War and it was clear it could not last long; prestige began to shift across the Atlantic; the high moral purpose of the Victorian age now faded. New behaviour patterns emerged which set new standards. The King of England abdicated for the love of a woman. The Duke and Duchess of Windsor became part of the international jet-set. The Mountbattens were very much part of this set too.

The Mountbatten marriage itself was the stuff of legend. In 1922 Lord Louis had married Edwina Ashley, daughter of Lord Mount Temple, a descendant of the former Prime Minister Lord Palmerston and of the social reformer Lord Shaftesbury. As the granddaughter of Sir Ernest Cassel she was heiress to a vast fortune. She and the dashing naval officer spent part of their honeymoon in Hollywood, where they stayed with the Hollywood film star, Douglas Fairbanks Jr. Charlie Chaplin, who was their host in Hollywood, made a short film called *Nice and Friendly,* starring the Mountbattens, Jackie Coogan and Chaplin himself.

The activities of this set provided a new entertainment for ordinary people emerging from the gloom of the First World War and experiencing the fears aroused by the rise of an aggressive Germany in the 1930s. The stories of sex, scandal and gossip emanating from this set provided a much-needed diversion. This élite was different from its predecessors: it was based on wealth and fame. Many of its members were genuinely beyond reach, beyond caring, beyond the morality of ordinary people. They were too exalted, too absorbed in themselves to be affected by the opinions of common mortals. Their actions were often carried out on the whim of the moment. As the darlings of society they felt they could behave exactly as they wanted to; sometimes their behaviour was grossly irresponsible. In the case of the Mountbattens and Nehru it cost millions of lives in the subcontinent and still creates problems between India and Pakistan.

But that is what celebrity is all about. It is a fire that consumes not only the individual but also those around. It burns with its own intensity, careless of the damage it is casually inflicting on those who happen to be in its vicinity.

Summer savagery

The celebrations of nationhood and the attainment of freedom from colonial rule were overshadowed by the shame and anger of the savagery in the summer of 1947. The founding fathers – all of them, on both sides – wept tears of grief as they surveyed the spectacle of human misery. Was this what they wanted?

Nehru, sensitive both in private and in public, expressed it with his usual eloquence in a Prime Minister's broadcast to the nation: 'My mind is full with horror of the things I saw and that I heard. During these last few days ... I have supped my fill of horror. That, indeed, is the only feast we can now have' (Seervai 1990: 213). Gandhi had declared a fast unto death to stop the killings of Muslims in Delhi. Jinnah, we know from Fatima, could barely control his tears at the sight of the endless stream of refugees from India.

With Mountbatten's announcement of partition things moved with bewildering speed. Unforgivably, Mountbatten removed British troops from effective duty, thus ensuring the collapse of law and order. Planned Sikh riots triggered a large-scale migration of Muslims from the districts of East Punjab towards Pakistan. These refugees arriving in Pakistan with harrowing tales of massacre generated riots in Muslim areas against Hindus and Sikhs. Refugees now began to pour from both areas in the opposite direction. They crossed the borders bringing with them stories of the most terrible atrocities against their community. These stories in turn created further violence. In the absence of law-enforcing agencies there was chaos. Had Mountbatten kept the steel frame in place and the regiments in position this mayhem would have been minimized and controlled.

Raping the enemy

Rape is one of the most infamous acts on man's long list of infamy, an act suggesting deep psychological and emotional disturbance. Because rape is so intimately tied to ideas of honour and disgrace, people are reluctant to discuss it. Yet to learn about the true nature of ethnic and religious conflict social scientists need to study ethnic rape or sexual intimidation.

Rape today is a modern instrument of war. In areas such as Bosnia and Kashmir the modern soldier, it appears, marches with gun in one hand and penis in the other. His victories and main activities are not on the battlefield. They are in darkened rooms, torturing and raping civilians. There is little honour left in soldiering today. Whether in the Balkans, in the Middle East or in South Asia the modern soldier is under intense psychological pressure. His role is unclear, as are his objectives. Government puts him in the field to solve the problem of dissidents and rebels. But he is now no longer the solution; he is the problem.

In Bosnia rape was used deliberately as policy, a fact confirmed by innumerable international organizations. Dogs, men infected with HIV and gang rapes were used against women in what have been exposed as rape camps. Small girls were raped in front of their mothers by soldiers. Rape is known as an ugly face of battle committed by soldiers in the heat of war. But in the twentieth century civilians, administrators, students – ordinary members of the public – have been involved as active participants or as spectators.

Bosnia was not alone in this regard. There is also considerable evidence gathered by international human rights organizations and by Indian writers that Indian troops in Kashmir are using the same tactics. After the destruction of the Ayodhya mosque the police were clearly implicated in organizing riots in Bombay and Surat against Muslims which involved rape (see chapter 8). Iraq and Israel have also used sexual tactics to intimidate minorities (Makiya 1993). Iraqi soldiers force Kurd women from camps and take them to be raped; Israelis lock up Arab women in security cells for the night with threatening men. An organization of brave Israeli women risked the wrath of the authorities and documented the widespread cases of sexual abuse by the Israeli police in *Women for Women Political Prisoners*, published in December 1989 in Jerusalem.

The spiral of violence

Rioting between Hindus and Muslims has been recorded in history since the early nineteenth century. From the 1920s onwards the increasing frequency and heightened intensity of the riots created a different kind of hatred. It none the less stopped short of the violation of women. But the collapse of law and order in 1947 changed that. In the summer of 1947 women were abducted, raped and killed on an unprecedented scale in large parts of northern India.

It is commonly accepted among those working with refugees that more than just self-esteem is involved. When a person has lost the family home, when friends and neighbours have become enemies, it creates an internal state of terror which quickly becomes external terror. If you want to abolish terror, you try to obliterate what you see as its source. Then the victim wants to turn on the perpetrator of the crime, not just wishing to kill, but to cut them up, torture them, torch their house and make sure they are utterly annihilated. They are burning with the desire to avenge what they see as palpable and gross injustice. This is what gripped the main communities in 1947.

In what are traditional agricultural societies in South Asia the honour, or *izzat*, of women is directly linked to the household and the clan or the tribe. The woman is made to suffer twice: first from the brutality of the rape itself and then from the horror of her family. It is a double burden. It violates the woman and it also alienates her from her own society as she is considered 'impure'. Honour, modesty and motherhood are all deemed to have been violated; in certain tribes, unlawful sexual acts are wiped out only by the death of the woman concerned (Ahmed 1980, 1991). Rape is thus deliberately employed by ethnic neighbours who are fully aware of its expression as political power and cultural assertion to humiliate the internal other.

The sociological implications are clear for the purposes of our argument: rape as a final line divides one group from the other; the state, through its forces, becomes the rapist, raping its own citizens, those it has sworn to protect. Bitterness is at a peak. So is the nature of hatred in the response. Blood and revenge follow. A spiral of violence is set in motion. All the key notions of modernity – justice, rule of law, rationalism, civic society – are negated by the criminal nature of ethnic rape. For the victim and her family it is no longer an age of modernity and progress but one of barbarism and darkness.

Because of the scale of the rape and abduction in the Punjab and the fact that it was a deliberate humiliation it has left permanent scars and explains the bitterness between communities until today (see, for example, *Embodied Violence: Communalising Female Sexuality in South Asia*, Jayawardena 1996). As is clear from reading Nirad Chaudhuri and other Indian writers, there is little doubt that as the drama began to unfold in 1947 large numbers of the Sikh community were alarmed at being caught in the middle, neither in India nor in Pakistan, and frustrated at not being able to obtain their own independent state. They were encouraged by Congress leaders to think about the elimination of the Muslims from their areas. They were supplied with weapons. Hostile propaganda fuelled their passions. Jinnah became the target of hatred and assassination attempts were planned.

In one of the most popular novels to be written in India, *Train to Pakistan*, Khushwant Singh described the sexual repulsion and fascination between the communities (1988). Appropriately it was set in 1947. The sexual relationship between a Sikh male and a Muslim female forms an important part of the book. It shocked people accustomed to thinking of communities as separate entities with no interaction between them, least of all a sexual one. But it touched a raw nerve. It brought to the fore what was known but not discussed, that is the use of sex as a weapon in communal violence.

The killings in 1947 are well documented and no credit to any community. Here, in another novel, Khushwant Singh describes the preparations to kill the Muslims of Delhi:

> The real problem was to find out who was Muslim and who was not. As soon as the Mussalmans of Delhi heard what had happened in Karnal and Ambala and Amritsar and Jalandhar, they burnt their red fez caps and furry Jinnah 'topees' and started wearing Gandhi caps instead. They shaved off their beards, gave up wearing 'sherwani' coats, loose pyjamas and learnt to tie 'dhotis' round their waists. Their women stopped wearing 'burqas' when they went out and started to put red dots on their foreheads and say 'namaste'. The only way we could tell if the fellow was a Mussalman was to see if his penis was circumcised. How could we stop everyone and say 'Show me your cock'?... We began by marking Muslim homes and shops with swastikas. Muslim 'goondas' got to know of this and put swastika marks on Hindu shops and homes. We changed our plans and decided to attack a few well-known stores owned by Muslims and watch the results. There was a big one in Connaught Circus in the centre of New Delhi. The chief approved of the plan and suggested a date for its execution. (K. Singh 1990: 359)

Jinnah saw Delhi erupt in the summer of 1947. The manner of the killings was unprecedented, as Nirad Chaudhuri records:

> Even more shocking than the scale of the massacres was the savagery of the murders. A friend of mine saw a Muslim boy of ten murdered in cold blood without being able to prevent it. The soldiers discovered a man tied to the electrical connector box of the tramlines, with a hole made in his skull so that he might die slowly by bleeding. I give another instance which was told to me.... A Muslim boy of about fourteen was passing through a Hindu locality and was seized. He was in Hindu dress and pleaded that he was a Hindu. He was stripped to find out whether he was circumcised or not, and when that proof of being a Muslim was discovered he was thrown into a pond nearby and kept under water by bamboo poles, with a Bengali engineer educated in England noting the time he took to die on his Rolex wristwatch, and wondering how tough the life of a Muslim bastard was. (Chaudhuri 1990: 810–11)

A deliberate attempt to cast Muslims as the aggressors who started the fight, so that their subsequent butchery became easier to justify, was noted by Chaudhuri:

> The newspapers reported that there had been pitched battles for twelve hours in Sabzi Mandi and large quantities of arms and ammunition had been discovered there in Muslim houses. The impression sought to be created was that the Muslims had been the aggressors and had defied the police and soldiers for a whole day. I still disbelieve the story. The upshot of the rioting in Sabzi Mandi was that after three or four days there was not a Muslim to be seen there. Almost all the Muslims houses had been set on fire or wrecked. The streets were literally lined, and the gutters choked, with corpses. Rumour puts the number of the Muslims dead there alone, leaving out the rest of Delhi, at thousands....
>
> Did they all die in a desperate defiance of authority? Not till all my observation of my countrymen is cancelled by direct personal experience to the contrary can I and shall I believe in that possibility. A friend of mine who has made careful inquiries has formed a different idea of the general pattern of these riots. According to him it was the Hindus who first tried to plunder the Muslim houses and murder the Muslims, and when the Muslims resisted or counter-attacked, the police and the soldiery came in, and they and the local Hindus (with Sikhs) between them made short work of the Muslims. I do not find the same inherent improbability in this hypothesis as I do in the standardized Hindu version given in the newspapers. (ibid.: 845)

Not only Delhi but all of India was in flames. Chaudhuri describes the scene in Bihar:

> The Hindus of Bihar rose and killed the Muslims who were a minority in the province, in masses. From October to November, the slaughter went on, with too few troops to bring it under control. The young British soldiers who were sent there had never imagined that in joining an army they would

have to do soldiering of this kind. They were horrified at what they had to see....

At the same time, the killings spread westward to the adjoining province of UP. Garh Mukteswar on the Ganges in western UP is a famous holy spot for bathing in the late autumn. That year the festival fell in November, and from the 6th to 15th November the enormous crowds of Hindu pilgrims completed their dip in the holy river by killing Muslims wholesale. (ibid.: 813)

The main leaders worked round the clock to calm their communities. We know of Gandhi's fast. Here is Jinnah calming his community:

I am glad that so far the Muslim majority provinces have been peaceful and immune from this virus of holocaust and I hope and trust that they will not lose their balance and will not stoop to the spirit of malice, revengefulness or retaliation, however deeply they may feel what they read and hear of the terrible happenings, especially in Bihar. (R. Ahmed 1993: 101)

Still, Indians blamed Muslim leaders like Jinnah for the killings in 1947: 'Pakistan ideologue Mohammed Iqbal and Pakistan architects Fazl ul-Haq, Mohammed Ali Jinnah and Liaqat Ali Khan, have caused the deaths of lakhs [hundreds of thousands] of people' (Elst 1992: 138).

Muslims were more vulnerable because they were less well armed, as illustrated by a note by Mountbatten in which he rejects Jinnah's complaints of violence against Muslims. In the official notes we see how the British view the two rival warring groups:

I [Mountbatten] told [Jinnah] that I considered it was wrong that the Sikhs had been given permission to carry these big swords, but since this wrong could not now be undone, I did not see how a second wrong could put it right. I said that if we allowed all parties to go armed in the Punjab, it was an invitation to civil war. (Zaidi 1993: volume I, part II, 651–2)

In Bosnia, in the early 1990s, the British would use exactly the same arguments, indirectly encouraging the genocide of the Muslims. One side is armed to the teeth, the other is defenceless; if both are armed there will be more, not less bloodshed. So do nothing.

Caught in the middle: the Sikhs

An important aspect of the story of partition and independence is the problem of the Sikhs, how it affected events in 1947 and its ongoing impact on relations between India and Pakistan (Akbar 1985; McLeod 1989; *Pacific Affairs* 1987; Pettigrew 1975, 1991, 1995; G. Singh 1987, 1991, 1993). When it came to dividing the Punjab, there was an intractable problem. The Punjab was shared by the three great religions of North India – Muslims, Hindus and Sikhs. The Muslims were in the majority, with over 50 per cent of the population; the Sikhs comprised about 13 per cent. If the Punjab was divided the international border would tear through Sikh territory and culture. For the Sikhs the Punjab was the only home they ever had.

The Sikh sense of nationalism and identity was linked to the Punjab. They had once ruled this area, however briefly, and their holy places were in it. Their sacred book had been formed here and their great capital had been Lahore. All this would be lost to them if the Punjab were to be divided and they were to move to India.

The Sikhs had helped make the province the bread-basket of India. Along with the Muslims they provided the backbone of the Indian army. From Attock to Lahore an arc of districts provided the cream of the fighting forces of the army. They developed a reputation as enterprising farmers, a martial people living by a defined code.

The Sikhs strongly opposed the partition of India. The Sikh leader Master Tara Singh warned: 'If the Muslim League wants to establish Pakistan they will have to pass through an ocean of Sikh blood' (Hamid 1986: 6). Jinnah became the main Sikh target, the figure of hate, and several attempts were made to assassinate him. Yet when Jinnah argued against the division of the Punjab and the need to keep British troops on to oversee the transfer of populations Mountbatten rejected both demands.

In the summer of 1947 the Sikhs drove Muslims from the districts of the Punjab that would fall in India. These Muslims arrived in Lahore with horror stories which provoked Muslims to attack Sikhs and Hindus, which encouraged their exodus to India. Punjabi Sikh, Punjabi Hindu and Punjabi Muslim societies were tearing themselves apart; it was a community in the throes of self-destruction.

Sikh history after independence in India is a disturbing one. They did well at first. They were honoured soldiers and something of a showpiece in the Indian army. Only about 3 per cent of the population, they got about 12–13 per cent of the jobs; for the Muslims the situation was reversed, since they held only about 3 per cent of the jobs although they had a population of about 13 per cent.

Fed on their own myth of martial valour and nursing dreams of independence, the Sikhs took on the might of Delhi. Sant Bindarwale raised the banner of revolt in the Punjab from his stronghold in the holy temple at Amritsar. In 1984 the attack on the Golden Temple, the holiest of the holies, enraged the Sikhs; the Indian army campaign, Operation Blue Star, left them bitter. The demand for their own independent country, Khalistan, grew, but the Indian authorities responded with escalating brutality. In a rash moment the Sikh bodyguard of the Prime Minister, Indira Gandhi, gunned her down. A massacre of Sikhs took place in Delhi. Sikhs were burnt alive, stabbed and killed in an orgy of violence. The Sikhs were back to square one. They were a people dispossessed, strangers in their own land. Once a pampered minority, now they became a suspect one. Ever since they have endeavoured to find a political and cultural balance in India.

Had the Punjab remained undivided there would have been no Sikh problem, there would have been no migrations, no killings, no communal madness. Above all there would have been more of a balance between India and Pakistan, more of a balance in the minorities they possessed so that neither country would become a monstrosity of one dominant culture or religion easily able to subjugate ethnic minorities.

Those who argue that the Sikhs could not have survived in Pakistan must recall that the Pakistan created by Mountbatten had in it Buddhists in the Chittagong Hill Tracts in East Pakistan and the Kalash Kafirs in the north of West Pakistan. Besides there were large numbers of Hindus, over 10 per cent of the total population. So why would the Sikhs have been out of place, especially when in a cultural sense they were as Punjabi as the Muslims?

The Sikh issue is far from over. In August 1995 the Chief Minister of the Punjab, along with a large entourage, was blown up outside the state government offices in the state capital, Chandigarh. Sikh separatists claimed responsibility. The Indians pointed a finger at Pakistan, and Congress intensified its campaign against the separatists. However, in the 1997 elections a coalition of Sikhs and BJP Hindus swept to power, routing the Congress party.

Today the Sikhs' struggle for identity is not over. It simmers on, exploding into violence with repeated force. India accuses Pakistan of helping and training Sikh militants. Once again we trace the tensions of a contemporary geopolitical flashpoint back to Lord Mountbatten.

Mountbatten's numbers game

On a visit to London in November 1947, Mountbatten, as Governor-General of India, said in a speech: 'Only a hundred thousand people had died and only a small part of the country had been affected' (Ziegler 1985: 437). He spent a considerable amount of his time and energy after he left India fudging the figures of those who had been killed in 1947. Presumably he thought 100,000 deaths would have been acceptable. Lord Ismay told his wife, 'I was horrified at Dickie's speech.' He was disgusted by this and is on record pointing out Mountbatten's attempts to distort history. Ismay was so repelled that he asked Lord Mountbatten to delete his name from a list of honours he was preparing. Ismay told Churchill's private secretary that over a million people had lost their lives. According to other reports, over 2 million died (Hewitt 1992: 25) and about 15 million were displaced. Yet Clement Attlee, the Prime Minister, who had given India Lord Mountbatten as Viceroy, wrote in 1961: 'Broadly speaking the thing went off well, I think.' It was remarkable that on Mountbatten's return from India in 1948 no one publicly discussed the disasters for which he was responsible. Mountbatten may have been criticized in private but in public there was a silence in Britain. Mountbatten's press attaché, Alan Campbell-Johnson, published *Mission with Mountbatten* in 1951. His enthusiasm for Mountbatten glows in his introduction:

> When originally published in 1951, this book was the first full-length inside story of one of the greatest world developments of our time – the transfer of power in India by partition and consent – the reconciliation of East and West, of ruler and ruled. This *tour de force* was primarily the achievement of Lord Mountbatten's dynamic diplomacy. (Campbell-Johnson 1985: 1)

Campbell-Johnson describes Mountbatten's staff meetings as an almost spiritual experience: 'He hammers out his thoughts on the anvil of discussion. It is most exciting to be a part of this creative process' (ibid.: 58). 'Never was Mountbatten's genius for informal chairmanship and exposition more signally displayed. His natural talent for this procedure had been enhanced by three years of almost daily discussion as Supreme Commander' (ibid.: 101).

According to Alan Campbell-Johnson, Mountbatten was not always so negative about Jinnah. Mountbatten's bitterness, he claimed, reflected his own changing personality towards the end of his life: it was the irascibility of an old man. But this was not entirely correct. Mountbatten's comments on Jinnah were made in 1947. Campbell-Johnson's argument that there were two distinct Mountbattens, one the golden boy of India, the other the bitter old man, is not borne out by the evidence. It seemed Ziegler was right when he remarked in the *Secret Lives* programme that Mountbatten was continuing to manipulate people from beyond the grave.

Campbell-Johnson gave me an article, 'Eight weeks that changed the world', by Woodrow Wyatt, the former Labour MP who was personal assistant to Sir Stafford Cripps on the Cabinet Mission to India in 1946 (published in *Reynolds News*, 9 December 1951). It shows the extraordinary hero-worship of Mountbatten in Britain after the independence of India:

> Mountbatten's assets were energy, charm ... and close relationship to the King.... Mountbatten's splendidly royal appearance, and conscious use of it, deeply impressed the confused and bewildered Princes.... But his regal background also touched the heart of all India particularly as it was allied, in both the Mountbattens, to an informality and human understanding which never radiated from the Viceroy's house before.... On August 15, 1947, when India and Pakistan were born as free nations, Mountbatten's popularity in the sub-continent was nearly as high with the multitudes as Jinnah's in Pakistan, and that of Gandhi and the Congress leaders in India. He had also persuaded both countries to stay in the Commonwealth.

To compound matters historians also failed to reassess Mountbatten and saluted 'Mountbatten's sincerity and energy' (Bayly in the authoritative *The Raj: India and the British 1600–1947*, 1990: 414). For the first decades after partition Mountbatten remained an imperial hero, a legend in his lifetime. Books such as *Mountbatten: Hero of Our Time* (1980), by Richard Hough, continued to be written about him until recently.

In the 1990s we saw the first signs of change in Britain. Christopher Beaumont wrote an article in the *Daily Telegraph* on 24 February 1992 describing how Mountbatten made Sir Cyril Radcliffe change the partition plans. His disclosure was significant as he was the last surviving member of the team responsible for partition. Shortly afterwards Andrew Roberts published his bestselling *Eminent Churchillians*, which savaged Mountbatten's reputation (1994a). Roberts devotes almost one-third of his book to Mountbatten in a chapter called 'Lord Mountbatten and the perils of adrenalin'.

Channel 4 followed this with the *Secret Lives* programme, broadcast on 9 March 1995, which further exposed Mountbatten as a hypocrite and a liar. It also offered clues as to why he tolerated his wife's affair with Nehru.

After seeing the Channel 4 *Secret Lives* documentary programme on Mountbatten, A. A. Gill wrote:

> Of all the men who weren't actually despots in the 20th century Mountbatten must have been responsible for the most needless deaths. He was, it seems, an exceedingly dangerous man to know or serve with, unless, of course, you were a German or Japanese, in which case you could go to bed

early, secure in the knowledge that he was probably tirelessly doing your job for you.

His precipitate and partisan handling of Indian partition resulted in untold deaths, but after every catastrophe he stepped out of the gore and walked away with a smile, covered in medals and glory and without doubts. He was not a callous man, just that most lethal of personality cocktails: an impatient enthusiast with one eye on posterity. ('Criminally inane' by A. A. Gill, *Sunday Times*, 12 March 1995)

Mountbatten's reputation is presently under a cloud. The pendulum may well be swinging the other way, with journalists scenting blood – as the example of Francis Wheen in the *Guardian* illustrates: 'He was also snobbish, devious and ruthless. "You're so crooked, Dickie," Sir Gerald Templer once told him, "that if you swallowed a nail you'd shit a corkscrew." Anthony Eden described him as "a congenital liar"' (*Guardian*, 26 October 1994).

At the best of times an operation of the kind envisaged in the summer of 1947 would be a nightmare business, since it meant cutting through religious, ethnic and cultural ties. It needed the handling of a master surgeon. It was the misfortune of the subcontinent that the surgeon was Lord Mountbatten.

In its passion the Mountbatten affair with Nehru helped to destroy the fabric of South Asian society in the summer of 1947. Its long-range implications are still with us today. Had the three been cooler, wiser in temperament, things might have been different. There might have been less bloodshed, less passion, less continuing violence.

What the killings of 1947 did was to create a permanent sense of hatred against the other. Each group saw the other as having started the savagery: this is what is firmly embedded in the mythology. It explains the deep-rooted suspicion in Pakistan, particularly in the Punjab, against India. It is useful to remember that it was the Punjab in Pakistan that took the brunt of the refugees, both incoming and outgoing. Memories are still sharp and few people are prepared to discuss what their families suffered. The issue of rape is especially sensitive. Similarly on the Indian side the refugees from Punjab and what is now Pakistan settled in the eastern Indian Punjab and Delhi. They brought with them the most bitter memories of losing homes and being violated. One of these, L. K. Advani, from the Sind, would become the leader of the BJP in India. His background would give a communal edge to his politics. Heading in the opposite direction to Advani was Zia ul-Haq, who became President of Pakistan and attempted to bring Islamic consciousness to Pakistan.

The shame of 1947 was not the fault of the British alone. Hindus, Muslims and Sikhs prided themselves on their sense of honour, and the respect they gave their women and children, of the fair play they believed in. In the summer of 1947 they disproved their own self-perception. They behaved with complete savagery, especially in North India. There was a total madness in the land. The fabric of British, Hindu and Muslim civilization had disintegrated. It is a wound that has not entirely healed half a century later.

Part III

A Tryst with Destiny?

CHAPTER 7

Pakistan: Ethnic versus Religious Identity

Unity, faith and discipline.

(Jinnah's motto for Pakistan)

In the following chapters I examine developments in the subcontinent after independence in 1947, bringing the story up to date. I shall continue to use Jinnah – and the Muslims – as a reference point. Over half a century later the South Asian countries are heading down the slippery slope of ethnic and religious violence. At the heart of the problem is the failure to resolve the central issues of identity in the spirit of mutual tolerance. The conflict in India revolves around religion and caste; in Pakistan around ethnicity and sect. In the first case the clash is *between* religions, in the second *within* one religion.

There is a sociological explanation for the failure. In India the dominant castes wish to impose a unitary vision on the land. A large number of Hindus are arguing – as, for instance, many in the BJP – that to be an Indian you must be Hindu. They insist that the minorities of India – like Muslims and Christians – were originally converts from Hinduism and must now revert back to Hinduism. Here, paradoxically, Gandhi and the BJP meet, as we saw above. The BJP even have a category for the reconverted Muslims: 'Hindu-Mohammadans'. Similarly they attempt to force the so-called 'lower castes' to revert to a more rigid and traditional schema. The lower castes are denied economic and political privileges although the constitution allows them such rights. Any changes to this thinking about the lower castes invites violence.

In Pakistan, because there is one main religion, the violence is generated within it. Because of the failure to develop a 'Pakistani' national identity, ethnic and tribal identities remain strong. Here the debate focuses on the relationship between a Pakistani identity and an Islamic one. In an Islamic identity the definition of what kind of Islam is important. Because the definition of Islam is important so is that of sect. Shia and Sunni clashes in Pakistan are not only regular but bloody. A member of the National Assembly of Pakistan, who heads a religious Sunni party, was on record on British television urging his followers to exterminate Shias. In southern Pakistan the strength of these identities means that groups like Sindhis and *muhajirs*, refugees from India, can clash with all the violence and savagery associated with the conflict of religions in India. Torture and brutality including rape are reported in these clashes.

From a distance, to Europeans or Americans, these cultures, and the people, may all look alike, but their customs, languages, religions are different; they demand respect; minorities must be given security and dignity. The essence of Jinnah's struggle is the struggle for the identity, dignity and security of the minorities.

Jinnah's Pakistan: the rising of the moon

'There is no solution in sight; once there was mirth in the heart, now nothing makes me smile.' Ghalib's despondent verses reflected the nadir of Muslim politics, the depths of the collapse. Within a century of those lines being written, Jinnah had pulled off the impossible. He had created an independent Muslim state. He had restored Muslim pride, given them a sense of destiny and secured them territory.

Pakistan, a modern Muslim nation

Pakistan, Jinnah said, was like the rising moon. The crescent would be on the Pakistan flag. Jinnah could have compared Pakistan to the sun. Indeed the sun is a common enough symbol of imperial statehood in the region. Iran used it; further east in Asia so did the Japanese. The sun represents power, authority, a dominating, irresistible force. In contrast the moon in South Asian literature is a symbol of softness, mystery, magic, romance, compassion, hope and promise.

The choice of moon over sun is obviously a deliberate, perhaps self-conscious, cultural selection making a political point. It is symbolic of Islam. It also reflects the mystical and romantic side of the usually pragmatic and practical Jinnah. In this selection he is illustrating a side usually kept guarded from the public.

The national anthem of Pakistan reflects Jinnah's Pakistan. It talks of the resolve of Pakistan, the focal point of faith, the pure land; it aspires for a destiny that is strong and shining; and it uses the Islamic symbol of the crescent and star on the flag to remind us of the glory of the past and the glory of the present and above all the shadow of the Almighty. It was never a popular demotic anthem because of the difficult literary words. Done in a hurry, it nevertheless reflects the high ideals of the founding fathers of Pakistan.

Once the nation was conceded, a capital had to be located. The older cities were not practical: Lahore was too close to the Indian border and Dhaka far too remote. Jinnah opted for Karachi. It was a port, it was away from the border and therefore India's armed forces, and it had space for accommodating the refugees. It was also Jinnah's birthplace. Overnight this small coastal fishing town became a major international city as hundreds of thousands of refugees poured into Karachi and the Sind province.

Jinnah's Muslim nation was not fully what he had wanted: it was 'truncated' and 'moth-eaten'. It appears Jinnah's willpower kept him going but in the last year of his life, after Pakistan had been created, he was seriously ill. He therefore focused his energies on the survival of the state, burning himself out in the effort to keep it alive. The unending problems were of such magnitude that they demanded his immediate attention (which gave his critics the opportunity to accuse him of concentrating too much power in himself, of becoming autocratic): the influx of millions of refugees from India; the horror of the communal violence in which about 2 million people – Hindus and Muslims – died; a state of undeclared war in Kashmir; a tattered defence and administrative structure, torn in two, needing to be rebuilt; the near bankruptcy of the state; and the refusal of an increasingly hostile India to send Pakistan the agreed division of assets. Besides, the awful reality of millions of Muslims stranded in India, as 'hostages', not easily able to enter his Pakistan, a nightmare he tried so hard to avoid, soon dawned on him. The savage scale of the killing of refugees on both sides shook him to the core, hastening his end. (This is precisely how Dina Wadia saw her father's death. She believed that he literally sacrificed himself for his nation. Her bitterness towards Pakistan is explained by the nation's failure to recognize his supreme sacrifice.)

Increasingly, Jinnah was opening his heart in an unprecedented manner to his people in the official broadcasts, abandoning the formal posture of the skilful but aloof lawyer. Now he shared their hopes, their sorrow, their sense of personal tragedy and their feeling of frustration at the injustices of the world. One senses his anger and outrage as he witnessed not only the machinations that would lose Pakistan the state of Kashmir but the attempts to kill Pakistan at its birth.

In the first winter of Pakistan's existence, a group of officers, in welcoming him, assured him that they were prepared to follow him 'through sunshine and fire' (Jinnah 1989: 118). Jinnah replied, 'Are you prepared to undergo the fire? We are going through fire, the sunshine has yet to come' (ibid.). He was aware of the dangers. The whole structure could rapidly unravel in spite of all the faith and commitment of the supporters of Pakistan. His question whether Pakistanis were prepared to undergo the fire is as relevant today as when Jinnah raised it. Pakistanis are still going through fire.

Jinnah's Gettysburg address

What was Jinnah's vision of Pakistan? Would Pakistan be a modern democracy or a closed theocracy? Would non-Muslims be safe in it?

Since Jinnah did not write a book or monograph, the main clue to his thinking comes through his speeches. If we put together two of his speeches in the crucial month of August 1947, when he had attained his Pakistan – indeed the first two speeches that he made in his new state – we are able to grasp his vision for the state he had created. The first was delivered on 11 August, when the Constituent Assembly of Pakistan elected him as their first President, the second on 14 August which is now celebrated as Pakistan or Independence Day (see plate 12). Together they comprise Jinnah's 'Gettysburg address' and would form the base for his subsequent speeches in the year that remained to him.

Perhaps his most significant and most moving speech was the first one. It is an outpouring of ideas on the state and the nature of society, almost a stream of

Plate 12   Jinnah replying to the address by Lord Mountbatten in the Constituent Assembly in Karachi, August 1947

consciousness. No bureaucratic hand impedes the flow because it was delivered without notes:

> Now, if we want to make this great State of Pakistan happy and prosperous we should wholly and solely concentrate on the well-being of the people, and especially of the masses and the poor. If you will work in co-operation, forgetting the past, burying the hatchet, you are bound to succeed. If you change your past and work together in a spirit that every one of you, no matter to what community he belongs, no matter what relations he had with you in the past, no matter what is his colour, caste or creed, is first, second and last a citizen of this State with equal rights, privileges and obligations, there will be no end to the progress you will make.
>
> I cannot emphasise it too much. We should begin to work in that spirit and in course of time all these angularities of the majority and minority communities, the Hindu community and the Muslim community – because even as regards Muslims you have Pathans, Punjabis, Shias, Sunnis and so on and among Hindus you have Brahmins, Vashnavas, Khatris, also

Bengalees, Madrasis and so on – will vanish. Indeed if you ask me this has been the biggest hindrance in the way of India to attain the freedom and independence and but for this we would have been free peoples long long ago. (Jinnah 1948: 9–10)

Building up from this powerful passage comes the vision of a brave new world, consciously an improvement in its spirit of tolerance on the old world he has just rejected:

> You are free; you are free to go to your temples, you are free to go to your mosques or to any other place of worship in this State of Pakistan.... You may belong to any religion or caste or creed – that has nothing to do with the business of the State.... We are starting in the days when there is no discrimination, no distinction between one community and another, no discrimination between one caste or creed and another. We are starting with this fundamental principle that we are all citizens and equal citizens of one State. (ibid.: 10)

If Pakistanis could follow these ideals, Jinnah would be confident of the future. Jinnah made a pledge: 'My guiding principle will be justice and complete impartiality, and I am sure that with your support and co-operation, I can look forward to Pakistan becoming one of the greatest nations of the world' (ibid.).

Two days later the Mountbattens flew to Karachi to help celebrate the formal transfer of power. In his formal speech to the Constituent Assembly on 14 August, Lord Mountbatten offered the example of Akbar the Great Mughal as the model of a tolerant Muslim ruler to Pakistan.

Akbar the Great as a model Muslim ruler...

Mountbatten had suggested Akbar advisedly. Akbar has always been a favourite of those who believe in synthesis or what in our time passes for secular. To most non-Muslims in South Asia, Akbar symbolized a tolerant, humane Muslim, one they could do business with. He avoided eating beef because the cow was sacred to the Hindus. The Rajputs gave his armies leading generals and his court influential wives.

But for many Muslims Akbar posed certain problems. Although he was a great king by many standards, he was a far from ideal Muslim ruler: there was too much of the wilful Oriental despot in his behaviour. His harem was said to number a thousand wives. His drinking, his drugs and his blood lust were excessive even by Mughal standards. In a fit of rage he had some 30,000 people massacred because they resisted him (in the siege of Chitor in 1567). Akbar also introduced a new religious philosophy, *din-e-ilahi*, a hotchpotch of some of the established religions, with Akbar himself as a focal religious point. This was imperial capriciousness, little else; but it made the *ulema* unhappy.

Mountbatten would have been aware that six Mughal emperors, beginning with Babar in 1526 and ending with Aurangzeb's death in 1707, had ruled India, giving it one of the most glorious periods of its history. The Mughal empire did not end until it was finally killed off in 1857 by the British, but its last great emperor was Aurangzeb.

They were remarkable men, these six, each one different and easily lending himself to popular stereotypes. There was Babar the warrior king, the founder; Humayun, good-natured but unlucky, who almost lost his father's kingdom; Akbar the Great, the man who joined together the various cultural and religious strands of India during his reign, thereby creating his own religion; Jahangir, artistic, drunken, troubled, who ruled mainly through his talented wife the empress Nur Jahan; Shah Jahan, who brought the empire to a pinnacle of artistic and architectural glory, the creator of the Taj Mahal; and finally Aurangzeb, whose long reign is seen as the watershed for Muslim rule in India and who himself evokes divided loyalties, orthodox Muslims holding him as an example of an ideal ruler, critics calling him a fanatic and pointing out his harsh treatment of his father and brothers.

So Mountbatten's choice was neither random nor illogical. Yet he could also have selected Babar, who after all opened a new chapter of history in India, not unlike Jinnah. The story of Babar – poet, autobiographer, loyal friend and devoted father – was perhaps too triumphalist for Mountbatten. But had Mountbatten and his staff done their homework they would have realized their blunder. In suggesting Akbar, Mountbatten was clearly unaware of the impression he was conveying. While his choice may have impressed some modernized Muslims, the majority would have thought it odd. Of the six great Mughal emperors from Babar to Aurangzeb, Akbar is perhaps the one most self-avowedly neutral to Islam. To propose Akbar as an ideal ruler to a newly formed and self-consciously post-colonial Muslim nation was rather like suggesting to a convention of Muslim writers meeting in Iran or Pakistan in the 1990s that their literary model should be Salman Rushdie.

Akbar was the litmus test for Jinnah. Perhaps a decade before he would have accepted Akbar as a model, but now he rejected the suggestion. In a rebuttal which amounted to a public snub – Mountbatten was after all still the Viceroy of India – Jinnah presented an alternative model.

… Or the Prophet of Islam?

Jinnah in his reply pointed out that Muslims had a more permanent and more inspiring model to follow, that of the holy Prophet:

> The tolerance and goodwill that great Emperor Akbar showed to all the non-Muslims is not of recent origin. It dates back thirteen centuries ago when our Prophet not only by words but by deeds treated the Jews and Christians, after he had conquered them, with the utmost tolerance and regard and respect for their faith and beliefs. The whole history of Muslims, wherever they ruled, is replete with those humane and great principles which should be followed and practised. (J. Ahmad 1976: 408–9)

Jinnah reverted to the themes he had raised only three days earlier. The holy Prophet had not only created a new state but had laid down the principles on which it could be organized and conducted. These principles were rooted in a compassionate under-standing of society and the notions of justice and tolerance. Jinnah emphasized the special treatment the Prophet accorded to the minorities. Morality, piety, human tolerance – a society where colour and race did not matter: the Prophet had laid down a charter for social behaviour thirteen centuries before the United Nations.

It is interesting how even scholars have misread these speeches of Jinnah. Wolpert, who analysed the first speech over several pages, concluded that what he termed the 'disjointed ramblings' suggested that Jinnah had lost his mind, that he was wandering (1984: 337–40). Was Jinnah aware, asked Wolpert, that he was abandoning his two-nation theory by talking of tolerance and so on? By asking this question and failing to link this speech with the one he made three days later Wolpert exposed his limitations as a scholar of Muslim culture and history (also revealed by his belief that Kanji was a Parsee when he was Hindu, and that the *tang* pyjama is Punjabi dress, etc.). In fact Jinnah's remarks must be seen in the context of Islamic culture and history. Jinnah, conscious that this was one of the last times he would be addressing his people because he was dying, would find himself echoing the holy Prophet's own last message on Mount Arafat. For him too this was the summing up of his life and his achievement. Wolpert's dismissal of the speech is interesting; he was aware of the comparison with the Arafat address but he did not follow it through.

The last testament

Let us compare the two newly independent countries, India and Pakistan. By the time Mountbatten arrived in India it was clear that Congress would be forming the government of an independent India, having worked towards this objective for almost half a century. Congress already had its leaders, a committed cadre, an all-India structure and networks that reached down to the village. It had struggled and sacrificed. Most important, it had a philosophy of how to run an independent India. The Pakistan movement, just a few years old in the 1940s, suffers in comparison.

Jinnah's ideas about Pakistan remained vague. Vagueness was both the strength and weakness of the Pakistan movement. It became all things to all men, drawing in a variety of people for different reasons; but it also meant that once Pakistan was achieved there would be no clear defining parameters. During the last year or two of his life, Jinnah had begun to sharpen his concept of Pakistan. He travelled extensively and spoke tirelessly on radio and in public.

An Islamic order

These speeches, together with what I have called his Gettysburg address, reveal that several themes are repeated again and again. The first is the unequivocal Islamic nature of Pakistan, drawing its inspiration from the Quran and the holy Prophet. This is the vision of an Islamic society which would be equitable, compassionate and tolerant (see also the last section in this chapter), and from which the 'poison' of corruption, nepotism, mismanagement and inefficiency would be eradicated. Pakistan itself would be based on the high principles laid down by the Prophet in Arabia in the seventh century. Although Jinnah had pointed out the flaws in Western-style democracy, it was still the best system of government available to Muslims.

Jinnah unequivocally did not want a theocratic state run by mullahs. In a broadcast to the people of the United States of America recorded in February 1948, Jinnah made his position clear: 'In any case, Pakistan is not going to be a theocratic State to be ruled by priests with a divine mission. We have many non-Muslims – Hindus, Christians and Parsees – but they are all Pakistanis. They will enjoy the same rights and privileges as any other citizens and will play their rightful part in the affairs of Pakistan' (Merchant 1990: 12; also in *Dawn*, 15 February 1948). When his enthusiastic admirers addressed him as 'Maulana Jinnah' he put them down, saying: I am not a *maulana*, just plain Mr Jinnah.

Protection of non-Muslims

Tolerance towards the minorities is another theme in his speeches. Jinnah had regularly reminded his Muslim audiences of what Islam maintains: 'our own history and our Prophet have given the clearest proof that non-Muslims have been treated not only justly and fairly but generously' (Merchant 1990: 10–11).

Jinnah's statements about the minorities (whether Muslims in India or Hindus in Pakistan) are significant: 'I am going to constitute myself the Protector-General of the Hindu minority in Pakistan' (Gandhi 1986: 178). He spent his first and only Christmas in December 1947 as a guest of the Christian community, joining in their celebrations. In that one act he incorporated the rituals of the minority community into Pakistani consciousness. (It is a far cry from the somewhat pointed distancing of Pakistani leaders from the rituals and customs of the minorities in contemporary Pakistan.) Although pressed for time, in Dhaka he met a Hindu delegation, in Karachi and Quetta a Parsee one, assuring them of his intention to safeguard their interests.

Indeed, even after the creation of Pakistan he not only continued to have British personnel on his staff but actively encouraged them. Sir George Cunningham, to whom Jinnah sent a telegram in Scotland inviting him to return to his post as the Governor of the North-West Frontier Province immediately after independence, is an example.

Opposition to provincialism

The other theme was the need to check provincialism which was already rearing its head. In his speeches Jinnah stressed the evils of provincialism, which he warned would weaken the foundations of the state, for example at Peshawar and Dhaka (Jinnah 1989). In Pakistan people assume that the movement for ethnic assertion is recent, a product of Pakistan. On the contrary, such movements existed *before* the creation of Pakistan, as is clear in a letter to Jinnah of 14 May 1947, from G. H. Hidayatullah, a Sindhi leader based in Karachi: 'Some enemies of my wife and myself have been making statements in the press that we two are advocating the principle that Sind is for the Sindhis only. This is entirely false and baseless. Both of us are ardent supporters of Pakistan, and we have given public expression to this. Islam teaches universal brotherhood, and we entirely subscribe to this.... All this is nothing but false propaganda on the part of the enemies of the League' (Zaidi 1993: volume I, part I, 760). A week later Abdus-Sattar

Pakistan: Ethnic versus Religious Identity

Pirzada issued a statement making clear that Pakistan would be the home for all Muslim immigrants from India: 'Sind has been the gateway of Islam in India and it shall be the gateway of Pakistan too' (ibid.: xxxiv).

Yet Jinnah sailed into an ethnic storm. In a momentous encounter in Dhaka, the capital of the province of East Pakistan (the future Bangladesh), he insisted that Urdu and Urdu alone would be the national language, although he conceded the use of the provincial language. Bengali students murmured in protest. The language movement would grow and in 1952 protesting students would be killed and provide the first martyrs. In time a far wider expression of ethnic discontent would develop at the imagined and real humiliation coming from West Pakistan and in particular the Punjab. But that was in the future. Jinnah had for the time being hung on to his idea of a united Pakistan, united in a political but also cultural sense.

Hope for the future

Jinnah often ended his speeches with a flourish. He reminded his audience that Pakistan was the largest Muslim nation in the world and the fifth largest in terms of population, that it had a special destiny and could become one of the most important states in the world. Jinnah did not want to create just another state; after all, even in his day there were many Muslim states. His dream was a grand one: what he wanted was nothing less than one of the greatest nations in the world, not just in the Muslim world. Even today the idea of Pakistan is greater than the reality of the country.

When he made these speeches he was an old man, and he knew he was dying; they were his last words. What makes a last testament valid is the fact that the speaker is about to die, about to meet his maker. A person's last words are therefore considered authentic; even the law accepts them as evidence. We can thus believe in the sincerity of Jinnah's speeches in the last months of his life which establish that he was moving irrevocably towards his Muslim culture and religion.

Those who argue that Jinnah was cynical and exploited religion and custom need to understand the one year he had in Pakistan before he died. Consider his position after the creation of Pakistan. He was by far the most popular and most powerful man in the country, the revered Quaid-i-Azam of Pakistan, respected by millions of people. If he had decided to defy tradition and custom, he would have got away with it. He could have dressed, spoken or eaten in any way he wanted and still been venerated. There was too much affection for him to be shaken by anything. The example of Kemal Atatürk, who rejected Muslim culture and tradition in Turkey – another father of the nation – comes to mind. But Jinnah took the opposite route. He may have started life at one end of the spectrum in terms of culture and tradition, but by the finish he was at the other end of it.

Diaspora: the plight of the refugees

The plight of the refugees, their lives for ever altered, moved Jinnah as nothing else in his life. Their killing, he repeated, was 'pre-planned genocide' (Jinnah 1989: 272). He constantly referred to them:

A few days ago, I received harrowing accounts of the terrible happenings in the Punjab and the situation, from all accounts, appeared to be so grave that I decided to come to Lahore. On my arrival here, I immediately got in touch with various sources that were available to me and I was deeply grieved to realize that unfortunately there was a great deal of truth in what had been told to me. I am speaking to you under deep distress and with a heavy heart. (ibid.: 96)

Even the joyous occasion of Eid became a moment of reflection:

For us the last *Eid-ul-Fitr* which followed soon after the birth of Pakistan was marred by the tragic happenings in East Punjab. The bloodbath of last year and its aftermath – the mass migration of millions – presented a problem of unprecedented magnitude. To provide new moorings for this mass of drifting humanity strained our energies and resources to breaking point. (ibid.: 275)

Jinnah mobilized everything at hand for the poor, especially among the refugees:

Let every man and woman resolve from this day to live henceforth strictly on an austerity basis in respect of food, clothing and other amenities of life and let the money, foodstuffs and clothing thus saved be brought to this common pool for the relief of the stricken. The winter is approaching and in the Punjab and Delhi particularly, it is very severe and we must provide refugees protection against it. (ibid.: 67)

Jinnah acknowledges the generous response of the local, indigenous Pakistanis to the refugees:

But for the spirit of brotherhood shown by the people of Pakistan and the courage with which the people as well as the Government faced the almost overwhelming difficulties created by a catastrophe, unparalleled in the history of the world, the entire structure of the State might well have crumbled down. (ibid.: 273)

The support for the refugees was inspiring. Nadir Rahim, whose father was Commissioner of Lahore, told me that locals and non-locals joined in, helping one another; the former became *ansaris*, helpers, the latter *muhajirs*, refugees. These were names revived from Islamic history when those who received the holy Prophet and his companions in Medina came to be called *ansaris* and those who had fled Makkah (Mecca) *muhajirs*. My own experiences in the early years of Pakistan confirm this. My father was a senior official in the new country, the first divisional superintendent of the Pakistan Railways at Karachi, its capital. The movement of refugees, troops and goods all depended on the railways (see plate 13). He had a large official house where dozens of refugees were camped for months and where families lived with us for years.

People seemed to appear from nowhere in our house and then disappear for ever. They looked dazed, uncertain and withdrawn. I remember in particular two men: one old, respectable and orthodox, the other young, barely in his teens. The first seemed to

Plate 13   Refugees coming to Pakistan in trains, summer 1947

have found strength in Islam. The young man was asleep most of the time wrapped in a white sheet as if he were a corpse enveloped in a shroud. When he woke he had little to say. An expression of permanent sorrow was etched on his face. He wished to shut out the past. I do not know where he came from and what happened to him.

Jinnah, Pakistan and India

To understand Jinnah's Pakistan, we need also to examine Jinnah's attitude towards Pakistan's relations with India, a crucial area which would determine the internal politics and external foreign policy of the country. Jinnah wished for cordial relations with the state of India. He never changed his will, which left part of his estate to educational institutions in Aligarh, Bombay and Delhi. He also kept his property in India, hoping to visit his beloved Bombay. Jinnah's view of friendly relations between India and Pakistan after partition was recorded in an interview with General Ismay, Chief of the Viceroy's Staff:

> Mr. Jinnah said with the greatest earnestness that once partition had been decided upon, everyone would know exactly where they were, all troubles would cease, and they would live happily ever after. He quoted me the case of two brothers who hated each other like poison as a result of the portions allotted to them under their father's will. Finally they could bear it no longer and took the case to court. Mr. Jinnah defended one of them and the case was fought with the utmost venom. Two years later Mr. Jinnah met his client and

181

asked how he was getting on and how was his brother, and he said: 'oh, once the case was decided, we became the greatest friends.' (9 April 1947, Zaidi 1993: appendices, volume I, part II, 647)

Jinnah's plan for a civilized discourse, maintaining standards, remained in his dealings with India. On his final flight from Delhi he conveyed this message:

> I bid farewell to the citizens of Delhi, amongst whom I have many friends of all communities and I earnestly appeal to everyone to live in this great and historic city with peace. The past must be buried and let us start afresh as two independent sovereign States of Hindustan [India] and Pakistan. I wish Hindustan prosperity and peace. (Jinnah 1989: 39)

Seervai, the Indian writer, comments on the Indian response to Jinnah's message: 'Jinnah left India for Pakistan on 7 August 1947, with an appeal to both Hindus and Muslims to "bury the past" and wished India success and prosperity. The next day, Vallabhbhai Patel said in Delhi, "The poison had been removed from the body of India"' (Seervai 1990: 134). Patel went on: '"As for the Muslims they have their roots, their sacred places and their centres here. I do not know what they can possibly do in Pakistan. It will not be long before they return to us"' (ibid.: 134). 'Hardly the words', concludes Seervai, 'to promote goodwill and neighbourliness either then or in the days to come.'

As for the Hindu citizens of Pakistan, there was never any doubt in Jinnah's mind that they would be protected as citizens and given full rights. Speech after speech confirmed this. When Pakistan was created, Jinnah had seven ministers in the Cabinet, one a Hindu.

In one of his first radio broadcasts as head of state Jinnah abandoned his normal reserve and opened his heart to the nation: 'I am speaking to you under deep distress and with a heavy heart. We have undoubtedly achieved Pakistan and that too without bloody war and practically, peacefully, by moral and intellectual force and with the power of pen which is no less mighty than the sword and so our righteous cause has triumphed. Are we now going to besmear and tarnish this greatest achievement for which there is no parallel in the whole history of the world by resorting to frenzy, savagery and butchery?' (R. Ahmed 1993: 99–100).

In early October 1947 Muslims in West Punjab began to react to the horror stories coming from India. Jinnah reminded the authorities in both countries: 'The division of India was agreed upon with a solemn and sacred undertaking that minorities would be protected by the two Dominion Governments and that the minorities had nothing to fear so long as they remained loyal to the State' (J. Ahmad 1976: 419–20). He urged the government of India to 'put a stop to the process of victimization of Muslims' (ibid.).

To calm the situation Jinnah flew to Lahore, which had borne the full brunt of the refugees arriving from India with their heart-rending tales, and in a public meeting urged restraint: 'Despite the treatment which is being meted out to the Muslim minorities in India, we must make it a matter of our prestige and honour to safeguard the lives of the minority communities and to create a sense of security among them' (R. Ahmed 1993: 101).

On the death of Gandhi on 30 January 1948, Jinnah issued a statement that angered and disappointed many Indians because it spoke of Gandhi only as a great Hindu leader. This was unfair to Jinnah, who used the word 'great' three times in his brief message. Once again, we need to read his full statement, especially in conjunction with the one made later in which he states that the Muslims of India had lost their main support. Here is the official version:

> I am shocked to learn of the most dastardly attack on the life of Mr. Gandhi, resulting in his death. There can be no controversy in the face of death. Whatever our political differences, he was one of the greatest men produced by the Hindu community, and a leader who commanded their universal confidence and respect. I wish to express my deep sorrow, and sincerely sympathize with the great Hindu community and his family in their bereavement at this momentous, historical and critical juncture so soon after the birth of freedom and freedom for Hindustan and Pakistan. The loss to the Dominion of India is irreparable, and it will be very difficult to fill the vacuum created by the passing away of such a great man at this moment. (Jinnah 1989: 128)

Just before his own death, Jinnah proposed a joint defence pact with India as the Cold War started to shape the world and the two power blocs began to form. Jinnah was still thinking as a South Asian nationalist. Since he had won the rights and security of his community through the creation of Pakistan, he thought the problem of national defence was over. Alas, it was not to be.

With relations souring so quickly at the creation of Pakistan, the relationship between the two countries – and therefore the two communities in the subcontinent as a whole – was set on a collision course and has unfortunately remained so ever since. As this conflict is rooted in history it is readily exploited by political parties who see an easy gain to be made.

Had Jinnah's vision prevailed – and found an echo in India – we would have seen a very different South Asia. There would have been two stable nations – India and Pakistan, both supplementing and supporting each other. Indeed Jinnah's idea of a joint defence system against the outside world would have ensured that there would have been no crippling defence expenditures. There would have been no reason to join one or other camp of the Cold War. There would have been open borders, free trade and regular visiting between the two countries. The lack of tension would have ensured that the minorities were not under pressure and, as both Jinnah and Congress leaders like Gandhi and Nehru wanted, lived as secure and integrated citizens. The fabric of society would have been different, and a more humane subcontinent might have emerged: a land truer to the vision of its leaders and spirit of its sages.

Jinnah's passing: growing crisis

There is a photograph of Jinnah on his way to inaugurate the State Bank of Pakistan in a gilded carriage drawn by horses and escorted by the Governor-General's bodyguard which is redolent of the Raj and its splendour (plate 14). This grand procession is

Plate 14   One of Jinnah's last public functions, the opening of the State Bank of Pakistan, July 1948

modelled on the British, who themselves had modelled it on the Mughals. Jinnah had gone back to his cultural roots via the British.

The state cavalcade, the erect horsemen with tall plumes in their turbans, long coats, high boots, white gloves, and gleaming golden braid on their shoulders and chests, provided a magnificent spectacle. Jinnah was wearing national dress with the *karakuli* cap on his head. The ceremony contrasted with the crowd watching along the streets, many of whom would have been ordinary refugees freshly arrived from India after having lost everything. As gilded carriages go, Jinnah's could not compete with the one used by the King of England on state occasions. But it was a period of scarcity in Karachi, still the early months of Pakistan.

Looking at the picture I understood what Jinnah was up to. At a time when refugees were pouring in, a time of severe economic hardship, bleak austerity and an uncertain future, with many people predicting the collapse of Pakistan, Jinnah chose to make a point. It was a statement of pride, of confidence, almost of defiance: we are here to stay, he appears to be saying.

Upon arrival at the State Bank, Jinnah was given a golden key to open the doors of the newly founded institution. It was 1 July 1948. It was to be his last public function. He would be dead within a few weeks.

Pakistan: Ethnic versus Religious Identity

The last days

When Jinnah died on 11 September 1948, he was 71 years old. Perhaps he might have lived long enough to plant firm roots in Pakistan had his health permitted, had he eased off, had his lungs not collapsed, had all the woes of Pakistan's birth not become his personal burden.

Frail and ill with TB, he received the news of rape and abduction and spent his last few months an unhappy man. Fatima described the effect of the stories on her brother:

> As he discussed with me these mass killings at the breakfast table, his eyes were often moist with tears. The sufferings of Muslim refugees that trekked from India into Pakistan, which to them had been the Promised Land, depressed him. Then there was the Constitution of Pakistan to be framed, to which he applied his mind as often as he could find time to sit in his study, surrounded by books dealing with constitutions of various countries of the world. The problems of Kashmir Muslims, who had been betrayed by an alien and tyrannical ruler, weighed heavily on his mind. (F. Jinnah 1987: 11)

The last year he survived on willpower alone. At the end he was desperately sick, his lungs barely functioning, his weight down to 70 pounds. His determination to ensure that Pakistan survived had kept him going during those extra months.

Shamsul Hasan, a devoted comrade from India, was alarmed when he saw him for the first time since the creation of Pakistan:

> When I was ushered into the presence of the Quaid, I was shocked to see him. Frail and weak he always was; but during the few weeks following August 14, 1947, he had become a spectre of his old self – a picture of utter exhaustion. He enquired about the happenings in Delhi. I narrated the gruesome details. In a voice choked with emotion, he told me that he had not been able to sleep for days, and that he was doing whatever was possible to improve the situation. He was very bitter with the Indian leadership. He accused them of having accepted Partition with reservations, and denounced them for trying to destroy Pakistan at the very outset. Making visible efforts to control his emotions, he added: 'The Musalmans of the Subcontinent cannot be destroyed by these tactics. They have now a homeland; and with hard work they shall, Insha Allah, make it powerful.' (Hasan 1976: 3)

Jinnah disguised his failing health from his followers, but during the last days in 1948 he said:

> I have been working fourteen hours a day for the last fourteen years. I have never known what sickness really is. However, for the past few years I get frequent attacks of fever and coughing. A few days' rest enables me to get over them. Recently they have become more exacting and more frequent and they have laid me low. (F. Jinnah 1987: 25)

Hassan Ispahani, Jinnah's disciple and Pakistan's ambassador to Washington, wrote to him just a few days before he died:

> You must rest and go absolutely easy until you regain the strength that you have lost through over-exertion and over-work. I shall not weary of telling you how important, nay essential, it is for the Nation that you have created to have you as its head for many, many years to come. You are its priceless jewel. (Zaidi 1976: 614–15)

When Ispahani finally saw Jinnah he was shaken by his mentor's condition. Fatima Jinnah described his visit:

> No visitors were allowed to see the Quaid-e-Azam, but when Mr. Hassan Ispahani, our Ambassador in Washington, visited our home in Ziarat, the Quaid was happy to see Mr. Ispahani, who had been his close associate for a number of years. As he came down after seeing his leader, Mr. Ispahani broke down in tears. He could not bear to see that veteran of many fights lay helpless in bed, struggling feebly for his life. (F. Jinnah 1987: 28)

Many critics accuse Pakistan of having killed the father of the nation. Remarking that the ambulance taking the dying Jinnah from the airport to the Governor-General's house mysteriously stalled in Karachi, on that humid September day, they claim it was part of a plot. However, vehicles available to Pakistan were generally in poor condition. India had frozen all the assets that it was to give Pakistan and the administration had few resources to fall back on. Indeed when Mountbatten and Jinnah in their Rolls-Royce – borrowed from the ruler of a state – came back from the Constituent Assembly on 14 August, after they had disembarked it caught fire because it was too old and the engine too heated. It is therefore unlikely that the ambulance broke down as a result of a conspiracy to kill Jinnah.

I thought of Karachi in the hot, sticky month of September and I thought of Jinnah old, sick and dying, so vulnerable in the capital of his own state. The broken-down ambulance was a pathetic reflection on those who had benefited the most – the Pakistanis in power. But his dignity did not desert him. When relief finally arrived and they came back to the Governor-General's house he still made an attempt to get up: he did not wish to be seen on a stretcher. Yet he was dead within a few hours.

Fatima was with him at the end: 'I intuitively felt it was like the last brilliant flicker of the candle-flame before it has burnt itself out.' In the silence she felt as if she was speaking to him in her mind. 'Oh, Jin, if they could pump out all my blood, and put it in you, so that you may live. If it would will God to take away all my years and give them to you, so that you may continue to lead our nation, how grateful I would be to Him' (F. Jinnah 1987: 37). Fatima describes his last moment: 'He made one last attempt and whispered, "Fati, *Khuda Hafiz* … La Illaha Illa Allah … Muhammad … Rasul … Allah." His head dropped slightly to his right, his eyes closed' (ibid.: 38).

When Jinnah died, Pakistanis were devastated: about a million turned up to pay homage (plate 15). They revered him as they would no other figure in their history. Today they look up to him wherever they live, from Los Angeles to Lahore. The airport in Karachi is named after him and prayers are said round the clock at his grand

Plate 15 Thousands accompanying Jinnah's cortege, drawn by naval personnel, on its last journey in Karachi in September 1948

monument in Karachi which is now a symbol of Pakistan and first port of call for any visiting VIP.

A grateful nation built him a mausoleum, a tribute to 'the last of the Moguls' (Collins and Lapierre 1994: 513). The opening lines of Stanley Wolpert's biography aptly sum up his life: 'Few individuals significantly alter the course of history. Fewer still modify the map of the world. Hardly anyone can be credited with creating a nation-state. Mohammad Ali Jinnah did all three' (Wolpert 1984: vii).

'A man born once in a millennium'

Jinnah died at the moment of his greatest triumph. His memory was therefore preserved in history as that of an untarnished hero. He did not belong to one caste or one ethnic group or one province; he belonged to everyone and to no one. Above all, he did not leave behind children and grandchildren who claimed power and allowed stories of corruption and nepotism to circulate. No land purchases, no back-room deals, no scandals relating to corrupt relatives, no dubious agreements mar his reputation. In this Jinnah is like the other giant of the subcontinent, Gandhi, who was shot only five months after the independence of India.

Had Jinnah lived, the growing problems facing Pakistan might have dented his reputation. Perhaps with his willpower and enormous prestige he could have changed things; perhaps not. We shall never know. Jinnah's death early in Pakistan's history preserved him in the minds of Pakistanis. They never knew him frustrated in office or foiled by the ambition of lesser leaders or facing the nepotism and corruption in society. To Pakistanis he remains the triumphant hero, defeating every enemy to attain a homeland for them. Since his illness was not generally known, he does not appear as a tragically sick man either. For Pakistanis he remains an almost mythical figure. They now look back nostalgically to a golden time when they were united and had a clear objective.

'By the time that he got Pakistan for the Muslims,' wrote Admiral J. W. Jefford, Pakistan's first naval chief, 'he was a demi-god to the masses' (Bolitho 1954: 201). The *Dawn* carried an editorial arguing he should be crowned Shah-in-Shah of Pakistan, imperial successor to the Mughals (also see A. Husain 1996: 60). In Pakistan Jinnah received 'adulation amounting almost to worship' (Callard 1958: 19). For E. H. Enver, Jinnah is 'The Modern Moses' (1990); for Professor Riaz Ahmad, 'the greatest leader of the Muslims of South Asia' (1994: 178). If Jinnah had asked his people to walk into the Arabian sea, they would have done so, said Dr Zaidi.

'A man like Jinnah is born once in a millennium; not once in a century but once in a millennium,' pronounced Dr Jaffar Qureshi of India. This from a Pakistani would have been fulsome praise; from an Indian it was an extraordinary tribute. Even making allowances for South Asian exuberance Dr Qureshi was making a point, going on to explain why Jinnah was unique. Devdas Gandhi, son of Mahatma Gandhi, declared that Jinnah was the greatest Muslim since the holy Prophet of Islam. The Aga Khan, not easily impressed, was as emphatic in his praise: 'Of all the statesmen that I have known in my life, Clemenceau, Lloyd George, Churchill, Curzon, Mahatma Gandhi − Jinnah is the most remarkable. None of these men, in my view, outshone him in strength of character and in that almost uncanny combination of prescience and resolution which is statecraft' (Merchant 1990: 6).

The secretary-general of the Arab League called Jinnah 'one of the greatest leaders in the whole world' (Mujahid 1981: 660). Even Jinnah's opponents acknowledged him after he died. The president of the Hindu Mahasabha in India wrote: 'In the death of Quaid-i-Azam, Muhammad Ali Jinnah, the Muslim world has lost a unique personality endowed with the highest qualities of head and heart' (ibid.).

The Times in its obituary captured the essence of his achievement:

> Mr. Jinnah was something more than Quaid-i-Azam, supreme head of the State, to the people who followed him; he was more even than the architect of the Islamic nation he personally called into being. He commanded their imagination as well as their confidence. In the face of difficulties which might have overwhelmed him, it was given to him to fulfil the hope foreshadowed in the inspired vision of the great Iqbal by creating for the Muslims of India a homeland where the old glory of Islam could grow afresh into a modern state, worthy of its place in the comity of nations. Few statesmen have shaped events to their policy more surely than Mr. Jinnah. He was a legend even in his lifetime. (*The Times*, London, 13 September 1948)

One of the brightest stars of the twentieth century, Nelson Mandela, was also an admirer of Jinnah. On arrival in Karachi in 1995 he headed straight for Jinnah's mausoleum and wrote in the visitor's book: 'To see Ali Jinnah Museum is a source of tremendous inspiration for all those who have struggled against all forms of racial oppression' (*Impact International*, April 1995: 47). He later remarked, 'Every sight related to leader Ali Jinnah is a source of inspiration' (ibid.).

What comes shining through half a century after his death, for the ordinary people of Pakistan – the servants in the large houses, the taxi drivers, the lower staff in the offices, the villagers in the rural areas – is Jinnah's integrity and commitment to the Muslim cause. He was untouched by the indifference of the rich and powerful.

In the last years of his life Jinnah had sacrificed his health, his property, his reputation – everything – for the ideal of a Muslim state. To me as a Pakistani, and as a Muslim, there can be no greater indication of his ultimate sincerity to the cause of the community. Jinnah became the father of the nation, the very symbol of Pakistan, his image honoured in every office, official building and function.

Similarly Gandhi, whatever his earlier position on Pakistan, in the last days of his life started a fast to death to protest against the killing of Muslims in Delhi. He was also protesting against the decision of the Indian government not to pay Pakistan its rightful funds and assets under the agreed terms of partition, the aim being to strangle Pakistan at its birth. Gandhi was shot in consequence by a Hindu fanatic who saw him as a 'Muslim lover'. Instantaneously Gandhi was acknowledged as a saint, globally recognized.

Jinnah's life must be seen in the context of the huge changes taking place in the world during the last century. Consider him as a young man pursuing his studies in London late in the last century – when Queen Victoria was at the height of her power, when the world was seen through the eyes of the British empire, when the dominant values and attitudes in India were formed by the British – to the last year of his life when we already discern the global themes that would engage Muslims up to our own times.

In his final years Jinnah was already talking about global Islam, about a common struggle taking place from Palestine to Indonesia. Early in Jinnah's life Muslims were still striving to assert themselves in sometimes incoherent if passionate movements. When he died they were emerging as a major world force and within a few years of his death could count many independent nations in their ranks.

Jinnah's lifetime covers a tremendous span. When Jinnah was born, the British empire dominated the world. When he died, Britain had already receded as a major power. The USA and the USSR had already begun to take positions that would set the pattern of global politics for the next half-century. The atom bomb had already been dropped and the age of nuclear confrontation had begun.

The Quaid's lieutenant

On Jinnah's death Liaquat Ali Khan, Pakistan's first Prime Minister, was left to carry on the struggle to survive. Liaquat is the unsung warrior of the Pakistan story. Although he is recognized officially, he has been caught up in the ethnic arguments of Pakistan and reduced to a *muhajir* leader, a refugee from India. Today people in Pakistan tend to knock Liaquat to knock the Muhajir Qaumi Movement, the main *muhajir* party. This is unfair: the man was a true hero of Pakistan and its creation, and deserves a proper place in the galaxy.

Liaquat, courteous and affable, had got on much better with Mountbatten than Jinnah did. But if Liaquat was seduced by Mountbatten's irresistible charm it did not mean that he was abandoning Pakistan. On the contrary, he remained a committed Pakistani, as a top secret record of an interview between Mountbatten and Liaquat Ali Khan on 3 April 1947 reveals. Liaquat observed: 'I consider the position now so intolerable that if your Excellency was only prepared to let the Muslim League have the Sind Desert, I would still prefer to accept that and have a separate Muslim State in those conditions than to continue in bondage to the Congress with apparently more generous concessions' (Zaidi 1993: appendices, volume I, part II, 633). This from a man who knew he would have to give up his considerable landed property in India if Pakistan was formed. It was, without doubt, a deep commitment to the cause of Pakistan that drove Liaquat – and indeed his wife.

One of Liaquat's first acts as Prime Minister was to issue a formal declaration in the Assembly on 12 August that henceforth all official correspondence would refer to Jinnah as Quaid-i-Azam. He pointed out in his speech that some people had been addressing Quaid-i-Azam as Shah-in-Shah of Pakistan.

Liaquat's integrity, his dedication and his affection for the Quaid are established. Yet through the incident of the ambulance which carried Jinnah on his last journey and broke down on the way from the airport many Pakistanis not only indulge in a sense of collective guilt but slyly criticize Liaquat, who after all was Prime Minister. It has even been rumoured – and in Pakistan rumour passes for fact, gossip for history – that Jinnah had fallen out with Liaquat and was on the verge of sacking him. Only a few years before his death, however, at the Karachi session of the Muslim League in December 1943 Jinnah expressed his confidence thus: 'Nawabzada Liaquat Ali Khan is my right-hand man. He has worked and served day and night and one could not possibly have an idea of the great burden he shouldered. He commands the respect and confidence of the Musalmans. Though a Nawabzada [aristocrat] he is a thorough proletarian, and I hope other Nawabs in the country would follow his example' (Z. Ahmad 1990: 305). There is no hard proof that Jinnah changed his opinion. On the contrary, the fact that right to the end he retained Liaquat as a chief executor of his will implies that he held him in the same high regard (ibid.). Moreover, Jinnah's doctor noted: 'I was moved by the Prime Minister's deep concern for the health of his chief and old comrade' (Baksh 1978: 11).

After Jinnah's death, tension with India increased dramatically: the one man India feared was dead. The next day India invaded Hyderabad, and people in Pakistan suspected a plan to destroy their country. At this point Liaquat emerged as a bold and committed leader. In a broadcast to the nation he declared: 'I again repeat, in the event of an attack on Pakistan no matter from which side, myself, my colleagues and every Pakistani will shed the last drop of his blood in defending every inch of the soil of Pakistan' (Z. Ahmad 1990: 71). But Liaquat's emergence now made him the prime target, as he was well aware. In a public speech in Karachi in 1950 on Pakistan Day, 14 August, he said:

> But there is still a class in India, term it as the Hindu Mahasabha, the RSS [extremist wing of Hindu communalism] or as you may, which is vomiting venom against the Pact, from the pulpit and the platform and in the Press.

They are inciting the Indian public. They are demanding police action against East Bengal. In other words, they are demanding war on Pakistan. (ibid.: 203)

A day before his assassination Liaquat delivered these prophetic words in a speech at Karachi:

I have neither wealth nor property, and I am glad, for these things weaken faith (*iman*). I have only my life, which I have dedicated long ago to my people and my country and when the need arises, I assure you, I will not lag behind others to shed my blood for Pakistan. (ibid.: 308)

Liaquat was shot as he rose to address a large audience on 16 October 1951 in Rawalpindi. The Afghan assassin was gunned down on the spot by the police but his motive was never established. The last words Liaquat spoke were the Muslim declaration of faith and 'God preserve Pakistan'.

Dawn's first editor wrote after Liaquat's death: 'With the *kalima* on his lips, Liaquat, successor of the Quaid-i-Azam, Prime Minister, leader unparalleled, is dead. The man who killed him was not just an individual, he was the symbol of that deadly enmity of the enemies of Islam who have always wanted to destroy Pakistan' (A. Husain 1996: 81). Nehru sent a gracious message: 'The news has filled all his old friends and colleagues in the Parliament of India with the deepest sorrow both in the personal aspect and in the larger background of the two peoples of India and Pakistan' (Z. Ahmad 1990: 291).

When Liaquat died he had the equivalent of £50 in his bank balance. Yet as the first Prime Minister of Pakistan he could have made himself a rich man. Liaquat had had a difficult time, mainly attempting to consolidate the Pakistan he had inherited. Perhaps his most famous image in the public mind is the photograph with his right fist clenched: he was telling India that Pakistan would not be bullied or pushed around. Pakistanis gave him the name of *Quaid-i-Millat*, leader of the nation; others called him *Shaheed-i-Millat*, martyr of the nation.

Struggling with identity

Liaquat's death deepened the crisis of identity which Pakistan had faced from the moment of birth. The consciousness of a 'Pakistani' identity was relatively unformed in many areas that actually came to Pakistan. For the vast majority of people in the villages the idea of independence, of a separate nationhood, was still abstract. The reality of their lives would change slowly over a decade or more. In the rural areas, traditional social customs still dominated life, transport and communications were poor and villages tended to be isolated even from neighbouring ones. The tribal areas in the North-West Frontier Province and Baluchistan saw themselves as a people apart; indeed they called their areas *azad* or independent.

Pakistan was far from being a monolithic society as is often suggested. In West Pakistan there were three distinct social structures: the states and large feudal estates ruled by dynastic families; the small peasant farmers mainly in the Punjab; and the tribal areas, semi-independent and autonomous regions where people lived according to the law of the tribe. In East Pakistan, Bengalis formed a distinct society. There were neither states nor feudal lords owning vast territories; the majority were mainly small farmers or landless tenants.

The influx of millions of refugees and the exodus of Hindus (and Sikhs from West Pakistan) caused a dramatic upheaval. The emergence of new classes, new political and social élites, and the clash of languages and cultures were reflected in politics and found ethnic expression. In East Pakistan this rapidly formed around the idea of a West Pakistani élite bullying and exploiting its eastern wing. In particular, Punjabi officials were accused of being almost neo-colonialist in their attitudes.

Pakistan had appeared with a flourish on the map of the world; but its quest for identity would never be quite resolved. Within two decades an irresistible ethnic movement split away Pakistan's eastern province, containing the majority of its population, into the new nation of Bangladesh (see chapter 8, last section). Serious ethnic rifts within what remained of Pakistan, in Baluchistan in the 1970s, in Sind in the 1980s and Karachi in the 1990s, continued to express themselves in the language of independence.

The Muslim relationship with and perception of Hindus varied considerably from province to province. The experience of those Muslims who had migrated from India – particularly as they travelled through the blood and fire in the summer of 1947 – had by and large not been pleasant; their memories of Congress rule in the 1930s were not happy ones. However, in many of the areas of Pakistan the story was the opposite. Where Hindus were in a minority, in most cases they had not only adapted to Muslim cultural life but even contributed to it. In provinces like the Sind, Hindus had been particularly well assimilated and were part and parcel of the culture, appreciating the Muslim saints, poets and scholars. Stories of Hindus on the rampage made little sense to these Muslims. After the initial sympathy for the Muslim refugees native Sindhis soon became indifferent, even hostile, as they saw jobs and land going to the refugees.

There were also positive attempts made by many Indians, such as Nehru himself, to help Muslims, to secure their support and assure them of a future in India. It was one important strand of Indian political life. After all, Maulana Azad, one of the best-known – and best-liked – Muslims of India, had been president of the Congress until just before independence and if he had stayed on he might well have become the first Prime Minister of India. As we have seen, Jinnah had included a Hindu in his small cabinet.

Nevertheless after Jinnah's death the problems continued to multiply. The fact that Jinnah had insisted on making Urdu the national language was resented by many ethnic groups with pride in their own language, such as the Bengalis, once the fervour of the Pakistan movement had abated. The Muslim League soon lost its way after achieving Pakistan. It did not possess the same grassroots organization as the Congress in India. Besides, its main leaders, like Liaquat, came from areas that were now in India and they were increasingly under challenge by home-grown politicians.

Jinnah, always the constitutionalist lawyer, had worked desperately hard to frame a constitution, with himself as head of the Assembly. But without him it took decades for the constitution to be written, and the delay allowed the intervention of and tampering by martial law, the first of which was led by General Ayub Khan in 1958 (challenged by Fatima Jinnah in the mid-1960s).

Pakistanis would never forgive Jinnah for one thing: his mortality. Had he not died he could have saved the nation: there would have been no martial law in the 1950s, no splitting away of East Pakistan in 1971 and no General Zia in the 1980s. The contrast with India is illustrative. Nehru, backed by a first-rate team and a solidly organized Congress, had almost two decades until his death in 1964 to guide and consolidate the new state. As a result India would emerge with a resounding voice on the international stage.

Shortly after the birth of Pakistan the Cold War began in earnest. Pakistan aligned itself early with the Western world. There were several reasons. On one level it was a response to the confrontation with the 'godless' Soviet empire. On another level it was the continuing influence of the British connection, for, in an important sense, America was seen to have taken over where Britain had left off as a global power. There were also cultural links with the Western world – particularly the use of English as an official language. Finally, the Soviet Union had begun to support India openly and strongly. It was therefore logical that Pakistan should find its way into the opposite camp. What it meant was that for the next couple of decades Pakistan would remain more or less a loyal ally – often little more than a camp follower – of America.

Jinnah as metaphor: 'secularist' or 'fundamentalist'?

Over the last decades the crisis of identity has remained severe. Should Pakistan be Islamic or secular? Or will it be more of the same, a muddle, a compromise, a continuing collapse?

Paradoxically, the self-consciously secular Pakistan People's Party (PPP) and the right-wing Jamat-i-Islami both claim Jinnah as their hero. In this exercise Jinnah's media images become important – what he wore, how he appeared and what he said. What processes explain the fact that both those categorized as secularists and those classed as fundamentalists use Jinnah as a model?

At the centre of this exercise is the quest for identity. Secularism and fundamentalism reflect opposing positions in the debate taking place in Muslim society from Morocco to Malaysia concerning the nature of society, its leadership and its future. One side wishes to modernize along Western lines by confining religion to private belief; the other side emphasizes the importance of religion in our times. Crudely put, one favours harmony (its critics say sycophancy) with the West, the other favours confrontation. The very nature of Islam is thus under debate.

The great debate

The heated debate over whether Jinnah was 'secularist' or 'fundamentalist' assumes more than academic significance. The line-up includes heavyweights on both sides. Those who have analysed him as 'secularist' include Eqbal Ahmed, M. J. Akbar, Hamza Alavi, Tariq Ali, Larry Collins and Dominique Lapierre, Emma Duncan, Ayesha Jalal and Christina Lamb. This position is summed up by Collins and Lapierre: 'A more improbable leader of India's Moslem masses could hardly be imagined. He drank, ate pork, religiously shaved his beard each morning and just as religiously avoided the mosque each Friday. God and the Koran had no place in Jinnah's vision of the world'

(1994: 102; this is quoted disapprovingly by Hashim Raza in 1982: 34). The Pakistan government responded to this statement not by research or academic refutation but by banning the book.

There is an opposed view. To many, even some of the *ulema*, Jinnah is depicted as a fundamentalist (Werbner 1990). Those who disagree with projecting Jinnah as secular although not necessarily suggesting he was a 'fundamentalist' include those who knew him, like Yahya Bakhtiar, S. S. Pirzada and Hashim Raza. They also include the scholars of Jinnah like Rizwan Ahmed, Liaquat Merchant, Dr Sharif al Mujahid and Dr Z. Zaidi.

Both groups are selective in their use of evidence and tendentious in their arguments. The secularists pick bits from Jinnah's early life and blithely ignore his last years when he took a distinctly Islamic position on various issues; the right-wing fundamentalists reverse the selection process, ignoring his early life and focusing on the last few years. This may be exciting polemics but in order to understand Jinnah we need to put both parts of his life together.

I believe that to ask whether Jinnah was secularist or fundamentalist is conceptually fuzzy and sociologically meaningless because we are taking current categories and forcing them on to people who lived over half a century ago in a different political and cultural context. Besides, to lift these terms from Western discourse, where they originated, and apply them to non-Western societies is misleading.

By the same token, where do we place Gandhi? Was he secularist or fundamentalist? To the Hindu extremists he is the former; to many Muslims he is the latter. Like Jinnah, he seemed to reflect both categories while transcending them.

The more interesting question, perhaps, is what kind of Islam Jinnah would have wanted to be practised in his state. Did he advocate what could be described as a more compassionate and tolerant form of Islam, one in accordance with the most scholarly thinking within the religion yet embracing all humanity, or a more literalist, rigid Islam in confrontation with other religions?

Neither secularist...

The intellectuals of Pakistan who divide themselves into 'secularist' and 'fundamentalist' camps are uncomfortable with the real Jinnah. The 'secularists' are frustrated because there is too much of Islam in the speeches, behaviour and public position of Jinnah's later years (see also chapters 3 and 4).

Secular is defined as 'not concerned with spiritual or religious affairs' (in the *Oxford Advanced Learner's Dictionary* published in 1993). Yet Jinnah constantly quoted the holy Prophet of Islam. As a young man, alone in London, he had decided to join Lincoln's Inn in preference to any other law college because it listed the holy Prophet among the greatest lawgivers of history. Later in life he quarrelled with his only child, pampered and loved, because she married a Christian and not a Muslim. He died with the Muslim declaration of faith on his lips.

Jinnah's last few years were a conscious attempt to move towards Islam in terms of text, purity and the scriptures, and away from village, folk or modern Westernized Islam. He constantly pointed to the principles laid down in the Quran and in the time of the Prophet as the basis for his state: 'Our bedrock and sheet anchor is Islam'

(R. Ahmed 1993: 22). In 1944 Jinnah declared: 'We do not want any flag excepting the League flag of the Crescent and Star. Islam is our guide and the complete code of our life. We do not want any red or yellow flag. We do not want any isms, Socialisms, Communisms or National Socialisms' (ibid.: 153). In 1946 Jinnah made the Muslim League members sign their pledges for Pakistan 'in the name of Allah the Beneficent, the Merciful' (Wolpert 1984: 261). After the creation of Pakistan the references to the Quran and the Prophet were prominent in Jinnah's speeches.

There is a story circulating surreptitiously that Jinnah did not and could not say his Muslim prayers. He was (as told to me by Dr Zaidi) supposed to have said to his secretary, standing to his right, as he bent to prostrate himself in the mosque, 'What next?' This has been disproved by many people including the evidence in court given by an eminent lawyer, an advocate since 1930 who had practised in the Bombay High Court until 1940 and testified that Jinnah prayed as an orthodox Sunni: 'Whenever the Quaid-e-Azam used to be in Bombay, I also joined in Eid prayers with him. On three of these occasions I had the opportunity to be standing close to him, and I saw him offering prayers as the Sunnis do, namely by folding the hands' (Merchant 1990: 48–50). He continued: 'I once took the Quaid-e-Azam to the Jama Masjid at Bombay which is a Sunni Mosque.... By this time he had become a person of great eminence.' Z. A. Suleri has described accompanying Jinnah to Friday prayers in London in 1946 ('Greatest of the century', *Jang*, 28 December 1996; for photograph of Jinnah offering prayers in a congregation, see Pirzada 1983: 23). Yahya Bakhtiar, who saw Jinnah at close quarters, concluded: 'To sum up, Mohammad Ali Jinnah was a very sincere, deeply committed and dedicated Mussalman' (*The News*, 1 July 1995).

Many but by no means all mullahs were with him, and they helped to swing the masses for the Pakistan cause. That is why from the mid-1940s the Muslim League won landslide victories throughout India. One dramatic example was that of the Pir of Manki Sharif, who snatched Pakistan from the jaws of the Congress in the Frontier Province. Within a few days after Pakistan was created Jinnah's name was being read in the *khutba* at mosques as the Amir-ul-Millat, a traditional title of Muslim rulers (Sayeed 1968: 256). The Sheikh-al-Islam Maulana Usmani's intense devotion to Jinnah was perhaps most eloquently expressed when he read his burial oration in September 1948 and compared Jinnah to Aurangzeb (Mujahid 1981: 659).

A British anthropologist has thrown light on where to place Jinnah by providing an insight into what she terms the 'political mythology' of contemporary Pakistanis in Manchester and offering the following thesis:

> Just as on the religious plane the Islamic nation, the *Ummat*, is constituted, above all, in the person of the Prophet, and secondarily in the persons of earlier prophets and latter-day *pirs*, so too the Pakistan nation is constituted in its visionary perfection in the person of Quaid-i-Azam. Quaid-i-Azam is the perfect model of a political national leader as the Prophet epitomised the qualities of religious leadership. (Werbner 1990: 52)

Religious leaders have themselves underlined the spiritual basis of Jinnah's political actions. A Maulvi (a religious figure), in explaining the processes whereby a Muslim is elevated to sainthood, recounted the freeing of the Prophet's slaves, and argued: 'So

195

when Quaid-i-Azam freed so many thousands of Muslims and gave them an independent country then think what his position must be in the eyes of God and the Holy Prophet' (ibid.: 58). The fact that Quaid-i-Azam was not a strictly observant Muslim, while not denied by the Maulvi, was dismissed as insignificant, an exterior reality hiding a much deeper truth:

> I studied Quaid-i-Azam's personality in the light of the Holy Quran, and the more I studied it in this light the more my respect for him grew. I never bothered to see if he had a beard or not [i.e. if he was a religious man or not], and it is my belief that he is better than a thousand of those bearded persons who sell the nation and fill their own pockets ... to know if he prayed or not, and in which way he prayed, what his beliefs were, and I have never bothered to find out what his opinions were. I only know that if he did not have deep respect and esteem in the eyes of God and the Holy Prophet [Peace be upon Him] then he would not have been born on this earth. (ibid.: 58)

The urban Pakistani so-called secular intellectuals would be apoplectic with rage at the ease with which religious leaders like the Maulvi reject their claim that Jinnah was not a good Muslim, that he was one of them. They would be further enraged at the strength of the Maulvi's argument and conclusion. Its echo in Muslim society is both universal and historical.

Other Muslims, more liberal and Westernized in their views than the Maulvi, use the same arguments (see title of E. H. Enver, a senior diplomat, *The Modern Moses: A Brief Biography of M. A. Jinnah*, 1990; Yahya Bakhtiar also calls Jinnah 'a modern Moses' in *The News*, 1 July 1995). As Dr Jaffar Qureshi, the Indian Muslim, put it: 'He was a *Waliullah*, a true friend of God. God says that if you help one Muslim I will reward you, how much reward would Jinnah get who helped millions and millions of Muslims.'

Jinnah's thinking on Islam has a contemporary ring to it. Speaking in a message to the nation on *Eid* on 27 August 1948, he linked Pakistan to international Islam:

> My *Eid* message to our brother Muslim States is one of friendship and goodwill. We are all passing through perilous times. The drama of power politics that is being staged in Palestine, Indonesia and Kashmir should serve as an eyeopener to us. It is only by putting up a united front that we can make our voice felt in the counsels of the world. (Jinnah 1989: 276)

Jinnah saw himself as a champion not only of Muslims in India. After the First World War he had championed the cause of the Turks; later he spoke on behalf of the Arabs; he met Hassan al-Banna, the founder of the Muslim Brotherhood in Egypt, and the Grand Mufti of Jerusalem and received admiring letters from them. (In the photograph of Jinnah in Cairo in 1946 published in *Impact International*, 24 December 1982 to 13 January 1983, he is seated in the centre of a group that includes Sheikh Hassan al-Banna, Idris as-Sanousi, the King of Libya, and the sheikh of one of the most prestigious universities of the Muslim world, Al Azhar University.)

The significance of Hassan al-Banna meeting Jinnah and writing to him in glowing terms is immense. The Muslim Brotherhood has over the last half-century grown in influence throughout the Middle East. Hassan al-Banna's ideas on Islam, on the revival within the community, on pan-Islamism, on challenging the cultural and political supremacy of the West, on asserting an Islamic identity, have had a huge influence well beyond the Arab world. Even today, al-Banna's ideas reverberate throughout the Muslim world, putting pressure on governments to move towards Islam. They inspire Islamic movements and they provide a charter of action for Islamic leaders. For Jinnah to be singled out and acknowledged as the Muslim leader *par excellence* by al-Banna is therefore something of an achievement for a man labelled by some as 'secularist'.

If there is still doubt about Jinnah's position then read what the Grand Mufti of Jerusalem wrote to him:

> I take this opportunity for the first time to write to you thanking you for your valuable efforts that you are making continuously for the services of Islam and Muslims, not only in India but all the Islamic countries, according to the command of God for Islamic brotherhood and cooperation between the Muslims ... the whole of the Islamic world values you and the Muslim League's stand and admires your continuous blessed efforts in the services of the Muslims. (Hasan 1976: 216)

A person who receives letters from the Grand Mufti, especially letters expressing thanks and admiration, must have passed the Muslim test. The nearest equivalent would be for a Christian belonging to the Church of England to receive a letter of thanks from the Archbishop of Canterbury, a South American Catholic from the Pope or a Tibetan Buddhist from the Dalai Lama.

Those who believe in a Westernized, secular future for Pakistan, with no place for Muslim tradition and belief, are strong in the media. To them Jinnah and his Muslim movement are an irrelevance and the last years of Jinnah's life are obliterated by the image of him as a secular man in a Western suit, a glass of whisky in his hand. Thus the entire creation of a country and the entire discovery of its identity are all dismissed in one superficial, simplistic stroke. This conveys the depth of the intellectual crisis in Pakistan.

Let Jinnah have the last word on his so-called secularism. While addressing the Karachi Bar Association on the holy Prophet's birthday, 25 January 1948, just months before he died, he declared that people were making 'mischief' when they rejected the idea of an Islamic state (see also Yahya Bakhtiar in *The News*, 1 July 1995, 'The making of Jinnah's Pakistan'). 'Some are misled by propaganda,' he pointed out. 'Islamic principles today are as applicable to life as they were 1,300 years ago.' He insisted that the constitution of Pakistan would be made 'on the basis of *Sharia*' (Jinnah 1989: 125–7). A few weeks later Jinnah once again repeated the same theme, using almost the same ideas and words: 'It is my belief that our salvation lies in following the golden rules of conduct set for us by our great law-giver, the Prophet of Islam. Let us lay the foundations of our democracy on the basis of truly Islamic ideals and principles' (Sibi Darbar, 14 February 1948).

... Nor fundamentalist

If the secularists are uncomfortable with Jinnah, so are the 'fundamentalists'. If we define fundamentalism according to the *Oxford Advanced Learner's Dictionary* as people advocating a 'literal' or 'strict' application of religion, then Jinnah is not a fundamentalist.

Indeed, for many on the right his personal tolerance and sense of fair play where non-Muslims were concerned smacked too much of Western liberalism (see Jinnah on minorities in 'Jinnah's Gettysburg address' and 'Protection of non-Muslims' earlier in this chapter). This was the man whose personal physicians were non-Muslim; whose steward at home was a Hindu; who married a Parsee; whose only child married a non-Muslim. These were seen as vulnerable points in Jinnah. He had to be safeguarded and projected as a straightforward Muslim warrior astride a white horse, with scimitar in hand, galloping inexorably to the triumph of Pakistan in 1947. His early life appeared irrelevant or uninteresting to those belonging to this school of thought.

Yet Jinnah's fight was not against Hindus, as he was at pains to point out. Even when taking on the Congress Hindu establishment he underlined the fact that he was fighting those among the Brahmin élite who for centuries had exploited not only Muslims but other Hindus. It was this line of argument that made him include in his cabinet a Hindu from the so-called lower or scheduled castes; this made him something of a hero among these Hindus (as the Dalit spokesman Krishna Gamre reported). In an exchange of letters between Jinnah and one of his non-Muslim doctors, Dr Dinshaw Mehta returned Jinnah's fees, explaining that he considered it an honour to treat him, but Jinnah wrote back to insist on payment (*Shamsul Hasan Collection*). In addition, Jinnah appointed a Christian, Pothan Joseph, as the first editor of the main Muslim newspaper, *Dawn*, in 1945. Just days after the creation of Pakistan, on 17 August, he attended a special church service in Karachi to celebrate independence. Later in the year, he would spend Christmas Day in the Christian community.

Even after the creation of Pakistan, Jinnah assigned British officers to his personal staff and to key posts like the commander-in-chief of the army and governors of the provinces. On Jinnah's visit to the regimental mess of the Royal Scots in December 1948 the commanding officer toasted the King and then, breaking tradition, toasted Jinnah: 'Your Excellency,' he began, 'it is such an honour to have you with us that I am going to break tradition. We consider ourselves good fighters; we consider you to be a good fighter also.' Moved by this, Jinnah replied: 'I shall never forget the British who have stayed in Pakistan to help us begin our work; this I shall never forget' (Bolitho 1954: 209).

Some Muslim religious figures were contemptuous of the title given to him by other Muslims, the Quaid-i-Azam, the Great Leader. They saw in him a dangerously modern Muslim, far too lax in his interpretation of Islam. They called him the *Kafir-i-Azam*, the great *kafir*, or non-believer (Khairi 1995: 468; G. H. Khan 1993: 77; Sayeed 1968: 199). Jinnah certainly did not want a theocratic state, a nation run by mullahs. The Taliban of Afghanistan, who were attempting just that in the mid-1990s, when meeting Pakistani bureaucrats in the north of Pakistan refused to conduct proceedings unless the picture of Jinnah hanging in the office was removed (*Jang*, London, 9 December 1996). Professor Abu Bakr Bagadar, a prominent Saudi social scientist, told me in 1996 in Jeddah that several South Asians believed Jinnah was not a Muslim; some even thought he was a Zoroastrian.

Jinnah's modern personality incurs the wrath of Muslims like the late Kalim Siddiqui, who styled himself the leader of the British Muslims. Siddiqui described Jinnah as one of the 'stooges of imperialism' (*Guardian*, 9 May 1992), and the extremist organization, the Hizb-ut-Tahrir, call him the 'Imperialist Collaborator' on their posters. For them Jinnah was too influenced by the West and not Islamic enough. The fact that he created the largest Muslim nation on earth is ignored. The Hizb-ut-Tahrir demand a pure theocratic Islamic state in opposition to a corrupt and decadent West. Living in the UK as permanent citizens, they have antagonized many by demanding Islamic law in Britain including the chopping off of hands as punishment for thieves and calling for the veiling of women.

'Jinnah defies Allah' screamed the subtitle of a special feature on Jinnah, 'Mohammed Ali Jinnah exposed!', in the December 1996 issue of the Hizb magazine *Khilafah*. Its main argument was that Jinnah had been influenced by the *kafir* because he insisted on democracy and indeed went as far as saying that Islam stood for democracy. They condemned and quoted Jinnah's statements: 'Islam believes in democracy' (speech at Aligarh Muslim University on 6 March 1940) and 'We learned democracy 1300 years ago' (presidential address, Muslim League session on 24 April 1943). The article indignantly claimed that 'Jinnah went one step further than most traitors, the man also had the audacity to justify his Kufr actions by Islam.' The article then went on: 'How dare this man associate a Kufr concept such as democracy with our Prophet (saw)!' They further accused him of 'inner secularism' because he had included a Hindu in Pakistan's first cabinet. They condemned the speech of August 1947 in which he spoke of tolerance for the minorities. The article concludes: 'These are only some of the examples where Jinnah clearly defied Allah (swt) and chose the way of the Kafir over the way of the Prophet (saw).'

While people like the Hizb argue that Jinnah's August speeches in the Constituent Assembly – and the one he gave at the opening of the State Bank in 1948 just a few days before he died – wandered away from strictly orthodox Islam, the secularists consider these his most important speeches because they stress tolerance for the minorities and economic welfare for the masses. Both interpretations ignore the context and content of Jinnah's speeches, which reflect not only Islam but also the nuances of the Islamic vision. Islam is concerned not only with theological matters, not only with ritual. It is also about relations with non-Muslims; it is also about bread and butter, about the stomach.

Some Pakistanis claim there have been attempts to conceal these speeches as somehow anti-Islamic in content (Khairi 1995: xix). It is like Lincoln's Gettysburg address being removed from the history of the USA. As part of the wider thinking of Jinnah, they are entirely consistent with both his larger vision of Pakistan and his understanding of Islam.

Anyone living in the British empire would know that social and cultural purity was virtually impossible, and Jinnah had many influences in his life. Under the British empire the subcontinent was very much a mosaic culture, of plural societies, ethnic and religious groups juxtaposed with each other; there was much mutual borrowing and overlap. Therefore the simplistic divisions and compartments will not do. They perhaps reflect the polarized world we have constructed for ourselves.

Whisky and ham sandwiches: tarnishing Jinnah

Zulfiqar Ali Bhutto in a well-known public statement admitted that he drank. But he added that he did not drink the blood of the poor. People applauded him for his frankness and his political position. Some supporters of Jinnah, however, have wished to avert the stigma of drink by blacking out this aspect of his life. It is not a defining part of Jinnah's character yet it has assumed a special place in the Jinnah mythology: his supporters on the right pretend it did not happen and his liberal champions exaggerate its importance. Dietary habits have come to symbolize major ideological positions in Pakistan. The fact that Jinnah drank alcohol is mentioned almost every time he is discussed outside Pakistan (usually as innuendo in writers like M. J. Akbar, Bolitho, Collins and Lapierre, Wolpert, Duncan and C. Lamb) and omitted from every book published in Pakistan (no discussion in Zaidi, Mujahid, Riaz Ahmad et al.); but in conversation the Pakistani élite invariably use innuendoes.

There is a subtext to the debate on Jinnah's drinking in Pakistan. The so-called secularists and liberals belonging to Pakistan's élite and living in urban areas mostly drink. They believe that it is their right to do so but feel restricted in a social climate which echoes Islam's prohibition on drinking. An image of the father of the nation as a drinker would exonerate and free them. It would also undermine the notion of a Pakistan based on Islam. If the leader of a Muslim nation drank, they argue, then how could the nation be Islamic in character?

Others, like S. S. Pirzada, believed there was a well-laid plot, a vigorous campaign, to project Jinnah as flawed – a man who was not a proper Muslim, who ate forbidden flesh and drank forbidden liquid. Tarnishing his reputation would weaken the base of Pakistan itself. Pirzada cited several articles that had appeared recently in this vein including those by Eqbal Ahmed in the *Dawn* (in June 1995). He claimed that this attempt was being made quite consciously and backed by Benazir Bhutto's government (*Impact International*, August 1995).

As a professional in Bombay Jinnah would have acquired the habits of the British élite. One of them was having a drink before dinner. Even if Jinnah drank only in moderation (as his daughter Dina maintained) drinking alcohol cannot be justified in Islam. But does this then mean that anyone drinking is to be excluded from the ranks of Muslims? If so, we obliterate large parts of the edifice of Islamic culture, the towering names from history – Babar, Ghalib and Iqbal. In Pakistan other leaders – not only Bhutto – were also known to drink. So why the fuss about Jinnah?

The answer may well come from Muslim history. Babar, the Mughal emperor, provides an interesting example of a Muslim's attitude to drink. Famous in history as a tippler, he was also a poet, autobiographer, warrior and a family man. But at a critical point of his career, when the fate of India was to be decided through a battle, he decided to make a personal sacrifice. He promised God that he would give up drink on the eve of the battle. He went on to win India. Perhaps something similar happened to Jinnah. Several sources indicate that towards the end of his life he had given up drink.

In August 1995 in Cambridge, Yahya Bakhtiar recalled that to the best of his knowledge Jinnah stopped drinking in his final years, and that Iqbal had done the same – that is, in spite of doctor's orders, they had 'gone Muslim'. S. S. Pirzada confirms this: 'It is on record that during his last illness when his physician advised him to take a little brandy, "as a medicine", he refused. "You want me to take it [alcohol] in the last days of my life, I would not do that," he said' (interview of S. S. Pirzada by M. H. Faruqi, *Impact International*, August 1995: 19).

Pirzada also rejects the often repeated story of Jinnah eating ham sandwiches. As

Jinnah's honorary secretary between 1941 and 1944, he never saw him eat forbidden flesh. However weak the evidence, the most widely read works on Pakistan – by Christina Lamb and Emma Duncan, for example – begin their accounts with a predictable catalogue of Jinnah's dietary habits.

Pirzada put the matter in perspective: 'Still there is this story about ham sandwiches which is being given currency in Pakistan now' (Pirzada interview, ibid.). 'The only source for this appears to be M. C. Chagla's book *Roses in December*.... After independence, he rose to become a Minister in the Indian Government and a virulent anti-Pakistani.' Pirzada explained Chagla's motivation as the need for revenge: Chagla had been both an honorary secretary to Jinnah in the 1920s and a secretary of the Muslim League, but when he welcomed the Nehru Report in 1928, which Jinnah opposed, Jinnah had him removed. When partition came in 1947 Chagla remained on in India, rising to the post of Chief Justice of the Bombay High Court and eventually becoming ambassador to the USA and Foreign Minister of India. Chagla needed to show loyalty to India and also wished to project Jinnah as 'secular' and a flawed Muslim.

According to Chagla's story (quoted in Wolpert 1984: 78–9), Ruttie offered ham sandwiches to Jinnah in the middle of a political campaign. If this were true it would mean that Ruttie was mentally retarded, that she had no idea about her culture and the sensibilities of her society. In fact she was an intelligent, supportive wife. Having become a Muslim after her marriage, she would have particularly appreciated the difference between what was forbidden and what was not. The last thing she would have done would be to embarrass her husband and damage his political career. As much for religious as for cultural reasons, she would certainly not have brought her husband ham sandwiches in the middle of a political campaign, even if she had wanted him to eat them in the first place. It is a silly story.

When I asked Dina Wadia in New York whether Chagla's story had any factual basis, she recalled that over sixty years ago they were travelling by train to a hill station when ham sandwiches were brought with the food as part of the menu. Her father had them sent away. (She also expressed her irritation about Pakistanis who only seemed to be interested in whether Jinnah ate ham and drank whisky.)

For Muslims the flesh of pig is *haram*, forbidden, because it is considered unclean. To eat it is also culturally symbolic of crossing a line. Even the Muslims who drink – and throughout the Muslim world many do – would be reluctant to eat pork. While some of the most famous Muslims drank, and with an arrogant flourish too, they would be revolted by pig meat. When asked whether he was a Muslim, Ghalib replied he was half a Muslim: he did not eat pork but drank alcohol. Even the most liberal of Muslims would not touch pork.

A ham sandwich, however trivial it may seem to secular Western readers, symbolizes to Muslims a cultural and religious crossing of boundaries. Salman Rushdie describes with some irony his loss of faith at 15 at Rugby and declares: 'to prove my new-found atheism, I bought myself a rather tasteless ham sandwich, and so partook for the first time of the forbidden flesh of the swine' (Rushdie 1991: 377).

Stanley Wolpert's book *Jinnah of Pakistan* was banned in Pakistan by General Zia ul-Haq (1984). It was banned perhaps for reasons that we will never know but can guess at. The story was that the authorities had not liked some lines in a book of more than 400 pages containing the most complimentary and favourable remarks about Jinnah.

The lines referred to his drinking and eating habits (ibid.: 78 and 79). All the ban did, however, was to fuel interest in the book. This created a diversion: from the scale of Jinnah's achievement the discussion shifted to whether he had eaten ham sandwiches.

Wazir Jogezai, Education Minister in General Zia's cabinet, told me that General Zia would present Wolpert's book to foreigners although he had banned it himself. He would give them the book with the notorious pages folded over at the corner so that the reader could not fail to find them. In contrast to Jinnah, Zia would thus appear as the champion of Islam. By being portrayed as not a good Muslim, Jinnah was reduced to apparently having led the Pakistan movement for purely personal reasons.

The ban ensured that the book was widely read in Pakistan; it was pirated and sold under the counter. We know from *The Satanic Verses* (1988) controversy that many more people read the book than if there had been no fuss – the book burnings, the violent protests – about it.

In the end, as the Indian Muslim Dr Qureshi asked, is it more relevant for a man to be rigidly orthodox and yet not care for his fellow human beings or for a man to dedicate his life – and health – to his community? Besides, from an Islamic point of view, he said, who gives the right – reserved by God alone – to anyone to judge another human being?

CHAPTER 8

Is Jinnah still Relevant?

Who says Jinnah is not relevant in Pakistan? Only Jinnah can make things work in Pakistan; nothing else works.

(Pakistani saying; 'Jinnah' refers to rupee notes)

In this chapter we shall explore how relevant Jinnah is to contemporary South Asia. We shall note that he remains a central symbol from which Pakistanis draw inspiration. In India Jinnah is also seen as a symbol, but a negative one. In Bangladesh, which was once part of Pakistan, Jinnah has been consciously obliterated from the national memory. With the changing symbolic perceptions, Jinnah's very ideas, character and the cause he fought for have also been distorted. This chapter will examine the three different views of Jinnah in contemporary South Asia and how they reflect developments in society.

From crisis to crisis: sidelining Jinnah in Pakistan

Jinnah gave the Muslims of the subcontinent their own territory; but he also gave them a sense of pride, of dignity, of identity and an awareness of a special destiny. Today most Muslims are indifferent about the former and have forgotten the latter.

The Internet and the latest computer technology on the one hand; trial by fire, child labour, female marriage to the Quran to prevent distribution of land, and death for suspected dishonour at the will of the male on the other hand: at the end of the twentieth century two different and incompatible systems, from two periods of history, seem to be running side by side in Pakistan. The resultant chaos and uncertainty are not unexpected. Pakistanis are maddeningly feudal one moment and impressively modern at the next.

A Tryst with Destiny?

Pakistan society never was – and is not now – monolithic or homogeneous. Different ethnic and social groups had differing relationships with each other which changed over time. There are Pakistanis in Lahore who go jogging, who are in touch with the world through computers, and whose educational background is Ivy League and Oxbridge; there are groups as well, also in Lahore, who would have nothing to do with the West and would reject it altogether. They wish to declare Pakistan a closed fortress of Islam. Both groups form Pakistan. Both participate in the sometimes acrimonious debate about its character and destiny.

The only consolation for Pakistan is that this anarchic disintegration is not just happening in Pakistan. South Asian society appears to be falling apart, torn by ethnic and religious violence (Ahmed 1990a, 1992a, 1992b; M. S. Ali 1995; Basu et al. 1993; Das 1992; Engineer 1991; Gopal 1991; Graham 1990; Pettigrew 1995). In too many cases the administration appears non-existent or takes on the role of tyrant, torturing and murdering its own citizens like organized gangsters.

The many problems of Pakistan

Although Pakistan today is in turmoil, its economy mismanaged, the country was never lacking in natural resources. In 1947 rice, cotton and wheat were already abundant – Punjab was known as the bread-basket of India; and jute and mangoes were plentiful in East Pakistan. Gas and oil were later discovered. As well as the spectacular mountain scenery in the north and west, Pakistan has the great river Indus and its tributaries full of fish. Even if Pakistan did not have the big imperial cities and higher level of development that India possessed, the resources were available for a strong economy to form the basis of a stable society.

The legitimate question is posed by critics: if Jinnah was such a political genius, why is his creation, Pakistan, beset with so many problems? From the moment of its birth Pakistan faced a series of life-threatening crises, splitting into two countries in 1971, when East Pakistan became Bangladesh. Jinnah had been forced to accept a Pakistan with such impractical boundaries that many Pakistanis were convinced that Mountbatten had set out to ensure its failure.

Pakistani insecurity is easily explained. Because Jinnah, their supreme Quaid, died when they needed him most, ever since there has been a crisis of leadership. Pakistanis have no faith in people in authority. They believe that the man holding the highest position of authority in India, the Viceroy, was a liar; that in the summer of 1947 he changed boundaries, conspired to airlift troops to Kashmir, approved the backdating of signatures in Kashmir, and did everything in his power to undermine Pakistan. They have seen districts and subdivisions change at the last minute from one country to another, they have seen killings and deaths on a mass scale, all of which could have been avoided had those in authority been more diligent and honest.

Pakistani character, politics and behaviour today are partly to be explained by the manner in which Pakistan was created. The trauma affected an entire generation, which in turn communicated this to the next. Pakistanis tend to believe in short-term solutions, in cutting corners, in taking unnecessary risks. This tendency is rooted in the belief that it is an insecure world, that people cannot be relied on, that things can change abruptly.

Is Jinnah still Relevant?

The creation of Pakistan in 1947 did more than just give the Muslims a new country. It also transformed their society almost as dramatically as did events in the middle of the nineteenth century. New élites sprang up overnight; old élites fell apart or faded away. A new breed of Muslims emerged. Mostly from the lower middle classes, enterprising, tough and opportunistic, they quickly made their way to power and wealth in the new state. The senior generals, the bureaucrats and the politicians who would dominate Pakistan in the next generation would come from this background.

In 1947 Pakistan was founded with the momentum that had been built up by the Muslim community; but nations are not sustained by enthusiasm alone. The Pakistan movement lacked organization and clarity of vision. What it had in abundance was spirit. Yet after the death of Jinnah, once the early euphoria had waned, the problems confronting the new state grew: the issues of ethnicity, corruption, nepotism and mismanagement, and a reversion to old-established tribal and feudal patterns in the areas that formed Pakistan. International problems like the Kashmir issue loomed large in foreign policy, threatening to drag Pakistan into a perpetual confrontation with a more powerful neighbour. Pakistan's leaders were not up to the task. In two decades they lost half the country, East Pakistan. Today they struggle with what remains, fighting first one ethnic community, then another. In the 1990s, it is the turn of the *muhajirs* – those who migrated as refugees from India – in Karachi to be attacked. Paramilitary or police are able to pick up *muhajirs* and declare them terrorists until they pay up ransom money (see below). This is anarchy, not an organized state.

It is easy to fall into the trap of imagining an ideal past and comparing it to a disintegrating present. Many of Jinnah's original disciples, many of those who created Pakistan, have done exactly this. Sirdar Shaukat Hyat Khan wrote his autobiography under the title *The Nation that Lost its Soul* (1995). Conjuring up an idealized Pakistan in its early days, he contrasted it with the rot and corruption of Pakistan today. Although reflecting a certain reality, this picture is not entirely correct. The past was never as admirable as Sardar Shaukat makes out; but the present may indeed be as gloomy as he has depicted.

By viewing Pakistan history as an ideal in that first year, reaching its climax with Jinnah's brief period as Governor-General, historians cause difficulties for the study of contemporary Pakistan. The actuality of Pakistan society will always be found wanting; no contemporary leader will ever quite match Jinnah. Marking off 1947–8 as one phase of Pakistan that was noble, good and pure (the true meaning of Pakistan) is not only a simplistic view of history but also misleading. Pakistan has produced a series of extraordinary leaders and for scholars to imply that after Jinnah there were nothing but pygmies is incorrect. It is true that most of those leaders faced almost impossible odds in trying to hold Pakistan together while moving it forward. For all of them the very question of survival was paramount. It is not surprising that some of them lost their lives while in office (Liaquat Ali Khan and Zia ul-Haq). It is also not surprising that many of them were military leaders. The Pakistan army would be one of the best-organized and best-motivated forces in the country; it also had a well-defined notion of what Pakistan was. Because Pakistanis sensed the insecurity, they often clutched at strong leaders, looking for a Saladin.

A Tryst with Destiny?

Martial law

The areas that comprised Pakistan had known a period of relative calm and stability for almost a century under the British. Law and order were maintained, and roads, railways and telegraph lines ensured communications. From its inception until today, Pakistan has experienced a series of crises interrupted by periods of relative calm. Because these periods have coincided with martial law, some people in the 1990s who prefer stability, even at the cost of military rule, look back with nostalgia to the time of Ayub Khan in the 1960s. His portrait is often seen in bazaars, or painted on the back of trucks.

Most of the 1960s were good years for Pakistan. General Ayub Khan had consolidated power and emerged on the international stage to project the image of a vigorous, confident Pakistan. Internationally, Pakistan's sphere of influence was at its greatest – from the military and political alliances of the Central Treaty Organization (Cento), which extended it to the shores of Europe, to those of the South-East Asia Treaty Organization (Seato). Agriculture flourished and trade grew; new strains of rice and wheat were introduced and model farms were set up. The Planning Commission in Islamabad attracted many Harvard and Oxbridge graduates. The World Bank cited Pakistan as a model growth economy and the South Koreans sent experts to learn its secrets. This gave Pakistan a sense of confidence and pride. Here was a tiger waiting to pounce in the Asian jungle.

But Jinnah had not made Pakistan for the Muslim élite. He specifically had in mind the community, the *ummah*. Iqbal had already incited the poor to revolt: in a famous poem called *Farman-e-Khuda* ('The Order of God to the Angels') the angels exhort the poor of the world to shake the foundations of society. Jinnah did not have time after Pakistan was created to implement these ideas. However, once Pakistan had been formed, Jinnah's concern for the *ummah* was quickly set aside and the traditional élite combined with a new emergent élite to seize power and perpetuate itself through marriages and political alliances. Pakistan politics have never really broken away from that stranglehold. In 1958 Ayub Khan, then the commander-in-chief of the army, declared martial law, and that was a major setback to Jinnah's concept of a democratic and free Pakistan.

Jinnah's reputation

Pakistan has been ruled by so-called democrats and self-proclaimed dictators for most of its half-century. Both groups have reasons to be uneasy about Jinnah – the democrats because their governments are usually steeped in corruption and nepotism, the dictators because they cast aside the principles of freedom and representation. Neither group sees Jinnah's impeccable integrity and unwavering loyalty to the idea of democratic and legal government as of much use.

Similarly the major political parties of Pakistan were ambiguous about Jinnah. The Pakistan People's Party (PPP) kept its focus firmly on the former Prime Minister Zulfiqar Ali Bhutto and loyalty to the Bhutto family. Both Bhutto and his daughter Benazir personally considered Jinnah a hero, but other members of the PPP, especially the sycophants, were less enthusiastic.

The Muslim League, which logically should have supported and propagated the ideas of Jinnah, was in a similar quandary. In the 1960s it was led by General Ayub Khan, who had little time for Jinnah and his talk of democracy. He had even less time for Jinnah when Jinnah's sister Fatima stood against him and almost toppled him. Once again Jinnah was sidelined. General Zia, who favoured not only the Muslim League but also the religious party, the Jamat-i-Islami, while accepting Jinnah's central role in the Pakistan movement, made it clear that his own understanding of Pakistan was much more explicitly Islamic. Jinnah, with his Westernized clothes, appearance and manners, did not entirely fit in with Zia's ideas.

While paying Jinnah lip-service, most of the leaders of Pakistan have ignored him. He is too much of a giant, too honest and firm in his moral correctness, to make them comfortable. This indeed is the perception of those who knew Jinnah and can compare him to his successors. Yahya Bakhtiar, a senator from Baluchistan, confirmed that all the leaders of Pakistan were in one way or another jealous of Jinnah's greatness and reluctant to acknowledge his stature. None of them paid him the tribute that he deserved. Scholars like Dr Zaidi agree with this view.

Every Pakistani, so Pakistanis say, wants to be *the* leader. Apart from the Quaid-i-Azam, there is the Quaid-i-Millat, the Leader of the Nation, Liaquat; there is the Quaid-i-Awam, the Leader of the People, Bhutto; and there is the Quaid-i-Sani, the second leader (after Jinnah), Nawaz Sharif, the Muslim League leader re-elected Prime Minister in 1997.

Besides, in Pakistan itself, political heroes tend to be ethnic. For example, Wali Khan in the Frontier Province and Bhutto in the Sind are identified more as local ethnic heroes than national Muslim figures. Iqbal is as much loved for his being Punjabi as for his poetry (although Iqbal was from Kashmir, he lived and died in Lahore). Jinnah was the outsider. Although he was born in Karachi he was not really a Sindhi in the strict sense as defined in contemporary Pakistan – that is, he was not from rural Sind (although many Sindhis claim he was born near Thatta in Sind and therefore a rural Sindhi). Jinnah thus stood outside both the ethnic traditions of Pakistan today and the larger North Indian Muslim culture as defined by Lahore and Delhi.

From the 1960s onwards Jinnah was subtly but quite consciously removed from mainstream political life by being placed on a pedestal. Fewer and fewer Pakistanis learned of Jinnah. Some scholars wrote about him with affection but for the most part Pakistanis saw him in the formal, stiff official portraits. They knew little of him or what he stood for. Worse, what they saw of him conveyed the impression of a distant, cold and aloof leader.

Looking at present-day pictures of Jinnah and comparing them to images from the 1940s, I see some significant changes in Jinnah's representation. I am not referring to the obvious differences in the quality and sophistication of the pictures. In the more recent images there is a strong sense of decorum, formality and authority. But something is missing. What has disappeared is the passion, the tumultuous feelings unleashed by Jinnah. The human, emotional dimension has gone; that *frisson*, that sense of elation, that spark which fired the Muslim masses is missing. After all, even Gandhi had acknowledged that Jinnah had 'mesmerized' the Muslims.

Jinnah wearing the national dress was favoured during Zia's time; the Western suit, depicting a 'secular' Jinnah, was popular during the time of the Bhuttos. The depiction of

Jinnah in the national dress, consciously painted in dark hues, conveys a 'fundamentalist' Jinnah; he is portrayed as grim and unsmiling; he looks like a stern headmaster. This makes a point: discipline is required; the headmaster's cane is to be kept at hand, and people have to obey. Both portraits still project a stiff, unsmiling figure. These are the subliminal messages conveyed by Jinnah's portrait, reinforcing the idea of strong authority. Pakistan was drifting away from Jinnah. He in turn was in danger of losing his nation.

Jinnah's relationship with his nation is illustrated by the grand mausoleum built for him in Karachi, the port of call for all visiting dignitaries and a recognizable symbol of Pakistan. As you walk up the wide stairs to the Turkish-design dome (characteristic because it does not have supporting towers around it), you are struck by its imposing architecture. But in fact it took Pakistanis several decades to achieve this ambitious expression of their affection. The gardens spread to over 60 acres but a few hundred yards from the mausoleum itself the grass runs out, not making it to the outer walls, and there is nothing but sand and broken bricks. Pakistani energy and consistency have been exhausted within the parameters of the mausoleum grounds. Failing to pay Jinnah tribute, they reflect their own failure to know the man while wishing to say something grand and noble about him. This ambiguity is at the heart of the Pakistani inability to understand the man and his contribution; it is also the inability to come to terms with their own identity.

Jinnah's vision of Pakistan – the rising moon – lies in the debris of the consumerism, cynicism and corruption of the 1990s. Jinnah's ideas of justice and compassion – ideas derived from the larger vision of Islam – are no longer visible. It is not only a political crisis but a serious moral crisis too. The Islamic Republic of Pakistan, its critics say, is neither Islamic nor a republic, nor much of a state; nor indeed is it the Pakistan Jinnah had dreamed of.

The only remaining lesson is Jinnah's motto for Pakistan: unity, faith and discipline. But Pakistanis have made a mockery of it with their disunity, lack of faith and lack of discipline. Yet the greater the crisis, the greater the reputation of Jinnah, who has assumed almost mythical, saintly proportions for ordinary Pakistanis. Pakistanis throughout the land, and indeed wherever they have settled, talk of him as the personification of honesty and dedication. He is the visible yardstick against which to compare the present leadership.

Gains and losses

Iqbal, Jinnah and those dreaming of a Muslim nation were reaching for the stars, a place in the universe. In his 'Gettysburg address', Jinnah had a vision of Pakistan joining the ranks of the great nations in the world. Today, those who have inherited Pakistan have forsaken this dream; their eyes are very much on the ground: they look for small plots of land given as government favours. It is a fall from the sublime to the ridiculous, as much a reflection on moral integrity as on political seriousness. They have squandered the legacy of the Muslims of South Asia.

If Jinnah returned today he would be proud of many things in Pakistan. He would be proud that Pakistan is a name recognized throughout the world, a nation with an identity. He would be pleased at how much progress has been made in the universities and colleges, the industries, the excellence of some of the training institutes, the standard of the defence services, the energy and initiative of the entrepreneurs, the solid base of middle-class Pakistanis.

When Pakistan was created there were entire districts without a single light bulb. There were whole divisions without tarmacked roads (Makran division, for example). Communications were non-existent in most of the country. Half a century later Pakistan is integrated as never before in its history. Roads, telecommunications and air flights link Pakistan from one end to the other.

An increasingly integrated Pakistani society had begun to take shape after the break from East Pakistan in 1971. Urdu, once the preserve of the élite from Delhi, became a common language spoken all over Pakistan. New classes emerged as the feudal élite began to disintegrate, and a new dynamism was apparent in society. Income per capita was almost double that of India and Bangladesh. Pakistanis made their mark in several international fields. They became renowned as world champions of sports like squash, cricket and hockey. A Pakistani, Dr Abdus Salam, won the Nobel Prize for Physics.

But Jinnah would not be so proud of the corruption, nepotism, mismanagement and plain inefficiency in Pakistan in the 1990s. He would be broken-hearted at the sight of Pakistanis killing Pakistanis. He would be despondent to hear of the long periods of martial law. He would also be saddened to discover that many members of minority communities complain of discrimination in Pakistan. It is ironic that the Pakistan of Jinnah, who fought for the security and rights of the minorities, should be accused of discrimination against Christians and Hindus in the 1990s. To him, Pakistan meant security for *all*, whether Muslim or non-Muslim, whether rich or poor. Jinnah fought for dignity and identity; today Pakistan is in danger of losing both.

The question of Islamic politics remains unresolved. There can be no doubt that Pakistan is demographically, sociologically and culturally a Muslim country. About 95 per cent of its 130 million people are Muslim. These Muslims vary in sectarian affiliation: they belong to different sects – although the majority are Sunni – and they belong to different tribes and political parties. Most Pakistanis are committed Muslims but many are not. Not all of them would want an Islamic state in Pakistan. Indeed, the religious parties have always done poorly at the polls, never gaining more than a handful of seats. While enthusiastically embracing the idea of being Muslim as individuals and as a society, Pakistanis have never been convinced they should adopt an Islamic character for the state itself. When the concept was energetically propagated during General Zia's rule in the 1980s, large sections of society were uncomfortable. In the elections that followed his death in 1988 Pakistanis voted for the Pakistan People's Party, which did not stand for an Islamic state.

Pakistanization and awam*ification*

Although Pakistan has lurched in unexpected directions, none the less it has been characterized by two distinct movements in nation-building: the 'Pakistanization' of culture and the '*awam*ification' of society.

Pakistanization means the development of a certain uniformity of values, clothes and aspirations – a homogeneity growing over the diverse ethnicity. It includes an understanding of Urdu as the national language. Even the most remote parts of Pakistan now understand and speak Urdu, a considerable achievement, since it is the mother tongue of less than 10 per cent of the population and regarded as a foreign language by many son-of-the-soil nationalists. The media, especially television, have ensured that Urdu is now the unchallenged language of Pakistan.

'*Awam*ification' derives from the word *awam*, meaning the people or masses. It was a term used frequently by Bhutto and the PPP in the 1970s to refer to an increase in the rights of the masses as distinct from the privileges of the élite. There has been a distinct '*awam*ification' in Pakistan in so far as ordinary people have gained power, wealth and rights as never before in history. Their expectations are high and the changing social structure allows them a greater say than they have ever had before. Regular elections mean that the common people, once despised, are now canvassed for votes by the privileged few from the big bungalows and estates.

After the establishment of Pakistan the governors and ministers would be the Nawabs, Khans and Chaudhrys (the first Prime Minister, Liaquat, was Nawabzada, or son of a Nawab). It is significant that the leaders of Pakistan – the governors, generals and secretaries – in the last two decades belonged mostly to the lower middle classes, bringing with them their world-view. Their fathers would have been junior clerical staff or junior army officers. President Zia was the son of a clerical mullah, and President Ghulam Ishaque Khan began his career in a junior clerical post (he was not from the Indian Civil Service as is often claimed). Nawaz Sharif, the Prime Minister, a protégé of General Zia, is from a humble background. Benazir Bhutto is one of the few exceptions. Her father had been Prime Minister; her grandfather was a knight of the British empire and a Chief Minister of an Indian state – but, her critics are quick to point out, it was a small, poor and unimportant state.

This sometimes quiet, sometimes noisy revolution has also meant that politicians are much more conscious of the needs of the *awam*, who demand schools, health facilities, transport and jobs. Their demands thus feed into ethnic politics, which has grown because of the need for politicians to placate their constituency or *awam*.

There has also been a vulgarization, a corruption, of the *awam*, as a kind of materialist blood-lust settles on them. In the 1980s under General Zia it was the *awam* who enjoyed the spectacle of members of its own community being whipped in public for violating minor Islamic injunctions.

We thus see several contradictory developments taking place: Pakistanization on the one hand and globalization through the media on the other, the '*awam*ification' on the one hand and the concentration of wealth among the élite on the other. Pakistan society in the 1990s is in flux: dynamic and growing, brash and confident, despondent and disintegrating. Lacking consistency it compensates with energy.

In the 1990s Pakistan society is joining the world stampede to project and display the images of consumerism – in food, clothes, pleasure. It makes for an uneasy and often violent juxtaposition of modernity and tradition, of Islamic and Western influences. It partly explains the anger and the easy violence that exist in Muslim society today.

Pakistani culture is mass culture, its expression is demotic and its gratification is immediate. There is little high-flown philosophy, esoteric idealism, or notions of literature or destiny anchored in it. This is appropriate: illiteracy rates are among the highest in the world. Images of consumerism are everywhere. Zee TV, Star TV and

Pakistan TV have kept the *awam* in a state of hypnosis round the clock, flashing the seductive charms of a consumerist world.

Through satellite television, in particular through Zee TV, Indian films, values, songs and culture came beaming into Pakistani living-rooms throughout the land. It was an irresistible flood and Pakistanis mopped it up. In public few would admit it but Pakistanis spend hours every day watching Indian TV. Jinnah's notion of separation – described in his historic 1940 speech in Lahore about separate culture, history and belief – is under threat from an unexpected quarter.

The Pakistani élite

A visit to the Rawal lake from which Islamabad draws its drinking water will illustrate how short-sighted is the Pakistan élite. The great and the good have built beautiful houses all around the lake. Visually, this is a picture postcard from Switzerland. In fact, by constructing the houses they have broken not only government law but also the law of common sense. By flushing their urine and faeces into the lake they ensure that along with all of Islamabad they too drink the polluted water.

To understand the élite in contemporary Pakistan you need to rise before dawn and go for a walk in their cities. Islamabad, like Lahore and Karachi, sleeps late. The élite, drinking and eating late into the night, rarely see the sun rise. The walk around Islamabad will tell us several things. It will show us the large, monstrous houses which reflect the wealth and corruption of the élite, and reveal the egos of those who built them. The most popular style is that of the White House in Washington; nothing less will do. There is no civic awareness: people living in the grandest houses just throw their rubbish outside their own walls. The eye sees houses that could be in Europe or the USA, but the nose reminds us we are very much in an Asian city with the smells from the sewage and the piles of dirt outside.

The élite in Pakistan are small in number, comprising the major politicians, the senior officials in the services, the big industrialists, the landlords and the influential journalists. Their petulance, myopia, caprice and snobbery are amazing, even by the standards of African and Asian élites. They are incestuous, marrying within, feeding on and patronizing themselves. Their aim in life appears to be the perpetuation of their privileges. They have repeatedly failed the nation, first losing half the country in 1971 and then, in the last two decades, constantly pushing it towards further disintegration. They appear to have no coherent vision of the future or of society. They are not even sure why Pakistan was created and what is its destiny.

The behaviour of some members of the élite contrasts with the simplicity, faith and generosity of the ordinary people of Pakistan. Talk to a villager in the Punjab or Sind or a tribesman in the Frontier or Baluchistan and then to those in the big cities who frequent the expensive hotels. It will be a lesson in contrasts and will present two different visions of Pakistan.

Although it is an Islamic nation, the parties in Gulberg in Lahore, or in Clifton and Defence in Karachi, or in Islamabad, might echo those of Rome in its decadent phase or the Mughal empire in its last days (for a rare published account of the domestic life of the élite, see Durrani 1994). Men and women drink themselves stupid and have to be carried to bed by their male servants. The idea of Muslim men picking up and carrying drunken women who are not their spouses to bed holds the potential for a social explosion. It is a sign of the power of the élite, an expression that they have arrived and can flout the rules. The paradox of a Muslim élite drunk, helpless, out of control, does not penetrate through to them. But it reflects their bankruptcy, both moral and intellectual.

The irony is that members of the élite provide the smart brigade, those who have been to Oxford and Cambridge, to universities in the United States, the shakers, the movers and the doers: this is the Who's Who of Pakistan. This is their understanding of modernity, of progress, of living like the West.

The Pakistani élite appear to have little brain and no heart, little *demagh*, no *dil*. What makes it worse is that they have a ravenous stomach, *pait*, which they must fill in any way possible – legal or illegal.

The diet of and the way food is eaten by the Pakistani élite are revealing. The impression of being overweight is confirmed by what they eat: rich sweets, meat and rice dishes dripping with fat. When the élite eat at a ceremonial function outdoors, the men rush to the tables, elbowing aside old people and women. In a few minutes the food will have disappeared. Bones and cutlery are strewn on the elegant lawns. It is not a pretty sight.

The Muslim élite like what they call 'show' – to spend money, to entertain lavishly, to display expensive jewellery. Prestige, wealth and appearances matter more than hard work, precision and talent, which count for little in society. Yet Jinnah represented those virtues. That is why in cricket, politics and journalism Pakistanis come with attitude: they appear to walk round with a chip on their shoulder. One minute they are capable of sublime heights, the next they are plunging to the depths of ridiculousness.

Stories of corruption have circulated widely in the 1990s and were supported by evidence, even if much of it was anecdotal. The reasons are not difficult to locate. Wages and salaries have fallen far behind the galloping inflation, with pay ranging from £50 to £100 a month, a span that ranges from the lowest to the highest in the public sector. The power of bureaucrats remains strong and their capacity to delay or reject a case is notorious. A customs official earning £50 a month can delay consignments arriving for an industry in Karachi by weeks. It is worthwhile for an industrialist to grease palms.

It is difficult to imagine a time when Pakistani leaders were honest – when Jinnah allocated himself one rupee a month as pay for his work as Governor-General of Pakistan (G. H. Khan 1993: 77) and Liaquat, the first Prime Minister, once a rich feudal lord who had to leave everything behind in India, had less than £50 in his bank balance at his death (interview with Akbar, son of Liaquat). When told about Jinnah, people ask: could a man like this have actually existed, a man of such unimpeachable integrity and moral authority? He took one rupee a month as his salary? they ask with disbelief, the question an implicit comment on the corruption they see around them.

In Baluchistan – where they do these things with tribal panache – when I visited the province in 1994 I was told about a minister who ran his official transport as a taxi service. He expressed his contemptuous attitude by insisting that the government pay for the petrol. Not wishing to leave any stone unturned in his efforts to line his pockets, he also had the tyres of his personal vehicles swapped with those of the official vehicles. This spoke not only of the depths of corruption but of a cynicism and collapse of morality on a scale not known before.

Is Jinnah still Relevant?

Jinnah often quoted a Dutch proverb (for instance in his presidential address to the Punjab Muslim Student Federation in March 1941; R. Ahmed 1993: 50):

> Money is lost nothing is lost;
> Courage is lost much is lost;
> Honour is lost most is lost;
> Soul is lost all is lost.

Cynics in Pakistan now reverse this proverb, reciting it with words suitably adjusted to the realities of Pakistan today:

> Soul is lost nothing is lost;
> Honour is lost much is lost;
> Courage is lost most is lost;
> Money is lost all is lost.

You still see the Quaid in portraits in every office and on banknotes; his mausoleum in Karachi is a symbol of the state itself, and important visitors to Pakistan invariably pay their respects there. On national days the Quaid's sayings are quoted in the press. But Pakistanis are cynical. They are aware that, although the Quaid appears to be everywhere, in fact very few know about him or what he stood for. There is little accessible and authoritative literature on him. Neither the tomes of the scholars nor the superficial, juvenile writing about him as Islam's warrior hero have penetrated society. In this vacuum his presence is marked by the humour and cynicism of Pakistanis. When Pakistanis speak of 'remembering' the Quaid we know what they mean: to get things done in Pakistan you have to pay large rupee notes with the Quaid's picture on them (see plate 16). That is how many people are familiar with him.

The young men and women who helped Jinnah create Pakistan, who sustained it in the early years with their fierce devotion to the state, are now in their seventies. They are bewildered and saddened by the rapid decline and cannot understand how the dream has soured. Many are so deep in despair that they are escaping to the West.

In the 1960s Jinnah's dream of Pakistan becoming one of the great nations of the world had appeared within grasp, and economic pundits were hailing it as a model for developing countries. Thirty years later Dr Mahbub ul-Haq, who had been chief economist of the newly formed Planning Division in Pakistan, now pioneered the *Human Development Report* for the United Nations Development Programme and pointed out in it that Pakistan was at the bottom of almost every set of statistics in the world – in education, in health, and so on (1995). It was, however, number two on the list of the world's most corrupt countries. (Pakistanis bribed the judges to remove them from the number one position, joked Pakistanis, still clinging to their sense of humour.)

Jinnah's city as hell on earth

In the 1950s up in the hills of North Pakistan in my school at Abbottabad we used to play cricket by dividing the main players into 'Karachi versus the Rest'. In spite of the upheavals of partition, Karachi was then the centre of commercial, political and

Plate 16   A cartoon in the *Friday Times* (30 May to 5 June 1996) of a 1,000-rupee note with Jinnah crying at the condition of his Pakistan

intellectual power. It was assumed that Karachi could easily take on the rest of the country.

By the 1990s, over a generation later, it was the turn of the rest of the country to get even with Karachi. Karachi had been hounded into a corner like an animal. In the early 1990s Karachi, the main city containing about one-tenth of Pakistan's population, had become a Beirut with hostages picked up at random in broad daylight and full-scale sectarian and ethnic killings taking place round the clock. The city was tearing itself apart.

All the major cities of the twentieth century have undergone dramatic transformation. In British or American cities, populations have swollen, some districts have become derelict and some areas are unsafe even before dark. Karachi is different. It has experienced the most radical structural and demographic changes in the last half-century. Within the space of fifty years it has been transformed from a sleepy coastal port with about half a million people to a fully fledged urban nightmare with almost 15 million people.

Over the last decade or two the sense of deprivation among those who had come to Pakistan as refugees forced the creation of a new ethnicity − an eclectic, inchoate but passionately held ethnicity called *muhajir* identity. It defied established ethnic traditions. It was based neither on tribe nor on common ancestry nor even on shared origin. Refugees from Bengal who spoke Bengali and Urdu-speakers from Delhi jostled with Gujarati-speakers from Bombay to form *muhajir* ethnicity. It found its expression in the

Muhajir Qaumi Movement (national movement of refugees), the MQM, which not only won most of the seats from Karachi and Hyderabad but dominated politics in those areas. It led to a direct confrontation with the centre in Islamabad and resulted in the violence that exploded in the 1990s in Karachi. With the collapse of the larger Pakistani identity, ethnicity was proving to be a deadly affair.

It was estimated that about a hundred people were being killed every day in Karachi in the mid-1990s. Wild rumours circulated about the identity of the killers. Some said that Benazir Bhutto's government was organizing the killings through its intelligence agencies; some said that the army was destabilizing the civilian government to pave the way for martial law; others said the killers were the Indians. No one seemed to know who was doing what to whom any more. Worse: no one seemed to care.

Whoever was organizing the killing was doing it in an egalitarian manner. Rich and poor, Shia and Sunni, *muhajir* and non-*muhajir* were all victims. The Muslims of Karachi looked back half a century and wondered whether it was all worth it. They appeared to have two choices: death and destruction by Hindu mobs in India or death and destruction by anonymous killers in Karachi.

In the summer of 1995 Benazir Bhutto, the then Prime Minister, made some provocative statement about the *muhajirs*, calling them 'rats'. The MQM leader, Altaf Hussain, in exile in London, gave a rare interview to an Indian journal in which he complained that *muhajirs* were treated as 'third-rate citizens' in Pakistan (*India Today*, 15 July 1995). He declared: 'We sacrificed two million lives. This country's foundations are soaked in our parents' blood.' He went on: 'Benazir Bhutto did not mean to call us cowards, as people say rats or chicken. It was more in the nature of calling us vermin. Now the world must accept that she is a fascist like Hitler. Hitler had said that Jews and Gypsies are like rats and should be exterminated. Then she said the *muhajirs* have different blood. That we have bad blood, it was this blood that built this country.' Altaf Hussain called for a general strike in Karachi, and the city came to a standstill. Then even more deaths were recorded, as the government tried to break the strike.

It was hell twice over for these *muhajirs*, the very Muslims who had fought for the Pakistan movement. Muslims in Delhi, Aligarh and Lucknow, at the vanguard of the Pakistan movement for a whole generation, were in 1947 suddenly faced with the terrible dilemma of having to decide whether to leave their homes and go to a Pakistan which only existed in their imagination, or, as relations between India and Pakistan rapidly deteriorated, be left behind in an increasingly hostile Indian environment. They were being punished by both countries. They had become foreigners in a land they had dreamed of, their Pakistan, and strangers in their own land in India. They have yet to make their peace with either. They are the visible sacrificial lambs of the Pakistan idea.

The *muhajirs*' attitude towards Jinnah has changed. In the 1990s the *muhajirs*, who had most to thank him for and had followed him from India to Pakistan, have contemplated life in the nightmare of Karachi, with its ethnic violence and the harsh actions against them of the administration, and become disillusioned with the Quaid-i-Azam and the Pakistan movement. On his mausoleum in Karachi they scrawled vulgar graffiti in Urdu. It was a comment not so much on the Quaid-i-Azam but on what had become of Pakistan.

215

A Tryst with Destiny?

Dodgem car culture

Pakistani commentators describe their society as a 'Kalashnikov culture', implying violence and breakdown of law and order from the time when the gun was introduced during the Afghan war in the 1980s. I prefer 'dodgem car culture'; it implies more than just the collapse of law and order: you may be hit in any place, sideways, from the back, from the front, by anyone at any time, anywhere. You will be hit for any reason however irrational or illogical.

Jinnah's high ideals for his nation, a nation of Pakistanis, of pure people, of Pakis, have become a joke in the 1990s. The very word Paki has come to signify a despised Asian immigrant in the UK. Pakis are the victims of bashing and Paki-bashing has become a sport. The irony is that even Indians are fair game. Imagine the chagrin of the poor Indian who was beaten up by some obnoxious white youth on the pretext that he was a Paki: the ultimate irony perhaps – a fanatical BJP member, a visitor to the UK, bashed for being a hated Pakistani.

In Pakistan in the 1990s, the sight of Pakistanis killing Pakistanis is an ugly one. The most vulnerable are those for whom Jinnah had created Pakistan – women, children, the minorities, the weak and the poor. Early in 1995, two Christians, one a mere boy, were condemned to execution by a court for insulting the holy Prophet of Islam in Pakistan. Such decisions were not based on Islamic law *per se*, but reflected several traditions.

In February 1995 BBC television in its *Correspondent* series interviewed the head of a religious group in Pakistan, a member of the Assembly, who openly declared that minorities like the Shias should be persecuted, threatened and, his rhetoric suggested, eliminated. Pakistan had split into sectarian factions. Cameras showed young boys in chains, tied to iron posts, virtual prisoners of religious teachers in rural Pakistan. About the same time, the BBC television programme, *Travelogue*, exposed the horrors of life in contemporary Pakistan. As if to confirm all this, unknown gangs in Karachi killed a record number of innocent people in bazaars and shopping malls.

In December 1995 a bomb blast in Peshawar stunned the nation and brought the anarchy home to me in Cambridge. Apart from dozens of other people, three members of the Governor's family, his daughter and grandchildren, cousins of my wife, were killed. A few days earlier the Chief Minister's brother had been brutally killed in Karachi. In what seemed an obvious retaliation, the brother of Altaf Hussain, the MQM leader, was found murdered shortly afterwards.

Imran Khan, the cricketer-turned-politician, accused Benazir Bhutto's government of banning advertisements for his cancer hospital in Lahore on the grounds that she was politically nervous of him. Hindrances were put in his path. In April 1996 there was a bomb explosion in his hospital. Half a dozen people died and dozens were injured. The explosion was a turning point for Imran Khan. Angry with the corruption and mismanagement around him, he formed a political party, the Tahreek-e-Insaaf or Justice Party. Ordinary people were already looking around for a hero figure and Imran's talk of Islam, national identity and cultural pride struck a chord. Almost overnight he was transformed from a cricket hero into a potential leader of Pakistan. Nevertheless, in the elections of February 1997 Imran Khan's party failed to win a single seat and its political credibility crumbled away.

Meanwhile the sectarian violence continued to grow. Over seventy people were killed when Shias and Sunnis fought each other in Chitral in North Pakistan. Over twenty were killed when unknown gunmen burst into a mosque in Multan and fired on the Sunni worshippers. Dr Zaidi was horrified. He was a young man when partition took place and recalls that, even during the worst Hindu–Muslim rioting, 'People fought each other but they did not invade places of worship. This is a new kind of violence.'

In September 1996, Murtaza Bhutto, brother of Benazir Bhutto, was shot dead by police officers outside the family home in Karachi. The Deputy Inspector General of Police, who took part in the police operation, was mysteriously killed a few days later ('suicide', according to the police). Pakistan had plumbed new depths.

My attempts to put on a brave face failed to convince even me, let alone viewers of *Channel Four News* on 23 September. The *Spectator* offered a solution to Pakistan's problems: 'Abolish it' (Tunku Vardarajan, *State of Nothing,* 12 October 1996). But this line of argument was not original: we had been hearing it since 1947. Paki-bashers and Islam-bashers were oozing out of the woodwork. The scent of a witch-hunt was in the air.

Early in November 1996 the President of Pakistan, Farooq Leghari, dismissed Benazir Bhutto's government and dissolved the assemblies citing 'nepotism', 'corruption' and 'mismanagement'. It was the second time her government had been brought down in this way. Her own father's government had been overthrown in 1977 by General Zia, and he had then been hanged in 1979 on what many suspected were trumped-up murder charges.

In the fresh elections held in February 1997 the electorate challenged the common perception that the more media-attractive candidate wins by supporting Nawaz Sharif and rejecting Benazir Bhutto in a convincing manner. The people of Pakistan were saying no not only to corruption and mismanagement but also to Oxford, Westerniza-tion and international media razzmatazz.

The retreat of Jinnah's Pakistan

Reading recent reports by Amnesty International on Pakistan, one wonders whether there is any justice left in the land. Rape, torture and kidnapping seem to be the lot of the ordinary citizen. The police are the worst perpetrators. The government appears to be helpless or else an accomplice, passive or active. It is a society that has broken down; there is little Islam, little justice, little balance. Looking at these reports, one finds it difficult to justify the word Islamic in the description of the country as the Islamic Republic of Pakistan; it is like any other society in the process of disintegration and racked by tribal genocide and violence – another Malawi, Burundi or Rwanda.

The paradox is that the world pointed a finger at Pakistan and declared that here was Islam disintegrating, an Islamic society corrupt, violent and sick. This was a paradox because the Islamic notion of a society rests on just leaders, people who heed the exhortations in the Quran to show justice, morality, piety and compassion. Pakistan society is in a state of anarchy, its old laws derived from the British decaying and falling apart. In its place there is a hotchpotch of laws that are simultaneously Islamic, Pakistani, tribal and state laws. In the end they often negate each other and lead to confusion and chaos.

Justice in Pakistan? Ask the women who are raped in the police stations by the police;

ask the tenants who are treated little better than bonded slaves on the estates of the feudal lords in the rural areas; ask the children who are sold into a lifetime of hard physical labour from which there appears no escape; ask the ordinary Pakistani living in an urban area trying to make ends meet, with soaring costs, a breakdown of services and the voracious mouths of bureaucrats demanding to be fed for the smallest public act.

Where are the genuine scholars and saints? It is a sad fact of Pakistani life that many of the outstanding scholars have simply been silenced or chased out of the country. The saintly Muslims keep to themselves, increasingly isolated in a society that is becoming more material and grasping with each year. People blame each other – the other ethnic group, the rich, the leaders and, invariably, Jinnah, the father who had died and left his children in the lurch, the ultimate desertion: not being there. But Jinnah has done his job. He had created the largest Muslim nation on earth. The mess has been made by subsequent Pakistani leaders. As Dr Jaffar Qureshi put it: 'Jinnah gave you a Rolls-Royce; you drove it straight into a wall and smashed it. It is not his fault.'

Pakistan in a profound sense is rebelling against the father, the founder of Pakistan, ignoring what he said, what he did and what he thought. Its fate is in the hands of a small élite situated in the north of the land alienated from the vast Muslim body in the subcontinent, no longer the embodiment of Muslim destiny but clinging neurotically to its own narrow parochial understanding of power. Abrasive, rapacious and unpleasant, the élite ensures that Jinnah's Pakistan is in retreat.

The supporters of the Pakistan idea have been changing. The big paradox is that after half a century the Punjab, which was initially slow to respond to the Pakistan idea, is now its main champion. Bengal, on the other hand, which led the Pakistan movement decades before the Punjab was interested, gave up the Pakistan idea in 1971. *Muhajirs* who were fanatical supporters of Pakistan in 1947 have by the late 1990s become ambiguous, even bitter about it, feeling they have not been given a fair deal. These great historical reversals are embedded in the politics of the subcontinent.

After half a century Jinnah's legacy is strongest in the region which converted last to his cause. It is now the Punjab versus the entire subcontinent, if we are to see it in the context of Jinnah's movement in the 1940s. It explains the sense of being beleaguered, of having one's back against the wall. Punjab in the 1990s is the last main bastion of the Pakistan idea in South Asia.

By not honouring the ideas that Jinnah was airing when he helped to create Pakistan, by not developing them into some coherent form of Pakistani nationalism, Pakistani leaders have preserved a weak and shaky overarching structure; hence the perennial uncertainty about the nature of the Pakistani state and the identity of Pakistanis. Pakistanis face the millennium with questions that have haunted them for a decade as they change prime ministers on average almost every year: 'Will it last?' and 'What will the future bring?'

From *Anandamath* to Ayodhya: Muslim fate in India

India is a grossly uneven society: it has the most virtuous individuals and the most violent mobs; the most sophisticated philosophy alongside the crudest materialism; the ambition to reach for the stars and the caste system which ties a yoke round the neck of the downtrodden. The modern leaders of India took one of the potentially richest areas in the world, a country of vast provinces with wheatfields and ricefields, mighty rivers full of fish, snow-capped mountains, people with intelligence, talent and patience, a civilization reaching back centuries; and they converted this into a drab, shabby, paralytic ruin. Yet the nuclear arsenal and the fourth largest army in the world make India a regional superpower with noteworthy geopolitical ambitions.

A random glance at the titles of the influential books on contemporary India – all written by Indians – confirms the sense of crisis in the land: *India: The Siege Within* (Akbar 1985); *Riot After Riot* (Akbar 1988b); *Mirrors of Violence: Communities, Riots and Survivors in South Asia* (Das 1992); *Communal Riots in Post-Independence India* (Engineer 1991); *Anatomy of a Confrontation: Ayodhya and the Rise of Communal Politics in India* (Gopal 1991); *The Colours of Violence* (Kakar 1995); *Bewildered India: Identity, Pluralism, Discord* (R. Khan 1994); *When Bombay Burned* (Padgaonkar 1993); *Freedom on Trial* (Singhvi 1991). Non-Indians too use similar titles: *Averting the Apocalypse: Social Movements in India Today* (Bonner 1990); *Democracy in India: A Hollow Shell* (Bonner et al. 1994); *India: A Million Mutinies Now* (Naipaul 1990; for my comments on modern India, see Ahmed 1990a, 1992b, 1993a, 1993b, 1993c, 1995a). I shall draw on Indian scholarship for material in this chapter.

Indian society is well served by its own world-class scholars. Planned genocide, the systematic terrorization of the minority through the media, the determination not to allow the minority to survive or flourish until it is broken and agrees to join the lower ranks of the caste system, the insidious accusations that all problems are the minorities' fault and linked to the events of 1947 and to Pakistan: these themes are illustrated in frank brutality in several books (see, for example, Akbar 1988b; Basu et al. 1993; Das 1992; Engineer 1991; Gopal 1991; Hasan 1997; Kakar 1995; Khalidi 1995; Madan 1992; Padgaonkar 1993; Phadnis 1989). The fact that the authors are also Indian makes their work an even more powerful testimony.

All very well, the reader will say, but how is this relevant to Jinnah? The answer is contained in India's complex relationship with its Muslims and its neighbour Pakistan. Riots and political debate invariably invoke the name of Jinnah. A Muslim who is too insistent about the community's demands is condemned a 'second Jinnah' (Rajshekar 1993: 48). For Indians to understand Jinnah is to exorcize his ghost; for scholars of Jinnah no study is complete without a look at that part of the Indian Muslim community he left behind when he went to Pakistan.

Jinnah himself did not forget them as we note from his emotional broadcast on the very first Eid of Pakistan on 18 August 1947:

> For many, Eid will be not an occasion of such great joy and rejoicing as in Pakistan. Those of our brethren who are minorities in Hindustan may rest assured that we shall never neglect or forget them. Our hearts go out to them, and we shall consider no effort too great to help them and secure their well-being, for I recognise that it is the Muslim-minority provinces in this subcontinent who were the pioneers and carried the banner aloft for the achievement of our cherished goal of Pakistan. I shall never forget their support, nor I hope the majority Muslim Provinces in Pakistan will fail to appreciate that they were the pioneers in the vanguard of our historic and heroic struggle for the achievement of Pakistan which today is an accomplished fact. *Pakistan Zindabad* [long live Pakistan]. (J. Ahmad 1976: 410)

A Tryst with Destiny?

Anandamath

Until recently the communal violence against Muslims in India has been blamed chiefly on Jinnah and the creation of Pakistan. However, there is now a growing awareness that the root causes of communalism may go back earlier than 1947 – for instance, to the rise of Hindu nationalism in the 1920s (as Jaffrelot 1996, argues). In this section I suggest that the roots go back further still.

From the time Bankim Chatterji wrote *Anandamath* (which contained 'Vande Mataram', the hymn to Mother India), and Tilak organized the Ganpati festivals, to the time the BJP leader L. K. Advani launched the campaign to demolish the Ayodhya mosque – a time during which first Golwalkar and then Bal Thackeray spoke with admiration about Hitler's treatment of the Jews and the lessons to be learned in order to dispose of the Muslims – there is a century of developing Hindu communalism. There is a direct causal relationship between *Anandamath*, written in 1882, and the destruction of the mosque at Ayodhya in 1992.

From the writers like Bankim Chatterji to the slogans in the bazaars in the 1990s it was a century of all-out war for many people in the subcontinent; in this war the elimination of Muslims was chillingly planned and executed. Hindu leaders today advocate a 'once and for all' battle which echoes the sentiments of leaders like Vallabhbhai Patel, who said the same thing to Lord Wavell (Basu et al. 1993: 99).

The seeds that were planted in the 1880s were to grow with rapidity one generation later. By the 1920s the RSS had been formed and communal rioting against Muslims had begun in an organized and regular manner. By the 1930s and 1940s there is documentary evidence of the systematic genocide of Muslim communities in northern India and Bengal, some of which was planned deliberately to create an exodus and permanently rid the land of the Muslims. Commentators then talk of a lull after independence. This is deceptive.

Nehru's comments in 1950 on the rioting against Muslims in Ayodhya and other places in the UP have a contemporary feel about them:

> But far from a solution being found to the problem in Ayodhya, the situation in the whole province, as Nehru saw, deteriorated. 'I have felt for a long time that the whole atmosphere of the UP has been changing for the worse from the communal point of view. Indeed, the UP is becoming almost a foreign land for me. I do not fit in there.... All that occurred in Ayodhya in regard to the mosque and temples and the hotel in Fyzabad was bad enough. But the worst feature of it was that such things should take place and be approved by some of our own people and that they should continue.' (Gopal 1991: 16)

The figures speak for themselves:

> According to official data during the ten years from 1954 to 1963, an average of sixty-two riots took place annually and the number of those killed in these riots was forty on average. From 1964 to 1970 the number of communal riots rose to an annual average of 425 and the number killed increased even faster, to a figure of 467 persons killed annually. With some improvements

from 1971 to 1978, the situation again deteriorated drastically from 1979. If we take the killing of Sikhs in the wake of the assassination of Indira Gandhi into account, the figure in the 1980s must have averaged more than 600 a year. (ibid.: 216)

Nehru and his colleagues made brave attempts to impose a genuinely more harmonious view of India on its peoples. The official rhetoric supported this but the reality is of riots that increased in frequency. They were often disguised. We thus heard of caste riots, language riots and regional riots. In their midst were communal riots, which became a code name for the killing of the minorities, especially the Muslims. As the century draws to a close the scale, frequency and organization of communal rioting reflects the high-tech world we live in. Ayodhya was the culmination of a process begun a century before.

Ayodhya

The destruction of Babar's mosque at Ayodhya in 1992 brought together the modern media, a thousand years of history and the notion of avenging it, religious emotions and modern nationalism. The destruction of the mosque had become a national imperative.

Popular slogans in the subcontinent are pithy, intelligent, topical and often witty. The contemporary popular slogan throughout India is '*Babar ki aulad – ya qabristan ya Pakistan*': the choice for the descendants of Babar is either the grave or Pakistan, that is, they must expect to be killed or else migrate to Pakistan and leave the land of Mother India. It sums up an entire political philosophy, which implies that Muslims are invaders, descendants of Babar now seen as the symbol of Muslim barbarism, invasion and aggression. Although there is scant historical evidence that Babar ordered the creation of the mosque at Ayodhya, it was built in his time and therefore he became the villain of the piece. He is therefore associated in the popular imagination with the destruction of the Hindu temple to Lord Ram at Ayodhya and the building of the mosque on its site. Babar, Lord Ram, Ayodhya: the Muslims were now inextricably linked to contemporary politics in India.

In December 1992, with the world watching on television, Hindu mobs attacked and demolished the sixteenth-century mosque, Babri Masjid, as paratroops stood by, many of whom were making gestures of reverence to the Hindu deities in a show of solidarity with the mob. Riots followed throughout India, the most gruesome, the most violent in form so far. In the wake of Ayodhya thousands were killed all over India. In Bombay men were stopped, forced to pull down their trousers and, if they were circumcised, stabbed. Women were gang-raped. This was not an ordinary breakdown of law and order, as many thought, but the opening into a new phase of communal barbarism in the subcontinent.

Just over half a century from the time Gandhi was writing with awe of the martial prowess of Muslims, they had been reduced in India to a quivering, huddled minority. This was the Hindu backlash acknowledged by Indian academics. The full power of the state was now in play to ensure that there would never again be a Muslim challenge at least from within the country.

What stopped the widespread orgy of rioting in India after Ayodhya were the bomb-blasts in Bombay in 1993. The shock effect froze the rioting. Highly placed Muslims in India remarked that this seemed to have been the only deterrent to the endless violence against them. The Hindus blamed the Pakistani Inter-Services Intelligence, the ISI. In the end, if the ISI were responsible, then they and they alone were the guardians of the Muslims in India. What tragic irony.

Krishna Gamre, the Dalit spokesman, believes that the explosions marked a new phase in Hindu–Muslim relations. The psychological impact was enormous. Hindus became aware that Muslims, however suppressed and miserable as a minority, could hit back. They would in future be far more careful about launching the pogrom-like attacks on Muslims. What was needed, Gamre argued, was for Muslims to stick up for their rights, to stand up and be counted and not allow themselves to be pushed around.

There were also immediate and serious international repercussions after Ayodhya: Hindus were attacked and their temples destroyed in Pakistan and Bangladesh, while angry mobs demanded a 'holy war' against India in retaliation. In Britain there was tension between the Hindu and Muslim communities and Hindu temples were mysteriously damaged. The geographical span of these responses confirms my argument that to understand contemporary ethnic confrontation we need to keep its global context in mind.

Although commentators singled out the BJP as the main culprit behind the ethnic violence, this is misleading; indeed, elements in the Congress had long compromised on its secular position. Others too – influential opinion-makers among bureaucrats, media commentators and academics – had abandoned their earlier secular neutrality on communal issues. Those who were dismayed by this trend were reduced to being powerless spectators.

Let us not make the mistake of the critics of the BJP by over-simplifying a complex phenomenon. Beneath every case of so-called 'ethnic cleansing' is layer upon layer of history and culture. The movement for a separate Muslim state, the creation of Pakistan (seen by many Hindus in a religious light as sacrilege, as the division of Mother India itself), the wars between India and Pakistan, the perception of a threatening Islamic revivalism (in neighbours on both flanks, Pakistan and Bangladesh, and also, of course, Iran) and the continuing problems of the Muslim minority in adjusting to the new realities of India all contributed to the violence.

The Hindu backlash was almost inevitable. The vast majority of the population was Hindu but in the post-colonial rhetoric – secularism, national progress, socialism – Hindu identity was in danger of being submerged. Hindus felt justifiably aggrieved. Among India's founding fathers were men of piety like Mahatma Gandhi and Sardar Patel but it was the first Prime Minister, Jawaharlal Nehru, who most influenced independent India with his secular, tolerant and modern ideas. However, in the eyes of the traditional and the orthodox, many aspects of modernity appeared to disempower and marginalize those who respected custom and belief. The Marxist vocabulary of the intellectuals added insult to injury. The globalization process and its aggressive cultural manifestation, especially of American origin, further alienated and threatened Indians – Hindus and Muslims – and forced them to hark back (a point perceptively raised by Iyer 1992; also see Amin 1994).

Is Jinnah still Relevant?

Turning point

The year 1971 was a turning point. In that year Indira Gandhi not only broke Pakistan in two but defeated it in a dazzling military victory, taking 100,000 Pakistani soldiers captive to languish in her jails. In a speech to Parliament she claimed she had avenged history.

It was left to a Hindu woman to shatter the myth of the Muslim macho warrior. The sociological stereotypes were not lost on the subcontinent. Indira was depicted in posters as Kali, the goddess of revenge, thirsting for the blood of her enemies. The myth of the Muslim warrior was finally laid to rest. Pakistan was no longer a threat.

'Every Muslim had a soft corner in his heart for Pakistan, and everyone was sad that the experiment had failed after less than 25 years. The dream had died,' said a Muslim, describing the impact of that year to V. S. Naipaul (1990: 370). 'The spell was broken in 1971' for the Muslims, according to Syed Shahabuddin (*Pioneer*, 27 September 1996); they finally gave up 'the useless emotional baggage – the attachment to Pakistan or to pan-Islamic or to Khilafat's revival'. Now Jinnah was seen in terms of 'betrayal', of having deserted them. Muslims blamed him publicly for their misfortunes and ridiculed him.

After 1971, once Hindus were no longer living under the threat of a militant Muslim Pakistan, complex and hidden forces were released in India which were religious, atavistic and psychological. V. S. Naipaul saw this as a million mutinies, an explosion of post-colonial assertiveness (1990). Stripped of binding ideologies and false affectations, the tensions removed, Indian society could be itself, declare itself, play and parade as itself. It became more relaxed, more anarchic, more fragmented, more materialistic. The emergent middle class, noisy and demanding, asserted themselves, to enjoy the good life. The underclass would remain suppressed in ghetto-like favelas.

Renunciation of materialism, never a dominant theme of Hindu culture, gave way to the notion of the householder (Madan 1987). It was a society unabashedly 'in pursuit of Lakshmi', the goddess of wealth (Rudolph and Rudolph 1987; also see Bonner 1990; Hardgrave, Jr 1984). 'The West', as Nandy writes, is 'the second colonization' (1983: xi; Madan 1987; see also Madan 1992 and 1994). The drive to acquire VCRs, televisions and fridges was hard and sustained. The arrival of the VCR put the cinema on the defensive. It now had to be even more attractive and glamorous. Free enterprise flourished and the spirit of entrepreneurship thrived; global consumerism now beckoned.

Smuggling (of guns and drugs) increased. The pursuit of pleasure and materialism reached obsessive heights. Raj Kapoor's films openly exploited, and set the trend for, explicitly sexual and hedonistic films: *Bobby* was the biggest box-office hit of the mid-1970s, and his *Satyam, Shivam, Sundaram* was an extravaganza. Gone was Raj Kapoor's earlier ragamuffin, pauper hero (as in *Awaara*; see Dissanayake and Sahai (1988) on Raj Kapoor's films). The trend tied in with the larger materialist milieu. In his interviews Raj defended himself, arguing that he was reviving a legitimate, ancient strain of erotica in Indian society.

Nehru's conscious policy of supporting minority and human rights issues was abandoned during the administration of his daughter, Indira Gandhi, who courted communalism. The use of Hindu symbolism now became part of the state. The new atmosphere in India after 1971 was a distinct departure from the style of Nehru. Ashis Nandy explains Mrs Gandhi's position: 'in private she was a devout Hindu who had to make her seventy-one – or was it sixty-nine? – pilgrimages' (in Das 1992: 76).

223

A Tryst with Destiny?

From British Raj to Ram Raj

It had taken over half a century from the time when Jinnah warned that the British Raj would be replaced by Ram Raj, that Muslims – and Christian and Dalits – would be vulnerable to communal violence and become a second-rate citizenry. But it had happened.

Since independence a central debate has enveloped India: whether homogeneity or a looser, plural society should prevail. From the time of Nehru, with his belief in a strong socialist centre, Delhi has attempted to steamroller the diversity and colour of the hundreds of different customs, languages and administrative organizations in the land. To an extent it has succeeded. By the 1990s one language, Hindi, one religion, Hinduism, and one people, the Hindus, have by and large emerged to dominate India (one economy is in the process of being abandoned). But at a cost.

The BJP, along with the Congress, is one of the two largest parties in Parliament. It insists that all those who live in India must demonstrate loyalty to the land and therefore accept Hinduism: Muslims would thus become something the BJP call 'Hindu-Mohammadans'. But it is not a simple Hindu-versus-Muslim clash. The Sikhs have also been 'taught a lesson' during the last decade. Christians have been persecuted and nuns raped. The so-called lower castes among the Hindus are still subject to humiliation and injustice.

Although Muslims are singled out, even Jains and Buddhists are not spared: 'Indian Christians are condemned for allegedly preferring the English language, instead of Sanskrit or Hindi. Jainism and Buddhism also come in for denigration: "they have never made any contribution to economic and philosophical thought as such"' (Basu et al. 1993: 28).

Yoga, abstention from alcohol, a universal caring for humanity, the notions of duty and respect for tradition: these were the positive aspects of Hinduism, something Hinduism has given to the world (see Madan 1987, 1992, 1994). But the transformation of what its devout and thoughtful followers see as a humane and universal religious tradition to a vehicle for ethnic hatred and political confrontation saddens many Hindus. Hindus themselves are aware of this predicament. Indeed, Rajmohan Gandhi, grandson of the Mahatma, in a dialogue with me organized by the *Indian Express* in Delhi, commented on the decline: 'After some years, looking back on the present moment, many Hindus will feel angry and ashamed' (*Indian Express Sunday Magazine*, 27 September 1992). 'Hinduism', he remarked sadly, 'has now been hijacked by the fundamentalists.'

In the summer of 1995 a controversy started when Ashok Row Kavi described Gandhi as a 'bastard *bania*' on Nikki Bedi's popular television show, *Nikki Tonight* (*Guardian*, 5 July 1995). The reaction was significant. There was no public outcry. Gandhi was more respected internationally than at home; he had brought the nation pride and identity abroad, but was reduced in contemporary India to an attractive idea, little more. Gopal Godse, brother of Gandhi's assassin, Nathuram Godse, openly terms Gandhi a 'bloodsucker', a 'fanatic', who betrayed the 'Hindu' cause. He was not the 'father of the nation' but the 'father of Pakistan'. Godse demanded that what is now Pakistan and Bangladesh must return to Akhand Bharat – that is, reunite with India (*Times of India*, 19 November 1993; Bonner et al. 1994: 2).

During 1947 Nehru complained that 'emotion and sentimentality have taken the place of reasoned thought and inquiry' (1961: 543). '"All of us", Nehru wrote, "seem to be getting infected with the refugee mentality or, worse still, the RSS mentality. That is a curious finale to our careers." But he realized that this communal feeling, if allowed to spread, would wreck India and destroy its future, and combating it became his prime task' (Gopal 1991: 15).

Fine words. But on extremism Nehru fudged. While formally denouncing communalism, he allowed Hindu communalists to organize functions and even patronized them. Quite early after independence, he allowed them to commemorate Somnath by rebuilding the temple where almost a thousand years ago Mahmud of Ghazni had defeated the Hindus. Gandhi had already blessed the project before his death. The Somnath celebrations generated the same kind of charged atmosphere created by the Ayodhya crisis. Nehru also failed to oppose the universal ban on cow slaughter, which was one of the directive principles of state policy, even though Muslims saw this as a concession to Hindu bigotry. Many Hindu communalists in the administration, active in their belief, were ignored by Nehru. For instance, after partition K. K. Nair, deputy commissioner at Ayodhya, was an RSS member. Babri Masjid at Ayodhya was quietly occupied by Hindus. But Nair's links were kept a secret and he was discreetly transferred (Bonner et al. 1994: 104). The roots of the explosion at Ayodhya in 1992 were nourished by people like Nair. Nehru also allowed RSS contingents in full military uniform to take part in national independence day parades in Delhi (for example in 1963).

The mood after partition had created a general climate of distrust and hatred for Muslims in general and for those who stood up for their rights in particular. Muslims were associated with Pakistan, and Pakistan rankled, as Golwalkar makes clear:

> There are those who tell us: 'Bygones are bygones. What is the use of raking up dead issues? After all, Partition is now a settled fact.' How is this ever possible? How can a son forget and sit idle when the sight of his mutilated mother stares him in the face every day? Forget? No true son can ever forget or rest till she becomes once again her complete whole. If Partition is a settled fact, we are here to unsettle it. (Golwalkar 1966: 91–3)

Every Muslim is regarded as a Pakistani at heart. Those Muslims who talk of rights for their community – even a Member of Parliament like Shahabuddin – are dubbed a 'second Jinnah' as we saw above (Rajshekar 1993: 48). Bal Thackeray, in fact, had said: 'If I come to power in the Centre, I would give 48 hours notice to Muslims and (solemnly) I will tell them: prove that you belong to this country. You can't remain here bodily if your mind and heart is in Pakistan' (Thackeray in *Muslim India*, June 1984: 155).

Sometimes this paranoia about Pakistan assumes absurd proportions. When a stalker began killing children in India's Uttar Pradesh state, people referred to a strange and frightening pig-faced monster which could jump 25 metres in one leap. Thirty children had been attacked by the middle of 1996 and seventeen died of their injuries. Parents lived in fear. People immediately blamed Pakistanis (*Time Magazine*, 'Talk of the streets', 15 July 1996).

The wars between India and Pakistan were not only fought on the battlefield. The cricket ground, for example, was seen by both Pakistan and India as an extension of the confrontation. Imran Khan's greatest ambition, he said in public, was to defeat India in India. This made him a national hero in Pakistan. It made him something of a star attraction in India too because he fitted the Muslim stereotype – bold and brash. But the Muslims of India cheering him and his team antagonized the Hindus, who considered this to be evidence of disloyalty. Muslims were failing the cricket test.

The idea of the cricket test came from a statement made by the British Conservative MP and former Cabinet Minister Norman Tebbit, in an interview with the *Los Angeles Times* in April 1990, the night before British MPs voted on whether to issue UK passports to Hong Kong citizens (which he was against). Tebbit, in what he called a 'lighthearted way' of finding out how much Asian immigrants genuinely integrated into British society, suggested they be asked: would you cheer for the English team or for the Indian or Pakistani team? It was an easy test to fail and many from India and Pakistan in Britain failed it. But in India failure meant riots, houses burned, torture, death and rape.

Bal Thackeray, who insisted on the cricket test, asked: 'But when Pakistan wins and my country is defeated, why Muslims should crack crackers? Why they should have that jubilation mood? ... They should shed tears for our country. That should be the spirit' (*Muslim India*, June 1984).

Genocide: the voices of the victims

The intensity of the violence in India against Muslims has been described by an Indian academic thus: 'The very meaning of communal riot changed into something very like genocide with official connivance' (Basu et al. 1993: 2; a similar message comes through in *India's Muslim Problem: Agony of the Country's Single Largest Community Persecuted by Hindu Nazis* written by V. T. Rajshekar, a Dalit, in 1993). Foreign journalists too use the word 'pogroms' ('Slow stirrings of a million mutinies' by John Rettie in the *Guardian*, 25 February 1995). But it is vital to hear the authentic voices of the victimized community itself, prominent Indian Muslim academics and writers like Asghar Ali Engineer, Professor Mushirul Hasan, Rasheeduddin Khan, Iqbal Masud, Syed Shaha-buddin and Omar Khalidi, who write as loyal Muslims and as loyal Indians.

Khalidi sets out to describe the history of his community in *Indian Muslims Since Independence* (1995; for a microcosmic study – of the Aligarh Muslims – see Mann 1992). The Indian Muslims are a large community, about 120 million (the census of 1981 recorded them as numbering 80 million), perhaps greater in number than even the Muslims of Pakistan, and they played a major role in India in the past. The difficulty in reconciling that role to their present plight is at the heart of the problem. Khalidi, backed by distinguished Indian authors, explains the processes whereby a newly independent Asian state attempts to absorb a large minority into the majority. Economic, linguistic and cultural policy – even the media – are powerful tools in this process. The pressures on the Muslims appear on several levels. On one level is straightforward communal rioting in which the police are the worst culprits. On another level there are smaller but equally significant cultural developments such as the insistence that all Indian soldiers, including non-Hindu ones, join in the Indian battle-cry which invokes Hindu deities. The same slogans are used by Hindu mobs attacking Muslims during riots.

The picture that emerges in Khalidi's book is of a beleaguered community. Constant riots – Khalidi uses the word 'pogrom' – media propaganda and implicit if not explicit government hostility make life difficult. The appendix gives a chronology of horrendous communal violence. In a devastating comment at the end of the book we learn that there is an 'ironic symbiosis' of the opposed views of the BJP leader Advani and the genuinely humanist and tolerant founding fathers like Gandhi. Both wish to reabsorb Muslims into the fabric of Hindu society – the first through intimidation, the second through seduction. But the world has no interest in the plight of the Indian Muslims, complains Khalidi. Even Amnesty International tends to ignore the gross violations. The fate of the Muslims in Spain is never far from Khalidi's mind (nor from some Hindus' minds, as 'How to exterminate Muslims in India: Hindu Nazis following Spanish experiment', by Rajshekar 1993: 38, illustrates; see also my discussion of the 'Andalusian syndrome' when discussing Indian Muslims, in Ahmed 1988).

Let us hear Syed Shahabuddin, the Member of Parliament:

> The Muslim community finds that its right to freedom of religion is sought to be curtailed on one pretext or the other. Land is not readily allotted for mosques; objections are raised to their construction; even their repair or maintenance is looked upon as an act of conspiracy attributed to the flow of foreign money! '*Azan*' (calling to prayer) is frowned upon as a public nuisance; sometimes objected to on the ground that it drives away the local gods! Mosques are readily locked up by the authorities, the moment some local elements raise an issue, e.g. that it has been built upon the ruins of a pre-existing temple.... Conversion to Islam is looked upon, despite the right to profess the faith of one's choice, as a denial of nationhood, an act of treason, a negation of Indianness. All this makes the impact on the Muslim mind that Islam does not in fact enjoy freedom and equality in India. (Shahabuddin, in Engineer 1991: 105).

Unending examples of atrocities like the following have been cited by Indian writers:

> A 19-year-old girl, with a shaven head, is convalescing at the Surat civil hospital. She was gangraped after being pulled out from a Bhusaval-bound train on December 10. Her brother, who was accompanying her to Dhulia, was stabbed and burnt alive in front of her.
>
> Another victim of gangrape at the hospital is a 20-year-old girl. She was married to a religious leader 15 days ago and had arrived here from Assam. Her husband was killed before her eyes and she was gangraped. Later, acid was thrown on her which brought her to the brink of death. (*Muslim India*, New Delhi, February 1993: 179)

Even a magistrate, a custodian of law and order, became a victim during the riots after Ayodhya because he was a Muslim:

> Zafar Salim, a special executive magistrate, was among those at the receiving end. 'At night they switched on the lights to provide a good target for their young boys to throw fireballs at. When we came out of our huts to

put out the fires, we were blinded by the strong beams,' he said. 'We were
not able to see any of them, but they could see us wherever we went to try
and escape.'

He accused some police officers of being partisan ... 'When we came out
of our houses to put out the fires, Inspector Thakur of Tardeo police-station
attacked us,' asserted Salim. 'When we complained about the Arya Nagar
attacks, he said "Bring out your weapons from Pakistan and Saudi Arabia
and use them."' (Padgaonkar 1993: 78–9)

Omar Khalidi has also pointed to the new element that has entered the well-
organized rioting: gangs raping Muslim women in groups and recording the event on
video to sell the cassettes in the bazaar. The following case, under the title 'The
pornography of communal violence', was documented in *Muslim India*, the journal
published by Shahabuddin, the Member of Parliament:

It was no ordinary film shooting in the riot-affected Ved Road area of Surat.
A group of women, naked to the waist, had run out of their houses chased
by a mob not with firearms in their hands, but with video cameras. Even as
Surat burned, these people had found a novel way of utilising the situation.
They were filming the molestation of women.... The women, now in the
relief camps of Muglisara and Rani Talav areas, are totally shattered. What
is more horrifying is that the police have still not arrested a single culprit
though they have been identified by the victims. In fact, the criminals are
moving around freely.

The mass rape and subsequent filming took place on the night of
December 8 when entire Surat was burning. The women recalled that while
they were being asked to strip before a group of men armed with knives and
swords, a video camera was whirring away and flash lights were being
turned on them. Their husbands had been herded out and some even killed.
(*Muslim India*, New Delhi, February 1993: 179).

Herding people into pre-constructed camps, gang-raping women, torturing, mutilat-
ing and killing men: all this on video to be seen again and again. Gandhi, *ahimsa*, non-
violence, tolerance, humanism appeared to have evaporated. Recent studies have
pointed to rape as an act of deliberate communal humiliation in South Asia (Jayawardena 1996). But the age of the media has provided a new vehicle for communal
violence: home videos to show the young how to hate early. They too could make their
own plans with junior camcorders in their own schools.

Shahabuddin draws a startling conclusion in his analysis of the Muslim situation in
India which goes back to Jinnah's struggle:

Perhaps the Hindu and Muslim communities are in some ways further
apart today than they were in 1947. The Hindu society is a closed society; the
Muslim '*mohalla*' is a cultural ghetto.... Both communities live apart in a
world of stereotypes, of make-believe. (in Engineer 1991: 113)

Is Jinnah still Relevant?

Three Hindu responses

Sudhir Kakar, one of the most perceptive of the Indian analysts, identifies three Hindu responses to Muslims (1995). The first response – that of the liberals and the left – posits that Hindus and Muslims were natural allies and good neighbours until the British arrived to divide and rule them. Once the British left they were friendly again up until the emergence of 'religion'. Religion therefore should be restricted to private life. This response fails to understand that culture and religion are of the utmost importance to South Asian society. For these people Jinnah's Pakistan movement was clearly inspired by the British, another attempt to divide and rule.

The ideas of the Hindu nationalists form the second response. Their argument is simple: Muslims must conform to the larger Hindu culture (including the caste system) or be branded traitors. For them the separation of Muslim identity is a crime. They will not accept a plural society. The solution is simple: Muslims must become Hindus, if they wish to remain in India.

The third Hindu response argues that societies must be accepted on their own terms; that differences must be recognized. So Jinnah is to be seen in realistic terms – once advocating Hindu–Muslim unity but, when that failed to protect the interests of the Muslims, eventually seeking a separate identity. Jinnah must not be dismissed; he must not be seen as a caricature. Kakar quotes Muslims in South India today, half a century after independence, who muse, perhaps not too loudly, that Jinnah's was the best answer for the Muslims, the only way out of the torture that is modern India.

I myself support Kakar's third position, approaching it from the perspective of Muslims and the West in *Living Islam* (1993a), where I wrote: 'Confrontation [between Islam and the West] is neither necessary nor desirable; besides, there is much in common both in ideas and in human societies. It is this which needs to be increasingly explored. We need to be able to see the other and say: "We understand you are different but we also understand your difference"' (ibid.: 11). Indeed, this was the spirit in which I wrote the dedication of the book: 'Only connect: In the hope that this book will help to connect different peoples and different faiths and thereby encourage understanding between them.'

The continuing impact of stereotypes

In chapter 2 we noted how communities in India, Hindus and Muslims, see each other in terms of historical stereotypes. On one point they meet. Both see Muslims as irresistible conquerors who, given a chance, would once again reassert their military supremacy over India.

One of the most authoritative anthropologists of India noted that Hindus saw Muslims as stereotypes, as *'mleccha'*, 'dirty', 'polluted', 'unprincipled', 'omnivorous', 'fanatic', 'merciless' and 'lustful' (Madan 1994: 191). Muslims are also seen as sex-crazed. This is largely because of the popular perception that they are polygamous. Paradoxically, it has been established that there are more polygamous marriages among the Hindus in India than among Muslims (Bonner et al. 1994).

Even the more tolerant and scholarly Hindus view Muslims through the prism of

229

stereotypes. Dr L. M. Singhvi, Indian High Commissioner in London in the mid- and late 1990s, believed that the problem stemmed from 1947, when 'the Muslims were not only left leaderless but also suffered from "a guilt complex and an inferiority complex"' (Singhvi 1991: 124) – guilt for creating Pakistan and inferiority to the Hindu majority. 'Unfortunately,' he continued, 'the Muslims in India continue to suffer from a minority syndrome. What is more unfortunate, a sizeable majority among them are led by the orthodox and somewhat communal leadership. The educated and rational elite appears to be in a hopeless minority' (ibid.: 124).

Like the standard anti-Semitic image of Jews in the 1930s and 1940s in Europe, Muslims are, an American professor tells us, depicted as filthy animals:

> They multiply like 'termites, grasshoppers, like dogs'. 'They do not send their children to school.' 'Muslims are bastards.' 'They sleep with their own sisters and why not; with their own mothers. They bugger them.' 'They are obsessed with sex'. (Bonner et al. 1994: 159)

Professor Bonner concludes: 'In the end the Muslim is unspeakably foul, the maggot that burrows in rot, the pathogenic agent in the body of the nation.... These ravings are similar to the obsessional themes of European anti-Semitism prior to 1940' (ibid.). But the cumulative effect is devastating for the Muslims since it encourages hatred and violence against them. Society is thus conditioned to disliking the Muslims and condoning action against them.

Asghar Ali Engineer, a respected Muslim commentator known for his liberal views, attempts to explain the situation:

> An average Hindu's prejudice against the Muslim community is because of his misconceived perception of firstly, the attempts made by the Muslim rulers in medieval times to destroy Hindu culture; secondly, the separatist role played by the Muslims in the freedom struggle; thirdly, their refusal to modernise themselves and accept the uniform civil code, family planning, etc., and lastly, their having extra-territorial loyalties.... School text books also unfortunately encourage anti-Muslim feelings by teaching and praising the culture and values of the majority community. (Engineer 1991: 59).

Hindu prejudices are mirrored among Muslims. The Hindu stereotype imagined by Muslims is a mean, cowardly and double-faced person who says one thing and does another, who practises the caste system and burns widows. The Hindu hates Muslims congenitally in the stereotype. For the Muslim the stereotype is of the hideous Hindu.

Hideous Hindu meets merciless Muslim in the stereotypes of contemporary Indian society. Reality is obliterated by a media image which is difficult to challenge because it is so pervasive and powerful. It is easy to burn down houses, rape women and torture and kill members of the opposite group when you can create such simplistic stereotypes of them. This has been one of the most insidious consequences of the mass media of the 1980s and 1990s.

Is Jinnah still Relevant?

Lord Ram as media superstar

The birth and activities of the Indian National Congress, *Anandamath*, the Ganpati festivals, the Arya Samaj movement, Gandhi's emergence after the First World War, the formation of the Hindu communalist parties like the Mahasabha and the RSS – all these were creating a national awareness of an Indian but also a Hindu identity which transcended caste and linguistic differences. But perhaps nothing – not even the great independence movement which took the entire subcontinent in its grip in the 1930s and 1940s – could rival the advent of the mass media in the 1980s which shaped a universal Hindu consciousness. Television, the VCR and the Internet have created for the first time in history a genuine Hindu cultural unity which never existed before on this scale.

The Muslim invaders from the north coming through the passes of the Frontier and Baluchistan from the tenth to the eighteenth century met resistance from two quarters: other Muslim groups, mainly the Pathans who had preceded them, and Hindus led by Rajput chiefs. They rarely encountered a monolithic Hindu opposition. Indian society was too divided by caste, regionalism, languages, and so on, to unite under one leader. This was the bane of Hindu leadership. Hindu unity would be the main objective of Hindu leaders, whether Gandhi or Advani.

It was partly in response to this problem and partly in an attempt to rectify history that Hindu ideologues focused on the Muslims as the main opposition. The Muslims provided a convenient answer. They allowed unity to be created among Hindus because they provided an opposition to Hinduism – a natural, cultural, political and social opposition against which Hindus could unite. In addition, by reviving memories of their rule, which Hindu ideology interpreted as tyrannical and blighted, Muslims would fuel a continuous anger. The irony of denouncing a fragmented and helpless minority – and attacking this minority with the help of all the instruments of the state – escaped the ideologues. The Muslims, operating on a different level of history, continued to move from one crisis to another, reinforcing their own isolation and the hatred against them. Each step that they took added fuel to the fire. They seemed to be sleepwalking into disasters.

The 1980s saw a new media phenomenon in the massively popular television drama series *Mahabharat* and *Ramayana*, which ran into numerous episodes and were seen at peak viewing time by 500 or 600 million people. The television series were no longer entertainment, they were national and cultural events. Traffic came to a standstill throughout the land when popular episodes were shown. (Almost 100 million Indians have access to satellite and cable television; in the last few years starting with one broadcaster – the state – there are now fifty private satellite stations.)

Had the matter ended there – that is, film as entertainment – it would have been admirable and innocuous. But Indian scholars argue:

> The serialized 'Ramayan' gave to the brand new phenomenon of high consumerism and media technology, imported by Rajiv Gandhi, an immediate culture together with a sense of rootedness. It provided to the new aggressive social class spawned in the 80s a packaged, collective self-image which, with the mobilizing by Hindutva [the idea of a dominant Hindu

culture and nation], became the motivating force for changing, by force and violence, the image of the country itself. (Basu et al. 1993: 109)

A subtext could be discerned: an ideal Hindu society was shattered by invaders from outside India; Muslims were to blame. It was the message of pride in Hindu culture, a pride that underlined a pre-British and pre-Muslim past. It pointed to the glory which once was. Implicit in this was the theme that India had been spoilt by subsequent invasions. The finger pointed, however indirectly, at the Muslims. While promoting unity and pride in the Hindu community, it none the less added to the political hysteria building up against the Muslims. The series helped to set a chain of events in motion. Some media pundits in the BJP, a party then floundering on the verge of extinction, at this point joined the emotions generated by the mass media to a political issue concerning the birthplace of Lord Ram at Ayodhya where a medieval mosque stood.

It was a masterstroke. The BJP had appropriated Ram. In Hindu mythology Ram defeats Ravana, the personification of evil, with whom Jinnah could be identified, since he had been demonized in Hindu society. Gandhi's Ram, a benign and attractive warrior figure standing for universal and noble causes, was now depicted as the exclusively Hindu avenger. Past injuries committed by the Muslims, the subtext implied, would be avenged. Within a few years the standing of the BJP in Parliament made the quantum leap from 2 to 119 and then to almost 200.

So while Hindus thrilled to the doings of the attractive warrior-hero figure of Lord Ram on television they were angered by the mosque at Ayodhya. A vigorous campaign daubed the legend 'Declare with pride your Hinduism' on walls, posters and hoardings all over India. A not so subtle subliminal message was contained in this slogan: vote for those who identify with Hinduism (like the BJP). The BJP notably, but also the Congress, then recruited the stars from the television series, who were treated almost like divine figures in India, as their parliamentary candidates. They helped mobilize public opinion in demanding that the mosque at Ayodhya be replaced by a Hindu temple. Widespread tension all over India resulted in frequent large-scale riots in the name of Lord Ram. The BJP was able to spearhead the destruction of the Ayodhya mosque with India and indeed the whole world watching, helpless.

Reputable Indian scholars confirm the links between media and rioting: 'The television versions of the "Ramayana" and the "Mahabharata" and, in sharp contrast, the failure to present a serious and non-partisan discussion of the Ramjanmabhumi issue, have all contributed to the heightened excitement which has led to the recent increase in communal rioting, with over a thousand Muslims killed in the last few months' (Gopal 1991: 16–17).

The battle for the future

Recent literature that we have cited above – mostly by Indians – should shatter all illusions about Indian society. Sadly the press reports incidents of communal violence yet is powerless to do anything about it. The government, which itself seems to be directly involved in many cases, appears to look the other way and often connives with the culprits.

Even the world's best-known Hindu writer, V. S. Naipaul, in a piece called 'The Hindu awakening' (1995), almost appears to justify the savage persecution faced by Muslims. Indeed, he condemns those Indians who call it a form of 'fascism' (ibid.: 140). He accepts the destruction of the mosque at Ayodhya, arguing that it was historically logical, since the same thing happened when the Christians reconquered Spain from the Muslims. As for the Indian Muslims, he concludes: 'Those people are considerably lost' (ibid.: 139). He criticizes Muslim revivalism as 'essentially a negative, last-ditch effort to fight against a world it desperately wishes to join' while applauding Hindu fundamentalism as 'a mighty, creative process' (ibid.: 137). Islam's revenge was not long in coming: Naipaul fell in love with and married a Pakistani nationalist.

The argument that if there had been no Pakistan the Muslims of India would have been guaranteed security in India is a shaky one. If 13 per cent of the population – and we must remember that population figures in the subcontinent remain at best estimates – cannot rely on a modicum of safety, then 30 per cent would also have been vulnerable. If the majority are united in denying rights to the minorities, then no guarantees or constitutional safeguards will work.

No, there has to be a change in the heart of the majority. There has to be more openness, more acceptance of a plural society. All the trends in India have been in reverse. The openly communal parties have gained strength spectacularly over the last decades; the secular elements in Congress have faded in proportion. There is no indication that if there had been no Pakistan the Muslims would have been any safer in an independent united India.

It was precisely this that Jinnah had understood by the late 1930s. He had succeeded in rescuing half the Muslim population of the subcontinent, but almost another half of the Muslim community still remained in India. To save them from Ram Raj, he reiterated in speech after speech, the Indian government needed to ensure their security as citizens of the state and enshrine such a guarantee in the Indian constitution. But government after government in India has failed to provide the Muslims with this security. Indeed government as represented by the paramilitary forces, police and officials on the spot appears to connive in the communal riots.

The Congress has been as much to blame as the BJP for the growing communalism in India. It was a Congress Prime Minister who helplessly watched the destruction of the mosque at Ayodhya and then in spite of his promises did not honour his commitment to rebuild it. It has been a story of appeasement, muddle and political pusillanimity. Faint hearts and weak minds govern the subcontinent.

In the 1990s no member of the minority community is safe. Rich or poor, noble family or ordinary folk, professional or unemployed, educated or uneducated, women or men, young or old – all are vulnerable to sudden, brutal physical attack. Whether they live in the north or the south, east or west of India their homes can be burned to the ground, the women in the house violated and they themselves killed or their bodies mutilated. Communal violence has reached a crucial point in its history. Where it goes from here is hard to guess. One road leads to sanctioned genocide, to the gas chambers; the other turns back from the brink, and perhaps leads to a return to sanity.

To their credit, many Hindu writers, lawyers and humanitarians are standing up to the forces of hatred now dominating their society. The battle is being waged on all fronts. To their credit, these warriors have not lost heart. It will not be an easy battle,

233

but it is not a hopeless one either. What would assist the fight for a more tolerant society would be the opening of India: as India attracted outside visitors, investments would arrive, media images would become important, and a more tolerant society would have to be shown to the world. The idea itself would act as a pacifying force: this, at least, is the hope. The alternative is a continuing descent in a barbaric spiral of violence. The cancer of communal violence will need curing if India is to emerge as a healthy body in the next century.

All is not lost. There are many who still believe in harmony and dialogue. The script of the *Mahabharat*, the most popular television series ever made about Hindu mythology, was written by a Muslim; a Hindu has written the authoritative study of Ghalib, the greatest Muslim poet (Varma 1989). To hear Jagjeet Singh singing Ghalib is to know the deep cultural synthesis between Hindus and Muslims, to feel the understanding. Muslim film stars in India like Dilip Kumar (Yusuf Khan), Madhubala and Naseeruddin Shah have been giants of the Indian cinema, loved by millions and imitated by their peers. In Pakistan, Indian film stars like Raj Kapoor and Amitabh Bachan continue to be admired.

It is a paradox of the subcontinent that the Muslims in India who are reviled as 'the children of Jinnah', the agents of Pakistan, are secretly perhaps the most ardent admirers of Jinnah, conscious of what he achieved (Kakar 1995: 165). These Muslims are aware that against impossible odds – which they now face themselves – he created a separate homeland for Muslims, even while they know they were sacrificed for that Pakistan. Dr Jaffar Qureshi, from Hyderabad in the south, described Jinnah as a man who created a nation and saved millions of people. Such a man, he said, 'is a *Waliullah*, a saint, for me'. He added: 'Whatever the narrow-minded say, there is no one like him in the history of South Asia.'

But other Muslims, some belonging to the élite, disagree; they are now fusing Islam with Hinduism, moving away from Jinnah's position. 'I do not hesitate to accept Shri Krishna (upon him be peace!) as a prophet,' wrote an Indian Muslim (R. Khan 1994: 190). Another Indian Muslim declared his faith as Islam and Hinduism (A. H. Khan 1995: 14). For M. J. Akbar, Nehru is the nearest thing to a prophet (1988a). These sentiments, honestly felt, raise important questions. Is this a genuine synthesis, a way forward in plural societies? Or is it the disintegration that comes with intimidation, defeat and retreat? The answers will occupy and shape India in the years to come.

Bangladesh: the struggle for identity

It is easy to forget that until 1971 Bangladesh was East Pakistan, part of the nation of Pakistan. The story of the Bengalis in the struggle for Pakistan and their growing disenchantment afterwards reflects the complex clash between an 'Islamic' and a 'Bengali' identity and is not yet fully resolved. Pakistan has only a small Hindu minority; but about 20 per cent of the Bangladeshi population of 120 million people is Hindu. This makes its relations with India difficult, especially in times of communal tension when Muslims are killed and injured in India. Indians, in turn, feel hemmed in by two 'Muslim' nations, Pakistan and Bangladesh, and their insecurity feeds Hindu revivalism. This has implications for South Asian geopolitics.

Is Jinnah still Relevant?

Misunderstanding Jinnah

The link between Jinnah and Bangladesh is easily missed. Commentators look at Bangladesh as a post-colonial phenomenon. What they ignore is that the Bengalis in fact led the movement for Pakistan in the first half of this century.

The Muslims of Bengal were the largest single category of Muslims in the subcontinent; they also accounted for over half of all Bengalis. They had succeeded in obtaining their own province in 1905, although it was reintegrated in 1911. The Muslim League was born in Bengal – in Dhaka – in 1906; the Nawab of Dhaka played a dominant role in the foundation of the Muslim League. Fazl ul-Haq, a Bengali and a major figure in the Pakistan movement, moved the Pakistan resolution in 1940. In 1946 the fervour for Pakistan was at a peak among Bengalis. The Muslim League swept the polls in Bengal winning 116 out of 119 seats. H. S. Suhrawardy, the Chief Minister of the Bengal province, moved the resolution calling for the formation of Pakistan at the Muslim League convention in Delhi. East Pakistan offered Jinnah a seat for him and his colleagues when they lost theirs in India in 1947.

Had there been no Jinnah to lead the Muslim movement there would have been no Pakistan and therefore no Bangladesh. Jinnah throughout was sensitive towards Bengali issues. At one point, late in the 1940s, he was even prepared to concede an independent Bengal as long as the Muslims of that area had freedom and got Calcutta. Jinnah's ideas on an independent Bengal are worth recording: '[Jinnah] said, without any hesitation: "I should be delighted. What is the use of Bengal without Calcutta; they had much better remain united and independent; I am sure that they would be on friendly terms with us"' (Zaidi 1993: appendices, volume I, part II, 668). In the event, part of East Bengal came to Pakistan, although it lost Calcutta.

Jinnah would have been dismayed at the way his Pakistan fell apart in 1971 – especially at the killings that Pakistanis inflicted on each other. But he would have preferred freedom and independence for the Bengali Muslims to the alternative of staying within India and of domination from Calcutta. Contemporary Bengali scholars and writers who appear to have written Jinnah out of Bangladesh history need to rise above their parochial understanding of politics and acknowledge Jinnah.

Present-day Bangladesh has reduced Jinnah to his position on the language issue. On his first and only visit to Dhaka he had insisted that Urdu would be the only national language of Pakistan. This one incident is enough to condemn him in Bangladesh today, where people do not remember his achievements and his battles on their behalf. Such is the level of politics and the intensity of the need for identity in Bangladesh.

In a public speech at Dhaka, on 21 March 1948, Jinnah had correctly emphasized that provincialism – or what is termed ethnicity by the social scientists – would be a particular danger to a united Pakistan. In the light of subsequent events he was correct to be concerned:

> There is a certain feeling, I am told, in some parts of this Province, against non-Bengali Muslims. There has also lately been a certain amount of excitement over the question whether Bengali or Urdu shall be the State language of this Province and of Pakistan. In this latter connection, I hear that some discreditable attempts have been made by political opportunists

to make a tool of the student community in Dacca to embarrass the administration. (Jinnah 1989: 180)

Jinnah pointed out the larger dangers facing the area:

> Let me warn you in the clearest terms of the dangers that still face Pakistan, and your province in particular, as I have done already. Having failed to prevent the establishment of Pakistan, thwarted and frustrated by their failure, the enemies of Pakistan have now turned their attention to disrupt the State by creating a split amongst the Muslims of Pakistan. These attempts have taken the shape principally of encouraging provincialism. (Merchant 1990: 12–13)

Once again, Jinnah echoes the themes from his first two speeches in the Assembly:

> As long as you do not throw off this poison in our body politic, you will never be able to weld yourself, mould yourself, galvanise yourself into a real, true nation. What we want is not to talk about Bengali, Punjabi, Sindhi, Baluchi, Pathan and so on. They are, of course, units. But I ask you: have you forgotten the lesson that was taught to us thirteen hundred years ago? You belong to a nation now, you have now carved out a territory, vast territory, it is all yours; it does not belong to a Punjabi or a Sindhi, or a Pathan, or a Bengali, it is yours. You have got your Central Government where several units are represented. Therefore, if you want to build up yourself into a nation, for God's sake give up this provincialism. Provincialism has been one of the curses; and so is sectionalism – Shia, Sunni, etc. (ibid.)

The testing time for Muslim destiny

It was not many years after the creation of Pakistan that the disunity, corruption and drift became apparent. In 1958 Ayub Khan, the commander-in-chief of the Pakistan army, declared martial law. That gave political and social life in Pakistan a different kind of direction from the one that Jinnah had envisaged. One direct consequence was the alienation of the Bengalis, who formed the majority population of Pakistan but lived far away in East Pakistan.

The inept and insensitive West Pakistani élite would drive the proud, gifted, sensitive and artistic Bengalis from Pakistan, complaining of not being given their share in the military, civilian jobs and industry. Besides, the cultural arrogance was resented by the Bengalis. Worse, they were angered by West Pakistani suggestions of racial inferiority. As President of Pakistan, Ayub Khan did not even bother to conceal his contempt for the Bengalis: they were 'down-trodden races', having 'complexes', full of 'suspicion' and 'a sort of defensive aggressiveness' (M. A. Khan 1967: 187). Bengalis exasperated him: 'I told an East Pakistani friend once, "You have such sweet music. I wish to God you were half as sweet yourself"' (ibid.: 27). This was an unprecedented public act of indiscretion for any sitting president. It was widely rumoured that a senior civil servant, a member of the élite administrative cadre of the Civil Service of Pakistan (CSP) and a sinister figure of the period, wrote Ayub Khan's autobiography. It is not surprising. Ayub Khan's view was also how the senior bureaucrats from West Pakistan perceived the Bengalis; they, more than anyone else, would be responsible for losing the Bengalis.

For most West Pakistanis, their eastern province was a land of inclement weather, of typhoons, cyclones and storms. It was also poor and overpopulated. As far as they could see, all the Bengalis seemed to do was organize strikes and demonstrations and whine about being exploited by West Pakistan.

For Bengalis their dreams of an independent, strong Pakistan in which they would be equal citizens had quickly dissolved. They felt slighted, their language, their culture and their dignity despised. They felt themselves to be second-rate citizens in their own land. Rumours that the income from the jute they produced was being siphoned off to the West, to feed the mainly West Pakistan army and Civil Service, gained circulation. There was no love lost between the two provinces by the 1960s.

By 1970, out of the twenty secretaries of the government of Pakistan, only three acting secretaries were East Pakistanis. The figures for the military were even worse: only one of the senior thirty-five generals was East Pakistani. Yet, in the first decades after partition, East Pakistan had a favourable trade balance while West Pakistan ran a deficit. Before 1965 East Pakistan earned about 60 per cent of Pakistan's foreign currency but received less than 30 per cent of imports. Little wonder then that East Pakistanis, conscious that they formed the majority population of Pakistan, felt humiliated and cheated.

Bengali intellectuals were quick to point out the innate prejudice in their West Pakistani compatriots. Even Iqbal's presidential address to the Muslim League in 1930 – in which he argued that 'the formation of a consolidated North-West Indian Muslim state appears to me to be the final destiny of the Muslims, at least of North-West India' – did not include Bengal. Similarly, Bengal was not to be found in Chaudhry Rahmat Ali's acronym, PAKISTAN. If P was for Punjab, A for Afghan or the North-West Frontier, K for Kashmir, S for Sind and TAN for Baluchistan, where was Bengal?

Missing Jinnah

For those Pakistanis who criticize Jinnah for the deal he struck in 1947, pointing out the loss of half the provinces of Bengal and Punjab, and also Kashmir and Hyderabad, let us look at a Pakistani example. In 1971 the President of Pakistan, Yahya Khan, facing conflict with India, needed to contain Bengali nationalism and preserve Pakistan. The goal of the Indians was to foster the former and damage the latter. In the event India succeeded and Pakistan failed miserably. For the Pakistani leadership it was a catalogue of disaster. It was a textbook case of how not to manage national and international affairs. From the outset the Pakistani leadership did everything it should not have done. Within a year it had lost more than half its population and its international credibility, and had created a legacy of bitterness in its own people, the Bengalis.

What went wrong? First, in March 1971 Pakistanis used the army to crush its Bengali civilian population, looting, raping and murdering. That was the turning point: the army action was the nail in the coffin of Pakistan. It inflamed the ethnic movement for independence.

Second, the Pakistani leadership walked into every trap set by the Indians. Pakistani flights between the two wings of Pakistan were suspended by the Indians after a suspect hijack attempt – organized, it was widely believed, by Indians. Pakistan now had no direct air link between its provinces. An international campaign pointing out human rights violations by Pakistanis was orchestrated by India; Pakistan did little to counteract this – even if it could, it had no idea of how to proceed. Besides, Pakistan was under martial law and generals are rarely successful at projecting a benign image of a Third World country.

Finally, too many in the Pakistani leadership were mediocrities, drunks and paper tigers. They were not prepared to listen to sensible advice and they attempted to carry out their own selfish agenda of self-preservation. They were no match for India. It was a short, swift, brutal year for Pakistan and it ended in total disaster. Two decades after his death, Pakistan would sorely miss Jinnah.

The break-up of Pakistan

The battle with India was not long in coming. India had co-ordinated a massive political and media campaign against Pakistan culminating in war. It ended in a decisive victory for India on both the military and the political fronts.

In the summer of 1971 Ayub Khan was ill. He only had a few years to live. Politically isolated, he lived in a big house on a hill in Islamabad. I had several long conversations with him, and he was one of the few Pakistanis then to tell me categorically that Pakistan had already lost East Pakistan, that there was no way it could pull out from what seemed a hopeless military and political situation with the present leadership and its policies. Ayub Khan argued that no leadership could fight a war on two fronts. Pakistan was in effect fighting both an external enemy and an internal one. Militarily it faced better-armed, better-motivated, better-prepared Indian forces, while simultaneously it was suppressing its own civilians through military action.

Ayub Khan's pessimistic but correct prognosis contrasted with the empty-headed bravado prevailing in Islamabad. A relative of Ayub Khan's, once an officer in the cavalry, did not agree with him. A Pathan, he dismissed the Bengalis as cowards. 'They will run when the first shot is fired,' he asserted. 'Do you know what an armoured regiment can do in Bengal? It will go through the Bengalis' (he used the derogatory term 'Bingo') 'like a knife through butter.'

The man in command of the campaign in East Pakistan was General Niazi, the martial law administrator of that province. He led a textbook campaign. Everything he did should be studied in military academies under the heading 'How not to conduct a military campaign'. Niazi began by alienating, and continuing to alienate, an already alienated local population. Rumours of looting and raping persisted throughout the province. There were even rumours that he delivered speeches to his soldiers advising them to impregnate Bengali women as a national – indeed Islamic – duty; it would improve the racial stock. This travesty of the Islamic notion of duty was an insult to Pakistani nationalism and Bengali cultural identity. It also fed into the negative international image of Pakistan as a brutal military power oppressing its own people. India orchestrated the campaign. Global sympathy was created for the Bengali cause. Even the Beatles performed for them.

Is Jinnah still Relevant?

When I asked General Niazi in Dhaka in the summer of 1971 what his strategy would be in the inevitable war that was looming, he looked surprised. 'Have you not heard of the Niazi corridor theory?' he asked. The other senior military officers present became tense. Who was this naïve young civil officer? Had he not heard of the general's ideas? I thought quickly, trying to work out what this could mean in the context of the politics of the subcontinent. 'Will you make a breakthrough in the north of East Pakistan to link up with China in order to allow Chinese ground troops access? Or perhaps make a break for Calcutta and capture it, thus providing a corridor to the main port of India and gaining a major bargaining chip?'

'No,' Niazi thundered. 'I will cross into India and march up the Ganges and capture Delhi and thus link up with Pakistan. This will be a corridor that will link East and West Pakistan. It was a corridor that the Quaid-i-Azam demanded and I will obtain it by force of arms.'

The idea was so preposterous, so absurd, even in the oppressive martial law atmosphere of the military mess where the conversation was taking place, that I assumed it was irony. I expressed an appropriate smirk, emitted a kind of gurgle, to suggest I appreciated the humour. There was dead silence. The other officials present looked at me disapprovingly. I was violating the first principle of these clubs. One did not challenge the hierarchy, especially not the most senior martial law administrator in the land. I realized with alarm that Niazi was serious. Only no one was saying so.

An officer far superior in intellect to General Niazi, General Shahibzada Yaqub Khan, had resigned from the same post a few months earlier. He had argued in what became a celebrated if confidential debate that East Pakistan could not be held militarily if its people were up in arms against the government in Islamabad. He maintained that the three military divisions deployed in Pakistan would be insufficient. It would be very different, he said, if the Bengali population was in harmony with the Pakistan army and they then jointly faced a united Indian army. After he resigned he had flown to West Pakistan. There were rumours that he would be arrested and shot.

General Yaqub was a poet, linguist and scholar who would later shine as Pakistan's Foreign Minister after holding the post of ambassador in Moscow, Paris and Washington. In a private conversation with me in Dhaka in early 1970, he had summed up the situation he faced before the military crackdown. Pakistan is like a Ming vase, priceless and delicate, he said. Mujib-ur-Rehman, leading the Bengali nationalist party the Awami League and later President of Bangladesh, is like a fly sitting on it. We have to smack the fly but make sure the vase does not break. Only a few months later his colleagues would use a hammer to swat the fly; they would smash the vase and the fly would be unharmed.

Notes of a subdivisional officer

The bureaucrats in Islamabad, always several years behind political reality, decided in the late 1960s that the Civil Service of Pakistan, the élite administrative cadre, were the best people to cement East and West Pakistan socially, culturally and politically. For their first posting, junior officials would therefore serve in the other province. About a dozen of us consequently found ourselves in East Pakistan. I was appointed assistant commissioner (subdivisional officer) in charge of Kishorganj, a subdivision of Mymensingh, containing about 4 million people.

Notes I wrote as subdivisional officer in 1970, contemplating the coming elections which would split Pakistan, reveal the extent of political disintegration already taking place:

> It is perhaps still too early to put mass politics in Pakistan into Left and Right compartments. This election will be fought mainly on ethnic and regional appeals. The Awami League still riding the crest with Sheikh Mujib-ur-Rehman in East Pakistan is uninhibitedly beating the Bengali drum. Its 6-point programme would virtually create East Pakistan into a semi-autonomous State. Learning from the Awami League's slogan of 'Bengal for the Bengalis' the Council Muslim League has recently begun to play its own 'Punjab for the Punjabis' tune. In the North-West Frontier Province Wali Khan, the son of the 'Frontier Gandhi' exiled at Kabul, also plays on Pathan sentiments. (Ahmed 1977: 161)

'The man of the moment and certainly the greatest crowd-puller in East Pakistan is Sheikh Mujib-ur-Rehman,' I observed in 1971.

> He wears an Indian-style waistcoat and sometimes tends to be carried away in public by the momentum of his own words. In a recent speech he thundered against Maulana Maudoodi, strong in West Pakistan and the head of the Jamat-i-Islami party, warning him that he would only be allowed into East Pakistan if the Sheikh so wished. Certain Bengali leaders have taken to labelling him as 'fascist' and a 'Bengali Hitler'. (ibid.: 163)

In East Pakistan I was horrified at the cultural insensitivity and plain arrogance of my colleagues. They were not only not seeing the coming storm but seemed to be inviting it. West Pakistanis in East Pakistan would routinely refer to the Bengalis as 'Bingo bastards' or 'black monkeys'. At the highest level too this name-calling was common: 'Bhutto told Yahya that Mujib was "a clever bastard"' (Sisson and Rose 1990: 67). 'Yahya declared in an important meeting on 20 February that Mujib was not "behaving", that he needed to "sort this bastard out"' (ibid.: 81). This attitude did not endear West Pakistanis to the Bengalis.

When I returned to West Pakistan in March 1971 after the army action for a few days' leave I was berated by my senior colleagues for challenging the idea that the military solution would not work. I was warned to keep my mouth shut or face serious consequences. My wife and I were dubbed 'Bengali-lovers' for talking sympathetically about the predicament of the Bengalis. With the urgency of youth we were acutely aware of the storm that was building up on the Bengal horizon but few in the senior hierarchy in Pakistan would listen. We were certain we would lose our lives in the imminent collapse of law and order. It was like Russian roulette. In the first wave, early in 1971, three of my batch-mates were killed in the most brutal manner possible. Some colleagues managed to escape to West Pakistan. By the end of the year just three of us were left, two being taken prisoner when the Indians marched into Dhaka in December.

I was able to escape purely by chance. I was on leave in Karachi in late November for the birth of my first child. Because her birth was delayed by a few days I missed the last flight to Dhaka, thus avoiding two years in an Indian jail. In 1947 I lost one home; in 1971 I lost another.

Creating a country from a country

One of the most penetrating accounts of the dramatic days of early 1971 when the fate of Pakistan was being decided appears in the authoritative book by Sisson and Rose (1990; for a Pakistani perspective, see Salik 1977 and Zaheer 1994; for the opposite perspective on Pakistan, from a Bengali who identified with the Pakistan movement, see Choudhury 1988; for a standard Bangladeshi nationalist point of view which blames Pakistan for all its ills and does not mention India at all in tracing the genesis of Bangladesh, see Karim 1994; for one that blames India, see Abedin 1995 and Hussain 1996).

When analysing Bangladesh we need to keep before us two sets of prejudices: the general religious prejudice between Hindus and Muslims (Sisson and Rose 1990: 5, 19 and 234); and the ethnic prejudice between races – between the people of West Pakistan and Bengalis (ibid.: 67 and 81). Terrible crimes were committed on both sides and a free-for-all resulted. Although the Indians – and Bengalis – claimed that about 3 million people became victims of Pakistani atrocities the figure is disputed. Experts – if there can be experts in such matters – believe it may have been around 300,000 (ibid.: 306), but this figure does not indicate how many Bengalis – Hindus and Muslims – were killed and how many non-Bengalis. It was once again, as in 1947, a breakdown of society.

Bangladesh was created both by Bengali political will and by Pakistani obduracy, by push and pull. Consider the following assessment; all the stereotypes of race, religion and gender are fatally on display:

> At another level of temperament, Pakistani military leaders commonly believed that the armies of 'Hindu India', as they were referred to in common parlance, were no match for those of 'Islamic Pakistan'. Pakistan had been created in the face of Hindu opposition; its independence had been successfully defended against Indian 'machinations'; and the larger Indian armies had been unable to defeat the smaller ones of Pakistan in battle. Any effort on the part of India to take territory in East Pakistan would be countered by Pakistani occupation of Indian soil in the west; and the Indian army had to labour under the control of a civilian government headed by a woman [Indira Gandhi]. (Sisson and Rose 1990: 5)

The deep-rooted stereotypes, the Muslim self-perception we discussed in previous chapters, would not die even in the face of the massive defeat in 1971:

> This renewed military planning, like that of the past, was bolstered by a firm conviction, held even through the end of the December war, that it was impossible for Pakistan to lose a war to India.... The belief was also commonly held that 'Muslims had never been defeated by the Hindus'. Muslims had created Pakistan against great odds and Hindu opposition;

Kashmir had not been lost to India, but was an unresolved and continuing conflict.... As one senior general officer forcefully observed: 'Never before had a Muslim sword been handed over to a Hindu. In Islam, surrender is taboo; you either return with the land, or you bathe it in your blood!' (ibid.: 223–4)

The final public humiliation for Pakistan came in the surrender ceremony in Dhaka: 'Ironically, it was here too that General Niazi, commander of the forces of Muslim Pakistan, surrendered his arms to three generals of "Hindu" India – one a Parsee, another a Sikh, and the third a Jew'. (Ibid.: 234)

Bangladesh in the 1990s

A Bangladeshi teacher was hacked to death in the south-west District of Narail and hundreds of students were hurt in battles with monitors and police trying to stop cheating in secondary-school final examinations, police said yesterday. ('Cheat kills teacher', *Guardian*, 11 July 1995)

Nothing seems to have changed since the quarter-century ago when Narail was part of my charge as a subdivisional officer. There is the same sliding into anarchy, the same lack of discipline, the same challenging of authority. The above report could be from my own diary of that time:

I called the Principal and his Vice-Principal and warned them that if on a sudden check of the Examination Hall I saw any sign of cheating I would hold the Invigilator on duty personally responsible and proceed against him....

The Principal is an amiable but ineffective character straight out of P. G. Wodehouse. He exemplified the mentality of his staff in requests that now degenerated into juvenile fantasies: could the East Pakistan Rifles patrol inside the Examination Halls? 'We are in mortal threat of our lives and demand round-the-clock personal protection'; the mounting hysteria and theme of the academic when confronted with physical violence. (Ahmed 1977: 158)

A comment on the current economic and political situation in Bangladesh appears pessimistic:

But with the economy in shambles and market forces sending up the price of consumer goods the government faces a difficult task.... Adding to the confusion ... are developments relating to the 25-year treaty with India signed originally by Sheikh Mujib-ur-Rahman.... The treaty has been termed as a 'treaty of slavery' but Sheikh Hasina points out that the Prime Minister has failed to secure an equitable share of the Ganges River water and curtail the flood of Indian goods all over the country. (Syed Neaz Ahmad and Lutful Kabir Saadi, 'A long hard winter of discontent', *Impact International*, March 1995: 10)

Another assessment, equally gloomy, once again linked the fate of Bangladesh to the larger geopolitics of the subcontinent:

> A more damaging by-product of this style of politics is visible growth in the agitation politics. Strikes at regular intervals have reduced the country's economy to a shambles; factories and mills have ground to a halt; almost day by day the volume of imports of essential goods from India without which people cannot survive is increasing … a group of quislings has begun to suggest openly that the best choice before Bangladesh is to abandon its pretence of independence and join the Indian Union as a province.
>
> This was the ultimate goal of those who, in 1971, succeeded in breaking up Pakistan. They knew then that plans for straightforward incorporation into India would not have carried any support at that time. Therefore, the process had to be divided into two phases. The first phase would see an independent Bangladesh with all the paraphernalia of sovereignty established for a time. As conditions deteriorate it would be time for the second phase to be put into effect.
>
> This is the game Awami League is playing. (Nassim Haider, 'Caught in a war of two women!', *Impact International*, March 1995: 8)

A recent book by a nationalist Bengali, once a leader of the movement against Pakistan in 1971, points out the widespread influence in his country of the Research and Analysis Wing or RAW, India's equivalent of Pakistan's ISI or the American CIA (Abedin 1995). Culture, religion and politics are the targets. The idea is to keep Bangladesh weak and dependent, the author argues.

Perhaps the final word on Bangladesh should be given to a Bangladeshi who in a frank and perceptive letter from Dhaka described the travails of his land. For me it echoes the larger crisis in South Asia; indeed, some of its later remarks could apply to other parts of the subcontinent:

> Now, a short commentary on Bangladesh. Since the Civil War of 1971, things have changed for the worse in almost every sphere of our national life. The country has virtually become an economic captive market for India. On top of it, the Farrakka Barrage built by India since 1975 is playing havoc with one-third of Bangladesh in the Northern and Western regions.… Already the affected regions are facing serious problems of creeping desertification. The situation is alarming because of India's unilateral withdrawal of water from the Ganges River.
>
> Present situation in Bangladesh is no good for law-abiding citizens. Only some marginal and positive results have taken place during the last 24 years. Reality is harsh and unpleasant compared to expectations of people. Corruption is very widespread in the body politic of the country. Quality of overall civil administration in the country has deteriorated alarmingly. Industry and education are in shambles. Law and order promotes lawlessness! Interestingly, some individuals and groups of families have flourished in this situation so fast and so well to make their fortunes at the cost of sufferings of millions since 1972. Rule of law is still a far cry. Rhetoric

is in abundance but action is in short supply. To me, the whole nation still appears to be facing 'Crisis of Identity' – the question is: whether we are Bengali first or Muslim first? It's a matter of shame indeed after so many years.... Our intellectuals are no better than our petty politicians. Our politicians act like mercenaries in their own country! (personal communication, Haroun Al-Raschid: 31 May 1995)

Suspended lives

In concluding this chapter I give a tragic example of South Asian politicians dealing with the ethnicity of the other: the Biharis of Bangladesh. These were mostly refugees from India who had migrated to what was then East Pakistan in 1947. Out of place in the intensely Bengali nationalist milieu after the creation of Bangladesh in 1971, and seen as supporters of Pakistan, they wished to migrate to what remained of Pakistan in the west. Technically they were Pakistanis, holding Pakistani passports. But Pakistan, with its increasingly ethnic politics, was not interested in more *muhajirs* arriving in Karachi. They were perhaps Jinnah's most loyal citizens, still believing in Pakistan and wanting to migrate to it, but they became its victims when Pakistan refused them entry. Bangladesh, offended, deposited about half a million of them in squalid temporary camps in Dhaka. Those who wished to return to India found they had burnt their boats. In the late 1990s, almost a generation after they declared their loyalty to Pakistan, their lives still remain suspended between the three countries of the subcontinent. Their fate – along with that of other unsettled groups like Sikhs and Kashmiris – is a damning indictment of the South Asian leaders.

South Asia is a region of menace and cruelty for the oppressed ethnic community. Much of the communal violence is evil; evil because it has no pressing cause and therefore no cure. We must move beyond this way of thinking. Perhaps the only way ahead is to go back to the past and try to understand it. Issues of religious and ethnic identity which were assumed to be settled half a century ago clearly need serious and committed resolution. In the present untidy and volatile form they create serious problems for millions of people from the Khyber to Chittagong. For such South Asians the promise of a new dawn in 1947 remains, in the words of the great Urdu poet, Faiz Ahmed Faiz, a false one.

Epilogue: Preparing for the Next Millennium

Our Hindustan [South Asia] is the best place in the world.

(Urdu verse of Allama Iqbal)

Nehru once observed that he felt out of place everywhere, at home nowhere. Today in South Asia many people share Nehru's sense of alienation: rich and poor, old and young, those in power and those out, those belonging to the majority and those to the minority. This is alienation on a vast scale. This is not the mood that makes people want to write poetry or take political action; this is what pushes societies towards disintegration. It forces us to pause and reflect. In this closing chapter I shall survey the South Asian situation and suggest a possible strategy for the future.

The manner of the birth of India and Pakistan helps explain certain characteristics associated with Indians and Pakistanis (as familiar to cricket commentators as to journalists and academics): the prickly sense of insecurity, the obsession with conspiracies, the desire to succeed, the lack of faith in the leadership (everyone is dwarfed at the side of Gandhi or Jinnah), the aggressive loyalty to a cause and by implication the need to assert a separate identity. There are differences yet similarities in the ways that India and Pakistan developed (the same argument applies to Bangladesh).

Globalization and traditional culture

The changes taking place in the last half-century have been more rapid and more bewildering than at any time in history. Just after the Second World War, when Mountbatten was winding up the Viceroyalty of India, the British empire on the map spread to one-quarter of the globe. Within a few years it was vanishing from the map. A totally opposed system, communism, emerged. A quarter of the world would soon be communist, with the Soviet Union and China dominating it. Within half a century, the Soviet empire had collapsed and China was seeking new directions. Once the Cold War was over, congealed ethnic and religious divisions began tearing apart many nations across the world.

Globalization draws in people all over the world who willingly or reluctantly participate in a global culture (see Ahmed 1992a, 1993d, 1996b; Ahmed and Donnan 1994; Ahmed and Shore 1995; Baudrillard 1995; Beck 1992; Fukuyama 1992; Giddens 1990, 1991; Huntington 1993; Mestrovic 1994; Moynihan 1993; Nash 1989; Robertson 1991, 1992; Turner 1994). It can be defined simply as the spread of contemporary Western culture to other parts of the world. Satellite television, the VCR, communications technology and developments in transport have made globalization possible. This expansion can take the form of a cultural imperialism and cause resentment as conflict develops between the indigenous culture and the pervasive world culture. The tension is heightened by the frustration that grows from attempting to stop what seems to be an irresistible force. Traditionalists are dismayed and not sure how to cope. Everything seems to be under challenge; all the old values seem to be threatened.

McDonald's and Mickey Mouse, Coca-Cola and Levis, as much as ideas of mass democracy and human rights, are now the universally recognized signs of this global culture, whatever their country of origin. 'Globalization', sighs one of the pundits studying it, 'is, at least empirically, not in and of itself a "nice thing", in spite of certain indications of "world progress"' (Robertson 1992: 6).

South Asia has changed more rapidly in the last two decades than it has in the last two centuries. In the next few years, and into the next millennium, it will change at an even more rapid pace through the processes of globalization. Muslims and Hindus cannot draw impenetrable boundaries around their societies. Information technology allows a local news item to be disseminated around the world within hours or even minutes. South Asian leaders have to wake up to the challenge of this global society of which they are now part.

We are living in a world of simulacra, of simulated surfaces, of replication of images that have lost touch with reality. Traditional religions, on the other hand, have to deal with reality. Islam or Hinduism or Buddhism ties its followers directly and closely with the rites of passage and everyday life. These religions include ideas on washing, hygiene, defecation, eating and sleeping. It is the disconnection between reality and illusion that traditional religion challenges; it is the reason why traditional religion and some forms of globalization appear to be on a collision course.

The new realities in the region

South Asia is at the crossroads, at a critical point in its history. The future looks bright but uncertain. There are more people living in middle-class comfort and more people suffering from poverty and deprivation than ever before in history. Women have never been so prominent – four female Prime Ministers – and yet cases of bride burning and abortion of female foetuses are on the increase. It is the best and worst of times.

Traditional economists fail to make sense of what is happening in South Asia. On the surface the statistics are positive. In spite of the rioting in India in the early 1990s, which acted as a temporary setback, investment, aid and trade in the mid-1990s continued to flow into India. People were talking about a future economic giant, an awakening titan. However, the social indices for education, poverty, health and population, for ecology, the destruction of forests, violence and corruption tell their sorry tale (see the *Human Development Report* 1995, United Nations Development Programme, Oxford University Press, Oxford and New York).

The population of India and Pakistan has been growing at an alarming pace and threatening to outstrip its resources. That rate will result in a population of 1.5 billion in the year 2000, nearly a quarter of the world's total population. Paul Kennedy in *Preparing for the Twenty-First Century* (1994) reveals the depressing statistics – population figures, ecological depletion, political instability and low education standards – that face developing societies. Kennedy calculates that by 2025 India might possess the world's largest population for the first time in recorded history, eventually reaching 2 billion people. In addition, Pakistan would have 270 million people. He further indicates that Calcutta, Bombay and Karachi would be among the twenty mega-cities of the world. On the other hand, South Asia's adult literacy rate is lower than that of any other region in the world: almost 400 million people are still illiterate.

The crumbling nation-state

With borders dissolving, with foreign satellite television beamed directly into South Asian homes, where are the once so jealously guarded boundaries of the nation-state? Once so possessive that they would not even allow photographs to be taken of sensitive bridges and roads, today South Asians cannot keep anything private or hidden. What does this mean for the future?

The modern state in Asia seems to be fading away. It lies in the wreck of its attempt to take off in the late twentieth century, dysfunctional and paralysed. Out in the streets, the state machinery – police, civil officials, civic amenities – can be bought or negotiated by the group. The group has become a surrogate state. Society is disintegrating into a collection of individuals and nuclear families with mafia networks reinforcing clan and tribal loyalties. People live, travel, socialize and marry within their own groups, each concerned with maximizing material, political and economic benefits for themselves.

The damning argument against Pakistan is that it took a community spread throughout the subcontinent, chopped it into several communities, gave it first one country and then two and left the others dangling in mid-air. People who once possessed the culture, customs and history of a whole subcontinent were left with neither a nation nor an idea of themselves as a community. Pakistan was a double disaster for the Muslims in India: first they lost their sense of coherence and political strength in the Indian union along with their leadership and middle classes which migrated to Pakistan by the thousands; secondly, they were for ever damned in India for having voted for Pakistan and broken the unity of India.

What if Jinnah were to come alive to see the mess that is his Pakistan, the killings, kidnappings, the corruption, mismanagement and despair? This question is repeatedly raised by Pakistanis wherever they live. But that question needs to be placed alongside another one. What if there were no Pakistan and Jinnah were to come alive in his native Bombay? There, the pogroms, the prejudices, the communal violence would have shaken him to the core. Then surely he would have been justified in saying that, however shaky and ramshackle – or, to use his words, 'moth-eaten' and 'truncated' – his Pakistan, it was still better than the living hell of Bombay.

In the 1990s Muslims in India were reduced to slum-dwellers and outcasts, their glorious monuments in ruins. They lived in clusters, in extreme poverty, around the shrines of the great saints in Ajmer and Delhi. If Pakistan is a poor answer to Muslim needs, India offers even less. The Muslim questions – would mosques be protected? would the worshippers in them be safe? would the *azan*, the call to prayer, be allowed? would Muslim culture and Muslim languages be preserved? – have been answered by recent events. In India they are all at risk in one way or another, sometimes directly, sometimes indirectly. Indeed Hindu extremists have a hit list of 3,000 Muslim monuments to be demolished (see, for example, 'Hindu threat to raze 3,000 mosques' by Derek Brown, *Guardian*, 6 November 1990). The Taj Mahal is on the list.

When I discussed the 'what if?' question with Pakistani students in Cambridge they provided a convincing argument. If there had been no Pakistan, they said, then among the hundred or so Indian students there would have been perhaps two or three Muslims – a few more than the present number. But because of Pakistan there were almost as many Muslims as there were Indians. Add to this the number of Bangladeshis and you can see why it was such a great advantage for the Muslims to have formed their own state.

Hostility towards Muslims

The global image of Islam as fundamentalist, terrorist and extremist has had an adverse affect on Muslims living everywhere. It is also difficult even for traditionally liberal and secular Hindus to support Muslims in India. This further isolates Muslims.

What the press called the fundamentalists – the fanatics, the extremists – played into the hands of those hostile to Muslims, who now only have to say that all Muslims are intrinsically fundamentalist in order to argue that Islam is a dangerous and uncontrollable civilization which must be stopped. This strengthens their position in dealing with Muslims in the most savage manner possible in their own countries and getting away with it. This would not have occurred even a generation ago, but so widespread and so global is the hostility to Islam that few people seem to be bothered about the excesses. Several cases present themselves – Bosnia, Palestine, Chechniya, Kashmir – where the killing, rape and torture were ignored by the world, Muslims believed, because the victims were Muslim: the world tacitly agreed to look the other way.

One Muslim response is to tie a bomb round the waist and set it off in proximity to a Jew; the other is to create self-induced hysteria against Salman Rushdie. Neither strategy has been effective in achieving Muslim objectives: the explosives do not even make a dent on Israeli security and Salman Rushdie remains alive. Indeed this response is counter-productive, since it reinforces the image of Muslims as violent fanatics.

Hinduism has been more successful with the media than Islam. It absorbs, mimics, subverts whatever other culture it comes in touch with; its philosophers and scholars are able to interact with the larger world. Muslim scholars in contrast appear inward-looking and defensive in their thinking, wanting to draw up barriers, to shut out the world.

A cursory glance at British literature during the twentieth century illustrates how with each generation Muslims are being pushed to the margins. Mehboob Ali in Kipling's *Kim* (1901) and Aziz in E. M. Forster's *A Passage to India* (1924) were both drawn with conviction and sympathy, both in their own way attractive if flawed characters. While Ali strutted about with the pride of the tribal warrior from the northern passes, in the 1920s Aziz was attempting to define a modern Indian in relation to the past. Over a generation later Muslims were mentioned in passing only to be described as possible rape suspects in Paul Scott's *The Jewel in the Crown* (1973).

By the present generation, India has subtly become 'Hindu' and the only Muslim in the play by Tom Stoppard, *Indian Ink* (1995), is the minor role of the thieving servant. It is Raj India and projects all its own romantic fantasy, prejudices and arguments on to a distant land and a past era. Flora Crewe is painted and seduced by Mirad Das and through the painting becomes Radha, the consort of Krishna, the Hindu god. Mirad's son complains half a century after independence that his countrymen are still 'hypnotized' by the British and their language. *Indian Ink* helps us to understand the relationship between the British, the Hindus and the Muslims from the perspective of the former. Muslims have simply begun, like the Cheshire cat, to fade away.

The crisis of leadership

It is a barren time for South Asian leadership. The ruling class does not believe in meritocracy, bureaucracy or democracy. It has reappropriated an Indian word which best describes it: lootocracy. In the age of globalization a dull, unimaginative leadership plays with – and preys on – ethnicity and religion. An arid mediocrity hangs over the land obscuring even the intellectuals and the great religious figures that the subcontinent has produced. The media discovered that most politicians were crooks, most holy men frauds, most academics idiots and most fathers tyrants. People, families, entire societies no longer had a moral centre. The South Asian leadership crisis reflected the larger crisis in the world as a whole – what social scientists were already labelling the 'risk society'.

Why are the leaders getting away with what they are doing? One obvious answer is the process of globalization. For the first time the local leader can easily transfer his or her illegal wealth abroad, acquiring property and buying into deals. For the first time he or she is able to live comfortably abroad and move around from one country to another, taking part in the regional culture. Another reason lies in the fact that the world media prefer broad simplification and superficial matters to profound complex issues. In any case most people in the West are cynical about leaders and have very low expectations of them. If stories of corrupt Third World leaders filter through, people are inclined to shrug their shoulders and say, 'What's new?'

Violence in South Asia has not spared saintly figures like Gandhi, let alone military dictators like General Zia ul-Haq or popular Prime Ministers like Indira Gandhi and

Zulfiqar Ali Bhutto. The idea of the subcontinent as a place of non-violence and peace propagated by Mahatma Gandhi's image is totally misguided. Irresponsible people led by extremists talk about final solutions, avenging history and wiping out the enemy. In brutality and in anarchy South Asia in the last years of the century has few equals.

While hundreds are being killed and thousands of lives are being disrupted, this is dismissed as a 'law and order' problem, as the work of the 'enemy' (read 'Pakistan' for India, 'India' for Pakistan). In Kashmir and in Karachi ordinary citizens suffer terrible privations; yet governments dismiss such ongoing atrocities as the work of enemy agents and attempt to use brute force to crush any expression of dissent or genuine demand. If the problem is not religion, as it is in India, then it is ethnicity in Pakistan. What we are seeing is the breakdown of society.

A dangerous rivalry

The risk of nuclear exchange has never been greater in South Asia than at the present time. According to experts, in the late 1980s and 1990s both countries were on the brink of nuclear exchange several times. In both countries it is mutual suspicion that creates the desire to have a nuclear programme. That is why, when in the early 1970s it was known that Indira Gandhi had exploded a nuclear device, Mr Bhutto, the then Prime Minister of Pakistan, immediately went on television to promise Pakistan its own nuclear weapon at all costs, even if it meant 'eating grass'.

The acquisition of an expensive nuclear programme makes no sense in the context of the general economic poverty of the subcontinent. But in the context of the deep suspicion and divisions between the two major communities it is logical. Pakistan believes it would be suicidal for it to give up its nuclear programme. It is the homologue of the Cold War between the Soviets and the USA during the second half of the twentieth century. The purpose of the so-called 'nuclear deterrent' is to prevent an all-out war, yet the notion of deterrence still requires people to envisage the actual use of nuclear weaponry. The idea of nuclear war in the subcontinent is madness, something Jinnah − and indeed Gandhi and Nehru − would have abhorred. Millions of people on both sides want nothing more than to live in peace, and are already leading poverty-stricken lives.

The collapse of the Cold War has meant that India and Pakistan are isolated in their own regional struggle and left by the world powers to fend for themselves. This situation has worked against Pakistan, which finds itself facing a far more powerful enemy without the comfort of knowing that America is backing it.

Pakistan and India are locked in a confrontation determined by their history. Pakistanis view themselves as the inheritors of the Muslim tradition of the subcontinent and see themselves in a far bigger role than their relatively small country and limited resources permit them to play. They will not accept a subordinate position to Indians, for that would mean negating their own history. Pakistan's problem is that it has never recognized itself as a lesser partner in the Indian subcontinent. India − larger, better known abroad, with a far greater depth of resources, both human and land − cannot acknowledge this. It sees Pakistan as a nuisance, an uppity newcomer. Pakistan's perennial political problems do not help its credibility with Indians. At the back of their minds there is the prediction of Nehru, Patel and Mountbatten that Pakistan – sooner rather than later – would collapse and come limping home to rejoin India.

Indian perceptions are also influenced by history. The idea of Kali Yog or a dark age has now taken hold of millions of Hindus: its central idea is a final showdown between the forces of good and evil. In the way it is interpreted in many eyes, good is symbolized by the Hindu and evil by the Muslim. The widespread idea of Kali Yog from the *Linguapurana*, a fifth-century Hindu religious epic, means an age of turbulence and uncertainty; it adds fuel to the communal fire. A dangerous mood of an inevitable once-and-for-all, all-out war that may settle things has grown and it has infiltrated the popular media.

Hindus see Muslims as threatening, as people who ruled them for a thousand years and who are ultimately their rivals. Although the disenfranchised Muslim minority in India is treated with contempt, Indians have mixed feelings of fear, respect and loathing for the Pakistanis. They do not know quite what to make of them.

There is an inherent contradiction in the foreign policy of both India and Pakistan which reflects their self-perception. India, which believes its finest cultural traditions lie in notions of non-violence and peace, is none the less a regional superpower bent on dominating its neighbours. It has used brute force to implement its foreign policy. Indian troops have been active in neighbouring countries (for example, in Sri Lanka). Instead of providing the soothing hand of the elder brother or father figure India competes with Pakistan. A spiral of attack and counter-attack, claim and counter-claim is thereby encouraged. Commentators have pointed out that 'politically, everyone of India's smaller neighbours has been the victim of Kautilyan [an ancient Hindu Machiavelli] intrigue' (Crossette 1993: 110).

Pakistani foreign policy has similar contradictions. On the one hand it acts as a middle-level nation struggling to survive, and on the other as the inheritor of the grand Mughal legacy. This contradiction was immediately apparent in the early 1990s when the Soviet Union disintegrated, causing half a dozen new Muslim states in Central Asia to be formed. Pakistan's Foreign Office was actively involved in exploring ways in which it could enhance its presence there. It was reviving memories of the Mughal emperor Babar's ancestral home. Indeed, the Foreign Office would echo this connection as it sought to create cultural and political alliances and recapture the lost glory of the Mughals. Pakistan was aiming at the stars but the reality constantly brought it down to earth.

Building a strategy for the next millennium

A radical reassessment of recent South Asian history is required. On the threshold of the new millennium will the future bring conflict or consensus, harmony or hatred? It is an appropriate time for stocktaking, to look at the past and contemplate the coming time.

We look at three possible scenarios for the future of South Asia. The first is further anarchy, turbulence and disintegration; the continued collapse of law and order; increasing repression by governments; inertia and disillusionment. Society will collapse into some great big black hole of complete barbarity, as occurred in the Balkans.

In the second possible scenario, the governments of South Asia will respond to the challenge of the new millennium and resolve to restructure their social and political policies and lead the people into a new phase of history, one which will allow them to fulfil their destinies. Justice will be exercised to all and minorities will feel safe. Corruption, nepotism and mismanagement will be challenged, tolerance and rule of law become widespread. India and Pakistan will normalize relations and the potential of the region will be fulfilled as it surges ahead as an economic power-house and political giant.

The third scenario is the present death-in-life existence, continuing to limp along, not quite a whole society, not quite dead but not living either. External events, the existing momentum and a tinkering with the structure will enable existing governments to survive; but there will be no meaningful changes. This probably is the most likely scenario for South Asia. But we can hope for the second possibility; we can dream dreams, see visions of destiny fulfilled.

In numerous forums it is suggested that once the Kashmir problem between India and Pakistan is solved there will be no other problem between them. This is ignoring the facts of history, sociology and culture. The issue is not Kashmir; it is people living together as tolerant neighbours, a humane society based on mutual understanding.

If we are to move ahead into the next century with any semblance of hope for the subcontinent, its leaders must understand and combat the poison of intolerance. They must stop genuflecting to unreasonable ethnic and religious demands. This intolerance does not restrict itself to Hindu versus Muslim. It includes minorities; it affects men, women, children, the poor, the less privileged, the outcast, the ignorant, the blind, the disabled, the elderly. The sense of bitterness between the two countries needs to be recognized as a central problem. There has to be a conscious de-escalation of hatred on all levels – cultural, social, religious and political. A strategy for the future needs to be multi-pronged and multi-layered. It must identify the problem not as the other, not as a religion or as a community, but as extremism and intolerance. Extremists – let us not use the word fundamentalist because not all fundamentalists are either extremists or violent – must be confronted in South Asia.

Perhaps the solution will come once again from outside. Rapid technological advances will force these traditional societies to readjust. Media and information technology which currently reinforce monolithic and inflexible religious positions will in time diminish them. People will be obliged to respond in neutral terms – assenting to merit, to law and order, to the rights of everyone, not just the family, clan or religious group.

If we are prepared to accept this proposition then the struggle of Jinnah – and indeed Gandhi – for the dignity of the community will not have been in vain. But we must move beyond Jinnah and Gandhi; their failure to reach an accommodation set the scene for further confrontation. We need to recognize that there was no ideal situation in 1947, that peace would have been unattainable however partition was implemented, and then to plump for a direction into the next millennium that combines pragmatism with fairness.

Stopping the media war

There is something of the Tom and Jerry about India and Pakistan. A large Tom chases little Jerry indefatigably, hitting and hammering him. But Jerry will not give up. He will constantly fight back, frustrating Tom first in one place, then in another; and so it goes on and on. It would be funny if the prospect of war that would devastate millions of people were not so frightening. Contemporary cartoons in Pakistan and India continue to use stereotypes of each other (see the two Pakistani cartoons reproduced in plates 17 and 18, one from the *Friday Times*, an influential English weekly, and the other from *Jang*, one of Pakistan's most popular Urdu newspapers).

South Asians must stop demonizing each other. Muslims must cease to think of Hindus as degraded *kafirs* to be subdued on the battlefield in a final showdown; similarly Hindus must stop thinking of Muslims as alien military invaders, unclean foreigners, to be finally defeated like the mythological demon Ravana.

The cultural diversity of the subcontinent must be acknowledged. Half a century after the events of 1947 it is pointless blaming individuals or sides. The main actors are long gone. Making ledgers of blame and credit will achieve little. Prejudices have hardened. The symptoms of the disease that Jinnah sought to check have now been exposed at the source – communal intolerance.

The hostile stand-off between India and Pakistan is the classic confrontation between two neighbours who know each other too well, who have interpenetrated each other's culture and religion and families through marriage. It is a conflict that echoes a larger confrontation over the last half-millennium in history. It is a conflict between two interpretations of two distinct ways of life which echo each other far more strongly than appears on the surface.

Plate 17   A cartoon in the *Friday Times* (16–22 May 1996) depicting an India obsessed with Pakistan

Plate 18 A cartoon in the *Jang* (26 May 1996) showing the corruption in Pakistan, with politicians fighting each other for plots of land while ignoring the Hindu menace

Epilogue

Understanding the other

It is time for Muslim historians to step outside their own culture and see themselves as others see them. This would help to give not only a more balanced picture of their own history but also allow them to develop a greater understanding of the environment in which they live. This in turn would help them work out a strategy for the future with more realism and compassion.

Hindus too simplify history dangerously. To them the stories of the Muslims of India is a straightforward one: barbaric invaders from outside India who destroyed Hindu temples and forcefully converted their populations to Islam (Ahmed 1993b, 1993c; Elst 1992; Oak 1965, 1990). This is not only a gross simplification but a completely inaccurate interpretation of history. As well as their religion Muslims brought to India their architecture, literature, poetry and painting. Most important of all, they offered a sense of unity, an idea of oneness, the notion of one land for over five hundred years when they ruled from Delhi.

Visiting each other

Getting to know each other is the best way to getting to accept each other. Cultural, trade and intellectual exchanges must be officially sponsored and encouraged. At the present time it is difficult to visit each other in groups and the hostile atmosphere vitiates individual attempts.

The problem of minorities

In all three countries – India, Pakistan and Bangladesh – the power, size and shortsighted intolerance of the majority create problems for the minorities. The Hindus in India, the Punjabis in Pakistan and the Bengalis in Bangladesh form large and powerful majorities. There is little hope for the minorities – whether the religious ones in India or the ethnic ones in Pakistan and Bangladesh – of challenging them at the polls. That is why democracy is seen to be such a sham in South Asia. Democracy means the perpetuation of misrule, corruption and nepotism by the majority; it means unlimited power in the state structure, the army, the Civil Service and the police; it means patronage, licences for industries and entrepreneurships; it means the constant misery and persecution of the minorities, both as quasi-official policy and as an unwritten but widely understood way. Torture, raids into private houses, positive discrimination against minorities, a media campaign to depict them as backward and even disloyal are all part of the official strategy. That is why Jinnah's struggle is so relevant today.

Jinnah emphasized again and again the need for minorities to feel secure, whether Muslims in India or Hindus in Pakistan. That is why he insisted that this security could only be guaranteed through cast-iron laws, written in the constitution and then rigidly upheld. But the rulers of the subcontinent today have been making the constitution irrelevant. It can easily be bypassed when it is evoked or interpreted according to what suits them. They are losing not only the law but also the spirit of the law.

255

Epilogue

In the general confrontation between India and Pakistan, between Hindus and Muslims, it is forgotten that Jinnah was in fact standing up for all minorities. Jinnah received great support from the lower castes among the Hindus. In India lower-caste Hindus and Christians are often physically attacked or even lynched if they are suspected of being uppity, if they begin to assert themselves in business or economics (Bonner et al. 1994: 232–8). The worst part is that there is no retribution: the administrative structure is entirely weighted against them. Perhaps the strangest paradox is that the emerging middle class, the affluent, educated, often Westernized section of society, are the worst culprits, insisting on their caste privileges in India, keeping the others down.

The question of Kashmir

One particular priority is to resolve the long-standing problem of long-suffering Kashmir. The Pakistani account of over half a million Indian troops raping, looting, killing and torturing Kashmiris indiscriminately may contain an element of propaganda. What cannot be denied is that Indians themselves are horrified at the human rights violations taking place in Kashmir. The summary and brutal nature of the punishments and the scale of the uprisings confirm that something is terribly wrong.

Kashmir is usually regarded as a post-colonial problem caused by 'fundamentalist' uprisings in the 1990s. In fact what needs to be known internationally is that the problem is over a century old. If there is one people the Kashmiris can blame for their present plight – even more than the Indians – it is the British. It was the British who first sold Kashmir for a few thousand pounds in the middle of the last century to a Hindu, Gulab Singh. (The sale worked out at 3 rupees per head and has always rankled: 'Each hill, each garden, field, / Each farmer too they sold, / A nation for a price, / That makes my blood ice-cold,' wrote the poet Allama Iqbal.) It was a British Viceroy who left the Kashmir issue hanging in mid-air between India and Pakistan in 1947 as the British hastily packed to leave.

Western powers, particularly Britain, can exert pressure to ease the suffering of the Kashmiris. This can be done in several ways: by highlighting human rights violations; by persuading the governments to reach a solution that would be acceptable to the three parties, that is India, Pakistan and Kashmir; and, above all, by using the power of the media to expose the atrocities. Too often the expediency of striking lucrative commercial deals in India overrides everything else.

Considering their role in Kashmir it barely exists in British consciousness in the 1990s (there are honourable exceptions such as Alastair Lamb 1991, 1994, and Schofield 1996; for an even more rare American comment, see Newberg's brief but perceptive book, 1995; for an Indian comment, see Singh 1995). The *Guardian* newspaper concluded a frustrated editorial thus: 'India has an appalling human rights record to correct, and some day will have to allow the people in the Vale to decide their own future' (25 August 1994; see also editorial of 15 August 1995). Kashmir only makes the news when a tourist is taken hostage.

Perhaps the masterstroke of the Indian government worked: Delhi labelled the uprisings as Islamic fundamentalist. Alarm bells began to ring in the West. The last thing it needed was another Islamic revolution to succeed. Whatever natural sympathy was felt for the cause of an oppressed people was drowned in the fear of an Islamic revolution in the making. Kashmiri youth themselves, not aware of how the Western media works, continued to talk of the glory of Allah and wave their guns about for foreign journalists.

Kashmir had reached an impasse. On both sides there was a deadlock. The people who ruled India believed that if an inch of Kashmir was conceded then India itself would be at risk. Besides, the Indian Muslims would be massacred all over the subcontinent. Wherever they were in a majority they would opt for the Pakistan solution, that is independence for themselves. Indian Muslims had to be diplomatic and in public support the Indian position over Kashmir. Even Hindu liberals, however shocked at the killings and torture in Kashmir, were none the less careful to point out that Kashmir was and would always be Indian. To criticize Indian policy in Kashmir is almost tantamount to declaring oneself a traitor in India.

Indian troops were now shifting tactics. They were not fighting the enemy in a traditional manner on battlefields but breaking into homes, picking ordinary women and men, torturing them, raping them and in many cases killing them. It was a nasty, vicious, dirty little war. The traditional honour that is associated with battle had evaporated. On both sides there was no quarter given; the hatred was intense.

In private, however, many sensitive and worried Indians agreed that something must be urgently done, that they had lost the people of Kashmir, that brute force could not keep a people enslaved. But they would not say so in public.

In Pakistan the perception was that Kashmir – where over 80 per cent of the population was Muslim – had always been ethnically, religiously, culturally, politically and legally Pakistan, that its absorption by India was a symbol of Indian duplicity. There was no way that Pakistan would concede Kashmir. Those who sometimes talked of an independent Kashmir, free from India and Pakistan, were singled out and attacked as betrayers of the cause.

Apart from geopolitics there were also close sociological reasons for Pakistan's involvement with Kashmir. Thousands and thousands of Kashmiris had migrated over the last half-century from their homes to Pakistan. Lahore, the capital of the Punjab and Pakistan's intellectual and cultural capital, was inundated by people of Kashmiri origin. Nawaz Sharif, who became Prime Minister three times, is Kashmiri; the national poet, Allama Iqbal, was Kashmiri. The visible presence of Kashmir in Pakistan politics kept the issue at a high emotional pitch. No political leader, however dove-like, could minimize or ignore the issue. There was a straightforward Kashmir test: political reputation was based on how hawkish you were on the issue by the population at large.

What is the solution which would be most acceptable to the three parties to the dispute? (It is easily forgotten in Delhi and Islamabad that the Kashmiris too are a party.) There is no easy answer. Perhaps the only way out is to go back to the origins of the problem and uphold the UN resolutions: let the Kashmiris decide.

The future of South Asia

It may be an unrealistic dream in the present climate but those thinking of the coming millennium need to create a South Asian renaissance whereby the great religions, cultures and traditions of the region can mutually benefit and flourish.

South Asia is living in times of growing regional competitiveness. Unlike Japan it does not have highly developed technology; unlike the Middle East it does not have abundant oil; unlike Europe and America it does not have high standards of living and strong infrastructures. What it does have are inventive, hard-working and imaginative people; against this it also has highly divisive religions, ethnicity and politics.

If South Asians can overcome their political, ethnic and religious divisions and become aware of a common destiny they can fulfil their destiny into the next century. If not, their meagre resources – already stretched to breaking point – and their vast populations multiplying at an alarming rate will keep them in the lowest statistics for everything from education to standards of living to health care. It is a bleak future and they will be firmly lodged at the bottom of the world league.

In looking at the future we must emphasize the cultural richness and diversity of South Asia, its tremendous potential on the world stage. From Amir Khusro living in the fourteenth century to Iqbal in the twentieth, poets have declared that there is no better place on earth than South Asia. It is a land that has produced some of the greatest religious figures (from Buddha to Khwaja Muinuddin Chisti, to Hujweiri, to Nizamuddin, to Guru Nanak, to Shah Waliullah), rulers (from Asoka to Akbar to Aurangzeb) and poets (from Amir Khusro to Tulsidas, to Kabir, to Ghalib, to Iqbal). It has produced the Taj Mahal and the Shalimar Gardens. Nobel prizes and other international awards have been won by South Asians. The stature and quality of the founding fathers are unrivalled anywhere in the world. Gandhi, Nehru, Patel, Bose, Ambedkar and Azad of India; Jinnah, Liaquat and Nishtar of Pakistan – these are extraordinary figures by any standards.

At the beginning of this book I raised several questions. By the end of the book we may not have found all the answers, but at least we have considered ways for further exploration. There is a large question mark hanging over the future of the subcontinent. It will not go away until South Asians confront their own past, honestly and truthfully. Fresh thinking and new ideas must be found that are in consonance with the best of tradition. Unless this is done urgently, South Asia itself will fall so far behind the other global regions that it may be a long, long time before it is able to assume a position of distinction in the world.

In 1971, when Pakistan was broken in two, its critics jubilantly cried, 'Jinnah's Pakistan is dead.' They were wrong. Jinnah's Pakistan will be alive as long as there are Muslims who feel for the dignity, the identity and the destiny of other Muslims, and who care for the oppressed and the minorities in their midst. In that sense Jinnah's Pakistan will remain alive for ever. Muslims must learn to say with pride: 'I am Muslim.' They must live up to the nobility and compassion of Islamic ideals; they must carry themselves with dignity in their identity as Muslims. Most important, they must stand up for their rights. This is the lesson that Jinnah taught them; this is their destiny and they cannot ignore it.

References

Abdullah, Sheikh Mohammad (1993) (Trans. from the Urdu by Khushwant Singh) *Flames of the Chinar: An Autobiography*, New Delhi: Viking, Penguin Books.

Abedin, Zainal (1995) *RAW and Bangladesh*, Dhaka: Fatema Shahab.

Afzal, M. Rafique (ed.) (1966) *Speeches and Statements of the Quaid-i-Azam Mohammad Ali Jinnah, 1911–36 and 1947–48*, Lahore.

Ahmad, Jamil-ud-din (ed.) (1976) *Speeches and Writings of Mr Jinnah*, Lahore: Sh. Muhammed Ashraf.

Ahmad, Riaz (1994) *Quaid-i-Azam Mohammad Ali Jinnah: Second Phase of his Freedom Struggle 1924–1934*, Islamabad: Quaid-i-Azam University.

Ahmad, Ziauddin (1970) *Mohammad Ali Jinnah: Founder of Pakistan*, Karachi: Ministry of Information and Broadcasting.

Ahmad, Ziauddin (1990) *Shaheed-e-Millat Liaquat Ali Khan: Builder of Pakistan*, Karachi: Royal Book Company.

Ahmed, A. S. (1977) *Pieces of Green: The Sociology of Change in Pakistan, 1964–74*, Karachi: Royal Book Company.

Ahmed, A. S. (1980) *Pukhtun Economy and Society: Traditional Structure and Economic Development in a Tribal Society*, London: Routledge and Kegan Paul.

Ahmed, A. S. (1988) *Discovering Islam: Making Sense of Muslim History and Society*, London: Routledge and Kegan Paul.

Ahmed, A. S. (1990a) 'South Asia: roots of decline', *Economic and Political Weekly*, Bombay, 13 January.

Ahmed, A. S. (1990b) 'The Perfect Englishman', *Guardian*, 28 April. Longer version as 'In Britain, Macaulay's chickens come home to roost', *Times of India*, 21 May.

Ahmed, A. S. (1991) *Resistance and Control in Pakistan*, London: Routledge.

Ahmed, A. S. (1992a) *Postmodernism and Islam: Predicament and Promise*, London: Routledge.

Ahmed, A. S. (1992b) 'Bombay films: the cinema as metaphor for Indian society and politics', *Modern Asian Studies* 26, 2, Cambridge: Cambridge University Press, pp. 289–320.

References

Ahmed, A. S. (1993a) *Living Islam: From Samarkand to Stornoway*, London: BBC Books. (Reprinted by Penguin in 1995.)

Ahmed, A. S. (1993b) 'The history-thieves: stealing the Muslim past?', *History Today* 43, January.

Ahmed, A. S. (1993c) 'Points of entry: the Taj Mahal', *History Today* 43, May.

Ahmed, A. S. (1993d) 'Media mongols at the gates of Baghdad', *New Perspective Quarterly* 10, Summer.

Ahmed, A. S. (1994) 'Jinnah and the quest for Muslim identity', *History Today* 44, September.

Ahmed, A. S. (1995a) '"Ethnic cleansing": a metaphor for our time?', *Ethnic and Racial Studies* 18, 1, January.

Ahmed, A. S. (1995b) 'Foreword' to *The Nation that Lost its Soul*, autobiography of Sirdar Shaukat Hyat, Lahore: *Jang* Publishers.

Ahmed, A. S. (1996a) 'The hero in history: myth, media and realities', *History Today* 46, March.

Ahmed, A. S. (1996b) 'Towards the global millennium: the challenge of Islam', *The World Today* 52, Aug-Sept, London: Chatham House.

Ahmed, A. S. (1997a) 'The Quest for the Quaid: Myth and Reality', Islamabad: Quaid-i-Azam Memorial Lecture Series 1, Quaid-i-Azam University.

Ahmad, A. S. (1997b) *The Quaid: Jinnah and the Story of Pakistan*, Karachi: Oxford University Press.

Ahmed, A. S. and Dr Hastings Donnan (eds) (1994) *Islam, Globalization and Postmodernity*, London: Routledge.

Ahmed, A. S. and Cris Shore (eds) (1995) *The Future of Anthropology: Its Relevance to the Contemporary World*, London: Athlone, University of London.

Ahmed, Jamil (1977) *Hundred Great Muslims*, Lahore: Ferozsons.

Ahmed, Rizwan (1993) *'Sayings of Quaid-i-Azam': Mohammed Ali Jinnah*, Karachi: Quaid-Foundation and Pakistan Movement Centre.

Akbar, M. J. (1985) *India: The Siege Within*, Harmondsworth: Penguin.

Akbar, M. J. (1988a) *Nehru: The Making of India*, London: Viking, Penguin Books.

Akbar, M. J. (1988b) *Riot After Riot*, New Delhi: Penguin.

Ali, Chaudhri Muhammad (1967) *The Emergence of Pakistan*, London and New York: Columbia University Press.

Ali, Chaudhry Rahmat (1940) *Pakistan: The Fatherland of the Pak Nation*, Cambridge.

Ali, K. (1990) *A New History of Indo-Pakistan Since 1526*, Lahore: Naeem Publishers, Urdu Bazaar.

Ali, Mahmud S. (1995) *The Fearful State: Power, People and Internal War in South Asia*, London: Zed Books.

Ali, Tariq (1983) *Can Pakistan Survive? The Death of a State*, Harmondsworth: Penguin Books.

Ali, Tariq (1985) *The Nehrus and the Gandhis: An Indian Dynasty*, London: Picador, Pan Books.

Allen, Charles (ed.) (1975) *Plain Tales From The Raj*, London: Futura Publications.

Ambedkar, Dr Baba Saheb (1987) *Riddles in Hinduism*, vol. 4, Bombay: Government of Maharashtra.

Amin, Samir (1994) 'India faces enormous danger from globalization, *Mainstream* XXXII, 9, 15 January, New Delhi.

Azad, Maulana Abul Kalam (1988) *India Wins Freedom*, Calcutta: Orient Longmans. (Originally published in 1959.)

Baksh, Ilahi (1978) *With the Quaid-i-Azam During his Last Days*, Karachi: Quaid-i-Azam Academy.

References

Ballhatchet, Kenneth (1980) *Race, Sex and Class under the Raj: Imperial Attitudes and Policies and their Critics, 1793–1905*, London: Weidenfeld and Nicolson.

Barr, Pat (1976) *The Memsahibs: The Women of Victorian India*, London: Secker and Warburg.

Basu, Tapan et al. (eds) (1993) *Khaki Shorts, Saffron Flags*, London: Sangam Books Ltd.

Baudrillard, Jean (1988a) *America*, London: Verso.

Baudrillard, Jean (1988b) *The Evil Demon of Images*, Australia: Power Institute Publications, No. 3.

Baudrillard, Jean (1995) *The Illusion of the End*, Cambridge: Polity Press.

Bayly, C. A. (ed.) (1990) *The Raj: India and the British 1600–1947*, London: Pearson-National Portrait Gallery Publishers.

Beaumont, Christopher (1989) 'The truth of the partition of the Punjab in August 1947', unpublished paper, 20 September (see also *Daily Telegraph*, 24 Feb 1992).

Beck, Ulrich (1992) *Risk Society: Towards a New Modernity*, (Trans. by Mark Ritter), London: Sage Publications. (Originally published in 1986.)

Beg, Aziz (1986) *Jinnah and His Times*, Lahore: Allied Press Ltd.

Blunt, W. S. (1909) *India Under Ripon: A Private Diary*, London: T. Fisher Unwin.

Bolitho, Hector (1954) *Jinnah: Creator of Pakistan*, London: John Murray.

Bonner, Arthur (1990) *Averting the Apocalypse: Social Movements in India Today*, Durham: Duke University Press.

Bonner, Arthur et al. (1994) *Democracy in India: A Hollow Shell*, Washington DC: The American University Press.

Callard, Keith (1958) *Pakistan: A Political Study*, London: George Allen and Unwin.

Campbell-Johnson, Alan (1985) *Mission with Mountbatten*, London: Hamish Hamilton Ltd & Co. (Originally published in 1951.)

Chaudhuri, Nirad C. (1988) *The Autobiography of an Unknown Indian*, London: The Hogarth Press.

Chaudhuri, Nirad C. (1990) *Thy Hand Great Anarch! India 1921–1952*, London: The Hogarth Press.

Choudhury, Golam W. (1988) *Pakistan: Transition from Military to Civilian Rule*, Essex, England: Scorpion Publishing Ltd.

Clément, Catherine (1996) *Edwina and Nehru: A Novel*, New Delhi: Penguin.

Collins, Larry and Dominique Lapierre (1982) *Mountbatten and the Partition of India*, vol. I: 22 March–15 Aug 1947, New Delhi: Vikas.

Collins, Larry and Dominique Lapierre (1994) *Freedom at Midnight*, New Delhi: Vikas. (Originally published in 1976.)

Crossette, Barbara (1993) *India: Facing the Twenty-First Century*, Bloomington, Ind: Indiana University Press.

Dalton, Dennis (1993) *Mahatma Gandhi: Nonviolent Power in Action*, New York: Columbia University Press.

Das, Veena (ed.) (1992) *Mirrors of Violence: Communities, Riots and Survivors in South Asia*, Delhi: Oxford University Press.

Dissanayake, W. and M. Sahai (1988) *Raj Kapoor's Films: Harmony of Discourses*, New Delhi: Vikas.

Dube, S. C. (1965) *Indian Village*, London: Routledge and Kegan Paul.

Dumont, Louis (1970) *Homo Hierarchicus: The Caste System and its Implications*, London: Paladin.

Duncan, Emma (1989) *Breaking the Curfew: A Political Journey through Pakistan*, London: Michael Joseph.

Durrani, Tehmina with William and Marilyn Hoffer (1994) *My Feudal Lord*, London: Corgi.

261

References

Dutta, Krishna and Andrew Robinson (1995) *Rabindranath Tagore: The Myriad-Minded Man*, London: Bloomsbury.

Edwardes, Michael (1962) *Nehru: A Pictorial Biography*, London: Thames and Hudson.

Elst, Koenraad (1992) *Negationism in India: Concealing the Record of Islam*, New Delhi: Voice of India.

Engineer, Asghar Ali (ed.) (1991) *Communal Riots in Post-Independence India*, London: Sangam Books.

Enver, E. H. (1990) *The Modern Moses: A Brief Biography of M. A. Jinnah*, Karachi: Jinnah Memorial Institute.

Evenson, Norma (1989) *The Indian Metropolis: A View Toward the West*, New Haven, Conn., and London: Yale University Press.

Farrell, J. G. (1973) *The Siege of Krishnapur*, London: G. Weidenfeld & Nicolson Ltd.

Forster, E. M. (1967) *A Passage to India*, London: Penguin Books. (Originally published in 1924.)

Fukuyama, Francis (1992) *The End of History and the Last Man*, London: Hamish Hamilton.

Gandhi, Mohandar Karamchand (1969–79) *The Collected Works of Mahatma Gandhi*, Delhi: Ministry of Information and Broadcasting, Government of India.

Gandhi, Rajmohan (1986) *Eight Lives: A Study of the Hindu–Muslim Encounter*, Albany, NY: State University of New York Press.

Giddens, Anthony (1990) *Consequences of Modernity*, Cambridge: Polity Press.

Giddens, Anthony (1991) *Modernity and Self-Identity: Self and Society in the Late Modern Age*, Cambridge: Polity Press.

Gill, Anton (1995) *Ruling Passions: Sex, Race and Empire*, London: BBC Books.

Gilmartin, David (1988) *Empire and Islam: Punjab and the Making of Pakistan*, London: IB Tauris & Co.

Golwalkar, Madhav Sadashiv (1938) *We or Our Nationhood Defined*, Nagpur: Bharat Prakashan.

Golwalkar, Madhav Sadashiv (1966) *Bunch of Thoughts*, Bangalore: Kesari Press.

Golwalkar, Madhav Sadashiv (1969) *Justice on Trial*, Bangalore: Prakashan Vibhag.

Gopal, Sarvepalli (1975) *Jawaharlal Nehru: A Biography*, vol. I, London: Jonathan Cape.

Gopal, Sarvepalli (1979) *Jawaharlal Nehru: A Biography*, vol. II, London: Jonathan Cape.

Gopal, Sarvepalli (1984) *Jawaharlal Nehru: A Biography*, vol. III, London: Jonathan Cape.

Gopal, Sarvepalli (ed.) (1980) *Jawaharlal Nehru: An Anthology*, Delhi: Oxford University Press.

Gopal, Sarvepalli (ed.) (1991) *Anatomy of a Confrontation: Ayodhya and the Rise of Communal Politics in India*, New Delhi: Penguin.

Graham, Bruce (1990) *Hindu Nationalism and Indian Politics: The Origins and Development of Bharatiya Jana Sangh*, Cambridge: Cambridge University Press.

Hamid, Shahid S. (1986) *Disastrous Twilight: A Personal Record of the Partition of India*, Barnsley: Leo Cooper, Pen and Sword Books.

Hannan, Qazi Sayyid Abdul (1995) *Meer-e-Karwan Mohammad Ali Jinnah* (Urdu), Karachi: Zahbar Publishers.

Hardgrave, R. L. Jr. (1984) *India Under Pressure: Prospects for Political Stability*, Boulder, Co., and London: Westview Press.

Hasan, Mushirul (1997) *Legacy of a Divided Nation: India's Muslims from Independence to Ayodhya*, London: Hurst & Co.

Hasan, Syed Shamsul (1976) *... Plain Mr Jinnah*, Karachi: Royal Book Company.

Hewitt, V. M. (1992) *The International Politics of South Asia*, Manchester and New York: Manchester University Press.

References

Hodson, H. V. (1985) *The Great Divide: Britain – India – Pakistan,* Karachi: Oxford University Press.

Hough, Richard (1980) *Mountbatten: Hero of our Time,* London: G. Weidenfeld & Nicolson Ltd.

Hough, Richard (1983) *Edwina: Countess Mountbatten of Burma. A biography.* London: G. Weidenfeld & Nicolson Ltd.

Human Development Report 1995, United Nations Development Programme, Oxford and New York: Oxford University Press.

Hunter, W. W. (1957) *The Indian Musalmans,* Lahore: Premier Book House, Club Road. (Originally published in 1872.)

Huntington, Samuel P. (1993) 'The clash of civilizations?', *Foreign Affairs* 72, 3, Summer.

Husain, Altaf (1996) *From Mutiny to Mountbatten: A Biographical Sketch of and Writings by Altaf Husain,* edited by Zeba Zubair, London: Kegan Paul International.

Hussain, Mohammad Tajammul (1996) *India's Farakka Barrage: Cold Blooded Murder of Bangladesh,* London: Al Hilal Publishers Ltd.

Ikramullah, Shaista (1963) *From Purdah to Parliament,* London: The Cresset Press Ltd.

Iqbal, Allama Muhammad (1986) *The Reconstruction of Religious Thought in Islam,* Lahore: The Institute of Islamic Culture, Club Road. (Originally published in 1930.)

Iyer, Krishna (1992) review of Ahmed 1992a in *Economic and Political Weekly,* 7 November, Bombay.

Jaffrelot, Christophe (1996) *The Hindu Nationalist Movement and Indian Politics, 1925 to the 1990s,* London: Hurst & Co.

Jalal, Ayesha (1985) *The Sole Spokesman: Jinnah, the Muslim League and the Demand for Pakistan,* Cambridge: Cambridge University Press.

James, William E. and Subroto Roy (eds) (1992) *Foundations of Pakistan's Political Economy,* New Delhi: Sage Publications.

Jayawardena, Kumari (1996) *Embodied Violence: Communalising Female Sexuality in South Asia,* London: Zed Books.

Jinnah, Fatima (1987) *My Brother,* Karachi: Quaid-i-Azam Academy.

Jinnah, Mohammed Ali (1948) *Speeches of Quaid-i-Azam Mohammed Ali Jinnah as Governor General of Pakistan,* Karachi: Sind Observer Press.

Jinnah, Mohammed Ali (1989) *Quaid-i-Azam Mohammed Ali Jinnah: Speeches and Statements 1947–48,* Islamabad: Government of Pakistan, Ministry of Information and Broadcasting, Directorate of Films and Publications.

Kakar, Sudhir (1995) *The Colours of Violence,* New Delhi: Viking, Penguin.

Karim, Nihal (1994) *Exploitation, Domination and Alienation: The Genesis of Bangladesh,* Dhaka: Osmania Library.

Kaura, Uma (1977) *Muslims and Indian Nationalism,* New Delhi: Manohar Book Service.

Kennedy, Paul (1994) *Preparing for the Twenty-First Century,* New York: Vintage Books, Random House.

Khairi, Saad R. (1995) *Jinnah Reinterpreted: The Journey from Indian Nationalism to Muslim Statehood,* Karachi: Oxford University Press.

Khalidi, Omar (1995) *Indian Muslims Since Independence,* New Delhi: Vikas.

Khan, Ansar Hussain (1995) *The Rediscovery of India,* London: Sangam Books Ltd.

Khan, Gul Hassan (1993) *Memoirs of Lt-General Gul Hassan Khan: The Last Commander-in-Chief of the Pakistan Army,* Karachi: Oxford University Press.

Khan, Muhammad Ayub (1967) *Friends Not Masters: A Political Biography,* London: Oxford University Press.

Khan, Rasheeduddin (1994) *Bewildered India: Identity, Pluralism, Discord,* New Delhi: Har-Anand Publications.

References

Khan, Sirdar Shaukat Hyat (1995) *The Nation that Lost its Soul*, Lahore: *Jang* Publishers.

Khurshid, K. H. (1990) *Memories of Jinnah*, edited by Khalid Hasan, Karachi: Oxford University Press.

Kiernan, V. G. (1972) *The Lords of Human Kind*, Harmondsworth: Penguin Books. (Originally published in 1969.)

Korejo, M. S. (1994) *The Frontier Gandhi: His Place in History*, Karachi: Oxford University Press.

Lahori, Ziauddin (1993) *Khudnawisht hayat-i-Sir Syad*, Lahore: *Jang* Publications.

Lamb, Alastair (1991) *Kashmir: A Disputed Legacy 1846–1990*, Hertingfordbury, Hertfordshire: Roxford Books.

Lamb, Alastair, (1994) *Birth of a Tragedy: Kashmir 1947* Hertingfordbury, Hertfordshire: Roxford Books.

Lamb, Christina (1991) *Waiting for Allah: Pakistan's Struggle for Democracy*, London: Hamish Hamilton.

Luhrmann, T. M. (1996) *The Good Parsi: The Fate of a Colonial Elite in a Post-Colonial Society*, Cambridge, MA: Harvard University Press.

McLeod, W. H. (1989) *Who is a Sikh? The Problem of Sikh Identity*, Oxford: The Clarendon Press.

MacMillan, Margaret (1988) *Women of the Raj*, New York: Thames and Hudson.

Madan, T. N. (1987) *Non-Renunciation: Themes and Interpretations of Hindu Culture*, New Delhi: Oxford University Press.

Madan, T. N. (1994) *Pathways: Approaches to the Study of Society in India*, Delhi: Oxford University Press.

Madan, T. N. (ed.) (1992) *Religion in India*, Oxford and Delhi: Oxford in India Readings in Sociology and Social Anthropology, Oxford University Press.

Majumdar, S. K. (1966) *Jinnah and Gandhi: Their Role in India's Quest for Freedom*, Calcutta: Firma. K.L. Mukhopadhyay.

Makiya, Kanan (1993) *Cruelty and Silence: War, Tyranny, Uprising, and the Arab World*, London: Jonathan Cape.

Malik, Hafeez (ed.) (1971) *Iqbal: Poet-philosopher of Pakistan*, New York: Columbia University Press.

Mann, E. A. (1992) *Boundaries and Identities: Muslims, Work and Status in Aligarh*, New Delhi: Sage Publications.

Mayer, A. C. (1970) *Caste and Kinship in Central India*, London: Routledge and Kegan Paul.

Menon, V. P. (1957) *The Transfer of Power in India*, Princeton, NJ: Princeton University Press.

Merchant, Liaquat H. (1990) *Jinnah: A Judicial Verdict*, Karachi: East & West Publishing Company.

Mestrovic, Stjepan G. (1994) *The Balkanization of the West: The Influence of Postmodernism and Postcommunism*, London: Routledge.

Morgan, Janet (1991) *Edwina Mountbatten: A Life of Her Own*, London: HarperCollins.

Moseley, L. (1962) *The Last Days of the British Raj*, London: Inter-Culture.

Moynihan, Daniel Patrick (1993) *Pandaemonium: Ethnicity in International Politics*, Oxford: Oxford University Press.

Mujahid, Sharif al (1981) *Quaid-i-Azam Jinnah: Studies in Interpretation*, Karachi: Quaid-i-Azam Academy.

Mujahid, Sharif al (1988) 'Jinnah and the Congress Party' in *The Indian National Congress: Centenary Hindsights*, edited by D. A. Low, Delhi: Oxford University Press.

Mukerjee, Hiren (1964) *The Gentle Colossus: A Study of Jawaharlal Nehru*, Delhi: Oxford University Press.

References

Naidu, Sarojini (1966) 'Mohammad Ali Jinnah – ambassador of Hindu–Muslim unity' in *Quaid-i-Azam as seen by his Contemporaries*, comp. Jamil-ud-din Ahmad, Lahore: Publishers United Ltd.

Naipaul, V. S. (1990) *India: A Million Mutinies Now*, London: Heinemann.

Naipaul, V. S. (1995) 'The Hindu awakening', in *At Century's End*, edited by N. P. Gardels, California: ALTI Publishing, La Jolla.

Nandy, Ashis (1983) *The Intimate Enemy: Loss and Recovery of Self Under Colonialism*, New Delhi: Oxford University Press.

Nash, Manning (1989) *The Cauldron of Ethnicity in the Modern World*, Chicago: The University of Chicago Press.

Nehru, Jawaharlal (1941) *Toward Freedom: An Autobiography*, New York: John Day. (Originally published in 1936.)

Nehru, Jawaharlal (1961) *The Discovery of India*, Bombay: Asia Publishing House. (Originally published in 1946.)

Neillands, Robin (1996) *A Fighting Retreat: The British Empire, 1947–1997*, London: Hodder and Stoughton.

Newberg, Paula R. (1995) *Double Betrayal: Repression and Insurgency in Kashmir*, Washington DC: Carnegie Endowment for International Peace.

Nichols, Beverley (1944) *Verdict on India*, London: Jonathan Cape.

Oak, P. N. (1965) *Taj Mahal was a Rajput Palace*, Delhi: Asiatic Printers.

Oak, P. N. (1990) *Some Blunders of Indian Historical Research*, New Delhi: Bharati Sahitya Sadan.

Pacific Affairs (1987) 'Politics in the Punjab' 60, 1, Spring.

Padgaonkar, Dileep (ed.) (1993) *When Bombay Burned*, New Delhi: UBS Publishers and Distributers Ltd.

Page, David (1982) *Prelude to Partition: The Indian Muslims and the Imperial System of Control, 1920–1932*, New Delhi: Oxford University Press.

Parekh, Bhikhu, (1985) 'The legacy of the partition', in *Punjab in Indian Politics: Issues and Trends*, edited by Amrik Singh, Delhi: Ajanta Publishers.

Parekh, Bhikhu (1989) *Colonialism, Tradition and Reform: An Analysis of Gandhi's Political Discourse*, New Delhi: Sage Publications.

Pettigrew, Joyce (1975) *Robber Noblemen: A Study of the Political System of Sikh Jats*, London: Routledge and Kegan Paul.

Pettigrew, Joyce (1991) 'Betrayal and nation-building among the Sikhs', *Journal of Commonwealth and Comparative Politics* 19, 1.

Pettigrew, Joyce (1995) *The Sikhs of the Punjab: Unheard Voices of State and Guerrilla Violence*, London: Zed Books.

Phadnis, Urmila (1989) *Ethnicity and Nation-building in South Asia*, New Delhi: Sage Publications.

Pirzada, S. S. (1983) *Film Gandhi and Quaid-e-Azam Jinnah*, Karachi: East and West Publishing Company.

Rabbani, Muhammad Ikram and Monawar Ali Sayyid (eds) (1989) *An Introduction to Pakistan Studies*, Lahore: The Caravan Book House.

Rajshekar, V. T. (1993) *India's Muslim Problem: Agony of the Country's Single Largest Community Persecuted by Hindu Nazis*, Bangalore, India: Dalit Sahitya Academy.

Raza, Hashim (1982) *Mountbatten and Pakistan*, Karachi: Quaid-i-Azam Academy.

Roberts, Andrew (1994a) *Eminent Churchillians*, London: Weidenfeld and Nicolson.

Roberts, Andrew (1994b) 'Why Mountbatten should have been impeached', *Sunday Times*, 24 July.

Roberts, Andrew (1996) 'Jinnah, star of the East reborn', *Sunday Times*, 18 August.

References

Robertson, Roland (1991) 'The globalization paradigm: thinking globally', in *Religion and Social Order*, edited by D. G. Bromley, Greenwich: JAI Press.

Robertson, Roland (1992) *Globalization: Social Theory and Global Culture*, London: Sage Publications.

Robinson, Francis (ed.) (1989) *The Cambridge Encyclopaedia of India: Pakistan, Bangladesh, Sri Lanka*, Cambridge: Cambridge University Press.

Robinson, Jane (1996) *Angels of Albion: Women of the Indian Mutiny*, London: Viking.

Roy, Asim (1983) *The Islamic Syncretistic Tradition in Bengal*, Princeton, NJ: Princeton University Press.

Royle, Trevor (1996) *Winds of Change: The End of Empire in Africa*, London: John Murray.

Rudolph, L. I. and Rudolph, S. H. (1987) *In Pursuit of Lakshmi: The Political Economy of the Indian State*, Chicago: The University of Chicago Press.

Rushdie, Salman (1988) *The Satanic Verses*, London: Viking, Penguin.

Rushdie, Salman (1991) *Imaginary Homelands*, London: Granta Books.

Rushdie, Salman (1995) *The Moor's Last Sigh*, London: Jonathan Cape.

Russell, Ralph (1992) *The Pursuit of Urdu Literature: A Select History*, London: Zed Books.

Russell, Ralph with Khurshidul Islam (1969a) *Ghalib: Life and Letters*, vol. I, Cambridge, MA: Harvard University Press; also London: Allen and Unwin.

Russell, Ralph and Khurshidul Islam (1969b) *Three Mughal Poets: Mir, Sauda, Mir Hasan*, London: Allen and Unwin.

Russell, Ralph (ed.) (1972) *Ghalib: The Poet and His Age*, London: Allen and Unwin.

Said, Edward W. (1978) *Orientalism*, New York: Penguin Books.

Salik, Siddiq (1977) *Witness to Surrender*, Karachi: Oxford University Press.

Saxena, N. C. (1991) 'The nature and origin of communal riots in India', in *Communal Riots in Post-Independence India*, edited by Asghar Ali Engineer, London: Sangam Books. (Originally published by Hyderabad: Sangam Books India in 1984.)

Sayeed, Khalid bin (1968) *Pakistan: The Formative Phase, 1857–1948*, London: Oxford University Press.

Schofield, Victoria (1996) *Kashmir in the Crossfire*, London: I. B. Tauris.

Scott, Paul (1973) *The Jewel in the Crown*, London: Panther Books.

Seervai, H. M. (1990) *Partition of India: Legend and Reality*, Bombay: Emmenem Publications.

Shaikh, Farzana (1989) *Community and Consensus in Islam: Muslim Representation in Colonial India 1860–1947*, Cambridge: Cambridge University Press.

Shaw, Tony (1996) *Eden, Suez and the Mass Media: Propaganda and Persuasion During the Suez Crisis*, London: I. B. Tauris.

Sherif, M.A. (1994) *Searching for Solace: A Biography of Abdullah Yusuf Ali, Interpreter of the Qur'an*, Kuala Lumpur: Islamic Book Trust.

Singh, Gurharpal (1987) 'Understanding the "Punjab problem"', *Asian Survey* 27, 12.

Singh, Gurharpal (1991) 'The Punjab problem in the 1990s: a post-1984 assessment', *Journal of Commonwealth and Comparative Politics* 29, 2.

Singh, Gurharpal (1993) 'Ethnic conflict in India: a case-study of Punjab', in *The Politics of Ethnic Conflict Regulation*, edited by John McGarry and Brendan O'Leary, London: Routledge.

Singh, Khushwant (1988) *Train to Pakistan*, New Delhi: Ravi Dayal.

Singh, Khushwant (1990) *Delhi: A Novel*, New Delhi: Penguin Books.

Singh, Tavleen (1995) *Kashmir: A Tragedy of Errors*, New Delhi: Viking, Penguin Books.

Singhvi, L. M. (1991) *Freedom on Trial*, New Delhi: Vikas.

Sisson, Richard and Leo E. Rose (1990) *War and Secession: Pakistan, India, and the Creation of Bangladesh*, Berkeley and Los Angeles: University of California Press.

References

Srinivas, M. N. (1952) *Religion and Society Among the Coorgs of South India*, Oxford: Clarendon Press.

Stephens, Ian (1963) *Pakistan*, London: Ernest and Benn Ltd.

Storr, Anthony (1996) *Feet of Clay: A Study of Gurus*, London: HarperCollins.

Suleri, Sara (1992) *The Rhetoric of English India*, Chicago and London: The University of Chicago Press.

Talbot, Ian (1984) 'Jinnah and the making of Pakistan', *History Today* 34, February.

Trench, Charles Chenevix (1987) *Viceroy's Agent*, London: Jonathan Cape.

Turner, B. S. (1994) *Orientalism, Postmodernism and Globalism: Intellectuals in the Modern World*, London: Routledge.

Varma, Pavan (1989) *Ghalib: The Man, The Times*, New Delhi: Penguin.

Ward, Andrew (1996) *Our Bones are Scattered: The Cawnpore Massacres and the Indian Mutiny of 1857*, London: John Murray.

Wasti, Syed Razi (1996) *At Quaid's Service*, Lahore: Jinnah–Rafi Foundation.

Wasti, Syed Razi (ed.) (1994) *My Dear Qaid-i-Azam (Jinnah–Rafi Correspondence)*, Lahore: Jinnah–Rafi Foundation.

Werbner, Pnina (1990) 'Exemplary personhood and the political mythology of overseas Pakistanis', in *Person, Myth and Society in South Asian Islam*, Adelaide, SA: University of Adelaide.

Wolpert, Stanley (1984) *Jinnah of Pakistan*, New York: Oxford University Press.

Wolpert, Stanley (1993) *Zulfi Bhutto of Pakistan: His Life and Times*, New York: Oxford University Press.

Wolpert, Stanley (1996) *Nehru: A Tryst with Destiny*, New York: Oxford University Press.

Woodruff, Philip (Mason) (1965) *The Men Who Ruled India: The Guardians* vol. II, London: Jonathan Cape.

Young, Robert (1994) *Colonial Desire: Hybridity in Theory, Culture and Race*, London: Routledge.

Zaheer, Hasan (1994) *The Separation of East Pakistan: The Rise and Realization of Bengali Muslim Nationalism*, Karachi: Oxford University Press.

Zaidi, Z. H. (1993) *Jinnah Papers: Prelude to Pakistan*, vol. I, parts I and II, Islamabad: Quaid-i-Azam Papers Project.

Zaidi, Z. H. (ed.) (1976) *M. A. Jinnah: Ispahani Correspondence 1936–1948*, Karachi: Forward Publications Trust.

Ziegler, Philip (1985) *Mountbatten: The Official Biography*, London: William Collins Sons & Co. Ltd.

Ziegler, Philip (1995) *Mountbatten Revisited*, Faculty Seminar on British Studies, Austin, TX: The University of Texas at Austin.

Index

Index

Index